Transition management for sustainable development

# Transition management for sustainable development

Edited by Kazuhiro Ueta and Yukio Adachi

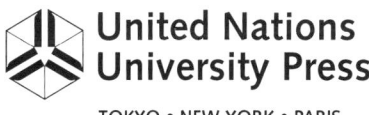

TOKYO • NEW YORK • PARIS

© United Nations University, 2014

The views expressed in this publication are those of the authors and do not necessarily reflect the views of the United Nations University.

United Nations University Press
United Nations University, 53–70, Jingumae 5-chome,
Shibuya-ku, Tokyo 150-8925, Japan
Tel: +81-3-5467-1212   Fax: +81-3-3406-7345
E-mail: sales@unu.edu   General enquiries: press@unu.edu
http://www.unu.edu

United Nations University Office at the United Nations, New York
2 United Nations Plaza, Room DC2-2062, New York, NY 10017, USA
Tel: +1-212-963-6387   Fax: +1-212-371-9454
E-mail: unuony@unu.edu

United Nations University Press is the publishing division of the United Nations University.

Cover design by Ian Youngs

Printed in the United States of America for the Americas and Asia
Printed in the United Kingdom for Europe, Africa and the Middle East

ISBN 978-92-808-1234-3
e-ISBN 978-92-808-7203-3

Library of Congress Cataloging-in-Publication Data

Transition management for sustainable development / edited by Kazuhiro Ueta and Yukio Adachi.
    pages cm
  Includes bibliographical references and index.
  ISBN 978-9280812343 (pbk.)
  1. Sustainable development.  2. Economic development—Environmental aspects.  3. Environmental policy—Economic aspects.  I. Ueta, Kazuhiro, 1952–  II. Adachi, Yukio, 1947–
  HD75.6.T73  2014
  338.9'27—dc23
                                                            2013050969

# Endorsements

"This volume by Ueta and Adachi, *Transition Management for Sustainable Development*, establishes in an impressive way the post-Fukushima agenda for Japan's energy transition, providing a rich theoretical overview with comparative and policy-relevant analysis of low-carbon and green growth trajectories. It is the most comprehensive and profound volume to date, allowing English language readers to study the thinking of outstanding Japanese scholars on transition processes."
**Mikael Skou Andersen,** Professor of Environmental Policy Analysis, Aarhus University, Denmark

"Our generation is the first to experience the reality of regional and global environmental dysfunction caused by our species. Previous generations inflicted upon themselves horrific problems by destroying their forests, soils and natural endowments, and polluting their water and air. But these destructive impulses were mainly local in their impacts – they did not impinge on the planet's life support systems. We are in a new world, where actions and impacts are simultaneously local and global, where economic and environmental interdependencies are pervasive, and extreme events seem to be becoming more frequent. These changes are triggering a re-think as to how we should manage our affairs. We are just beginning to work out how to manage this transition.

This book is an important effort by scholars to both learn from the past, and develop ways of thinking and doing that move us forward. Although its authorship is by Japanese scholars, and is shaped in part by the Great East Japan Earthquake and massive tsunami that hit north-eastern Japan on 11 March 2011, its intellectual and practical reach is global. It will be of interest and value to all who are interested in the intellectual and practical challenges we face in finding a better way to live on the earth."

**Frank J. Convery,** Chair and Senior Fellow, UCD Earth Institute, University College Dublin, and Honorary President, European Association of Environmental and Resource Economists

"Given the worldwide attention on the crisis of Fukushima, with its implications not only for Japanese environmental policy but for many other countries as well, this volume arrives as a timely addition to the literature on sustainability and the critical task of transition management.

Leading Japanese experts, working at the intersection of technology and political policymaking, offer both environmental policy academics and professional practitioners an agenda for coming to grips with the fundamental challenges of our time. Particularly welcome is the emphasis on sustainable development as a form of human development. This book should be widely read and discussed."

**Frank Fischer,** Distinguished Professor of Politics and Global Affairs, Rutgers University, USA, and Research Associate at the Environmental Policy Research Centre, Free University of Berlin, Germany

# Contents

List of figures, tables and boxes .......................................... x

Contributors .............................................................. xii

Preface ................................................................... xiv

Introduction: From green growth to sustainable human development ...... 1
    *Kazuhiro Ueta*

**Part I: Environmental governance for sustainable human development** ............................................................. 7

1 On the concept of sustainable human development ..................... 9
    *Hiroki Nogami and Kazuhiro Ueta*

2 Environmental policy integration for sustainability and its contemporary policy implications ................................... 28
    *Kazuo Matsushita*

3 The state transformation in environmental governance: From the viewpoints of environmental regulations ..................... 47
    *Shin-ichi Yatsuki*

4 Governance of sustainability transition management at the local, national and global levels ............................................ 57
    *Tatsuro Niikawa*

**Part II: Transition management for sustainable development: Case studies**............................................................. 79

5 Environmental governance strategies and transition to a sustainable society: Integration of environmental and energy policies in Germany and Japan.......................................... 81
   *Minoru Tsubogo*

6 Environmental governance failure and environmental metagovernance for local sustainable development: Local Agenda 21 in Japan................................................ 105
   *Kentaro Miyanaga*

7 Transition to sustainable urban development in Japan: A case study of an antipollution movement in Nishiyodogawa Ward, Osaka City ...................................................... 121
   *Mayuko Shimizu*

**Part III: Democracy and institutional reforms for sustainable development**............................................... 135

8 Democracy in transition management for sustainable development............................................................. 137
   *Yukio Adachi*

9 Does better governance make for a better environment?................ 154
   *Kosuke Oyama*

10 Deliberation, expertise and sustainability ............................... 189
   *Makoto Usami*

11 The restructuring of society around environmental education: From education for economic development to education for sustainable development.................................................. 205
   *Wataru Sano*

12 Is contemporary capitalism sustainable? ................................. 222
   *Satoshi Niioka*

13 Decentralization and local governance for sustainable development............................................................. 234
   *Katsutaka Shiraishi*

**Part IV: Social movements and social learning in transition
   management for sustainable development** .......................... 249

14 Anti-nuclear movements in Japan: Before and after the Fukushima
   nuclear disaster....................................................... 251
   *Koichi Hasegawa*

15 Social learning for endogenous development and sustainable world:
   From the viewpoint of experiences and discussions in Japan........... 273
   *Takayuki Ota*

16 Undesirable facility siting and democracy: A comparative
   analysis of radioactive waste repository siting in Japan,
   South Korea and France ................................................ 293
   *Shunsaku Komatsuzaki*

17 The reintegration of welfare, the economy and the environment:
   Governance of post-productivist welfare ............................... 317
   *Taro Miyamoto*

Index .................................................................... 338

# List of figures, tables and boxes

**Figures**

| | | |
|---|---|---|
| 1.1 | Resources and capital in two economies | 14 |
| 9.1 | Number and proportion of democratic regimes | 156 |
| 9.2 | The analytical framework | 158 |
| 9.3 | The state of Japan's governance in World Governance Indicators (WGI) data | 161 |
| 9.4 | The Comprehensive Environmental Indices in the Third Environmental Basic Plan by the Ministry of Environment | 177 |
| 9.5 | Worldwide Governance Indicators (WGI) and Environmental Performance Index (EPI) | 178 |
| 9.6 | Per capita gross domestic product (GDP) and Environmental Performance Index (EPI) | 181 |
| 12.1 | Post-war public policy characterized by combinations of the four basic social values | 230 |
| 13.1 | Conceptual relativity of the social system and the ecosystem | 236 |
| 14.1 | The triangular structure of social movement analysis | 255 |
| 14.2 | Network structure of anti-nuclear energy movements | 260 |
| 15.1 | Multiple-loop learning | 278 |
| 15.2 | Number of organizations involved in YWPA and the YWPA's budget | 280 |
| 15.3 | The Yahagi River Method for large-scale developments | 282 |
| 15.4 | Total number and area of prior consultations under the Yahagi River Method | 284 |
| 15.5 | Biochemical oxygen demand shift, 1971–2002 | 286 |

| 15.6 | Suspended solid shift, 1965–2004 | 286 |
| 16.1 | A two-step framework of attitude formation | 296 |
| 16.2 | The residents' attitude formation throughout the dispute in Toyo-cho | 299 |
| 16.3 | The residents' attitude formation throughout the siting process in Gyeongju | 303 |
| 16.4 | The residents' attitude formation throughout the siting process in Bure | 308 |
| 17.1 | Paired relationships of welfare, the economy and the environment | 322 |

**Tables**

| 1.1 | Indicators of sustainability and human development | 18 |
| 2.1 | The distribution of EPI instruments within and across 30 OECD countries | 34 |
| 2.2 | Conventional versus twenty-first century power supply systems | 44 |
| 9.1 | The sources of governance data used in the 2008 World Governance Indicators (WGI) update | 163 |
| 9.2 | The distribution of data points by type in World Governance Indicators (WGI) 2008 | 169 |
| 9.3 | The Environmental Performance Index system | 171 |
| 9.4 | The numerical results: Environmental Performance Index (EPI) and World Governance Indicators (WGI) | 179 |
| 9.5 | The numerical results: Environmental Performance Index (EPI), World Governance Indicators (WGI) and per capita gross domestic product (GDP) | 183 |
| 14.1 | Number of nuclear reactors (1995 and 2010) | 252 |
| 17.1 | Diversity of social inclusion strategies | 329 |

**Boxes**

| Box 15.1 | Principles of endogenous development by Miyamoto (2007) | 276 |

# Contributors

**Yukio Adachi** is Professor Emeritus, Kyoto University, and Professor of Public Policy in the Faculty of Law, Kyoto Industrial University, Japan.

**Koichi Hasegawa** is Professor of Sociology in the Graduate School of Arts and Letters, Tohoku University, Japan.

**Shunsaku Komatsuzaki** is Assistant Professor of Civil Engineering in the Graduate School of Engineering, The University of Tokyo, Japan.

**Kazuo Matsushita** is Professor Emeritus of Environmental Policy, Kyoto University, Japan, and a Senior Fellow, Institute for Global Environmental Strategies (IGES), Japan.

**Taro Miyamoto** is Professor of Political Science in the School of Law, Chuo University, Japan.

**Kentaro Miyanaga** is Senior Researcher of Environmental Governance and Policy in Lake Biwa Environmental Research Institute, Japan.

**Tatsuro Niikawa** is Professor of Public Policy in the Graduate School of Policy and Management, Doshisha University, Japan.

**Satoshi Niioka** is Professor of International Political Economy in the Faculty of Economics, Kanto Gakuin University, Japan.

**Hiroki Nogami**[†] was a Senior Researcher at the Institute of Developing Economies, Japan External Trade Organization, Japan.

**Takayuki Ota** is Associate Professor of Regional Policy in the Faculty of Humanities and Social Sciences, Shizuoka University, Japan.

[†]*The author is deceased.*

**Kosuke Oyama** is Professor of Public Administration and Policy in the Faculty of Law, Keio University, Japan.

**Wataru Sano** is Associate Professor of Public Policy in the Graduate School of Human and Environmental Studies, Kyoto University, Japan.

**Mayuko Shimizu** is Lecturer of Environmental Policy in the Faculty of Policy Science, Ryukoku University, Japan.

**Katsutaka Shiraishi** is Professor of Public Policy in the Faculty of Policy Science, Ryukoku University, Japan.

**Minoru Tsubogo** is Professor of Comparative Environmental Politics in the Faculty of Social Sciences, Waseda University, Japan.

**Kazuhiro Ueta** is Professor of Environmental Economics in the Graduate School of Economics, Kyoto University, Japan.

**Makoto Usami** is Professor of Philosophy and Public Policy in the Graduate School of Global Environmental Studies, Kyoto University, Japan.

**Shin-ichi Yatsuki** is Associate Professor of Environmental Economics in the Faculty of Economics, Kyushu University, Japan.

# Preface

It was during the course of our research project entitled "Multilevel Environmental Governance for Sustainable Development" between 2006 and 2012 that the Great East Japan Earthquake struck in March 2011, a disaster unprecedented in terms of its magnitude and the extent of the areas affected by the earthquake and resultant tsunami and nuclear accident. Recovery and reconstruction efforts are under way to restore the lives of the victims and revive the disaster-stricken regions. We cannot, however, blindly engage in such efforts. There are questions to be answered. What does reconstruction mean in the first place? What should be the goal? How should it be achieved? To answer these questions, the theoretical basis of the policy for post-earthquake disaster reconstruction must be clarified.

Consider post-earthquake disaster reconstruction as the recovery and improvement of people's quality of life. Then the appropriateness of such policy can be judged by applying sustainable development theory. This is because sustained improvement of quality of life – or per capita well-being – is the goal of sustainable development. Sustainable development can be assessed through the productive base, which is a determinant of quality of life. A society's productive base is the source of its well-being (quality of life). An economy's productive base includes not only manufactured capital, human capital, natural capital and knowledge, but also its institutions. Trends and changes in this productive base can be used to assess sustain ability and the effectiveness of reconstruction policy.

In this context, the damage caused by the earthquake disaster and nuclear accident can be regarded as destruction or depreciation of the productive base. Furthermore, the reconstruction policy must promote investment in the productive base of the affected economy in the Tohoku region in a broader sense and make such investment positive in net terms between the pre- and post-earthquake periods. Sustainable development can function as the theoretical basis for the assessment of damage and the direction of the reconstruction policy.

Our project aims to develop sustainable development theory by taking into account the idea of human development for environmental governance. The two concepts of human development and sustainable development have for the most part been proposed separately. Although the two concepts overlap and share many arguments that are counter to existing mainstream development initiatives, it is important to insist that they are different from each other. What is crucial is to look at the ways in which the actions and changes demanded by the two concepts can be integrated and to see the conditions under which they are consistent with each other.

How do sustainable development and human development coincide or differ? One view is that they share perspectives on opportunity and quality of life. We also attempt to combine the two into a single concept of sustainable human development and discuss how to make sustainable human development operational.

In evaluating the performance of a society, we have to do so not only in terms of achievement of the respective indicators, but also in terms of range of opportunities available for the people. Emphasizing the expansion of freedom of an individual suggests a trend towards the use of strong sustainability indicators, such as endowment of natural capital in a comprehensive manner. Thus, in putting together the indicators for sustainable human development, priority should be given to critical levels of natural capital.

Our project also aims to clarify how the structure and function of multilevel environmental governance contribute to sustainable human development. Governance for sustainable development refers to social, economic and political processes of governance towards the attainment of sustainable development. It encompasses public debate, policy formation and implementation, as well as complex interactions among government, private business and civil society. The establishment of longer-term operational goals for sustainable development, the extension of co-management arrangements both vertically and horizontally, and the development of pluralistic networks for reviewing social and environmental trends and policy performance can help reduce uncertainties about future development trends.

The publication of the research results in the five volumes of this series by the United Nations University Press is financially supported by the Japan Society for the Promotion of Science Grant-in-Aid for Publication of Scientific Research Results.

*Kazuhiro Ueta*

# Introduction
# From green growth to sustainable human development

*Kazuhiro Ueta*

## Limits to growth

If green economic growth (hereafter, green growth) were achieved, it could solve certain problems which have shackled the process of building a low-carbon society. Since green growth is a combination of greening the economy and economic growth, achieving such growth would help win over some opponents of the building of a low-carbon society who think that at least one aspect cannot be realized. For example, let us suppose there are people who oppose the building of a low-carbon society for the reason that even though the reduction of greenhouse gases emissions itself is preferable, it hinders economic growth. However, if green growth is achieved, the reason for the opposition is eliminated. Therefore, progress would be made in reaching consensus for building a low-carbon society. In other words, the feasibility of realizing a low-carbon society increases because the amount of obstacles in its path is reduced.

One may ask whether the goal to be achieved along with the maintenance and protection of the environment (such as the reduction of greenhouse gas emissions) is simply economic growth. Certainly, economic growth has been regarded as desirable, at least by economists. This is because the increase of per capita real gross domestic product (GDP) is considered to be linked with improvement in people's lives. However, some limitations have been pointed out regarding economic growth. One is the natural limit to growth. This is associated with the question of whether unlimited growth is feasible without destroying the environment and ecology, which are the foundation of human existence. The question

---

*Transition management for sustainable development*, Ueta and Adachi (eds.), United Nations University Press, 2014, ISBN 978-92-808-1234-3

has been posed numerous times. The report *The Limits to Growth* by the Club of Rome warned about the pattern of economic development in post-war industrial society (Meadows, 1972). As clearly seen in the climate change problem and the biodiversity problem, the possibility that problems involving the environment and natural resources impose constraints on economic growth seems to have become obvious. If nature as a basis of human society becomes vulnerable as the economy grows, the permanence of economic growth is not guaranteed.

Of course, human society seeks ways to overcome such environmental constraints or resource constraints, and these can be utilized as new driving forces for economic growth. The concept of green growth advocates that innovations be created to overcome natural limitations and that economic growth be realized based on such innovations. In an extreme case, however, there is the structural problem where growth destroys its own foundation, which cannot necessarily be avoided.

Another question posed regarding the limits to growth may show a more fundamental problem. It is the question of whether continued pursuit of economic growth will actually improve people's quality of life. Here, quality of life is considered synonymous with well-being (Dasgupta, 2001). Welfare is another synonymous term (Sen, 1987). It is quality of life or well-being that human society has pursued and will continue to pursue into the future, and economic growth has been meant to be a tool to realize a society where people enjoy high levels of well-being. Therefore, if the original goal cannot be attained with the tool, naturally there is no point in using it.

## Implications from happiness research

If economic growth leads to higher income levels but not to improvement in peoples' lives or in their quality of life, pursuing economic growth becomes meaningless. This might be called a social limit to growth, and this problem has become a central topic in recent happiness research.

Still many issues are to be studied regarding the measurement of quality of life and well-being. Discussions in this section are based on research focusing on the level of happiness measured through individuals' subjective evaluation of their well-being. Surveys on the level of satisfaction in life are conducted in various parts of the world, such as World Values Survey, and studies on factors of happiness are actively being conducted. Let us first examine the relationship between the level of happiness and economic growth or an increase in income.

Easterlin (1974, 1995) provides the most important observation regarding the relationship between happiness and economic growth, and his (unexpected) finding that a nation's income level and the average level of happiness of its people are not necessarily correlated is referred to as the Easterlin Paradox or happiness paradox. What the Easterlin Paradox suggests fundamentally affects the concept of green growth. This is because the level of happiness does not necessarily increase even if green growth is achieved (or if economic growth is achieved while overcoming environmental constraints and resource constraints).

Facing stagnant economic growth, countries, particularly advanced ones including Japan, have adopted various strategies for economic growth. However, under the Easterlin Paradox, even if growth strategies yield some positive effects, their significance is small. One thing that can certainly be said is that it has become important to examine the objectives to be achieved through economic growth as well as the significance and quality of economic growth.

What are determinants of happiness? Recognizing the Easterlin Paradox, Frey and Stutzer (2005) focused on the effects of democracy and political participation on happiness. They considered that once materialistic affluence exceeds a certain level, political conditions become more important in people's lives than economic conditions. They pointed out that although happiness is often considered as a purely personal issue, it is actually affected significantly by the society in which people lead their lives. Conducting an empirical analysis of the case of the Switzerland, they then provided evidence that the level of people's happiness increases as a country becomes more democratic and decentralized.

Although one should be careful in making generalizations, subsequent studies on happiness find the following with regard to the relationship between the politico-economic system and the level of happiness (Frey, 2008). For instance, the effects of economic freedom are greater in the poorest countries than in rich countries, whereas the effects of political freedom are greater in rich countries. It is also pointed out that stability of the political regime is associated with the level of happiness.

In addition to political and economic conditions, conditions in society are also considered relevant to the level of happiness. A concept that is attracting attention at present is social capital. According to Putnam (1993), social capital refers to the civic tradition in society, including trust, norms and networks. The level of happiness and economic performance depend on how much social capital is accumulated. The United States is facing a problem that the level of happiness is declining despite rising GDP. One reason is said to be deterioration of social capital. Trust among people is being lost, and the rate of participation in, for example, local volunteer activities is decreasing. Because of these situations, increased income does not necessarily lead to a rise in the level of happiness.

It must be noted, however, that there are two aspects to the relationship between social capital and the level of happiness. Since social capital is associated with connections between people, its increase would raise the level of happiness. Also, the accumulation of social capital results in deeper networking and so-called institutional thickness, which would give rise to industrial agglomeration and efficiency in resource allocation as the potentials of the nature and talents of people are discovered and connected with one another.

## Sustainable development

As the preceding discussions clarify, what we should pursue is improvements in people's lives, quality of life and well-being, not merely economic growth. According to Dasgupta (2001), sustainable development of an economy means sustainable improvement of per capita well-being (quality of life).

Several "lineages" exist for the economic models of sustainable development. But the most important question in modelling sustainable development is what has to be sustainable. Is it the level of natural capital stock, or is it the consumption or utility level? One of the important characteristics of the Dasgupta model is that it specifies sustainable development as sustainable improvement in per capita well-being. Because of this, the results of re-examining the concept of development conducted by Sen and sustainable development can be understood in a unified manner, and the guidelines for policy making have become comprehensive. The concept of development used by Sen (1999) is one associated with the expansion of human freedom. The term *human development* represents the concept. This concept has had an impact on the activities of international organizations, and since 1990, the United Nations Development Program has published the Human Development Report and created the Human Development Index.

What becomes an issue in Dasgupta's specifications for sustainable development is the concrete nature of well-being. In considering well-being, Dasgupta (2001) separates its constituents from its determinants, which is another important characteristic of the Dasgupta model. The constituents of well-being are health, happiness, freedom to live and act and (more broadly) basic freedom. The determinants of well-being are capital assets and institutions, which form a basis for producing goods and services supporting (the constituents of) well-being. Capital assets include man-made capital (factories, machines, etc.), human capital, knowledge and natural capital. Institutions include economic actors such as households, firms, markets, communities and governments, which are considered to perform, as a whole, the function of the resource allocation mechanism that combines different capital assets and generates well-being.

As discussed earlier, Dasgupta specifies sustainable development as sustainable improvement in per capita well-being. Examining such well-being by separating its constituents from its determinants enables separate analyses on the sustainability of the constituents and the sustainability of the determinants, and subsequent unified examinations of them. This provides numerous implications for public policy design. Public policies aimed at improving well-being must realize sustainable development. In designing such policies, it is essential to acquire deeper knowledge about the constituents of well-being, such as happiness and freedom and the factors that contribute to them, as well as to clarify the actions to be taken and the manner in which such actions will realize well-being improvement. At the same time, systematic efforts must be made to examine how a mechanism should be built so that it can enhance and maintain the determinants of well-being or the foundation that improves and supports well-being.

## Transition management for sustainable human development

What is suggested by environmental problems and fundamental limits to economic growth is that responses to environmental problems become effective by being conducted as part of the process for realizing sustainable development, and not as individual environmental measures. Let us call this method of engaging in environmental problems an "environmental economic strategy for realizing sustainable development". The reason why it is called an environmental economic strategy is that the realization of sustainable development requires a unified strategy that goes beyond simple environmental measures or simple economic policies because in sustainable development the conflict between the environment and development are integrated from the standpoint of sustainable improvement of well-being.

A concrete attempt to realize sustainable development, which goes beyond the realm of socio-economic visions or models of sustainable development, requires clarification of the method used, which would incorporate issues found at the global, national, regional and local levels and their multilayered, mutual relationships.

If the framework by Dasgupta is to be followed, attention should be paid to institutions that produce well-being-supporting goods and services by combining various capital assets. The reason is that in making a necessary shift from the traditional high-carbon processes to low-carbon ones in producing goods and services, the relevant know-how that determines the quantity and quality of the goods and services produced, the quantity and quality of the capital assets used in production and the combination of such assets depends greatly on institutions.

Our project aims to clarify the issues and tasks of transition management for sustainable human development taking into account the idea of human development for environmental governance. Although the two concepts of human development and sustainable development overlap and share many arguments against existing mainstream development initiatives, it seems important to look at the ways in which the actions and the two concepts demand can be integrated and to see the conditions under which they are consistent with each other. We attempt to combine the two concepts into a concept of sustainable human development, and discuss how to make sustainable human development operational.

This book also aims to clarify how the structure and function of multilevel environmental governance contribute to sustainable human development. Governance for sustainable development refers to social, economic and political processes of governance towards the attainment of sustainable development. It encompasses public debate, policy formation and implementation, and complex interactions among government, private business and civil society. The establishment of longer term operational goals for sustainable development, the extension of co-management arrangements both vertically and horizontally, and the development of pluralistic networks for reviewing social and environmental trends and policy performance can help reduce uncertainties about the future development trends.

REFERENCES

Dasgupta, P. (2001) *Human Well-Being and Natural Environments*, Oxford: Oxford University Press.
Easterlin, R. A. (1974) "Does Economic Growth Improve the Human Lot? Some Empirical Evidence", in P. A. David and M. W. Reder (eds.) *Nations and Households in Economic Growth: Essays in Honour of Moses Abramowitz*, New York: Academic Press, pp. 89–125.
—— (1995) "Will Raising the Incomes of All Increase the Happiness of All?", *Journal of Economic Behavior and Organization*, 27, pp. 35–47.
Frey, B. (2008) *Happiness: A Revolution in Economics*, Cambridge, MA: MIT Press.
Frey, B. and A. Stutzer (2005) *Happiness and Economics*, Princeton, NJ: Princeton University Press.
Meadows, D. H. (1972) *The Limits to Growth: A Report for the Club of Roma's Project on the Predicament of Mankind*, New York: New American Library.
Putnam, R. (1993) *Making Democracy Work: Civic Tradition in Modern Italy*, Princeton, NJ: Princeton University Press.
Sen, A. (1987) *Commodities and Capabilities*, New Delhi: Oxford University Press.
—— (1999) *Development as Freedom*, Oxford: Oxford University Press.

# Part I
# Environmental governance for sustainable human development

# 1
# On the concept of sustainable human development

*Hiroki Nogami[†] and Kazuhiro Ueta*

The purpose of this chapter is to modify the concept of sustainable development by focusing on sustainability of improvement of quality of life (the Human Development, as proposed by United Nations Development Programme [UNDP]).

The two concepts of human development and sustainable development have been mostly proposed separately and from different authors and organizations. Although the two concepts overlap and share many arguments against existing mainstream development initiatives, treating them as distinct concepts is important. In this chapter, we look at the ways in which the actions and changes the two concepts demand can be integrated and determine the conditions under which they are consistent with each other.

The chapter is organized as follows: the second section discusses how the sustainable development and human development concepts coincide or differ. There, the view that they share perspectives on opportunity and quality of life is discussed. The third section attempts to combine the two concepts into a new concept of sustainable human development. Issues regarding the sustainable human development are also discussed. The fourth section is concerned with the question, How to make the sustainable human development concept operational? There, concepts and indicators of savings in human development and sustainable development are discussed. The final section provides our concluding remarks.

## The concepts of sustainability and human development

*Sustainability and sustainable development*

Sustainable development is a broader concept than is the sustainability of economic growth. Sustainable development stresses both the idea of sustaining activity for current and future generations as well as the linking of such activity to well-being rather than to economic growth per se. Authors on sustainable development argue that the scale of economic growth has to be controlled within the limit of natural environmental capacity and that an improvement of human livelihood conditions has to be achieved without heavy reliance on economic growth and resource depletion. In addition, protecting species and biological diversity has to be integrated into the development process.

Sustainable development seems to have two aspects. The first is the long-term possibility of reproducing present modes of production and consumption (the reproduction aspect). The second is maintaining and expanding the opportunity set of the future generations (the opportunity aspect). The first aspect relates to economic formulation of sustainable development. Two variations in economic formulation of sustainable development exist: weak and strong. In the weak formulation of sustainable development, the total endowment of natural and human-made capital is important. In the strong formulation of sustainable development, endowment of natural resource is important. The strong formulation relates not only to the endowment of capital but also to the conservation of natural resources and the protection of biological diversity and species. Authors favouring human development sometimes refer to the possibility of substituting natural resources and human-made capital because they think of the natural environment as an important instrument for the improvement of the quality of life.

On one hand, in the first aspect of the sustainability, attention is focused on the instrumental values of environment and natural resources. On the other hand, in the second aspect, the intrinsic value of the natural environment must be taken into account. In addition, for the second aspect, values and preferences of the future generations are unknown, and it is important to maintain the range of options in utilization of environment as wide as possible. If we focus on the range of options available for the future generations, we must pay attention not only to providing new options but also to preventing contraction of existing sets of options (avoiding changes that cannot be recovered by the environment). In this sense, if the opportunity aspect of sustainable development is important, the intrinsic values of nature and species, as well as the cultural product, have to be managed carefully, and the view of strong formulation of sustainable development will be important.

## Human development and capability

The concept of human development can be interpreted as a process of social and economic change whose main motive is to produce a radical improvement in the material and cultural lives of people. Authors supporting the human development approach share the general recognition that although a poor country may take a very long time to become a rich country through economic growth, the conditions for quality of life can change much more rapidly through intelligent policy-making. For example, by properly targeted social intervention, the average life expectancy in poor countries can be brought quite close to that of the richest countries in the world. Similar achievements can be made in other fields as well, such as basic education and health conditions. Therefore, the needed economic development should be justified by its contribution to human welfare, and economic growth has to be carefully promoted without contracting the opportunity set of current and future generations.

The opportunity set, which is a focal point of the human development concept, is sometimes referred to as "capability" in the human development literature (Sen, 1993; UNDP, 2010). Capability is a broad concept, and it incorporates not only the concerns that are associated with the notion of standard of living, but it also includes the notion of quality of life. Therefore, the human development (capability) approach has the following two features:

1. Distinction of well-being and resources: One of the features of the human development approach, which focuses on opportunity and freedom, is to be sensitive to the distinction between freedom and the means to achieve freedom (such as income or resources). This is because the relationships between income or resources and well-being may vary because of personal diversities in the possibility of converting income and resources into achievement of well-being (effective consumption, or "functionings", in Sen's [1993: 31–32] terminology). For example,
   - women are more exposed to high levels of indoor air pollution due to the fact that they traditionally spend more time at home, especially in the kitchen. As farm work is one of the important activities of women in developing countries, female farmers seem to be increasingly subject to the ill health effect of pesticides. In converting energy and fertilizer into their well-being, women have to cope with additional cost. Women in developing countries also tend to cope with limited outdoor activity. Although development initiatives construct roads in rural and remote areas in developing countries, women cannot convert the roads into their capability such as "going to remote areas freely".
   - people with disabilities suffer from limited access to opportunities. This is because society is often prejudiced against them and does not make the

necessary arrangements for people with disabilities to make full use of their potential. The handicaps, such as age or disability or illness, that reduces one's ability to earn an income can also be more difficult to convert into one's well-being (Sen, 1992).

These examples suggest that development initiatives have to be evaluated in terms of outcomes (what people can do or what people can be) rather than of input (such as income, budget or resources) or output (consumption of goods and services) of the development process. Individuals' capability depends not only on the goods and services consumed but also on variations in their utilization. Variations in utilization can arise from the biological and social characteristics of persons. Besides income, factors affecting consumption options include availability and infrastructure of essential goods and services, information, social barriers and autonomy of decision making in household matters (UNDP, 1998). Even when these factors affecting consumption options are not influenced greatly by policy, these factors have to be taken into account in policy planning.

2. Opportunity oriented: Development initiatives have to be evaluated in terms of not only achievement of outcomes (years of schooling, longevity, income etc.), but also a range of valuable alternatives from which people can choose. Sen proposes the concept of "capability", which reflects the degree of freedom in choosing alternative lifestyles a person can achieve. The capability is a set of activities and situations of an individual, and the individual can choose one collection of activities and situations ("functionings" in Sen's articles) from the "capability" (Sen, 1993: 31). For example, suppose that, in a society, an individual A can apply and engage in all types of jobs, and his or her wage is 80. Another individual B, who suffers from disadvantages, can apply for only one type of job, and his or her wage is 100. In monetary terms, individual B is better off than A, but in terms of freedom and opportunity, the well-being of B may not be superior to that of A. This example suggests that, in assessment of the standard of living in the human development, perspectives on opportunities and options are needed.

The perspectives of opportunity, which is one of the features of human development, can provide a channel that connects the notions of sustainable development and human development. The first implication is on empirical studies. If the opportunity aspect of the human development is taken as a focal point, indicators relating poverty, welfare and sustainability per se cannot provide sufficient information regarding states of an individual or a society. This is because indicators such as per capita income and life expectancy cannot tell why the values are realized, and they cannot provide enough information about the context and the process in which states of the individual or the society are realized. The second implication is related to welfare assessment. If the values of an individual's freedom are taken into account, planning of policy intervention must not depend on one or two outcome indicators. For example, total endowments of food and water at the macro level certainly influence the possibility in which an individual can obtain food and water to support his or her livelihood. However, the ability by which the individual can obtain necessary food and water in existing institutional framework depends not only on total resource endowment, but also on his or her labour and assets, as well as on his or her opportunity set of exchange. This is because the individual must work or sell his or her assets in order to buy food, water and other necessities. If the individual has to cope with deterioration of employment condition, the terms of trade between his or her labour and the necessities would also deteriorate, and the individual has to cope with difficulties in meeting his or her needs, even though total endowment with food and water remains unchanged. Therefore, in order to provide food and water to the population continuously, policymakers have to attend to not only food production and water management but also to social security and employment promotion.

*Mutual support between sustainable development and human development*

Many authors investigate conditions under which the notion of sustainable development and that of human development are consistent with each other. However, the concept of sustainable development is related to the assessment of performance of an economic system as a whole, and the concept of human development is related to the assessment of an individual's well-being. Therefore, the two concepts can be seen as complements rather than substitutes. For example, performances of an economic system have to be evaluated not only in terms of aggregate measures, such as the gross domestic product (GDP) or traditional sustainable measures, but also in terms of its impacts on people's standard of living. This is because any economic system cannot survive without an active and healthy population enjoying a decent standard of living. In addition, individuals can only lead their own lives once, and performances at the macro level are meaningless unless the economy can provide them with a good standard of living. Therefore, the concept of sustainable development must be complemented by that of human development. In addition, the concept of sustainable development tends to be considered as an appropriate balance between natural resources endowment and population.[1] This conceptualization seems to be derived from the Malthusian theory, which explains poverty by the unbalance between food production and the population. The capability approach criticizes this theory. First, we have to focus on terms of trade between goods and services and individuals' assets (labour, savings and entitlement). Second, we have to focus on inequalities in efficiency, by which an individual transforms goods and services into his or her well-being. By rejecting the Malthusian theory, the capability approach attempts to overcome the conflicts between environmental sustainability and social sustainability, namely, sustainability of human livelihood. As Mahbub ul Haq (1995) holds, if the present is miserable, it must be changed before it is sustained, and what must be sustained are worthwhile life opportunities.

## Towards sustainable human development

### *The meaning of opportunities in sustainable human development*

In order to clarify the relationship between the two criteria of sustainability and the notion of capability, the following example is discussed.

Suppose that there two economies, case A and case B, in which there is a renewable resource (such as bio-energy), a non-renewable resource (such as oil) and human-made capital (see Figure 1.1). The renewable resource can compensate the loss of 5 units by its reproduction capacity. The endowment with the non-renewable resource is 10 units. People utilize renewable and non-renewable resources to accumulate and utilize the human-made capital.

Case A

|  | Period 1 | Period 2 |
|---|---|---|
| RR | ▼5 | 0 = (▼5 + 5) |
| NRR | 0 | 0 |
| HMC | 0 | 0 |

Case B

|  | Period 1 | Period 2 |
|---|---|---|
| RR | 0 | ▼5 |
| NRR | ▼10 | ■ |
| HMC | 10 | 10 |

Figure 1.1 Resources and capital in two economies
*Note:* Figures in the matrix mean increases or decreases in resources and capital. RR = renewable resources; NRR = non-renewable resources; HMC = human-made capital, ■ = not available; ▼ = negative. In case A, people utilize RR by 5 units, but due to the reproduction capacity of the RR, in period 2, endowment of the RR remains unchanged (▼5 + 5 = 0). In case B, people utilize 10 units of NRR in order to accumulate 10 units of HMC, and NRR depletes. In case A, monetary value of RR decreases by 5 in period 1, and in period 2, RR increases by 5 by RR's reproductive capacity, as a result that total value of resource and capital remain unchanged. In case B, NRR decreases by 10, but HMC increases by 10, as a result that total values of resource and capital remain unchanged. In period 2, RR decreases by 5, but the decreases can be recovered by reproductive capacity of RR.

Suppose that, in case A, people utilize renewable resources by 5 units within the limit of reproduction capacity of the renewable resources (the resources can compensate the loss of 5 units), and levels of income and human-made capital remain unchanged (a case of stationary state). In case B, people utilize 10 units of the non-renewable resource in order to accumulate human-made capital of 10 units in period 1 and in period 2, after depletion of the non-renewable resource, people utilize the renewable resource to make the human-made capital work. As a result, in period 2, volume of human-made capital and resources of case B exceed those of case A. As for the weak criterion of sustainability, both cases can be regarded as "sustainable", but in case A, although the achievement of human-made capital is lower than in case B, people have the option of utilizing renewable resources in period 2. In case B, although the achievement of the human-made capital is high, people have to utilize the renewable resource in period 2 because the non-renewable resource is not available. Dimensions of opportunities in period 2 are inferior to those in period 1. Therefore, in order to qualify the development pattern in case B as ethically sustainable in the sense of strong sustainability, the overall development of a society should leave many more options open than the common approach regarding sustainable development tends to advocate.

In order to examine whether case B is a reasonable model of sustainable development, we have to examine for what kind of purposes the human-made capital is utilized. If the human-made capital is used for meeting basic human needs, case B can be regarded as a success in terms of basic human needs satisfaction, but it is not regarded as a case of sustainable human development in the strong sense. This is because, in period 2, the set of alternatives people can choose from is contracted, and no room remains for the people to choose using the non-renewable resource. Although facing more alternatives need not invariably be seen as an expansion of a person's freedom, the recognition that choice is an important component of human life has to be taken into account (Sen, 1992).

This example illustrates that, when evaluating performance of a society, we have to evaluate the performance not only in terms of achievement of the respective indicators but also in terms of range of options available for the people. As Comin et al. (2007) argue, using the capability perspective to modify sustainable development policies implies focusing on the weak sustainability criterion (in which a constant or increasingly high level of consumption can be maintained over time through the substitution of physical capital for natural capital) as instrumental, but the strong sustainability criteria (closer to the principles of environmental conservation and involving decreasing or constant levels of natural capital over time) can reflect, together with principles of quality of life, goals of sustainable human development policies. Therefore, emphasizing the expansion of freedom of an individual suggests a trend towards the use of strong sustainability indicators, such as endowment of total natural capital. Thus, in making the sustainable human development indicators, priority should be given to critical levels of natural capital.

## Equality or expansion of basic capabilities?

As for the concept of human development, it is important to notice the fact that there are two different formulations regarding the prescriptive content of the capability approach, as explained in Alkire (2002). One formulation argues the goal of development as the promotion and expansion of valuable capabilities. The second considers the goal as equality in the space of basic capabilities. In the second formulation, the goal of development is accomplished if there is equality in basic capabilities, regardless of the effect the achievement of such equality might have had on other valuable capabilities. Given the capability approach's attention on valuation, it is necessary to pay attention to the possible contraction in other valuable capabilities that might be associated with an expansion of the basic capabilities they identify (Alkire, 2002).

In order to clarify the problem, let us modify the example of case B in Figure 1.1, and let us denote modification of case B as case B+:

Case B+: In period 1, the most deprived person suffers from illness, and in order to make the person survive in period 2, it is necessary to build a health care system, which requires at least 10 units of the human-made capital. Whether depletion of the NRR is accepted depends on social valuation of sustainability of the most deprived person's life. The preceding discussion assumes that there is an agreement regarding identification of the most deprived person. There are persons with illness, disability and other disadvantages. They all need social assistance. In addition, in reality, the most deprived person often pays the cost of depletion of the non-renewable resource, rather than the benefit of depletion of the non-renewable resource. Therefore, the extent of the trade-off between the sustainability and poverty reduction depends on the context of the society.

In case B+, it is possible to promote expansion of the basic capabilities of the most deprived persons. This case may be justified in terms of equality of basic capability to survive. However, in period 2, the same capability expansion cannot be reproduced, and the most deprived person, who can survive in period 2, may not be able to enjoy the capability of "being able to live with concern for and in relation to animals, plants and the world of nature" (Nussbaum, 1999: 235). In case A, persons enjoy a wider range of options because of the availability of the renewable resource and the non-renewable resource, but the most deprived person cannot survive in period 2. Thus, the human development approach has to confront choice between assuring basic quality of life (in Sen's words, capabilities) for all individuals and improvement of overall quality of life (in Sen's words, capabilities) for a portion of the people.

The most important issue in the preceding example is the fact that present development initiatives may be associated with contraction in non-basic capabilities including cultural and environmental opportunities of future generations. Spending more attention on reducing social inequality does not justify entirely disregarding the cultural and the environmental considerations. This is because, even in a number of deprived communities, people value non-material impacts (unity, helping others, religion and others) as well as impacts that affect their material poverty (health, savings, education and others; Alkire, 2002). Even in case B+, the society has to spend attention for improving the quality of the most deprived person in period 2. Development initiatives, whether focused on income or on basic needs, may be defined as exogenous and may undermine other valuable capabilities in the long term. Even in the case of initiatives based on the human development perspective, development may expand choice only in some dimension while constricting choice in others.

In an interesting paper by Satō (1997), he emphasizes the importance of focusing on contraction of the capability sets, in which the development initiatives reduce the number of alternatives from which people can choose. This is because, in the development process, new additional alternatives replace traditional and existing alternatives people can enjoy, i.e., "Development by Displacement" (Grabowski and Shields, 1996: 76–79). In addition, people cannot have a clear image of additional new alternatives, whereas people can easily imagine the value of existing alternatives. Satō's argument suggests that the priority of the development initiatives must be an equality of the basic capability rather than an enlargement of the capability sets.

## Making sustainable human development operational

### Is human development in Japan sustainable?

This section attempts to search for the way that makes the concept of sustainable human development operational.

Table 1.1 shows indicators regarding sustainability and human development (Human Development Index, or HDI). The Japanese adjusted saving rate exceeds that of Australia and Norway. In addition, Japan belongs to a group of countries with a very high HDI. If we accept the figures as true, Japan seems to be on a path towards sustainable human development.

However, the majority of Japanese people do not think that their economy and society are on a path towards sustainable human development. This is because the HDI series is a combination of a few social and economic indicators, and they cannot cover information regarding the present situation of Japanese people.

We can imagine some examples:
- The high savings rate in Japan may be interpreted as a sign that people are anxious about their livelihood in old age and that they have to prepare for expenditure associated with housing, educating children, illness and unemployment.

Table 1.1 Indicators of sustainability and human development

(1) On sustainability

|  | NNS | EE | ED | MD | NFD | CDD | PED | ANS |
|---|---|---|---|---|---|---|---|---|
| Norway | 25.4 | 7.0 | 23.0 | 0.0 | 0.0 | 0.1 | 0.1 | 9.2 |
| Australia | 6.8 | 4.7 | 3.6 | 5.1 | 0.0 | 0.4 | 0.1 | 2.4 |
| Japan | 13.4 | 3.1 | 0.0 | 0.0 | 0.0 | 0.2 | 0.5 | 15.8 |
| Russian Federation | 23.7 | 3.5 | 37.5 | 1.9 | 0.0 | 1.4 | 0.3 | −13.8 |
| Low income countries | 21.5 | 3.4 | 9.4 | 1.3 | 0.6 | 1.0 | 0.7 | 11.9 |
| Middle income countries | 19.6 | 3.5 | 12.8 | 1.6 | 0.0 | 0.9 | 0.8 | 7.0 |
| High income countries | 6.9 | 4.7 | 1.5 | 0.2 | 0.0 | 0.3 | 0.3 | 9.3 |

(2) On human development (Human Development Index: HDI)

| Year | HDI 2005 | HDI 2009 | HDI 2010 |
|---|---|---|---|
| Norway | 0.932 | 0.937 | 0.938 |
| Australia | 0.925 | 0.935 | 0.937 |
| Japan | 0.873 | 0.881 | 0.884 |
| Russian Federation | 0.693 | 0.714 | 0.719 |

Developed countries (average)

| Year | HDI 2005 | HDI 2009 | HDI 2010 |
|---|---|---|---|
| Developed OECD countries | 0.868 | 0.876 | 0.879 |
| Developed non OECD countries | 0.829 | 0.840 | 0.844 |

Developing countries (average)

| | HDI 2005 | HDI 2009 | HDI 2010 |
|---|---|---|---|
| Arab States | 0.562 | 0.583 | 0.588 |
| East Asian and the Pacific | 0.600 | 0.636 | 0.643 |
| Europe and Central Asia | 0.679 | 0.698 | 0.702 |
| Latin America and the Caribbean | 0.681 | 0.699 | 0.704 |

Table 1.1 (cont.)

| | | | |
|---|---|---|---|
| South Asia | 0.481 | 0.510 | 0.516 |
| Sub-Saharan Africa | 0.366 | 0.384 | 0.389 |

*Source:* Panel 1: World Bank (2008) *World Development Indicators 2008,* Washington, DC: World Bank, pp. 188–191. Panel 2: UNDP (2010) *Human Development Report 2010,* New York: UNDP, pp. 148–151.

*Note:* NNS = net national savings rate (% of gross national income [GNI], 2006); EE = education expenditure (% of GNI, 2006); ED = energy depletion (% of GNI, 2006); MD = mineral depletion (% of GNI, 2006); NFD = net forest depletion (% of GNI, 2006); CDD = carbon dioxide damage (% of GNI, 2006); PED = particulate emission damage (% of GNI, 2006); ANS = adjusted net savings rate (% of GNI, 2006). ANS = NNS + EE − ED − NFD − CDD − PED. In panel 1, "0.0"means very small expenditures, and figures are for 2006. "Low income countries", "Middle income countries" and "High income countries" are based on classification of World Bank (2008). In panel 2, classification of countries is based on UNDP (2010).

In addition, some monetary expenditure by ordinary consumers represent not additions to welfare but attempts to offset some change in social, environmental or individual circumstances that are causing a decline in welfare.
- The Japanese economy consumes a large volume of imported mineral and fuel resources, and the adjusted net savings rates of the World Bank do not take into account the consumption of the imported resources as depletion.
- Many Japanese students go to university, and this is because, in their view, although a person at 15 years of age can work, he or she will have difficulties in obtaining employment opportunities for decent work without any diploma. The HDI is composed of education, life expectancy and per capita income, and the HDI does not reflect employment opportunities of the younger generation.
- The Japanese economy has to cope with international competition, and the government cannot provide effective action due to fiscal constraint.
- Due to rapid population aging in Japan, together with the fiscal constraint, people tend to think of the Japanese socio-economic development as being not sustainable.

The preceding discussion suggests that factors affecting people's perception of possibility of sustainability and human development are broader concepts than are those reflected in the indicators. In order to realize sustainable human development in Japan, we have to look at the mechanism of human development, rather than at indicators of human development and sustainability.

## A proposal of policy framework

Alkire (2002) revised the traditional formulation of capabilities to incorporate consideration of the full menu of choices that people face, and the amendments can be modified to incorporate opportunities of the future generations in the following manner. According to Alkire (2002: 174–176), for policymakers and governments, the long-term goal is to increase the basic capabilities of people, including the future generation, without contracting their overall capability set, which requires one (1) to identify long-term valued capability goals and strategies, using participation; (2) to work in the short term to establish functionings instrumental to these goals; (3) to implement a strategy that safeguards people's overall freedom; and (4) to mitigate the contraction of wider capabilities that occur as a result of expanding basic capabilities (where possible, to allow both to expand).

This proposal of Alkire (2002) seems to be useful, but relationships between capabilities have to be examined. This is because sustainable human development requires sustainable expansion of basic capabilities (such as being educated and longevity) or enlargement of sets of the basic capabilities, and balances between the process of promoting capabilities would be important.

Suppose that elements of the basic capability sets have intrinsic and instrumental values. For example, the capability of "being educated" has not only intrinsic value but also instrumental value of income generation. The instrumental value of the education cannot be realized without employment opportunities for decent work. The process of improvement of standard of living requires balanced development of the economy and the society.

In order to make a cycle of basic capabilities, such as "being educated" → "being employed" → "income generation" → "consumption of goods and services" → "well-being", balance and consistency of the development policies have to be provided. For example, Taylor et al. (1998: 442–450) describe two processes: (a) a virtuous circle of income poverty reduction, social development and economic growth and (b) synergies between policies and outcomes within the social sectors which contribute to social development. They attempt to demonstrate that policies which do not focus on at least two of the three variables (income poverty reduction, social development and economic growth) will have serious difficulties in realizing the desirable outcomes initially set out. In order to create the virtuous circle, one option, which links sustainability and human development, is employment for environmental protection. Ecosystem maintenance increasingly calls for active intervention rather than simply minimizing damage. Mere neglect does not necessarily yield restoration. Much of the anthropogenically modified environment requires maintenance (McNicoll, 2007).

As for strategies of poverty alleviation, several authors emphasize the role of distribution of income and resources in poverty alleviation. This is because, in their view, the present state of productive capacity can ensure sufficient volume of goods and services for the population. However, there are two issues to be emphasized. First, in the human development perspective, income and resources are inputs rather than ends (ultimate outcome) in human livelihood. Investment in people must be allocated not only to increasing income-earning capacity but also to enhancing the individual's ability of utilizing income and resources (the extent to which an individual transforms the income and resources into the individual's activity). Comin et al. (2007) refer to the view that it is necessary to distinguish between consumption of products and services to meet current demands and needs, and the consumption of resources (the extent to which materials and energy are used). Comin et al. (2007) emphasize from the capability perspective not only resource-earning ability but also their resource-using ability. Thus, in order to make human development sustainable, we pay attention to not only saving resource use but also investing in enhancing resource-using ability (the efficiency of resource use in meeting current demands and needs) and to identifying basic elements of human well-being. Debates between the strong and weak versions of sustainability refer to the possibility of substitution between natural and human-made capital. Factors determining the possibility of substitution must be discussed. One of the important determinants of the degree of substitution is the ability of human beings. For example, in order to reduce energy consumption, firms and households must provide alternative forms of production and consumption. In addition, people must have opportunities to choose alternative lifestyles. This is because the information of income and consumption can provide very limited description of social status. As the advocates of the strong criterion for sustainable development hold, the possibility of substitution between natural capital and other human-made capital in production may not be perfect. However, if we can improve efficiency of utilization of resources in the livelihood of the people with disadvantage, we can improve the quality of life of the people with disadvantage within the constraint of resources.

Second, in addition to an individual's income and resources, social infrastructures and common property resources are also important in human livelihood, and policies for sustainable human development must pay attention to provision and management of social common capital and commons (Uzawa, 2005). The social common capital includes institutional arrangement of the society.

*Poverty reduction and savings*

One of the focal points regarding the sustainable development and the human development concepts is savings. This is because finding the appropriate balance between consumption for the present generation and the saving of resources for future generations has been a central issue in the sustainability literature. Sustainable development focuses on the appropriate level of genuine (or the adjusted) saving so that the total endowment of human-made and natural capital is kept constant (see for example, World Bank, 2003). Initiatives regarding poverty reduction tend to focus on the appropriate consumption which meets the basic needs of the population. In this sense, there seems to be a conflict between sustainable development and poverty reduction. This is because sustainable development requires control of utilization of resources and the poverty reduction demands maximum utilization of resources for the present generation. However, in the case of human development, investments in education and health are considered as high priorities because they enlarge the opportunities of the population. Therefore, in order to make the initiatives for the sustainability and human development to be consistent, the role and meaning of the savings in the poverty reduction may be reconsidered.

There might be some point at which consumption by the poor was more socially valuable than savings. It may be necessary to incorporate some value for the social cost of consumption, because savings should be promoted in order to obtain resources for investments. For example, employment would have led to an increase in income, most of which, in all cases, was consumed. However, according to Alkire (2002), savings are usually valued more highly than present consumption, even among the poor. In the case of a lack of credit institutions, the development of the habit of saving might enable the poor to decrease their need for credit. Families who save can manage consumption throughout the year and so possibly decrease their vulnerability to absolute poverty in the period of shortage. Sustainable development requires saving and allocation of saving to natural capital, whereas the concept of human development concerns transformation of consumption and to the quality of life. Nussbaum (1999: 235) argues that opportunities to live with concern for and in relation to animals, plants and the world of nature is one of the central elements of decent quality of life. Therefore, protection of natural environment improves the quality of life of the present generation.

The minimum level of the standard of living, the so-called poverty line, has to be reconsidered to incorporate the perspective of the capability approach. In addition, the poverty line also has to be consistent with the conditions of sustainable development.[2] The traditional method of determining the minimum income level, which is the threshold line to poverty, is to identify the adequate nutritious requirement and other necessities to support a decent life of a particular individual. The method provides information regarding the appropriate minimum level of an individual or of a family to pay for consumption as such. In this process, it is very important to identify the contents of phrases such as "adequate requirement" and "a decent life". On this issue, Krongkaew (1979) attempts to define an income level which relates to a break-even point of zero savings, and which is converted into an upper limit of poverty threshold using computation of a consumption function, a relationship between consumption and income (see also Takayama, 1980). According to Krongkaew (1979), besides food, there are additional expenses for clothing, shelter, relaxation and entertainment, and so on. Thus, Krongkaew (1979) argues that the real income level of the poor must always lie below the break-even point, and the best proposition is to use a "poverty band" instead of using only a single line or index. Upper limits on income level are sets which prevent families from suffering from inconveniences stemming from insufficient income. Lower limits are families' minimum income level for survival.

The discussion by Krongkaew (1979) can be extended to the determination of the poverty band in the sustainable development, and this is because the method of poverty line determination proposed by Krongkaew (1979) takes savings into consideration. In order to ensure sufficient income and resources for investment in people's capacity, savings in terms of income and resources are needed. In addition, although the poor have to rely on public assistance, the poor have a right to promote their potential by utilizing their savings, and the poverty line or minimum wages have to be arranged so that the poor can achieve a minimum level of savings. Therefore, at the macro level, per capita income below the break-even point (a zero savings rate) cannot provide sufficient savings for further development. In addition, if we accept the weak criterion of the sustainability, income level, which cannot provide sufficient savings to meet the requirement for maintenance and recovering the depletion of natural resources, is not sustainable. Balances between the per capita income which relates to zero net savings rates, and the per capita income level which relates to zero genuine (or adjusted net) savings rates are important in sustainable human development.

Suppose that a consumption function between per capita income, $Y$, and per capita consumption, $C$, is identified.

$$C = a + bY, a > 0 \text{ and } 0 < b < 1. \tag{1}$$

Then, $Y^* = \dfrac{a}{1-b}$ is the break-even income level at which the savings rate is zero (savings means net savings, which cover depreciation of fixed capital). At this income level, people can afford expenditures for survival, and economic growth is impossible because the economy cannot provide savings for investment and development. However, the expenditures may include non-necessities and the real minimum level for stationary state seems to be below the $Y^*$. Therefore, Krongkaew (1979) proposes that $Y^*$ be multiplied by the Engel coefficient, a proportion of expenditure spend for food consumption, as a lower limit of the minimum income. At least, national poverty line (or the basic income) may set levels between $Y^*$ and $Y^*$ multiplied by the Engel coefficient.

If we pay attention to natural capital, savings provided at the income level of $Y^*$ may not be sufficient to cover the requirement necessary to recover and maintain the depletion of natural capital and resources. Suppose that natural resource depletion follows the equation

$$Dep = d + eY^2, d > 0 \text{ and } e > 0. \tag{2}$$

Equation (2) means that resource consumption is increasing more rapidly than income growth. The genuine savings, or adjusted net savings (ADJS), which is the difference between the net savings and cost of natural resource depletion, are determined as follows:

$$ADJS = -eY^2 + (1 - b)Y - (a + d). \tag{3}$$

If appropriate balances between the parameters (such as $a$, $b$, $d$ and $e$) are realized, then there are two income levels: $Ym$, which refers to the lower value of income at which the ADJS is zero, and $YM$, which refers to larger value of income at which the ADJS are zero.[3] If the per capita income is below $Ym$, the economy cannot achieve sustainable economic development, and this is the situation of some of the least developed countries (e.g., UNCTAD, 2002: 87–97). If the income level is between $Ym$ and $YM$, the economic growth is sustainable because savings cover the cost of natural resource depletion. If $Y^*$ is below $YM$ (the maximum sustainable income level), the economy, which is sustainable, can provide a per capita income which covers necessary expenditure for people's survival. The surplus (the different between $YM$ and $Y^*$) can be utilized for maintenance of nature and social common capital.

The implication of the preceding discussion is that, even though we focus on dimensions of income and consumption, there are ambiguities and fuzziness in determining the minimum income appropriate for the sustainable human development. This is because a decent livelihood requires a lot of goods, services and activities. In addition, it is important to keep the appropriate balance between a civil minimum standard of living (the poverty line and minimum wages) and a sustainable income level. Promoting savings, as well as improving resource utilization efficiency, is required.

As for the management of savings and investments, authors on human development and sustainable development share the view that public policies are needed for sustainable human development. For example, Sen emphasizes the role of social arrangement for optimal saving. Sen's argument for the non-optimality of market savings is based on the assumption of a situation of the type of the isolation paradox. In this case, an individual will not engage in saving even if he or she knows that others are doing so, resulting in the non-optimality of the market outcome (Sen, 1967). In order to guide private savings to a sufficient level for sustainable development and direction, policy intervention will be crucial.

*Role of the government*

In a discussion concerning social security, Drèze and Sen (1989) propose two strategies in enhancing people's well-being. One approach is to promote economic growth and take the best possible advantage of the potentialities released by greater general affluence including not only an expansion of private incomes but also an improved basis for public support (growth-mediated security). Another alternative is to resort directly to wide-ranging public support in domains such as employment provision, income redistribution, health care, education and social assistance in order to remove destitution without waiting for a transformation in the level of general affluence (support-led security). This scheme is useful for the achievement of sustainable human development. In addition, Drèze and Sen (1989) distinguish two aspects of social security, namely, protection and promotion. The former is concerned with the task of preventing a decline in living standard, and the latter refers to the enhancement of general living standard and to the expansion of basic capabilities of the population. If we pay attention to the possibility of the livelihood reproduction as a condition of the sustainable human development, resilience (capacity to prevent rapid reduction of standard of living) to cope with economic recessions and natural disaster has to be taken into account. Even if a country has to rely on natural resource exploitation, the country can accumulate revenue and save it as a fund for improving human capacity.

## Synthesis and conclusion

This chapter attempts to identify a link connecting the concepts of sustainable development and human development. The UNDP's *Human Development Report 2010*, which is the 20th anniversary edition, explores how the past *Human Development Reports* drew attention to sustainable development and environmental issues. The report insists that human development and sustainable development cannot be separated, and the broader scope, which is emphasized in the human development perspectives, complements conventional approaches to sustainable development. This is because traditional discussions regarding sustainability tend to focus on future growth and consumption, as well as the survival of the species and the intrinsic importance of the ecosystem.

However, there seems to be still a gap between views expressed in the past *Human Development Reports* and those expressed in original formulations of the capability approach by Sen and others. Therefore, *this* chapter attempted to bring attention to the issues, which were not emphasized in the *Human Development Reports*. Then, the chapter showed a way to make the capability approach work for reconsideration of the sustainable development concept.

The original formulation of the capability approach emphasizes the opportunity aspects of freedom, and this can be extended to sustainable human development. The implication is that if development initiatives, which focus on the promotion of the basic dimensions of human development (such as components of the UNDP's Human Development Index), neglect the values of non-basic dimensions of human development, such as freedom to enjoy clean air and water of the population, then the initiatives may deteriorate the quality of life of the future generations. Therefore, in order to prevent the possibility of contraction of opportunity sets of future generations, sustainable human development may pay more attention to the strong version of sustainable development.

Finally, the examples, which explored difficulties in making the sustainable human development operational, were discussed. The difficulties are partly due to difficulties regarding identification of a decent standard of living and a decent quality of life. The list of central human functional capabilities, proposed by Nussbaum (1999), certainly provides useful guidance for the arrangement of basic standard of living in the sustainable human development concept.

## Notes

† The original manuscript of this chapter was written mainly by Hiroki Nogami who passed away very unexpectedly before completing this work. Therefore, one of the volume editors, Kazuhiro Ueta, who had proposed a similar idea in the study group, led the completion of the chapter. We pray for the repose of our admirable friend who held a deep interest in the human development concept and devoted his work to finding ways to integrate such a concept, both in theory and practice, with sustainable development.

1. For example, Herman E. Daly (1996: chap. 9) views sustainable development in terms of balance between population and population-supporting capacity of the natural environment. Although Daly refers to the importance of distribution and institutions, his view, which is focusing on the macro economy and neglecting inequality in an individual's access to utilization of energy and natural environment, has to be complemented by a sociological approach.

2. There are measures which incorporate the notion of sustainability and well-being. For example, the ISEW (Index of Sustainable Economic Welfare) or the GPI (Genuine Progress Index) attempt to measure sustainable income and consumption for advanced countries (see Daly, 1996; Hamilton, 2007). In my view, this notion is interesting because it enables combining the notion of a sustainable level of decent standard of living and a sustainable poverty line, which is indispensable for the social policy formulation in sustainable development. We can find recent studies based on the notion of Hick's definition of sustainable income (consumption). Osberg and Sharpe (2002) and Torras (1999, 2001) attempt to measure economic well-being corrected for inequality, poverty, resource depletion and environmental degradation. Torras (1999, 2001) creates revised measures based on GDP but that are corrected for both distributional bias and resource depletion for Indonesia, Costa Rica and Brazil. The measures are derived from depletion-adjusted domestic product (DADP) by allocating the DADP among the different quintiles with poverty weights suggested by preceding studies (for example, the weights are the inverse of the income share). This assumption is based on the observation that it is the poor who disproportionately absorb welfare losses resulting from natural resource depletion.

3. $ADJS = -eY^2 + (1-b)Y - (a+d) = -e\left(Y - \frac{1-b}{2e}\right)^2 + K$
$K = \frac{(1-b)^2 - 4e(a+d)}{4e}$

If $K$ is positive, then adjusted net savings (ADJS) takes maximum value ($K$) at the income level of $\left(\frac{1-b}{2e}\right)$.

Derivative of the ADJS with respect to $Y$ ($-2eY - (1-b)$), when $Y$ is at the level of break-even point (zero net savings), becomes $\frac{-2ae}{(1-b)} + (1-b)$. If $(1-b)^2 > 2ae$, although the ADJS at the break-even point of $Y^*$ is negative (not sustainable), the ADJS is increasing, and $0 < Y^* < Ym < YM$. This condition implies that the marginal propensity to save $(1-b)$ has to exceed sufficiently the subsistence consumption ($a$) and the rate of natural resource depletion ($e$).

## REFERENCES

Alkire, Sabina (2002) *Valuing Freedom: Sen's Capability Approach and Poverty Reduction*, New York: Oxford University Press.

Comim, Flavio, Rie Tsutsumi, and Angels Varea (2007) "Choosing Sustainable Consumption: A Capability Perspective on Indicators", *Journal of International Development*, 19(4), pp. 493–509.

Daly, Herman E. (1996) *Beyond Growth: The Economics of Sustainable Development*, Boston, MA: Beacon Press.
Drèze, J. and A. K. Sen (1989) *Hunger and Public Action*, Oxford: Clarendon Press.
Grabowski, Richard and Michael P. Shields (1996) *Development Economics*, Cambridge: Blackwell.
Hamilton, Clive (2007) "Measuring Sustainable Economic Welfare", in Giles Atkinson et al. (eds.) *Handbook of Sustainable Development*, Cheltenham: Edward Elgar, pp. 307–318.
Haq, Mahbub ul (1995) *Reflections on Human Development*, New York: Oxford University Press.
Krongkaew, Medhi (1979) "The Determination of Poverty Band in Thailand", *Philippine Economic Journal*, 18(4), pp. 396–417.
McNicoll, Geoffrey (2007) "Population and Sustainability", in Giles Atkinson et al. (eds.) *Handbook of Sustainable Development*, Cheltenham: Edward Elgar, pp. 125–139.
Nussbaum, Martha (1999) "Women and Equality: The Capabilities Approach", *International Labour Review*, 138(3), pp. 227–245.
Osberg, L. and A. Sharpe (2002) "An Index of Economic Well-Being for Selected OECD Countries", *Review of Income and Wealth*, 48(3), pp. 291–316.
Satō, Jin (1997) "Conceptual Methods for Assessing the Standard of Living: A Critiques and Extension of Amartya Sen's Approach", *Ajia Kenkyū* (Asian Studies), 43(3), pp. 1–31.
Sen, Amartya (1967) "Isolation, Assurance and the Social Rate of Discount", *Quarterly Journal of Economics*, 138(3), pp. 112–124.
—— (1992) *Inequality Reexamined*, Oxford: Clarendon Press.
—— (1993) "Capability and Well-Being", in Martha Nussbaum and Amartya Sen (eds.) *The Quality of Life*, Oxford: Clarendon Press, pp. 30–53.
Takayama, Noriyuki (1980) *Fubyōdō no Keizai Bunseki* [Economic Analysis of Inequality], Tokyo: Tōyō keizaishimpō sha.
Taylor, L., S. Mehrotra and E. Delamonica (1998) "The Links between Economic Growth, Poverty Reduction and Social Development", in S. Mehrotra and R. Jolly (eds.) *Development with a Human Face*, Oxford: Oxford University Press, pp. 435–467.
Torras, M. (1999) "Inequality, Resource Depletion, and Welfare Accounting: Applications to Indonesia and Costa Rica", *World Development*, 27(7), pp. 1191–1202.
—— (2001) "Welfare Accounting and the Environment: Reassessing Brazilian Economic Growth, 1965–1993", *Development and Change*, 32(2), pp. 205–229.
UNCTAD (2002) *The Least Developed Countries Report 2002: Escaping the Poverty Traps*, New York and Geneva: United Nations.
UNDP (1998) *Human Development Report 1998*, New York: UNDP.
—— (2010) *Human Development Report 2010: The Real Wealth of Nations: Pathways to Human Development*, New York: UNDP and Palgrave Macmillan.
Uzawa, Hirotumi (2005) *Economic Analysis of Social Common Capital*, Cambridge: Cambridge University Press.
World Bank (2003) *World Development Report 2003: Sustainable Development in a Dynamic World Transforming Institutions, Growth, and Quality of Life*, Washington, DC: World Bank.

# 2
# Environmental policy integration for sustainability and its contemporary policy implications

*Kazuo Matsushita*

The world is on the brink of a paradigm shift from energy-intensive to low-carbon societies. "Low-carbon societies" are those where people can enjoy rich and humane lifestyles while reducing dependence on fossil fuels and carbon dioxide emissions. In order to develop low-carbon societies, consistent policy packages must be laid out, and efforts must be made to ensure these policies are realized.

Global warming mitigation is reputed to put new burdens and costs on household budgets and companies. However, on the flipside are business opportunities for new investments. A prerequisite is that our societies are stimulated and employment expanded through investments in the environment and that the shift to a low-carbon industrial structure will be promoted. For this, reform of social institutions and tax systems is required.

This chapter scrutinizes the present-day definition of environmental policy integration (EPI), a policy principle designed to realize sustainable development. Policy integration is necessary for the creation and implementation of consistent policies, and prioritization of policy is required to achieve the shift to sustainable low-carbon societies. From this viewpoint, concepts and instruments are reviewed, and how these stand up to the criterion of EPI is determined. Further, the potential for deployment in various countries and in local environmental administration is examined.

## Why address environmental policy integration?

The five points that follow, previously made by Matsushita (2007), outline issues that must be deliberated when considering strategic approaches to environmental governance aimed at the formation of sustainable societies.

1. How can standards for sustainability be woven into the processes and institutions of environmental governance?
2. What kind of democratic processes exist for relevant parties to take advantage of their diversity and plurality and get actively involved in problem-solving?
3. Promotion of decentralization based on the view that community initiatives are the basis for addressing environmental problems, that decision-making at a level nearer to citizens should be stressed and that work that can be accomplished by foundational administrative units should be left to these administrative units (subsidiarity principle).
4. Establishment of the cooperative principle, whereby citizens and private companies get involved in problem-solving from the stage of policy-making.
5. In order to ensure environmental sustainability, policy integration with sustainability at its axis should be promoted. Then, application of various policy instruments and a policy mix should be promoted in order to improve the effectiveness and efficiency of policy.

Of the preceding issues, this chapter focuses particularly on point 5. Further, implications for research and practice of environmental policy integration in Japan, based on the normative debate on environmental policy integration in the European Union (EU) and the German National Sustainable Development Strategy, are discussed.

## What is environmental policy integration?

Policy integration is generally considered to be the planned integration of differing policy objectives and instruments from the initial stages of policy formation. It removes inconsistencies between policies, creates common benefits and is expected to bring about mutually reinforcing results.

Although policy integration in general does not indicate a defined policy direction, EPI is a policy principle designed to realize sustainable development (SD), and it has a more pronounced normative implication (Jordan and Lenschow, 2008). This type of policy, through deliberate integration of environment-related objectives and environmental concern with policy-making in other areas (e.g., energy, transport, agriculture), is key to realizing sustainable development. In contrast, traditional environmental policy has treated environmental problems as an individual area separate from other policy areas and tends to impose end-of-pipeline treatment after problems arise.

A standard definition for environmental policy integration does not exist; however, historically in the process of EU integration, EPI was included in the draft of the Single European Act of 1987. Furthermore, the Treaty of Amsterdam (which was adopted in 1997 and went into effect in 1999) sets forth sustainable development as one of the EU's objectives and most important issues. Article 6 gives a legal foundation to EPI, said to be the only quasi-constitutional foundation related to EPI: "Environmental protection requirements must be integrated into the definition and implementation of the Community policies and activities . . . in particular with a view to promoting sustainable development."

Moreover, in the EU, the decision of the Commission of the European Communities (Jordan and Lenschow, 2008) in Cardiff in June 1998 called for a shift to environmental policy integration that stresses interdepartmental cooperation among each government department in charge of public policy. The movement that ensued following this decision was called the Cardiff Process, and accordingly, the movement to integrate environmental policy objectives in the policy areas of transportation, energy and agriculture accelerated. The EU Sustainable Development Strategy, drafted in 2001, allots a central role to EPI in achievement of policy issues such as climate protection, health, natural resource management and transportation. Moreover, the European Environment Agency (EEA) defines environmental policy integration for practical purposes as follows:

> EPI . . . is a continual process to ensure environmental issues are taken into account in all policy phases, from the very beginning of the policy process. Importantly, EPI needs to lead to overall improvements in policy, policy implementation and policy outcomes. Environment will not necessarily come out on top in every policy that is adopted and implemented, but the overall trend should certainly be in the direction of sustainable development. (EEA, 2005: 13)

## Origins of environmental policy integration

The principle of environmental policy integration has two origins. Historically, in the EU (including its predecessor, the European Community (EC)), the debate on the principle of environmental policy integration can be traced back to the first Environmental Action Plan (EAP) of 1973. In the successive second (1977–1981), third (1982–1986), fourth (1987–1992) and fifth (1992–1997) plans, the idea of EPI developed as experience was accumulated. Then EPI was incorporated into the draft of the Single European Act of 1987 and was given legal basis in Article 6 of the Amsterdam treaty (which was adopted in 1997 and went into effect in 1999), thus giving sustainable development and EPI a role in the political integration objectives of the EU.

The other stream of development was the World Commission on Environment and Development (WCED; also known as the Brundtland Commission) report (1987) and the processes of the Earth Summit (Grubb, 1993), which was held with the concept of sustainable development advocated in this report as its central concept. In other words, EPI has a background related to sustainable development. Due to its relationship with sustainable development, environmental policy integration has become more universalized.

The WCED (1987) report describes sustainable development to be "a process of change in which the exploitation of resources, the direction of investments, the orientation of technological development, and institutional change are made consistent with future as well as present needs". It also states that "technology and social organization can be both managed and improved to make way for a new era of economic growth", and cites "the possibility for a new era of economic growth, one that must be based on policies that sustain and expand the environmental resource base", as it stresses integration of environmental objectives in economic policy areas. Thus, the report stresses the necessity for policy integration to realise sustainable development, in order to formulate and implement policy not only in the field of environment, but in the fields of economics, trade, energy and industry as well, in an integrated manner.

The fourth principle of the Rio Declaration on Environment and Development, adopted at the Earth Summit in 1992, states that "[i]n order to achieve sustainable development, environmental protection shall constitute an integral part of the development process and cannot be considered in isolation from it".

Additionally, chapter 8 of the simultaneously adopted Agenda 21 (Integrating Environment and Development in Decision-Making) contains the following passage:

> 8.3. The overall objective is to improve or restructure the decision-making process so that consideration of socio-economic and environmental issues is fully integrated and a broader range of public participation assured. (omission)
> (a) To conduct a national review of economic, sectoral and environmental policies, strategies and plans to ensure the progressive integration of environmental and developmental issues;
> (b) To strengthen institutional structures to allow the full integration of environmental and developmental issues, at all levels of decision-making;
> (c) To develop or improve mechanisms to facilitate the involvement of concerned individuals, groups and organizations in decision-making at all levels;
> (d) To establish domestically determined procedures to integrate environment and development issues in decision-making. (United Nations Secretariat, 2000: 64–65)

Thus, this passage addresses the need for mutual adjustment between policies and plans related to economics, society and environment and the arrangement of conditions to allow these adjustments. It should be noted that in comparison with the WCED report, this passage does not refer to "environmental policy integration for sustainable development" but to "the integration of environment and development".

## The definition and concept of environmental policy integration: Debate on a norm

Because EPI has been designated a policy principle for realizing sustainable development, attention has been drawn to the existence of a standard for the concept.

Collier (1997) defines environmental policy integration based on the following three objectives. The first is to realize sustainable development and to prevent environmental destruction. The second is reciprocal policy and the removal of inconsistencies in policies. The third is to realize the benefits of reciprocal policy and to mutually reinforce policy objectives.

Lafferty and Hovden (2003), although calling this definition a good starting point, raise the following criticisms of Collier's definition based on the objectives. The first objective refers to the overarching aim of environmental policy in general. Regarding the second objective, it is an issue related to all policy coordination and, thus, is not a unique feature of EPI. On the third, concerning issues of actual environmental problems and environmental policy, there are many instances of real, conflicting interests with the policy objectives of other areas. Accordingly, although Collier's definition is intellectually significant, his definition falls short of a more precise and applicable conception.

Then Lafferty and Hovden return to Underdal's concept of policy integration. Underdal (1980) proposes comprehensiveness, aggregation and consistency as the conditions required for policy integration.[1] Comprehensiveness refers to time, space, actors and issues. Aggregation implies making assessments on policy formation from an all-encompassing viewpoint. Consistency occurs when all levels of a specific administrative department conform to promote policy objectives (vertical integration) and when all related governmental agencies perform in a unified manner (horizontal integration) on a specific policy. From this perspective, Underdal (1980: 162) defines an integrated policy as one in which "all significant consequences of policy decisions are recognized as decision premises, where policy options are evaluated on the basis of their effects on some aggregate measure of utility, and where the different policy elements are in accord with each other".

Lafferty and Hovden (2003) assert that this definition is applicable to all types of policy integration and not confined to environmental policy. Thus, they argue that a "hierarchy of values" is needed to usher in environmental policy integration that confronts reality. Namely, a priority ranking among policy objectives is called for, and without strong emphasis on environmental objectives, EPI is devoid of meaning. Thus, they provide the following definition of environmental policy integration:

1. The incorporation of environmental objectives into all stages of policy-making in non-environmental policy sectors, with a specific recognition of this goal as a guiding principle for the planning and execution of policy.
2. Accompanied by an attempt to aggregate presumed environmental consequences into overall evaluation of policy, and a commitment to minimize contradiction between environmental and sectoral policies by giving principled priority to the former over the latter. (Lafferty and Hovden, 2003)

In the background of this proposed definition is the long period over which environmental policy was relegated to the fringe of policy-making. In addition, there is recognition that sustainable development cannot be achieved by simply maintaining a balance with other policy objectives, considering the issue of irreversible risks faced by the life support system.

Lafferty and Hovden (2003) further assert that based on the WCED report, the core of EPI is, "in the context of sustainable development, to ensure that the long-term carrying capacity of nature becomes a principal or overarching societal objective", and they stress the normative significance of this characteristic. In other words, an ordinary policy integration theory places importance on a balance between environment and other objectives, from a value-neutral and rational perspective aimed at removal of inconsistencies among policies, mutual benefits and mutually reinforcing effects. In contrast, in the context of sustainable development, maintenance of the carrying capacity of nature is at the heart of achieving social objectives, and therein lies the significance of EPI.

Jordan and Lenschow (2008) call the theory of Lafferty and Hovden "strong EPI" and assert that in selection of policy in various sectors, simply aiming for synergy with environmental objectives and win–win solutions is not sufficient. Rather, the significance of environmental policy integration lies in the intentional effort to prioritize environmental objectives when trade-offs arise among policy objectives (Jordan and Lenschow).

Furthermore, Lafferty and Hovden categorize environmental policy integration into "vertical integration" and "horizontal integration" as an analytical framework. Vertical environmental policy integration signifies integration of environmental preservation objectives as targets into individual policy areas (e.g. energy, transportation, agriculture), with the extent of integration relinquished to the discretion of each ministry or agency (Lafferty and Hovden, 2003). Meanwhile, horizontal environmental policy integration signifies that the central government determines the course of environmental policy integration and allots objectives related to policy integration and responsibility to all policy departments (Lafferty and Hovden, 2003). In other words, at the stage of horizontal environmental policy integration, EPI is the foundational principle of all public policy of the government (Kim, 2008).

## Environmental policy integration instruments and the state of implementation in various countries

Jordan and Lenschow (2008) selected a variety of instruments as indicators of realization of environmental policy integration, as they compared and contrasted the progress in EPI in 30 Organisation for Economic Co-operation and Development (OECD) member states (Jordan and Lenschow, 2008). Table 2.1 shows the state of adoption of these environmental policy integration instruments in 30 OECD member states.

Table 2.1 The distribution of EPI instruments within and across 30 OECD countries

| | General Framing and communicative tools | | | | | | Organizational EIP measures | | | Procedural EPI tools | | |
|---|---|---|---|---|---|---|---|---|---|---|---|---|
| | Constitutional provision | NEP | NSSD | Sectoral strategies | Reporting obligation | Independent institutions | Amalgamation of departments | Green cabinet | Interdepartmental working groups | Green budgeting | SEA (data until 2007) | Impact assessment |
| Australia | | | • | | | • | | | | | • | |
| Austria | • | • | • | | • | | | | | | • | |
| Belgium | • | • | • | | • | • | | | | | • | |
| Canada | • | • | • | • | • | • | | | | | • | • |
| Czech Rep | • | • | • | | | • | | | | | • | |
| Denmark | | • | • | • | | | (dismissed in 2002) | | | • (dismissed in 2002) | • | |
| Finland | • | • | • | • | • | • | | | | | • | |
| France | • | • | • | | | • | | | • | | • | |
| Germany | • | • | • | | • | • | | • | • | | • | |
| Greece | • | • | • | | | • | | | • | | • | |
| Hungary | | • | • | | • | • | | • | • | | • | |
| Iceland | | • | • | | | • | | | • | | • | |
| Ireland | | • | • | | • | • | | | • | | • | |
| Italy | • | | • | | | • | | | • | | • | |
| Japan | • | • | • | | • | | | | | | • | |
| Korea | • | • | • | | | | | | • | | • | |

| Country | | | | | | | | | | | |
|---|---|---|---|---|---|---|---|---|---|---|---|
| Luxembourg | • | | | | | | | | | | |
| Mexico | • | • | • | | | | | | | | |
| Netherlands | • | • | • | | | • (experimental) | | | | • | |
| New Zealand | | • | | | | | | | | | |
| Norway | • | • | • | | • | • | • | • | | • | |
| Poland | • | • | • | • | • | • | | | | • | |
| Portugal | • | • | • | • | | • | | | | • | |
| Slovakia | • | • | • | | | | | | | • | |
| Spain | • | • | | | | | | | | • | |
| Sweden | • | • | | | | • (dismissed in 2006) | | • | | • | |
| Switzerland | • | | • | | | | • | • | | • | |
| Turkey | • | • | | | | | | | | | |
| United Kingdom | | • | | • | | • | • | • | | • | |
| United States | | | | | • | • | | • | • | • | • |
| Count | 17 | 20 | 26 | 7 | 14 | 23 | 4 | 18 | 4 | 25 | 4 |

*Source*: Jordan and Lenschow (2008).

*Note*: EIP = environmental integration policy; NEP = National Environment Plan; NSSD = National Strategies for Sustainable Development; SEA = strategic environmental assessment.

The policy integration instruments employed as indicators can be divided into the three categories. The first is communicative instruments at the comprehensive policy level. This type of instrument attempts to orient efforts in the direction of reform through broad communication and sharing of visions of an ideal society, objectives, strategies and accumulated knowledge. The actual content of environmental policy integration initiatives is left to individual governments and organizations.

Concrete examples include putting environmental provisions into constitutions, creation of national environmental plans or strategies, drafting of sustainable development strategies and sectoral environmental strategies; environmental performance reporting obligation and review of environmental performance by an external and independent institution. As these instruments represent comparatively soft approaches, they have been implemented by the most countries.

Already, 17 of the 30 OECD member states (Austria, Belgium, the Czech Republic, Finland, Germany, Greece, Hungary, Korea, the Netherlands, Norway, Poland, Portugal, Slovakia, Spain, Sweden, Switzerland and Turkey) have environment-related provisions in their constitutions. The addition of environmental provisions to a constitution is a potentially strong political commitment. However, specific content differs considerably by country. A large portion of constitutional provisions refer to environmental preservation objectives in a broad sense of the term, but do not grant environmental objectives priority in relation to other objectives. Hence, although constitutional provisions contribute to a shared vision, they do not result in change of the actual state of real EPI in individual areas. Further, they do not lead to a higher priority for the environment. Of these, the EU's provisions (Article 6 of the Amsterdam treaty) are the clearest ones.[2] Likewise, Norway put a provision regarding EPI into its constitution in 1992.

National environmental plans (or strategies) clarify the comprehensive objectives of long-term environmental policy and priority areas. Of the OECD member states, 20 have drawn up national environmental plans. As such, the role these plans play in EPI warrants discussion.

Consistency among environmental plans and other plans at the national level are an issue. The Japanese government's Third Basic Environment Plan (Ministry of the Environment, Government of Japan, 2006) states that "[w]hen the nation draws up a plan recognized to have impact on the environment, it must give consideration to preservation of the environment". It also states that "[it] is therefore essential that between the Plan and other national plans, harmony with the Basic Environment Plan should be ensued relating to environmental conservation". Further, it states that "as for other national plans which include provisions on environmental conservation, these are to be compatible with the principal directions of the Basic Environment Plan relating to environmental conservation, so harmonious coordination shall be ensured with the Plan" (Part III, Section 3, Coordination between plans). However, no institutionalized guarantee exists to coordinate between Japan's Basic Environment Plan and existing national level plans targeted at areas other than environment. Thus, the relationship between plans is as yet unclear (Otsuka, 2002).

National sustainable development strategies are not only targeted at the environment, but also have economic and social facets that cover a broader range than environmental plans. A large majority of OECD member states (26 countries) have drawn up national sustainable development strategies.

Of these, Germany's National Sustainable Development Strategy (2002) is reputed to also be a strategy for environmental policy integration, and has provided many suggestions for research on environmental policy integration (Kim, 2002). This point is examined in the following section.

The second category is organizational reform. Organizational reform is reform of existing organizations or the establishment of new organizations to promote policy coordination among environment-related departments. Concrete methods include amalgamation of ministries and agencies, green cabinets, the establishment of a unit in charge of environment in each ministry and the establishment of interdepartmental working groups. These instruments intend to change policy-making patterns, for example, by attempting to promote EPI by strengthening the authority of the environment ministry. There is a variety of forms for this type of instrument. The most common form is the inter-departmental working group, which has been established in 18 OECD member states. Green cabinets are usually made up of vice-ministerial-level officials from relevant ministries and agencies and have been established in Germany, Hungary, Norway and the United Kingdom.

Actual effects on environmental policy integration through organizational reform are not very clear. However, of late, some outstanding examples of EPI based on organizational reform can be found. For example, after re-election of the coalition government of the Social Democratic Party and the Green Party of Germany (the so-called red-green coalition) in 2002, jurisdiction over renewable energies was transferred from the Ministry of Economics to the Ministry for the Environment. As a result, a dramatic expansion of renewable energies, including Germany's wind power generation, took place under environment minister Jürgen Trittin of the Green Party.

In the United Kingdom, in October 2008, the energy administration of the Ministry of Economics and the climate change administration of the Ministry for Environment were transferred to the newly established Department of Energy and Climate Change. Further, the Obama administration in the United States named Carol Browner (former administrator of the Environmental Protection Agency) to the newly established post of energy and climate advisor in order to guarantee integration of climate protection policy and energy policy through structural enhancement of government. However, she was later discharged.

The third category is procedural instruments, such as green budgeting, strategic environmental assessment (SEA) and including environmental concerns when assessing new policy and regulations (policy impact assessment). These instruments directly intervene in policy-making to change its direction and are intended to support EPI.

Green budgeting, as a part of the budget-drafting process, involves detailed environmental assessment to specify and screen for expenditures inconsistent with environmental objectives.

SEA arose from insufficient consideration of alternatives in conventional assessment at the project stage. Environmental assessment is performed, including impacts on society and on the economy, at the initial planning stage, which precedes the stage of decision-making.

Policy impact analysis is applied to all new policy and is not limited to programmes or plans that could have an impact on the environment. However, content is not as rigorous as that of SEA.

Because an EU directive was issued on SEA, many countries have adopted this instrument; however, green budgeting has been implemented only in four countries, including the United Kingdom and Norway. Only four countries, including the United Kingdom and the Netherlands, have adopted policy impact assessment.

The following is an interpretation of Table 2.1, which compiles survey results on the state of adoption of environmental policy integration instruments in 30 OECD member states.

Comprehensive frameworks and communicative instruments have been adopted in a relatively large number of countries. Further, strategic environmental assessment, influenced by the EU directive, has been implemented in 25 OECD member countries. On the other hand, the amalgamation of departments, green cabinets, green budgeting and policy impact assessment have been adopted in only a portion of OECD member countries.

This exemplifies the fact that the environmental policy integration initiatives in a large majority of countries are limited to soft and symbolic actions that do not attain the intended nature of EPI in the WCED report. Namely, they are not initiatives that bring about opportunities for reform of policy and institutions that are incorporated into actual decision-making processes. Of course, even if initiatives are soft and symbolic, when political interest and support for environmental policy integration are high, environmental policy integration can function. However, if that is not the case, they are in danger of becoming devoid of meaning (Jordan and Lenschow, 2008).[3]

Compared to other OECD countries, the instruments adopted in Japan for promotion of EPI are quite limited. The table shows that the following instruments have been adopted: the national environment plan (corresponding to the Basic Environment Plan), the national sustainable development strategy (submitted to the UN Commission on Sustainable Development), reporting obligation, review by independent institution interdepartmental working groups and SEA.

Regarding the effectiveness of adopted instruments, systematic assessment has yet to be carried out domestically. For example, the Basic Environment Plan does not specify a framework for coordination with other development-related national plans. Furthermore, analysis of the policy integration of the Basic Environment Plan itself, as well as its contribution to sustainable development, apart from follow-up on the Basic Environment Plan by the Ministry of the Environment, is uncommon. A variety of administrative frameworks (ministerial meetings, liaison conference of relevant authorities and working groups) have been adopted, but questions remain as to the extent of effectiveness these frameworks have exhibited as EPI. Rather, more frequently pointed out are the ill effects of a vertically segmented administration (Imamura, 2006). Amid the striking ill effects of a vertically segmented administration at the national level, it is in the movements toward policy integration aimed at community sustainable development at the local government level where future potential may lie instead.

## Germany's National Sustainable Development Strategy and environmental policy integration[4]

Since the early 1990s, in Germany, policies aimed at technological innovation, economic growth and creation of employment have been adopted based on strategic investment in environmental areas according to the "ecological modernization theory".

Ecological modernization theory is an ideology that interprets sustainable development as a new stage in modernization, and attempts to solve environmental problems that have arisen as consequences of modernization and rationalization, through the political innovation of social systems.[5] Enhancement of environmental regulations, adoption of environmental taxes, promotion of green consumerism movements, promotion of environmentally sound technological innovation and development of aggressive environmental diplomacy have been proposed as policy frameworks to realize ecological modernization. Consensus-building among government, the private sector and citizens is essential for the realization of these policies.

Based on this idea, Germany was the first to set forth the type of green new deal policy that has now become a global trend. As such, based on aggressive investment in the environment and regulation frameworks, initiatives designed to expand renewable energies and support economic development have been built up to the present day.

Germany's climate and environment policy strives for policy integration and coordination between economic policy and energy policy. Based on a long-term vision, this policy is being advanced based on legally binding frameworks, backing with revenue sources and appropriate controls, a feed-in-tariff system for renewable energies and appropriate information provision to citizens.

Underlying these processes is the idea that good climate protection policy is good economic policy, the basis of ecological modernization theory. On this idea, the integration of political strategy with economic strategy is designed. Specifically, renewable energies are diffused and dependence on fossil fuels is curtailed through pricing of $CO_2$ and a gradual increase of the price of fossil fuels, leading to decreased energy import costs and a guarantee of energy security. Further, through promoting development of environmental and energy technologies and the creation of markets, new employment is created and international competitiveness is enhanced.

"Perspectives for Germany; Our Strategy for Sustainable Development" (Federal Government of Germany, 2002), which is the National Sustainable Development Strategy (NSDS) of Germany, drafted in April 2002 by the German federal government, provides numerous hints for research in environmental policy integration. This strategy corresponds to the Agenda 21 called for by each country at the Earth Summit in Rio de Janeiro, and was a proposal by Germany oriented towards the World Summit on Environment and Development held in Johannesburg, South Africa, in September 2002.

Thus, questions arise regarding the significance of Germany's NSDS contribution to the development of environmental policy integration and what clues can be gained. Germany's NSDS treats sustainable development as a cross-departmental issue and, through integration of ecological, economic and social objectives, attempts to achieve intergenerational equity, improved quality of living, social cohesion and international contributions. According to Kim (2008), it was confirmed that the treatment of sustainable development, index system, and content on priority issues of the NSDS in particular follow the storyline of environmental policy integration.

Specifically, the NSDS does not stop at a traditional plan for environmental protection. Rather, its main content is environmental policy integration, and integration of environmental values into public policy is set as a priority issue. In other words, sustainable development is redefined from the perspective of environmental policy integration, and the strategy has been praised for encouraging integration of environment and economy through the greening of public policy. Furthermore, it is systematic and concrete concerning the indication of targets. It examines issues of sustainable development, focused on the four pillars of intergenerational equity, quality of living, social cohesion and international responsibility. Each pillar is allotted 12 indicators that set forth environmental, economic and social targets, with numerical targets and goal achievement times specifically stated. Kim (2008: 7–8) appraises this quantitative index system in that it made possible the quantitative management of the NSDS process in Germany.

Moreover, in the process of NSDS drafting and implementation, institutional change for cross-departmental coordination was evident, such as in the green cabinet functioning as an institutional adaptation to carry out environmental policy integration across each ministry.

In addition to the preceding, it has been pointed out that top-down initiatives, such as those of the prime minister's office, and the bottom-up political will of local environment minister meetings, environmental non-governmental organizations and the Green Party were indispensable to environmental policy integration (Kim, 2008: 15).

## Implications for research and practice of environmental policy integration in Japan

There is some research accumulated on environmental policy integration in Japan (Teranishi and Hosoda, 2003; Yatsuki, 2007), but very little research exists equal in perspective and scope to Jordan and Lenschow (2008). Appraisal of Japan's environmental policy itself from the perspective of policy integration is a task for the future.

On the one hand, policy integration activities at the local government level aimed at community sustainable development have attracted attention. For example, in the city of Tajimi, administrative and financial system reform was implemented in 2001 for environmental policy integration. A "policy formation hearing" system was developed whereby the environmental department screened the budgets of all departments, as the city produced results in sustainable city planning (Yoshizumi, 2005). According to Jordan and Lenschow's categories, this falls under green budgeting.

Additionally, compact community building in the city of Toyama centred on revitalization of public transportation with light rail transit at the core (Toyama Light Rail and Environmental Transportation Policy; Ministry of the Environment, Global Environment Bureau, 2007) is an example that has attracted attention from the perspective of policy integration of environmental and transportation policy. Community-building from the perspective of global warming mitigation is aimed at making a contribution to the realization of improved convenience for those who cannot use private vehicles, such as the elderly; lessening of financial burden, such as administrative and maintenance costs of infrastructure; and revitalization of the city centre and local communities. This policy has been praised for aiming to comprehensively improve the environment, lifestyles and the economy; to enhance coordination among various policies; and to become an example of EPI that transcends the vertical divisions between departments.

In general, examination of the present administrative reality at national and local levels reveals the strikingly ill effects of the vertically segmented administration of each ministry at the national level. Meanwhile, setting up local government structure allows the administration to implement policies in a comprehensive and unified manner under the head of government chosen by citizens in an election. Personnel changes for employees are centrally managed, and there are human resources that have experience in multiple policy areas. Utilizing such mechanisms and human resources, there is hope for the potential to advance environmental policy integration toward achieving sustainable development.

Likewise, in comparison to the practice and accumulation of research on environmental policy integration in the EU, as well as the green new deal proposal of US president Obama, Japan requires the establishment of a policy system with consistency in order to achieve sustainability. Accordingly, the development of policy research toward this aim is also warranted.

In particular, green new deal policy that is at present being put into effect in various countries aims to create new green jobs and to develop growth industry by strategically making large-scale investments in the environment. This policy intends to integrate environmental policy, energy policy and economic policy, that is, policy integration.

Meanwhile, the so-called Japanese version of a green new deal (which featured facilitation of replacement purchasing of green home appliances [eco-points] and facilitation of replacement purchasing of eco-cars [new car purchase subsidy], etc.) drafted under the Aso administration (2009), on the whole, was limited to a medley of environmental measures as part of its short-term economic stimulus policy. It lacked a clear vision for a future low-carbon society. Moreover, it was exceedingly deficient on the point of policy and institutional reform in order to compatibly combine tax systems, financing and incentives from a long-term perspective to guide society to a low-carbon economy.

Green new deals as environmental policy integration are designed to create green jobs and develop growth industry, and to contribute to energy security and regional revitalization, through strategic investment in the environment. The creation of a system of public policy that consistently promotes these objectives is essential. What is needed is a wise government that is capable of promoting consistent fiscal spending and structural reform and the entrepreneurial spirit to be aware of environmental constraints, accept the challenge of environmental targets, and expand innovation.

Ideally, efforts should not stop at elimination of wasteful administration and moving away from dependence on bureaucrats, but should lead to the establishment, through political initiative, of a system to promote environmental policy integration toward the creation of a low-carbon society.

## Issues of environment and energy policy integration: Lessons learned from the Fukushima nuclear power plant accident

Germany's experience in advancement of climate change policy and rapid diffusion of renewable energies backed by environmental policy integration and ecological modernization theory reveals that, "with a clear sense of direction and effective policies, rapid change is possible" (World Watch Institute, 2009: 147).

Meanwhile, the nuclear accident in Fukushima caused by the Great East Japan Earthquake of 11 March 2011 exposed the fragility of our society, with its mass consumption and mass supply of energy reliant on nuclear power. Fundamental reconsideration of the safety and economics of nuclear power is warranted, including evaluation criteria and evaluation systems. The lessons that must be learned from this accident concern not merely technical issues of nuclear power but are also closely related to power supply systems in general, as well as energy security and climate change policy. For this reason, the life cycle of power supply systems as a whole must be examined, and energy policy, environmental policy and resource policy must be thought of in an integrated manner. In other words, an approach based on policy integration is required.

Hitherto, Japan has promoted nuclear power generation based upon the reasons of its economic efficiency, safety and contribution to climate change policy. Concerning safety and contribution to climate change policy, the foundation of this reasoning is shaky. As far as economic efficiency is concerned, when considering the back-end cost, the cost of treating radioactive waste, the cost of pumped-storage hydroelectricity plants built alongside nuclear power plants and the massive fiscal burden put out for nuclear power under various pretexts, it is clear that the cost of power generation has been underestimated (Oshima, 2010). Namely, the question of the economic efficiency of nuclear power generation was, in fact, based on massive fiscal expenditures. These expenditures are a hindrance to the practical application of various power generation technologies, such as renewable energies, and have distorted competition.

Furthermore, Japan's power supply at present is a vertically integrated type performed by regional monopolies. Power generation and power transmission are not separated. This structure is a peculiar one worldwide. A future issue is the creation of an institutional framework that enables equitable competition by power source. Such a system is expected to have separated power generation and power transmission, and participation in appropriate competition in power generation based on small-scale decentralized renewable energies.

## Shift to a 21st-century energy and environmental system

In order to avoid the risks of climate change and nuclear power, dependence on fossil fuels and nuclear power must be decreased as soon as possible. When stated according to the type of power source, it is a shift from the conventional "fossil fuel + nuclear power" to "renewable energies + energy conservation + smart grids + energy storage". The latter is named the futuristic system, or "21st-century power supply system" (see Table 2.2).

Promotion of energy conservation and power-saving subtracts from energy and power consumption, and thereby increases the supply capacity of energy and power, in that the energy saved is thus produced in an equivalent amount. That is to say, conservation of energy is equivalent to the construction of a power plant.

Table 2.2 Conventional versus 21st-century power supply systems

| Conventional power supply systems | 21st-century power supply systems |
|---|---|
| Nuclear power + fossil fuels | Renewable energies + energy conservation + smart grids + energy storage |
| Large-scale centralized power sources | Decentralized and two-way (greater resilience to large-scale disasters) |
| Regional monopolies and vertical integration | Electricity deregulation, separation of power production from power transmission |
| Vested interests | Industrial structure transformation and new industries, consumer's choice |
| RPS (renewable portfolio standard) | FIT (feed-in tariffs: fixed-price buy-out system), new business models |
| Top down | Bottom up (←citizen movements, consumer movements, policy innovation from local governments) |

Energy conservation and power-saving mechanisms must be integrated into the economy and the society. Also, creation of the institutional infrastructure to promote investment in energy saving is essential.

Smart grids (next-generation transmission networks) utilize information technology to manage demand and supply of energy, and are indispensable to capitalize on renewable energies and the capacity of multiple decentralized storage devices. Through utilization of smart grids and smart meters, as well as the spread of smart communities, two-way communication between power users and suppliers becomes possible, balance of supply and demand in real time can be attempted and a shift in peak demand (levelling) becomes easier.

The energy and power supply system based on "renewable energies + energy conservation + smart grids + energy storage" signifies a switch from conventional large-scale centralized power sources to decentralized network power sources. By being small-scale and decentralized, risk to large-scale centralized locations is avoided in the event of a large-scale disaster, and an entire shutdown of the system can be avoided. Accordingly, resilience to disasters is improved and contribution is made to the creation of a reduced risk society. This system would also lead to local production for local consumption of energy and expansion of local economies and employment that conforms to nature.

With the Fukushima nuclear accident as its impetus, the government has declared that it will conduct a fundamental revision of existing energy policy, including the Basic Energy Plan. Whether or not the shift to a 21st-century energy and power supply system can be realized, starting with separation of power generation and transmission, is an issue of environmental and energy policy integration.

## Conclusion

This chapter examined the implications of EPI, particularly its normative aspect. It also evaluated the experiences of EPI in OECD countries, particularly the German experience. Contrasting to these experiences, current practices of EPI in Japan for promotion of EPI are quite limited. This chapter also proposes a direction of energy and policy integration after the nuclear power plant accident in Fukushima, which is a more decentralized and resilient, more renewable energy-oriented and bottom-up approach.

## Notes

1. Yatsuki (2007) also discusses this point.
2. Nevertheless, despite the quasi-constitutional commitment to EPI in the EU, it has become clear that implementation is vastly more difficult. The European Commission recognizes that EU policy in many important areas is lacking in EPI (Jordan and Lenschow, 2008).
3. However, arguments here are limited to extrapolation. In order to come to a clear conclusion, details research on individual countries is required.
4. Kim (2008) and Tsubogo (2009) contain excellent introductions to and discussions of the national sustainable development strategy of Germany. Many of the accounts in this section rely on these works.
5. Refer to Mol et al. (2010) for a discussion on the latest ecological modernization theory.

## REFERENCES

Collier, U. (1997) *Energy and Environment in the European Union*, Aldershot: Ashgate.

EEA (European Environment Agency) (2005) *Environmental Policy Integration in Europe*, EEA Technical Report No2/2005, Copenhagen: European Environment Agency.

Federal Government of Germany (2002) *Perspectives for Germany. Our Strategy for Sustainable Development*, Berlin: Federal Government of Germany.

Grubb, M. et al. (1993) *The Earth Summit Agreements: A Guide and Assessment*, London, Earthscan.

Imamura, T. (2006) *Government Agency Sectionalism*, Tokyo: University of Tokyo Press (in Japanese).

Jordan, A. J. and A. Lenschow (eds.) (2008) *Innovation in Environmental Policy?: Integrating the Environment for Sustainability*, Cheltenham Glos : Edward Elgar Publishing Limited.

Kim, K. (2008) "German National Sustainability Strategy and Environmental Policy Integration", Paper presented at the Society for Environmental Economics and Policy Studies 2008 Convention in Osaka (in Japanese).

Lafferty, W. and E. Hovden (2003) "Environmental Policy Integration: Towards an Analytical Framework", *Environmental Politics*, 12(3), pp. 1–22.
Matsushita, K., ed. (2007) *Environmental Governance Theory*, Kyoto: Kyoto University Press (in Japanese).
Ministry of the Environment, Global Environment Bureau (2007) "Report of the Investigative Commission on Global Warming Mitigation and Community-Building". Tokyo: Ministry of the Environment, Government of Japan (in Japanese).
Ministry of the Environment, Government of Japan (2006) *The Third Basic Environment Plan*. Tokyo: Gyosei (in Japanese).
Mol, A. P. J., D. A. Sonnenfeld and G. Spaargaren (eds.) (2010) *The Ecological Modernisation Reader*, London: Routledge.
Oshima, K. (2010) *The Political Economy of Renewable Energies*, Tokyo: Toyo Keizai (in Japanese).
Otsuka, T. (2002) *Environmental Law*, Tokyo: Yuhikaku Publishing (in Japanese).
Teranishi, S. and E. Hosoda (eds.) (2003) *Policy Integration Toward Environmental Preservation*, Tokyo: Iwanami Shoten (in Japanese).
Tsubogo, M. (2009) *The Political Science of Environmental Policy*, Tokyo: Waseda University Press (in Japanese).
Underdal, A. (1980) *Integrated Marine Policy: What? Why? How?*, Marine Policy.
United Nations Secretariat (2002) "Agenda 21".
WCED (World Commission on Environment and Development) (1987) *Our Common Future,* Oxford: Oxford University Press.
World Watch Institute (2009) *State of the World 2009*, New York: W.W. Norton & Company.
Yatsuki, S. (2007) "Subsidization of Grants and Environmental Policy Integration", *Economics Research*, 74(1), pp. 159–181 (in Japanese).
Yoshizumi, M. (2005) "Sustainable City Planning through Policy Integration and Citizen Participation", Dissertation, Doctoral Program in Global Environmental Studies, Graduate School of Global Environmental Studies, Kyoto University, Kyoto: Kyoto University (in Japanese).

# 3
# The state transformation in environmental governance: From the viewpoints of environmental regulations

*Shin-ichi Yatsuki*

Public governance as it relates to public problems and public policies is characterized by a focus on the state in the steering position. Within this focus, there are two analytical frameworks: one that focuses on state transformation while supposing the state as steering position, and another that focuses on different social networks among different sectors, while being centred on hollowing out the state.

Discussions about the superiority of these frameworks have continued, but there are some common features. First, against the backdrop of public authority, the state has had difficulty solving public problems within a governance structure. Second, governance has focused on a function which is made through institutions built by agencies including the state. Finally, governance occurs as a dynamic process that would be able to remake pro-governance adaptive.

Environmental governance is reflected by these features of public governance in the field of environmental policy. Here, through the occurrence of the transformation of environmental problems, environmental regulations which have been central position in environmental policy are being criticized. But, in response to this viewpoint, how can the steering position of the state be transformed in environmental governance? This chapter analyses such state transformation and environmental regulations through three cases: the Porter hypothesis, a policy mix with new policy instruments, and multi-level regulatory governance.

*Transition management for sustainable development, Ueta and Adachi (eds.), United Nations University Press, 2014, ISBN 978-92-808-1234-3*

## Characteristics of public governance as an analytical framework

Among studies on governance, public governance is characterized by a focus on the steering position of the state. In there, two main analytical frameworks are provided.[1]

One framework stands on the limited infallibility of the state but still supposes that the state is in a steering position, which means it sets policy goals while in new collaborations with other agencies, such as firms and civil society, during the policy-making process. The other framework supposes that the formulation and the development of new social networks are based on trust and dialogue among different sectors and through deepening civil society and global economy.

Discussions on the superiority of these frameworks continue, but there are some common features in these discussions.[2] First, the purpose of governance is problem solving. This purpose is also reflected by states' difficulties in solving public problems. These difficulties stem from the deficiency of resources owned by states and the change of public problems. This chapter focuses on the latter especially. Second, to achieve this purpose, public governance focuses on the function of agencies and institutions rather than on the structure by which the state has governed. Agencies are state, firm and civil society, and institutions play an important role in coordinating different interests among these agencies. Thus, if these institutions cannot work to coordinate these interests enough, public governance will not contribute to solving public problems. Hence, we can see clearly the difference between function-centric governance and structure-centric governance. Finally, governance is not a static process but a dynamic one. Concretely speaking, through reflecting on the appearance of new public problems and the complexities of these problems, the two frameworks share the common idea that it is possible to make pro-governance adaptive.

## Transformation of environmental problems and the problem of environmental regulations

The appearance of environmental governance in the field of public governance has a background in the transformation of environmental problems and the limit of environmental regulations. That transformation has three important characteristics.[3]

First is the complexity of environmental problems. For example, global warming has deep linkages with other public problems related to traffic and energy; thus, this means that an interconnection exists for each problem. For example, that the possibilities of toxic substances and genetically modified technologies could not be foreseen shows the uncertainty of environmental problems. This uncertainty stems from that the influences of these substances and technologies on the environment are unknown in the short term and cumulative in the long term.

Second is the diversification of problem-making factors. These factors are both direct, such as those made by a specific agency (e.g., emission gases created by a firm), and indirect, such as those created by the public (e.g., carbon dioxide emitted by daily-life activities or an increase in garbage from each household). It is important to understand the latter because as problem-making factors, their portion has been increasing.

Finally, there are multi-level problems. In addition to the progress of the global economy deepening environmental problems at the global level, these problems have a spatial interconnection to other environmental problems at the national and local levels. A typical case would be the increase of global warming gases, mainly in developed countries, inducing the risk of flooding on islands and damaging the ecology in specific areas in developing countries.

Environmental regulations have been the main policy instruments for solving environmental problems. But it has become clear that such a position regarding environmental regulations is not adaptive enough for transforming environmental problems.[4] The transformation on which I especially focus is about the complexity, diversity and multi-level dimension of environmental problems in modern society.

In relation to the complexity of environmental problems, the effectiveness of environmental regulations to the end-of-the-pipeline treatment of individual problem declines, along with the interconnections of each problem. Many environmental regulations that include enforcement are convenient when accounting for a policy's performance on overt problems in the short term, but if problems have uncertainty for the medium or long term, then we cannot treat these problems properly over time.

With these diverse problem-making factors, problems caused by a large number of unspecified people increase the costs of acquiring information or of enforcing the process of regulatory policy, and this increase could be a source of declining efficiency. If we consider equity among those being regulated, as the number of them increases, the transparency of institutional management decreases. Finally, multi-level problems create a spatial unbalance in the benefits and costs of environmental policies. This unbalance makes it difficult to recognize who gets gains or losses and to measure how many gains or losses occur correctly in these environmental policies. Thus, this problem not only decreases the effectiveness and efficiency of policies but also makes it more difficult for the state to perform accountability checks.

## Characteristics of environmental governance and new viewpoints of environmental regulations

What are the characteristics of environmental governance as public governance are given by such transformations of environmental problems? And in relation to these characteristics, how we can consider new viewpoints of environmental regulations?

The first characteristic of environmental governance is sustainability. Sustainability is the normative dimension common in environmental governance.[5] In the first place, environmental regulations are policy instruments for solving environmental problems; thus, these regulations have focused mainly on environmental sustainability. But the decline in effectiveness induced by the complexity of environmental problems and the decline in efficiency caused by the diversification of making-problem factors may disturb economical sustainability. On the other hand, the decline in transparency incurred by that diversification and the decline of accountability from multi-level problems could cause some effect on the social sustainability crisis relating to suspicions about the legitimacy of environmental regulations. Hence, environmental regulations must achieve the compatibilities of a "triple bottom line".

A second characteristic of environmental governance is the function of problem solving performed by environmental governance.[6] This function in public governance is performed by some agency through an institution that solves a public problem, but it is important to grasp the many functions provided by natural or historical environmental resources because environmental problems are induced by damaging these functions. In general, these functions are composed of the supply of natural resources, the purification of pollutants, and the supply of amenities made by nature and by the built environment. In particular, it is very important that we recognize the integrated feature of these functions, for example, the multi-functionality of agriculture. Because this integrated feature diversifies the agency that benefits from or that bears the cost burdens of conserving those functions, then it is easier to make environmental governance a means of promoting institutional building in accordance with this diversification.[7]

The third characteristic is multi-level environmental governance that means multi-level governance in response to the transformation of environmental problems. I have already suggested that the diversification of problem-making factors and of multi-level problems attend this transformation. To coordinate different interests among agencies, multi-level environmental governance is formed simultaneously through horizontal and vertical relations. "Horizontal relations" means collaboration between states and other sectors including firms and civil society at same spatial level. On the other hand, "vertical relations" means intergovernmental relations or those agencies mentioned earlier collaborate at different spatial levels.

Institutions would play an important role in coordinating different interests; thus, it is necessary to build these institutions in multi-level environmental governance for solving multi-level problems. Concretely speaking, it means forming multi-level institutions[8] which deploy institutional subsidiaries among formal institutions, or between formal institutions and informal ones at same, and at different spatial levels. But being multi-level hinders the achievement of some public policies, including environmental ones, because of the increase of veto points made by these characteristics, as in the case of regional policy in European Union.[9]

## Reconsideration of environmental regulations: Cases

These new viewpoints about environmental regulations needed in environmental governance have already been reflected in some study fields on environmental regulations. In this section, I introduce the Porter hypothesis as a case of environmental regulations and sustainability, the policy mix as a case of function and institutional building for problem solving and multi-level regulatory governance as a case of multi-level environmental governance. By surveying these cases, we will glimpse state transformation in environmental governance through reconsideration of environmental regulation.

### *The Porter hypothesis*

Environmental regulations might reduce the competitiveness of firms in some cases because firms, in being regulated, must bear the costs of complying with environmental regulations. Such an opinion about environmental regulations and competitiveness is a conventional wisdom, but the Porter hypothesis confronts that opinion.[10]

The Porter hypothesis suggests that not all environmental regulations might reduce competitiveness of firms uniformly, but well-designed regulation can have the opportunity to trigger innovation to offset the costs of complying. But many theoretical and empirical studies find fault with the Porter hypothesis; hence, we cannot gain a consistent conclusion on the Porter hypothesis until now.[11] From the viewpoint of environmental governance, it is better to focus on some assumptions to create well-designed environmental regulations. In total, there are six conditions.[12]

First, regulation signals to companies that resource inefficiencies and potential technological improvements are likely. Second, regulation focused on information gathering can achieve major benefits by raising corporate awareness. Third, regulation reduces the uncertainty that investments made to address the environment will be valuable. Fourth, regulation creates pressure that motivates innovation and progress. Fifth, regulation levels the transitional playing field. Related to this assumption, Porter and van der Linde indicate that regulation provides a buffer until technologies become proven and learning effects reduce their costs. Sixth, regulation is needed in the case of incomplete offset, because innovation cannot always completely offset the cost of compliance, especially in the short term before learning can reduce the cost of innovation-based solutions.

As already mentioned, these assumptions mean that the problems of environmental regulations, which have occurred as a result of not being adaptive to the transformation of environmental problems, can be solved by coordinating different interests between states and firms flexibly in the process of making regulatory design. The Porter hypothesis offers a good reference because this hypothesis suggests how to make dynamic collaboration between states and firms in regulatory design for solving environmental problems.

*Policy mix*

As there are some questions about the results of environmental regulations in which the state was in the steering position, we have focused on new policy instruments such as market-based instruments (eco-taxes, tradable permit, etc.) and voluntary approaches by firms (eco-labels, environmental management systems, voluntary agreements, etc.). Do these changes of environmental policy instruments make environmental regulations useless?

Shout and Jordan (2005) analysed the present situation of environmental policy instruments from relations between environmental regulations and new policy instruments previously mentioned.[13] The main purpose of their study was to analyse change in environmental regulations by strong government on the rise of new policy instruments. They categorized four typologies of environmental governance, but it becomes clear that two are extreme. One involves a strong government that determines societal goals and selects the means of policy. In traditional environmental regulations, there is hierarchal steering from the centre. The other extreme typology involves strong societal governance in that society determines societal goals and selects the means of policy. In this typology, strong governance is based on the idea that society is self-steering and self-organizing. Between these typologies, Shout and Jordan indicated hybrid types which combine government with governance.

As the result of their analysis, environmental regulations are still the most widely used policy instruments. Environmental regulations play an important role in setting rules and imposing penalties on offenders. But if use of only environmental regulations cannot work enough to solve environmental problems, then new policy instruments play a complementary role to these regulations, and vice versa. This indicates that the former characteristic of environmental regulations is a compulsory function and that the latter is a supportive function. Present environmental regulations in policy mix need both wise regulation as in the Porter hypothesis and the transition to a mixture of steering states and enabling states.

*Multi-level regulatory governance*

Multi-level regulatory governance means that real rule making, implementation and compliance in the field of environmental regulations cause three levels of relations simultaneously. The first level is vertical intergovernmental relationships between national government and local governments. The second level is horizontal intergovernmental relationships among local governments. The third level is multi-level relationships between the state as the regulator and other sectors including some agencies that are being regulated.

In vertical intergovernmental relations, the kinds and degrees of regulatory responsibilities that are delegated to local governments are important. According to Delia et al. (2009), the next four categories are used to assign these responsibilities.[14] First, local governments have no discretion when applying regulations developed at the central level (Hungary). Second, local governments have some discretion to implement regulations developed at the central level (the Czech Republic, Belgium, Denmark, Ireland, Finland and the United Kingdom). Third, local governments have limited powers to create regulations (the Netherlands). These powers often concern local policy issues (Greece). Fourth, local governments have extensive regulatory powers (Australia, Canada, Switzerland, Mexico and the United States).

From these categories, we can grasp that degrees of responsibilities of implementation and other regulatory processes of delegating to local governments are very important in vertical intergovernmental relations. The increase of these degrees harmonizes with decentralization of environmental policy based on the subsidiary principle. But, on the other hand, we have the opportunity of inducing "race to the bottom" which is a central controversy in environmental federalism.[15]

Intergovernmental relations regarding environmental regulations tell that it is not enough to recognize the state in a steering position only. But this viewpoint cannot capture enough multi-level governance in multi-level regulatory governance, because intergovernmental relations focus only on domestic regulation. Based on environmental problems and on firm activities at the global level, we must coordinate the contents of each domestic regulation internationally and build an international framework for regulations made by each national government. In response to these challenges, we must make clear the dynamic interconnections of intergovernmental relations in environmental regulations from the viewpoints of each regulatory institution and of a mutual relation among institutions.

In particular, social capital plays a very important role in this situation. Social capital is composed of trust and of networks that coordinate social relations smoothly to realize some societal mission. If this capital is invested and accumulated by public policy or through voluntary actions related to regulation, it is, hence, expected that consensus building for regulatory content and for compliance to regulations will proceed smoothly.

In addition to this, when firms recognized as being regulated can actively self-regulate, for example, with voluntary agreements, it means that soft law becomes more important when promoting firms to do these activities. To make soft law is the role of enabling states, and performance of soft law depends on the situation of social capital because soft law does not have the compulsory feature such as hard law. The key factor in multi-level regulatory governance is the situation of social capital that could respond to multi-level characteristics of regulatory institutions.

## Conclusion

In this chapter, I discussed the state transformation in environmental governance which is reflected in discussions about public governance, especially from the aspect of environmental regulations. Through an understanding of the characteristics of public governance as the state in a steering position, I analysed the role of the state in environmental governance from the viewpoint of environmental regulations, which are a policy instrument that reflects the steering position.

Certainly, environmental regulations can not only be caught in compulsory characteristics such as hard law; thus, if we adapt environmental governance, we also need to turn environmental regulations into soft law. These changes in environmental regulations also express the state's transformation in the field of environmental regulations. But it is not proper to recognize these changes as a hollowing out of the state by diminishing the state's role in solving public problems. Rather, it is better to focus on making environmental regulations adaptive to environmental governance. The Porter hypothesis, the policy mix and multi-level regulatory governance introduced in this chapter indicate the direction for making environmental regulations and reflect the transformative figure of the state through the channel of environmental regulations.

This chapter has discussed not focusing on the details of the differences among environmental regulations. For example, there are different stakeholders between regulations for economic activities by firms and those for consumption or daily living by the public. This also reflects the difference of contents and multi-level institutions that coordinate different interests among agencies. The Porter hypothesis fits the former cases, but, on the other hand, there is little doubt that we need to analyse and evaluate the regulatory impact at specific local areas in the latter cases. At the theme of multi-level regulatory governance, I could not concretely analyse cases that indicate the coordination of the contents of each domestic regulation internationally and the building of an international framework for regulations made by each central government; thus, my suggestion remains very abstract. But extending analytical frameworks and objects of regulations related to environmental governance is needed increasingly; hence, the present situation means that environmental regulations by the state are still major subjects and that environmental governance also might not indicate some ideal figure, but a dynamic concept related to a transitional process to sustainability.

## Notes

1. See Jessop (2004) or Jordan et al. (2005).
2. Regarding these features of governance, see de Loë et al. (2009).
3. See Jänicke and Jörgens (2009).

4. Regarding the norms of regulatory evaluation, see Doern and Johnson (2006).
5. See de Loë et al. (2009).
6. Regarding institutions related to environmental governance and functions, see Paavola (2007).
7. See Paavola (2008).
8. For multi-level governance and multi-level institutions, see Yatsuki (2013).
9. For performance of governance are influenced by veto points in multi-level governance, especially the case of European Union regional policy, see Benz (2000).
10. See Porter and van den Linde (1995).
11. For the latest study on survey of the Porter hypothesis, see Ambec et al. (2011).
12. Porter et al. (1995: 99–100).
13. See Shout and Jordan (2005).
14. Delia et al. (2009: 12). The author used "local governments" instead of "sub-national governments" to emphasize local characteristics in this chapter.
15. See Wälti (2010).

REFERENCES

Ambec, S., Cohen, M. A., Elgie, S. and P. Lanoie (2011) *The Porter Hypothesis at 20*, REF Discussion Paper 11-01, Resource for the Future, Washington, DC.

Benz, A. (2000) "Two Types of Multi-Level Governance: Intergovernmental Relations in German and EU Regional Policy", *Regional and Federal Studies*, 10(3), pp. 21–44.

Delia, R., Allio, L. and A.-A. Pedoro (2009) "Multi-Level Regulatory Governance: Polices, Institutions and Tools for Regulatory Quality and Policy Coherence", Organisation for Economic Co-operation and Development Working Paper on Public Governance 13, Paris.

de Loë, R. C., Armitage, D., Pulmmer, R., Davidson, S. and L. Moraru (2009) *From Government to Governance: A State-of-the-Art Review of Environmental Governance*, final report prepared by Rob de Loë Consulting Services for Alberta Environment, Environmental Stewardship, Environment Relations, Guelph, Ontario, Canada.

Doern, G. B. and R. Johnson (2006) "Conclusion", in G. B. Doern and R. Johnson (eds.), *Rules, Rules, Rules, Rules: Multilevel Regulatory Governance*, Toronto: University of Toronto Press, pp. 348–368.

Jänicke, M. and H. Jörgens (2009) "New Approaches to Environmental Governance", in A. P. J. Mol, D. A. Sonnenfeld and G. Spaargaren (eds.), *The Ecological Modernization Reader*, London: Routledge, pp. 156–189.

Jessop, B. (2004) "Multi-Level Governance and Multi-Level Metagovernance", in I. Bache and M. Flinders (eds.), *Multi-Level Governance*, Oxford: Oxford University Press, pp. 49–74.

Jordan, A., Wurzel, R. K. W. and A. Zito (2005) "The Rise of 'New' Policy Instruments in Comparative Perspective: Has Governance Eclipsed Government?", *Political Studies*, 53(3), pp. 477–496.

Paavola, J. (2007) "Institutions and Environmental Governance: A Reconceptualization", *Ecological Economics*, 63(1), pp. 93–103.

―――― (2008) *Explaining Multi-Level Environmental Governance*, SRI Papers 10, University of Leeds.

Porter, M. E. and C. van der Linde (1995) "Toward a New Conception of the Environment-Competitiveness Relationship", *Journal of Economic Perspectives*, 9(4), pp. 97–118.

Shout, A. and A. Jordan (2005) "Coordinated European Governance: Self-Organizing or Centrally Steered?", *Public Administration*, 83(1), pp. 201–220.

Wälti, S. (2010) "Multi-Level Environmental Governance", in H. Enderlein, S. Wälti and M. Zürn (eds.), *Handbook on Multi-Level Governance*, Cheltenham: Edward Elgar, pp. 411–422.

Yatsuki, S. (2013) "Multi-Level Environmental Governance and Intergovernmental Relations: The Case of Minuma-Tambo Conservation Policy", in K. Ueta (ed.), *Sustainable Development and Environmental Governance*, Kyoto: Minerva-Shobo, forthcoming (in Japanese).

# 4
# Governance of sustainability transition management at the local, national and global levels

*Tatsuro Niikawa*

This chapter investigates and clarifies the conditions under which governance can achieve the necessary structure and function for sustainability in the current transition period to be realized as a social goal in the future. Generally, governance theory proposes that the influence of the government has become relatively small and that it is the social actors of the second and third sectors (excepting the government) who now participate as decision makers at the centre of policy-making and influence the policy directions as stakeholders. Yet, it is a nuanced theory. There are various understandings about the theoretical connotations of governance. Although one of the more cogent lines of scholarship points to the existence of a horizontal policy network without government (Rhodes, 1997), another addresses the central role of government among relevant stakeholders (Pierre and Peters, 2000). Generally, governance theory identifies a horizontal constellation of actors including the government, and states that the overall policy process is composed of actors from multiple sectors (Bell and Hindmoor, 2009). This point is touched on in greater detail in a later section.

Such governance situations have important implications for environmental issues and policies. However, on the specific matter of sustainability—so contested on local, national and global levels—it is uncertain whether the governance theory is applicable. Regardless, it remains necessary to examine which process of governance can achieve the aim of future sustainability, which means it is necessary to adopt the viewpoint of transition management (Loorbach, 2007b). In turn, the objectives being examined are how the structures of governance are changing and set up in order to manage the process of transition. In addition, the relationship and differences between the transition management process and the governance process must be examined. It is recognized that a specific policy process (e.g., that pertaining to environmental policy) has unique characteristics in terms of the governance process which controls the decision process. Then, the transition management process controls the governing process of policy (Rotmans et al., 2001). It is an outstanding question of whether the environmental policy can, in fact, be controlled by the transition management process and associated governance structure.

These questions are the subject of the present investigation and are laid out sequentially. First, the purpose of this chapter is to make clear what are the issues surrounding the policies of environmental sustainability in the context of multi-level governance. Second, we ask whether the transition management approach can guide governance processes in particular, if the sustainability policies at global, national and local levels take mutually opposing stances to problem-solving an environmental issue. Can governing transition management work in practice for providing the measure for finding the resolution?

To examine these questions, after precisely identifying what is meant by the theory of transition management and governance, we look at the multi-level governance of the European Union (EU). Then, it is possible to sketch the strategy of transition management.

## Transition management for sustainability

The transition management approach is considered effective for promoting sustainability. A trial by the government of the Netherlands has particularly garnered favourable attention. The Dutch transition management scheme delineates a process towards the ultimate aim of sustainability, which stresses the socio-technical transformation of the policy system, for example, research and development of a renewable energy system and its installation into the social system.

There are a variety of governance challenges to achieving sustainability. In other words, such governance collectively surveys a feasible goal of sustainability, discovers the seemingly effective niche approach, forms a population of vested actors and the systems directing the market and the government sector and continuously learns and adapts itself to the surrounding environment. It is recognized that the transition management approach is about adjusting the dynamics of socio-technical change to those that are specifically goal-oriented. This is a continuous process in which further adjustments are carried out when environmental conditions change because the change is partially the result of a previous intervention. The cycle of feedback, monitoring, action and reaction includes factors which cannot be separated from each other in the overall frame of this process (Rotmans et al., 2001; Jere, 2012).

Because a governance system reduces opposition to and uncertainty about the aim of the sustainability in environmental policy, and provides possibilities to unify public policies that were once fragmented, it can be said that transition management has been successfully adopted and that the governance itself is adaptive and interactive. The governance associated with environmental policy implies transition management as a part of its essence, but investigating a governance condition under which transition management functions is necessary. In addition, the investigation has to consider the multi-level governance context, because environmental governance is likely to touch all levels. Multi-level governance thus prescribes the framework of transition management (Lorbach, 2007a).

In turn, the question is whether multi-level environmental governance can foster the conditions necessary for fulfilling the requirement of operating transition management. The conditions related to the potential and basic steps and processes are described next (Kemp and Loorbach, 2006).

The network responsible for developing the vision of sustainability pursued by a given governance system is organized by a host of actors across sectors who are mobilized to carry out and continually evaluate the transition project. This network not only develops the path to sustainability, but also implements the transition process including monitoring evaluation and re-evaluation.

The elements that are particularly important in this process are as follows (Kemp and Loorbach, 2006):
- Clear definitions of the problem
- A sound vision of the transition
- Means and ways of measuring transition steps and commitment within an organization
- Evaluation and learning
- An ability to research the innovation program of the socio-technical system and put it to use
- A broad base of public support and
- The creation of a nexus transition, which is likely to be a social network and system of governance.

The requirements of transition management demand following the operation specifically (Kemp et al., 2007), handling uncertainty using case scenarios, maintaining open choice and treating the fragmented policy, stimulating changes of knowledge and skill, pursuing innovation and progressive improvement, paying attention to the multifaceted perspective of all actors and stakeholders, enacting short-term policy with long-term orientation, observing the changing process of global society and discovering a solution with a proper standard. The government in particular has its own problems to tackle with, namely to steer the work of stimulating mediation and partnership to cultivate the appropriate condition for accomplishing transition management and executing the laws and ordinances concerned.

At this point, it bears mentioning that there are some criticisms of transition management (Shove and Walker, 2007). Although the transition management approach ends with sustainability, its adaptive governance characteristics may mean that the approach effectively stops working at a certain insufficient level, and it cannot achieve its future aim (Smith and Stirling, 2008). On the other hand, it is uncertain whether or not a given government can manage such transition and can fully supervise transition management. There is yet a further question about whether the governance of transition management is democratic and legitimizes citizen participation (Skelcher and Torfing, 2010). One more serious problem, particularly salient for the purpose of this analysis, underlies the question of whether the transition management approach can work in multi-level governance contexts, especially as far as environmental sustainability is concerned. Because environmental governance cannot be isolated from different levels of governance, transition management has to function inherently at all levels in such a system (Loorbachs, 2007b).

If transition management remains within a particular governance (e.g., the national governance), the environmental governance suffers disturbances of policy implementation from another governance. Even if individual governances can cope with the transition management, it is difficult for them to respond to the environmental problem in a manner that is in concert with other levels in the multi-level governance. The transition management approach must assume the characteristics of network-type and policy-centred governance to function across administrative and state borders within the multi-level governance. The globalization or internationalization of the transition policy is easy to address, but transition management in the globalized society is difficult to practice; it is a big challenge for the approach when it transcends the borders. For sustainability, the aspect of multi-level governance problem is the most difficult to solve in a transition management model. However, transition management is applicable for all environmental policy efforts directed toward building a sustainable society, because all government actors at least believe the transition process is necessary for stakeholders to have different interest. The approach melds with certain conditions of multi-level governance in that it considers different domains (multi-domain), different levels of scale (multi-level) and different system states (multi-phase); it encourages adopting a long-term perspective as a framework for short-term actions, employs a multi-actor approach, utilizes both back-casting and forecasting to reconcile uncertainties and to plan for surprises, and focuses on social learning through learning by doing and doing by learning simultaneously (Loorbach, 2007a). Although multi-level governance should be democratic and supported by the public, for environmental governance, it must support harmonized environmental policy and identify a future goal which is to be flexibly pursued (Skelcher and Torfing, 2010).

## The opposition between policy values for sustainability

Environmental transition management focuses on achieving sustainability in an age of conflicts among the local, national and global governances. Existing policies concerned with sustainability focus on realizing social value, economic value and environmental value simultaneously. However, these values may not be mutually agreeable; rather, they may in fact oppose one another. In the domain of policy-making remain many more contradictions that are critical to resolve in order to realize sustainability targets at each level of governance. Specifically, it is often mentioned that sustainability must satisfy three objectives; growth of the economy, fairness of society and environmental value. Because sustainability targets have introduced many conflicts pertaining to competing values, a serious fight concerning the present priorities in the goal-seeking process is likely to occur (Newig et al., 2008).

Since 1987, the aim of sustainability has included the value opposition when the concept of sustainable development first gained traction as a proposition by the Brundtland Committee. It has been said that sustainable development was an expression coined to mitigate the opposition between North and South and between the environment and the economy; the North has historically intended to regulate the environmental pollution in the developing countries, and the South has insisted that it wishes to seek economic development and that the North has violated its collective right of economic prosperity (Speth and Haas, 2006).

The opposition phenomenon may occur between the national target and the local target for sustainability as well as at the global level, expressed as conflict between developed and developing countries. Frequently, local and national sustainability targets prove contradictory. Although the central government may seek economic development from sustainability, a local community may want to preserve its natural environment for sustainability and vice versa. With such conflicting situations the interest of the nation may oppose those on a local level, and the central policy may therefore oppose local, too (Kirton and Hajnal, 2006).

The governance tensions between central and local governments create another complex problem of global governance. Because policies pertaining to social, economic and environmental problems transcend borders easily, environmental governance has to deal with the multi-faceted relationships among nation states, and environmental policy frequently feels the impact of policy priority change from other governance systems (Kutting and Lipschutz, 2009). Achieving the policy objectives depends on the success of environmental governance in organizing the process of the sustainability's goal-seeking. This success of governance seems to be found at the local, national and global levels individually, in which each governance operation is necessary to learn the mutual dependent relationships. In the scheme of multi-level governance, the local has an interactive relationship with the national and the global, and generally, in terms of legal authority, the local is put under the control of the national. Yet, in addition, it is well known that local power politically influences national and global policy-making (Kutting and Lipschultz, 2009).

Regarding economic issues, the greatest opposition may be between national and local levels of governance, whereas for social and environmental problems, conflicts are perhaps more likely to occur between the national and the global levels of governance. The issue of sustainability, then, brings in a wide spectrum of domains (social, political and economic) and associated differences of opinion at each level. Yet, although multi-level governance occasionally hampers intergovernmental relations, it also sometimes functions in a cooperative and complementary manner, according to the policy field and the precise policy mix. Even if the multi-level governance achieves sustainability, from the standpoint of policy-makers and governments, multi-level governance itself may be concerned about the complicated problem that must be resolved (Oberthur and Ghering, 2006).

It is critical for environmental governance that the transition management process works for and builds a sustainable society. Yet, it is questionable whether transition management can in fact yield progress towards sustainability in a multi-level governance context. As for governing sustainability, it seems that there is plain agreement about an ideal target in the far-off future and plenty of disagreement about the present goals. There also seems to be opposition among the values in the policy network promoting sustainability in the short term and value disagreement among the levels of governances. To find the means of breaking through such a situation is a mission of environmental governance and the role of transition management.

## Structure of the governance and its conflicting stance toward sustainability

The concept of multi-level governance has become an international buzzword during the past two decades. The original theory of multi-level governance was based on the European unification process and was formulated by European political scientists and the field of international relations (Bache and Flinders, 2005). The multi-level governance theory deals with those functions of global governance (in the case of the EU, regional governance) which transcend the purview of national governance. The concept of multi-level governance means the presence of intergovernmental relationships in both the horizontal and the vertical direction. Global decisions affect national and local decisions and vice versa. There are mutual two-way influences and interactions among the global, national and local governance levels.

The preeminent characteristic of this multi-level governance is that it tends to bypass the level of national governance and seeks to make a direct connection and policy coalition between global and local governance. When local and global levels of governances are committed to environmental policy formation and relevant decision-making, it proves useful to introduce the concept of the multi-level, or multilayered, governance (Winter, 2006).

Another characteristic of multi-level governance is that the function of transboundary governance can be activated through multi-level governance, and each governance can interact with each other as well. Each actor in the governance structure behaves not only as a member of one level of governance but also as a member of another level, regulating the interest of both governances based on his or her common membership. Each actor connects with mutual members of governance and organizes a governance network while he or she coordinates cooperation and settles conflicts among the multi-level governances (Le Prestre and Stoett, 2006). From the viewpoint of the policy-process analysis, such governance is estimated as being midway between disorder and order of decision-making. Besides, it is observed that this governance has been experiencing institutionalization of sorts and becomes a delinquent adaptation at the same time.

Multi-level governance has to solve the problem of sustainability, or sustainable development. This concept of sustainable development, however conciliatory, is born from the value opposition between the developed country and the developing country, as previously mentioned. The basic idea of sustainability is a tautological one: a society which is sustainable and does not exploit the existence of future generations. The policy for sustainability aims at achieving environmental, economic and social targets, which are the standard for concrete developmental action (Okereke, 2008). These three standards are the so-called "triple bottom line".

Sustainability policy includes goals for economic growth, environmental conservation and social fairness at the same time and tries to inspire the policy measures, institutions and organizations in order to realize those ideals. For such an idea or policy orientation, the actors of the governance network are required to hold those ideals as the premise, but it is uncertain whether such a consensus exists. Although such an idea or policy orientation is generally understood by the governance network, it is difficult to make clear the definition of sustainability more specifically (Kirton and Hjnal, 2006). In the type of policy formation process that names sustainability as the basic objective, it is necessary for governance to continue to review and reorganize environmental policy, economic policy and social policy from the point of view of developing a sustainable society.

Under the condition of multi-level governance, if the interpenetration of different policy objectives for sustainability occurs, inconsistent policy targets may arise among governments and basic contradictions in value orientation among governances may be introduced. In other words, the opposition among local, national and global sustainability policies is regarded as resulting from governances' realizing the value of sustainability. It is important that a network of decision-making and governance function in tandem to solve the problems or disturbances that may prevent a sustainable society from being achieved (Kennett, 2008). It is widely recognized that the decision-making function of governance is critical in achieving the targets of sustainability policy.

There may be many cases in which the local use of resources, the local implementation of environmental conservation and the local program of economic development conflict with the standard use of resources and the environmental protection at the global or national level. In such a case it may be possible to control local exploitation of resources by the regulation of the national government or an international organization. In addition, there may be reverse cases, in which it is likely that global and national environmental conservations are in fact spoiling the sustainability at the local level.

If the local governance structure relates with their global and national counterparts on the matter of environmental protection, the multi-level governance may be said to function vertically. However, the direction of work and the relationships of control among governances are variable in each case. Generally, in a given locality, the policy priorities for sustainability among the social, economic and environmental values are easy to change, because the speed of the policy response to the voice of the citizen in the local governance tends to be accelerated by the local government which is characteristic of the democracy and is responsible for their citizen's needs (Stoker, 2000). Although local governance is both complemented and controlled by the global and the national governance, the local does not passively accept the vertical impact of multi-level governance, which shows essentially the characteristics of vertical and hierarchical governance. Rather, it is necessary to focus on the possibility that multi-level governance can realize the values of local policy, in which the global governance may tend to support the local interest despite facing an opposition or interruption from national government. It must be noticed that one of the functions of multi-level governance is to connect local values with national and global values, so that the local value set becomes globalized or nationalized while the national and global value sets become localized.

It is taken for granted that the governance structure at each level and their actors do not participate in an easy relationship in multi-level governance (European Commission, 2001b). For example, at the national level, government has its own interest for the sustainability, and it is apparent that the national government and its governance structure cannot respond to the demands for sustainability at the global and local levels, each of which has different priorities. Rather, it happens that the national government cannot coordinate the relationships between global and local governances and cannot transmit the information in the multi-level governance as a sovereign state.

The environmental and multi-level governance for sustainability is in the transition process. The problem of sustainability cannot be solved completely at present, and none of the environmental, economic and social contradictions will be settled in the near future; simultaneously, it must be recognized that governance structure cannot completely realize policy integration for sustainable development. It is the strategy of transition that is critical to the goal of achieving sustainability in the far-off future, because it both inspires and manages the incremental change of policy with the long-term perspective. The governance system can implement transition management as needed (Kemp and Loorbach, 2003). There must be a mode of governance that initiates change and leads the way to an appropriate future aim through managing the dynamics of the policy change; however, there is a question about whether the governance process can ever function properly.

In confronting the problems of governing sustainability, it should be recognized that transition management faces some critical issues. Per Kemp and Loorbach, (2006): (1) The first issue is that governing transition management for sustainability requires appropriations for a different phase in the transition process. The transition management approach recognizes different stages, which include stagnation and the big-leap phases.

(2) The second issue is the changing actors in the governance network trying to manage the transition. In the transition process, these actors continually develop new value orientations toward policy decisions for sustainability; also, the actors are leaving and their replacements are entering. The actors and their roles change continuously according to the environment in which the multi-level governance operates and with the introduction of opposition from other actor groups.

(3) The third issue is that multi-level governance must cope with the transition management system at different levels, such as the micro and the macro, the simple and the complex system, and so on. The transition management system itself shows different characteristics according to whether it is controlled from the outside or spontaneously from within. Transition management cannot work without the spontaneous participation of the actors, while the management component cannot function without regulation.

(4) The fourth issue is, as we have touched on, the multi-level governance itself. Transition management must cope with the circular and horizontal relationships among the local, national and global governances. In the transition process, multi-level governance should resolve the opposition among competing governance systems.

Governing transition management works in two directions: one direction is making the target shared and accepted, and the other is adaptive in terms of the management process. The former represents the basic idea of governing the transition management. Although there may be different values, techniques and goals of sustainability, transition management seeks to identify the common aim and implements the process of reaching social consensus of future objectives. As an adaptive governance, the latter is more practical and realistic. If it is difficult to agree on the policies and overarching goal of sustainable development, using the adaptive management approach is much more important than other idealistic measures. Adaptive management is a practical way to proceed with implementing sustainable policy and avoiding the critical conflict to stop the policy process. It is wise to carry out what the environmental governance can do for the sustainability by adaptive governance approach in the step-by-step way.

## Multilevel governance of transition management for sustainability

The theoretical backgrounds of the theory of multi-level governance have been originated in the political process analysis of the unification of Europe.

In the 1950s, the principle of new functionalism by Haas (1958) stated that the government of every country in Europe was merging in an interdependent network, which was growing and gaining traction. The theory of new functionalism goes a long way toward explaining European unification. In the 1960s, Hoffmann (1995) addressed the intergovernmentalism by which the nation state was regarded as a gatekeeper and the arbiter of national interest as well as the centre of the process of unification. In the 1970s and 1980s, the Intermestic (international and domestic) theory had been proposed by Rosenau (1983). It provided an important viewpoint discussing the issue of domestic administrations' relationships to foreign policy. Intermestic theory addresses that foreign policy influence domestic policy decision-making and vice versa, and the theory is also called Lincage politics between national and international policies.

During and since the 1990s, the multi-level governance theory has emerged as a dominant trend in the literature. The background of the argument was that external factors propelled the theory and practice of the political economy under the globalization, the deepening of the interdependence, the increasing risk and uncertainty in the world and the technical innovation and the knowledge accumulation (Boyer, 1988).

On the other hand, there were inherent structural reasons why multi-level governance became a popular explanatory theory: the collapse of the social base of corporatism at the nation-state level, the gradual change of political behaviour, and the emergence of newer pattern in a collective action and the bargaining process of interest (Majone, 1998).

Since 2000, a new behaviour pattern in multi-level governance has been identified in several directions (Pierre, 2000; Pierre and Peters, 2000): (1) the first one is that there has been a switch from the principle of the interventionist state to that of the regulation state (Dingeldey and Rothgang, 2009). The growth of multinational enterprises and the proliferation of multinational outbreak of interests have needed regulation across the nation states.

(2) The second direction is a tendency by non-profit organizations (NPOs) and non-governmental organizations (NGOs) or public-interest groups active in the decision-making process to prefer choosing international regulation across many countries over changing the structure of interest in one country (Chhotray and Stoker, 2009). They find that it is economical and effective for resolving the environmental issues and consumers' problems in this manner. Therefore, they are accustomed to utilizing sub-national resources for global lobbying.

(3) The third direction is the emergence of newer values that are changing a simple value-opposition scheme to the values of a post-industrial society and post-materialism, and to pluralistic and complex values like in the human rights campaign and environment movement (Pierre and Peters, 2000).

The operation of local, national and global governance and multi-level governance itself is changing the behavioural pattern and composition of the governance network in the field of environment policy and of its transition management. The change has come from the interrelationship of governance structures among the local, national and global (Schuppert, 2006). The characteristics of each governance, in turn, dictate the relationship and the behaviour of multi-level governance.

For local governance, realizing the value of local sustainability is relatively easy, because local governance is influenced by the changing priority of the local residents, and the prioritization of local social, economic and environmental values is easy to change. The speed with which the local governance replies to the input and demands from governance network actors is prompt, and the behaviour pattern of local governance varies, corresponding to the changes in the policy and value environment. The responses of local government also show the democratic and sometimes popularized character of local governance (Stoker, 2000). Then, the national governance system is more difficult to change than the local, because the actors of the central governance network are usually such huge organizations and so have a stable, collective vested interest as to not change the decision promptly (Sanford, 2005).

National governance structures "above" local governance may indeed control the local in the vertical or hierarchical relationships. The control mechanism between the local and global governance structures works in the forms of subsidy and regulation from the central government and so on. There are some interdependencies to consider when examining the relationships between local and central governance.

The capacity of global governance is generally limited, because the actors are fragmented and decentralized in the realm of global politics. Decisions at the level of global governance need consensus from nation states and international organizations. Thus, global governance functions in carefully specified policy arenas which are likely to tightly align with the interests of each country.

If a multi-level governance scheme is to work, there must be close, mutual relationships among the local, national and global levels of governance. In the case of environmental policy, a number of the national-level governments cannot intercede between their local and global counterparts, because these national governments do not have the singular ability to negotiate directly as an agent of the global or the local governance; moreover, these national governments also often have different interests from the local and the global governance actors. However, the multi-level governance can work in another way in which the local governance system directly adopts the global value so that, in turn, the global accepts the local value set. Sometimes this chain of interaction operates without national governance structure, or with opposition or support at the national level. If there is a contradiction between the local values and the national values in a given context, multi-level governance occasionally intervenes and coordinates the relationship between the national and local governance structures. Then, as already mentioned, the local value may become the global value and vice versa (Prakash and Hart, 1999).

The idea of multi-level governance is likely to adequately adjust each level by introducing a more democratic mode. For example, the sub-national conflict is discussed at a global level directly, and vice versa. As a result, the multi-level governance extends the ability and the impact possibility of smaller entities and local actors in addition to that of global actors.

## Multi-level governance in EU environmental policy

The European Union (EU) is a typical example of multi-level governance and environmental governance for sustainability, and the EU is well known to the environmental initiative of global governance and local government (Paraskevopoulos et al., 2006). In this section, the multi-level governance aspect of the EU environmental policy and governance is examined from the viewpoint of the EU, national and sub-national governments and the civil society organizations at each level. The rise of multi-level governance as it applies to EU environmental policy is particularly examined and analysed from both the practical and theoretical perspectives.

First, let us examine the methods by which EU environmental regulation is decided and implemented. Oberthur and Gehring (2006) explain the process well: the most important policies are proposed by the EU Commission, and the member states and the special interest groups committed to the proposals make adjustments according to their interests. When the proposals are judged to be feasible, they are sent to the Council of the European Union and to the European Parliament, and the proposals are submitted for public comment by stakeholders. Any suggestions or corrections are incorporated before the proposal adoption by the Council of the European Union, which is composed of cabinet ministers of member states. When an EU directive is provided, the member state must incorporate its provision into the national law within the time limit which is indicated by the statement clearly (Cafruny and Rosenthal, 1993).

In order to harmonize conflicts between the provisions of the EU directive and the laws of the member states, there are a number of means of coordination. After a grace period of several months for various legal delays, in observance of the time limit for the domestic legislation to be implemented, the EU warns the member state three times every few months. Nevertheless, if the violation continues, the European Court of Justice, under the EU Commission, is instituted. The judgement of the judicial court is to confirm the non-fulfilment of the directive. If the government of the member states does not obey and non-fulfilment has been confirmed, the stronger second round of three warnings by EU Commission commences. If the national law is not appropriately harmonized and the directive is not carried out, the matter is once more submitted to the European Court of Justice, and the EU can impose fines for noncompliance in some cases (Amull, 2006).

As a matter of course, it is often said that EU environmental policy does not have the authority of compulsion, and it is generally recognized that the Directorate-General of Environment and the European Environment Agency does not have a critical decisive authority of forcible execution. For the EU Commission, which likewise does not have sufficient direct power, the recourse to the European Court of Justice becomes the important means simply because the EU commission does not have the ability to enforce environmental policy execution without court decision (Diedrichs et al., 2011). This can be confirmed by the fact that about one-third of the instances in which the EU Commission has called upon the EU Court of Justice relate to environmental issues (Oberthur and Gehling, 2006). Each deficiency which occurs in member states is caused basically by the imbalance: the capability gaps within each state to practically administer the EU-level environment policy. Another factor to influence the difference of environmental policy implementation greatly is an internal composition of each government: its stated issues and values. Against this complicated backdrop, the EU has to pay attention to each member state's implementation of environmental policy in each member state and in each domestic law and ordinance enacted. The EU must assess domestic goals and the plan about the environment policy, and ensure such plans are carried out on schedule. To these ends, the monitoring and inspection are indispensable (Oberthur and Gehling, 2006).

Another problem happens with monitoring. Not having data for observation and comparison with an equal database is problematic, owing to the unevenness in the data-gathering among the country of the EU. This is recognized as a risk of further EU enlargement.

It is a matter of course that various organizations and agencies have been set up for making EU environmental policy effective and harmonized. In particular, the leading organization in Europe for environmental policy is the European Environmental Agency. The European Environmental Agency is an organization that provides environmental information and is the premier source of information about policy formation, decisions, enforcement and environmental evaluation, but it has been called "the watchdog without the teeth" at the same time (Diedrichs et al., 2011). The European Environmental Agency coordinates and runs the European Environmental Information and Observation Network (EIO-NET), which is an organization giving intelligence that aids substantially in the processes of environmental policy formation (EIONET, 1997). In addition, an informal network among environmental regulation organizations cooperating with each other on matters of environmental regulation gathers under the umbrella IMPEL (EU Network for the Implementation and Enforcement of Environmental Law), which works on the task of the communication and policy adjustment among the member states (IMPEL, 2012).

On the other hand, there is an international meeting of local governments regarding environmental policy (International Council for Local Environmental Initiatives: ICLEI Local Government for Sustainability). ICLEI has approximately

1,100 organizations or entities globally, in which the active members of Europe and a few other core members who affiliate ICLEI Europe are 175 entities. In addition, the Climate Alliance was established in Europe, and approximately 1,400 local governments or authorities participate (ICLEI, 2009). As there is a high degree of initial cooperation among local governments for preventing global warming proceeds, these local governments and ICLEI Europe have tried to extend their influence on international compliance and have worked at the COP15 of Copenhagen in particular (ICLEI Europe, 2012).

The development of the environmental movement among local governments includes promoting the transition management for sustainability goals in the multi-level governance structure. The information disseminated from the local entities is used to influence the formation of global and national environmental policy. The cooperation between local organizations or between regional organizations with the local groups is influential for the development of global governance and multi-level governance. One of the most significant is the ICLEI, which aims to complete the Local Agenda 21 and Local Action 21 (the internationally recognized proposition and action plan intended to contribute to sustainable development at the local level). The ICLEI also proposes the Sustainable City Program which provides a scheme for realizing a sustainable city in each local government. It seems that the transition management by ICLEI leads local governments in implementing their own sustainable city plan (Evans et al., 2005). Local initiatives may then influence the central governments and the global society, preparing the introduction strategy of environmental policy for sustainable goals and fostering the transition management in central governments.

These local governments and the central government may often develop their activities in cooperation with private environmental action groups, namely, an environmental NGO or an NPO, although sometimes these groups stand in direct opposition to the government policy options. The same is true within the EU. For example, at the conference about the emission trading system, an environmental NGO has the ability to participate and each governmental member has the opportunity to cooperate with NGO or NPO. Nevertheless there are some closed meetings limited to government representatives only, so the public and the private sectors are kept at arm's length (Kirton and Hjnal, 2006).

The characteristics of multi-level governance in the environmental policy of the EU are summarized as follows: (1) first, from the viewpoint of organizational and governance characteristics, the states' positions in the governance scheme are becoming not absolute but relative, so that it may be observed that the influence of a given state is parallel and coessential with that of other social actors as NGOs and NPOs. Of course, this does not mean that a nation state finishes its role in the decision-making process of the environmental policy, but that the decision-making system for environmental policy and the policy enforcement system are changing largely in which the national government has lost its power as a central organ of policy-making (Lafferty, 2002).

(2) Second, it is critical that the policies and the organizations transcend the boundaries of the nation state and become more influential, as has been a trend. This is so not only within the EU itself, but also within the Directorate-General Environment of the EU and other administrative organizations for environmental protection that have been growing year by year. Then, through the growth of such organizations, state power tends to decline relatively (Schuppert, 2006).

(3) Third, it is natural that a horizontal network for environmental policy is composed of the governments of every member state. It happens that the environmental administration organization or the regulation authority of each country come into close contact with each other and sometimes cooperate and support mutually in their actions (Jeffery, 1996).

(4) Fourth, it is important that a network between the international organization and the local government is built. If the coalition of the local governments expresses the unified purpose and the common interest and takes action, environmental issues are one of the areas that can be most easily agreed on at a national and global level. The EU is groping for cooperation and collaboration with the allianced organization of the local governments. Specifically, as the Climate Alliance has been trusted by the EU, the environmental affair has been pushed forward by the partnership between the local government network and the EU (Climate Alliance, 2012). Another example is the Covenant of Mayors, which bound together the mayors of approximately 400 cities from different nations, and, through cooperation with the EU, aimed to reduce the discharge of greenhouse gases by more than 20 per cent in 1990 (Covenant of Mayors, 2007).

(5) Fifth, there are the negotiations and the continual networking between the governmental sector and the non-governmental sector. The environmental NGOs in particular are given formal seats in the international conferences and a voice, which has been influential. As is similar in an EU context, and in the meetings about various environmental problems, a number of relevant NGOs are generally invited. Not only because of increasing concrete influence of the NGO and NPO, but also, ideally, because of the need for close relationships with the civil society sector, an international organization might sometimes ally itself with environmental NGOs in order to adjust the balance between it and each national government and to reach the decision that is advantageous to its individual aims (European Commission, 2009).

Kohler-Koch and Larat (2009) outline the characteristics of the network and the actors in the multi-level governance that seem common in EU environmental policy.
- The first characteristic is that the network is pluralistic.
- The second is that the weak compelling force between each actor acts mutually.
- The third is that the initiative and voluntarism of each actor are thought to be significant. The actors are also participating in the network voluntarily.
- The fourth is that there is consensus, which means the general policy perspective, but there is a difference in opinion about the details which are included

at the same time. In other words, the separation and unification between the general remarks (at EU level) and the detailed exposition (of member states) are integrated in a cross-linked policy that includes the differences and contradictions between the macro policy and the micro policy.
- The fifth is that the initiative of each government and the network among the local, national and international at the different levels can be identified.
- Finally, sixth, although there is the feasibility of the formation of the environmental policy, the basic agreement about the policy value and the goal between the governments, and the agreement between the public and private sectors, there still exist plenty of opportunities to discuss the shared value and goal to set the range that can form a mutual agreement in order to prevent contradictions among the actors at the same time.

The policy process mentioned earlier includes the transition management of environmental governance in the EU. It seems that the transition management is working in the EU multi-level environmental governance, and EU environmental policy has been established, although not expressly declared, as a transition management policy for the goal of sustainability (European Commission, 2009). Local, national, regional and global governance of environmental policy regimes interact and are interrelated; if the EU wants to achieve the goal of sustainable environmental policy at each level of government, it must seek the feasibility of implementing such policy and hold a good balance between the centralization and decentralization in the redistribution of authority and/or jurisdiction (Marks, 1993).

In some cases, EU environmental policy leads the local, national and global policy formations to pursue sustainable development, whereas the EU governance of environmental policy works as multi-level governance. The development of environmental policy in the EU coincides with functioning multi-level governance which prompts the local and national governments to adopt the policy in line with the EU decisions. For this to further a kind of integration work, the EU has equipped governments with some tools and measures which are unique (Sbragia, 1992):

1. The common environmental policy proceeds with the aim at achieving "the high-level protection" based on a preventive action and the polluter-pays principle.
2. Based on the common policy, the laws and directives of the EU have been established and many regulations have been implemented. The laws and directives concerning environmental problems already number more than 200, and the proportion of the "rules" and "decisions" to have a directly legal binding force is increasing.
3. In addition, the establishment of the European Environmental Agency has been critical of environmental policy for realizing a sustainable target and for unifying each agency. The environmental administration has proceeded with the key agency who organizes environmental policies and distributes the financial

resources of carbon emission trading. The annual revenue by that trading has been increasing, and the expenditure for environmental protection is growing largely.
4. A policy-making procedure also has changed. By adopting majority rule, the decision-making system of the Council of European Union has changed from a unanimous to the current co-determination procedure, and the domain of co-decision with the European Parliament has likewise been enlarged. The European Commission has found participating in that decision-making process difficult, although the commission had the power to influence before the establishment of the Single European Act and its amendments.

## Reconstruction of idea, policy, institution and organization of multi-level governance for sustainability in the age of transition management

In the case of the EU, if transition management can be broadly understood, the elements of transition management have partially been fulfilled. Transition management is not only the socio-technical program for sustainability but also the management of transition for the sustainability in a broad sense in Europe. Basically, European environmental policy has defined the issues and has identified the purpose of reaching sustainability. This also means to adopt the measure and manner of transition and to respect the goal commitment of each organization in which policy integration has been sought and policy evaluation has been tried, although they may not necessary have public support (Atkinson et al., 2011). The Directorate-General Environment and European Environmental Agency have been enlarging their ability to research the innovation programme which breaks through the deadlock of sustainable development, and providing the opportunity of information exchange among the stakeholders.

The practical requirements of transition management are satisfied partially in EU environmental governance: the uncertainty has been handled through examining the effects of policy implementation. Regarding treating the fragmented policy, the policy integration approach has been introduced as a principle (Diedrichs et al., 2011). The EU system is stimulating the exchange of knowledge and skills among actors and stakeholders who have different perspectives on sustainability issues. It is not certain that the short-term policy set introduced will contribute to the long-term orientation while the changing process of global society is observed and a solution with a clear standard is discovered. It is also unclear whether the government of a member state in particular will further attempt the transition management and its execution (Loorbach, 2007b).

The transition management of environmental policy has to control both the regulation of policy and the system design for sustainability in general. The structure of the sustainable society and the process of its formation may depend on the present conditions of the organizational ability and the policy-making ability of the governance. There are both external conditions and inherent conditions of governance which are able to initiate change in the governing process and its outcome. A nation state is influenced by the global market, by the international organizations and NGOs and by the local government and its constituents, the governance of which is changing with the impact of disappearing the borders (Kirton and Hjnal, 2006).

The change in policy frameworks appears in the change from a regulation-and-redistribution-type policy to an alternative policy plan that activates NGOs and the market, which is so-called the Public-Private-Partnership (PPP) policy type (Bull and McNeill, 2007). There may also be the appearance of new actors and new values that assist this fundamental reorientation. A functional condition of multi-level governance in the transition management is defined by the bottom-up and top-down power and the mixture with which the actors and network of stakeholders can work.

If the social, economic and environmental values are at odds among the local, national and global governances, the multi-level governance may not function. To avoid a dysfunction of multi-level governance which disrupts the process of sustainability policy, the new rule of transition management must be accepted by the actors who compose the governance network (Atkinson et al., 2011). The success or failure of the transition management depends on the creation of a new design of governance network for the sustainability (Bovens et al., 2001). Resolving contradictions and integrating policies in environmental policy for the sustainability will be promoted by the governance of transition management, making the unification adaptive and the multi-level governance harmonious (Paraskevopoulos et al., 2006).

The governance of transition management appears to be one of the special forms of multi-level governance. Therefore, the transition management of local, national and global environmental policy has to resolve the contradiction among the local, national and global governance. Although at the three levels of governance the transition management policy has to be shared and coordinated to complete the future aim for the sustainability, each level has its particular priority according to the geographical scale, the character of actors and its own issue (Winter, 2006).

Transition management breaks down a long-term, complicated issue into the midterm, partial problem and breaks down the midterm, partial problem into short-term action items. It has to reorganize the different issues and goals into those which are mutually related by providing the arena of coordination (Bovaired and Loffler, 2009). The structure of governance that can subsume the new and dispersed demands will be able to resolve a complicated social problem such as sustainability (OECD, 2005) and will craft the environmental policy effectively and efficiently.

The dual tendencies of decentralization and dispersion in the multi-level governance prove a serious and critical impediment for the governance of transition management. Policy-making is losing its transparency, and the division of the power in multi-level governance makes responsibility and accountability obscure (Vari and Tamas, 2011). Although the proper operation of multi-level governance for sustainability is difficult to practice, transition management can solve problems through enabling democracy to function well, by securing the public support and by allowing for flexible decision making about the future goal (Sorensen and Torfing, 2008).

REFERENCES

Amull, A. (2006) *The European Union and Its Court of Justice*, Oxford: Oxford University.

Atkinson, R., G. Terizakis and K. Zimmermann (eds.) (2011) *Sustainability in European Environmental Policy: Challenge of Governance and Knowledge*, Abingdon: Routledge.

Bache, I. and M. Flinders (2005) *Multi-Level Governance*, Oxford: Oxford University Press.

Bell, S. and A. Hindmoor (2009) *Rethinking Governance: The Centrality of the State in Modern Society*, Port Melbourne: Cambridge University Press.

Bovaired, T. and E. Loffler (eds.) (2009) *Public Management and Governance*, London: Routledge.

Bovens, M., P. Hart and B. G. Peters (eds.) (2001) *Success and Failure in Public Governance: A Comparative Analysis*, Cheltenham: Edward Elgar.

Boyer, R. (1988) *The Search for Labour Market Flexibility*, Oxford: Clarendon Press.

Bull, B. and D. McNeill (2007) *Development Issues in Global Governance: Public-Private Partnerships and Market Multilateralism*, New York: Routledge.

Cafruny, A. and G. Rosenthal (eds.) (1993) *The State of European Community Vol. 2: The Maastricht Debate*, Harlow: Longman.

Chhotray, V. and G. Stoker (2009) *Governance Theory and Practice: A Cross-Disciplinary Approach*, Hampshire: Palgrave Macmillan.

Climate Alliance (2012) "Climate Alliance", available at http://www.klimabuendnis.org/.

Covenant of Mayors (2007) *Covenant of Mayor: Committed to Local Sustainable Energy*, available at http://www.covenantofmayors.eu/.

Diedrichs, U., W. Reiners and W. Wessels (eds.) (2011) *The Dynamics of Change in EU Governance*, Cheltenham: Edward Elgar.

Dingeldey, I. and H. Rothgang (eds.) (2009) *Governance of Welfare State Reform: A Cross National and Cross Sectoral Comparison of Policy and Politics*, Cheltenham: Edward Elgar.

EIONET (European Environmental Information and Observation Network) (1997) *EIONET Newsletter*, May 1997 No. 0.

European Commission (2001a) *White Paper on European Governance*, Brussels: European Commission.

—— (2001b) *Networking People for a Good Governance in Europe*, Brussels: European Commission.

—— (2002) *General Principles and Minimum Standards for Consultation*, Brussels: European Commission.

—— (2003) *Interactive Policy-Making Initiative*, Brussels: European Commission.

—— (2009) *Review of the European Union Strategy for Sustainable Development*, Brussels: European Commission.
Evans, B. et al. (2005) *Governing Sustainable Cities*, London: Earthscan.
Fine, B., C. Lapavitsa and J. Pincus (eds.) (2001) *Development Policy in the Twenty-First Century: Beyond the Post-Washington Consensus*, London: Routledge.
Haas, E. B. (1958) *The Uniting of Europe, Political, Social and Economic Forces*, Stanford, CA: Stanford University Press.
Hix, S. (1994) "The Study of the European Community: The Challenge to Comparative Politics", in *West European Politics*, 17.
Hoffmann, M. J. (2011) *Climate Governance at the Crossroad: Experimenting with a Global Response after Kyoto*, Oxford: Oxford University Press.
Hoffmann, S. (1995) *The European Sisyphus, Essays on Europe 1964–1994*, Boulder, CO: Westview Press.
ICLEI Europe (2012) "Europe ICLEI Local Governments for Sustainability", available at http://www.iclei-europe.org/home/.
IMPEL (European Union Network for the Implementation and Enforcement of Environmental Law) (2012) *Exploring Qualitative and Quantitative Assessment Tools to Evaluate the Performance of Environmental Inspectorates Across the EU*, Final report: 30 March 2012, available at http://library.impel.eu/.
International Council for Local Environmental Initiatives (ICLEI: Local Government for Sustainability) (2009) *ICLEI Local Government for Sustainability: Local Solutions to Global Challenges*, available at http://www.iclei.org/.
Jeffery, C. (ed.) (1996) *The Regional Dimension of the EU*, London: Frank Cass.
Jere, W. A. (ed.) (2012) *Transition Management (Governance)*, EQU Press (online publisher).
Keating, M. (2004) *Who Rules? How Government Retains Controls of a Privatized Economy*, Sydney: Federation Press.
Kemp, R. and D. Loorbach (2003) "Governance for Sustainability through Transition Management," paper for EAEPE 2003 Conference, 7–10 November, 2003 Maastricht: the Netherlands.
—— (2006) "Transition Management: A Reflexive Governance Approach", in J.-P. Voss, D. Bauknecht and R. Kemp, *Reflexive Governance for Sustainable Development*, London: Edward Elgar, pp. 121–139.
Kemp R., D. Loorbach and J. Rotmans (2007) "Transition Management as a Model for Managing Processes of Co-Evolution towards Sustainable Development", *International Journal of Sustainable Development & World Ecology*, 14(1), pp. 1–15.
Kennett, P. (ed.) (2008) *Governance, Globalization, and Public Policy*, Cheltenham: Edward Elgar.
Kirton, J. J. and P. I. Hjnal (eds.) (2006) *Sustainability, Civil Society and International Governance*, Burlington, VT: Ashgate Publishing.
Kohler-Koch, B. and Larat, F. (eds.) (2009) *European Multi-Level Governance: Contrasting Images in National Research*, Cheltenham: Edward Elgar.
Krasner, S. (ed) (1983) *International Regime*, Ithaca, NY: Cornell University Press.
Kutting, G. and R. Lipschultz (eds.) (2009) *Environmental Governance: Power and Knowledge in Local-Global World*, Oxon: Routledge.
Lafferty, W. M. (ed.) (2002) *Sustainable Communities in Europe*, London: Earthscan.

Le Prestre, P. and P. Stoett (2006) *Bilateral Ecopolitics: Continuity and Change in Canadian-American Environmental Relations*, Aldershot: Ashgate Publishing Ltd.

Loorbach D. (2007a) "Governance for Sustainability", *Sustainability: Science, Practice, & Policy* 3(2), pp. 1–4, available at http://sspp.proquest.com/.

—— (2007b) *Transition Management: New Mode of Governance for Sustainable Development*, Chicago: IGP Press.

Majone, G. (1998) "Europe's Democratic Deficit: The Question of Standards", *European Law Journal*, 4(i), pp. 5–28.

Marks, G. (1993) "Structural Policy and Multilevel Governance in the EC", in A. Cafruny and G. Rosenthal (eds.) *The State of the European Community Vol. 2: The Maastricht Debates and Beyond*, Harlow: Longman, pp. 391–410.

Newig, J., J-P. Voss and J. Monstadt (eds.) (2008) *Governance for Sustainable Development Coping with Ambivalence, Uncertainty and Distributed Power*, Abingdon: Routledge.

Newman, J. (ed.) (2005) *Remaking Governance: People, Politics and the Public Sphere*, Bristol: Policy Press.

Oberthur, S. and T. Gehring (eds.) (2006) *Institutional Interaction in Global Environmental Governance: Synergy and Conflict among International and EU Policies*, Cambridge, MA: The MIT Press.

OECD (2001) *Fiscal Design across Levels of Government Year 2000 Surveys*, Paris: OECD.

—— (2005) *Modernizing Governance: The Way Forward*, Paris: OECD.

—— (2009) *Governance at a Glance 2009*, Paris: OECD.

Okereke, C. (2008) *Global Justice and Neoliberal Environmental Governance: Ethics, Sustainable Development and International Co-Operation*, Abingdon: Routledge.

Paraskevopoulos, C. J., P. Getimis and N. Ress (eds.) (2006) *Adapting to EU Multi-Level Governance*, Burlington, VT: Ashgate Publishing.

Pierre, J. (eds.) (2000) *Debating Governance*, Oxford: Oxford University Press.

Pierre, J. and B. G. Peters (2000) *Governance, Politics and the State*, Basingstoke: Macmillan.

—— (2005) *Governing Complex Societies*, Basingstoke: Macmillan.

Pierson, C. (1996) *The Modern State*, London: Routledge.

Pollitt, C. and G. Bouckaert (2000) *Public Management Reform: A Comparative Analysis*, Oxford: Oxford University Press.

Power, M. (1997) *The Audit Society: Rituals of Verification*, Oxford: Oxford University Press.

Prakash, A. and J. Hart (eds.) (1999) *Globalisation and Governance*, London: Routledge.

Rhodes, R. A. W. (1997) *Understanding Governance: Policy Network, Governance, Reflexivity and Accountability*, Buckingham: Open University Press.

—— (2007) "Understanding Governance: Ten Years On", *Organization Studies*, 28(i), 1243–1264.

Rhodes, R. A. W. and M. Bevir (2003) *Interpreting British Governance*, Oxford: Oxford University Press.

Roseneu, J. N. (ed.) (1997) *Along the Domestic-Foreign Frontier: Exploring Governance in a Turbulent World*, Cambridge: Cambridge University Press.

Rotmans J., R. Kemp and M. van Asselt (2001) "More Evolution than Revolution: Transition Management in Public Policy", *Foresight*, 3(1), pp. 1–15.

Salamon, L. (2002) *The Tools of Government: A Guide to the New Governance*, Oxford: Oxford University Press.
Sanford, M. (2005) *The New Governance of the English Regions*, Hampshire: Palgrave.
Sbragia, A. (ed.) (1992) *Europolitics: Institutions and Policymaking in the New European Community*, Washington, DC: Brookings Institution.
Scharpf, F. (1998) *Governing in Europe: Effective and Democratic?*, Oxford: Oxford University Press.
Schuppert, G. F. (ed.) (2006) *The Europeanisation of Governance*, Baden-Baden: Nomos.
Selin, H. (2010) *Global Governance of Hazardous Chemicals: Challenge of Multilevel Management*, Cambridge, MA: MIT Press.
Shove, E. and Walker, G. (2007) "CAUTION! Transitions Ahead: Politics, Practice and Sustainable Transition Management", http://eprints.lancs.ac.uk/.
Skelcher, C. and J. Torfing (2010) "Improving Democratic Governance through Institutional Design: Civic Participation and Democratic Ownership in Europe", *Regulation and Governance*, 4(i), pp. 71–91.
Smith, A. and A. Stirling (2008) *Social-Ecological Resilience and Sociotechnical Transitions: Critical Issues for Sustainability Governance*, STEPS Working Paper 8, Brighton: STEPS Centre.
Sorensen, E. and J. Torfing (eds.) (2008) *Theories of Democratic Network Governance*, London: Palgrave.
Speth, J. G. and P. M. Haas (2006) *Global Environmental Governance*, Washington, DC: Island Press.
Stoker, G. (2000) *The New Politics of Local Governance*, London: Macmillan.
Tullock, G. (2005) *Public Goods, Redistribution and Rent Seeking*, Cheltenham: Edward Elgar.
Vari, A. and P. Tamas (eds.) (2011) *Environment and Democratic Transition: Policy and Politics in Central and Eastern Europe*, NY: Springer.
Winter, G. (ed.) (2006) *Multilevel Governance of Global Environmental Change*, Cambridge: Cambridge University Press.
World Bank (1992) *Governance and Development*, Washington, DC: World Bank.

# Part II
Transition management for sustainable development: Case studies

# 5

# Environmental governance strategies and transition to a sustainable society: Integration of environmental and energy policies in Germany and Japan

*Minoru Tsubogo*

A sustainable society is achieved by means of a transition involving the implementation of various policies and systems to change corporate activities and people's lifestyles. The task is to change the current structures of industrial society to those of a sustainable society by implementing those policies and systems and to develop a political and administrative structure capable of managing this transition process. In order to discuss this transition to a sustainable society, this chapter summarizes the factors affecting environmental governance strategies with a focus on integrated environmental policy and then considers the issues related to innovation in environmental policy and the roles played by policy experts in environmental governance. The integration of environmental and energy policies in Germany and in Japan is introduced as case studies. Policy making by governmental agencies and private research institutions as well as advocacy activities by environmental organizations and other non-profit organizations (NPOs) are included in the discussion about policy experts. The two countries were chosen for examination in this chapter because both Germany (in 1998[1]) and Japan (in 2009) have seen a recent change in government as a result of the opposition party winning a majority of seats, which resulted in environmental and climate change policies coming to the forefront. Innovations in environmental policy were seen in Germany, whereas new measures were initiated in climate change policy in Japan. Another reason for choosing the German and Japanese cases is that although the nuclear accident at Fukushima Daiichi nuclear power plant in March 2011, now known as "Fukushima", triggered energy transitions in Germany, Italy and Switzerland, it led Germany to make a political decision to withdraw earlier from nuclear energy. In Japan, the issue of "energy shift" has become highly politicized.

The Great East Japan Earthquake and massive tsunami that hit northeastern Japan on 11 March 2011 caused the accident at the Fukushima Daiichi nuclear power plant. Triggered by the Fukushima accident, the Merkel conservative–liberal coalition government in Germany (2009–2013) came to a political decision to withdraw earlier from nuclear energy, nine months after it announced prolonging the life span of the nuclear reactors in Germany. In Germany, the previous Social Democrat/Green Party coalition (red-green coalition, 1998–2005) had already made the decision, in 2000 and in 2002, to withdraw from nuclear energy. As opposed to these clear political decisions seen in Germany, Japan is still at the stage of re-evaluating its energy policies and has not made any clear plans to change energy or nuclear power generation policies. By comparing the cases of Germany and Japan, I clarify important questions and issues surrounding future environmental and energy policy in Japan while assessing the current state of the transition to a sustainable society.

First, I outline the key discussion points regarding environmental governance strategies as a framework for analysis. Second, I discuss the establishment of environmental governance systems, the integration of environmental and energy policies, and the roles of policy experts in environmental governance by examining the cases of Germany and Japan. In the case of Germany, the period between the red-green coalition led by then chancellor Gerhard Schröder and Angela Merkel's current conservative–liberal coalition is examined. In the case of Japan, the main focus will be on the coalition administrations led by Prime Ministers Yukio Hatoyama (2009–2010) and Naoto Kan (2010–2011) of the Democratic Party of Japan (DPJ).

## Key factors in environmental governance strategies

Around 1970, environmental policy emerged as one coherent policy field. Germany has been working on its integrated environmental policy since the beginning of environmental policy. After the 1990s, environmental policy has been significantly influenced by arguments about governance and New Public Management (NPM). This is relevant to the question, Why has environmental policy not yielded results? (Jacob et al., 2007, pp. 13–17). In this area, past governmental activities to adjust for market failure have not been fully successful due to inadequacies in administrative structures, legal systems and policy design; lack of knowledge; and the need for a long-term approach to environmental issues that is beyond the capacity of most governments. Therefore, breaking free of the existing common practices and traditions is required by transitioning from a government-centred approach to a governance approach led by multiple actors in the government sector, market sector and civil society sector, while implementing administrative reform in government sectors to establish effective environmental policy.

As Kooiman (2002, p. 73) describes in the collection of theses on "participatory governance", governance is intended to solve social issues and is focused on generating "social opportunities to solve social issues". One of the important points in Kooiman's argument is the issue of democracy in governance or "democratic legitimacy", which has two aspects: the participatory aspect of "input-legitimacy" and the aspect of "output-legitimacy", which constitutes "satisfactory results" (Benz and Papadopoulos, 2006). Participation in democratic political systems has generally been considered to be the best means of legitimating procedures in the policy-decision process. Furthermore, because bringing the knowledge and skills to the table by various actors is useful for both policy decisions and policy implementation, participation undoubtedly brings more widely accepted results. Participation here includes not only participation through elections but also participation in the process of formation, decision, implementation and evaluation of policies. It is a process of communication and learning, and consensus formation through free and open public debate (or dialogue) is emphasized.

Thus, among governance approaches, participatory governance is one that creates opportunities to solve problems by various actors from government sectors, market sectors and civil society. It is also an approach for developing a new style of democracy that emphasizes consensus formation through participation and debate.

The key elements of environmental governance strategies are "target and results-oriented governance", "integrated environmental policy (integration of environmental policy into each policy field)", "cooperative governance by various actors" and "multilevel governance".[2] As such, environmental governance incorporates a great diversity of approaches for "consensus formation, broad-range of goal setting (economic, social and ecological goals), strategy formation to solve issues, and participation by civil society actors" (Jänicke and Jörgens, 2006: 177, 181–194) and emphasizes the transition to a sustainable society and roles of policy experts including universities, research institutes and civil think tanks. Environmental governance, which creates strategies to achieve the policy ideal of sustainable development, can be positioned as a strategy to shift to a sustainable society. In the following, I discuss the key points in environmental governance strategies and systems aimed at achieving the transition to a sustainable society.

The first point is target- and results-oriented governance. Policy schemes implemented by environmental policy pioneers such as the Netherlands have new approaches of setting targets with specified time limits and then monitoring results. This is because effective environmental policy accompanied by well-coordinated, continued actions is required to solve persistent, complex and long-lasting environmental issues. Management through target-setting is effective in breaking down common practices and traditions in public administration and in other relevant organizations. In order to set environmental targets, the processes of mutual learning, negotiation, discussion and consensus formulation among actors are important. For these purposes, an adaptable, systematic framework that allows the participation of policy experts and citizens needs to be established. Setting strategic goals that are consistent is useful for investment and corporate activities; they can determine their direction for new technology innovation. The capacity to address environmental issues can be increased through technological development. Technologies related to environmental policy have now advanced from the stage of "end-of-pipe technologies" to the stage of structural change in production systems.

The second point is the integration of environmental policy into other policy fields. Because the main causes of long-term burden on the environment lie in economic activity, an objective of environmental policy should be to focus on those causes by restructuring economies and changing industrial structures. The effectiveness of environmental policy can be ensured by integrating it with economic and social policies. The debate on this integration is reflected in the principles of the environmental program that was initiated in the 1970s in West Germany, and in the third Environment Action Programme of the European Community (EC) of 1982. However, these actions did not reach the stage of structural change at the time. It requires a shift from environmental policy based purely on technology to policies featuring more extensive instruments and processes for political negotiation/discussion and communications among citizens. The "dialogue strategy" about long-term vision, in which stakeholders participate to integrate the economy and the environment based on the policy strategy drafted by policymakers and policy experts, is useful.

Strategies for integrating different policy fields need to include clarification of accountability and procedures, mandatory reporting, and monitoring by the legislative and executive branches of government. The shift from "horizontal policy integration" implemented by the environment ministry and applied to other ministries to "vertical policy integration" applied by a strong environment ministry toward the legislature, other ministries and the chief executive is key for the integration of environmental policy (Jänicke and Jörgens, 2006: 187–189). In this context, Jordan and Lenschow (2008b) cast a spotlight on the institutionalization of integrated environmental policy. By comparing developments across Organisation for Economic Co-operation and Development (OECD) countries, they discuss tools to manage the process of integrating environmental policy. First, using communicative instruments, information about concept, target, strategy and knowledge is shared. Next, an organizational reform is implemented to strengthen environment ministries, open up and expand existing networks, and identify new actors. Finally, policy-formation procedures, such as environmental impact evaluation on formation and enforcement of laws (e.g., green budgeting) and strategic assessment of environment are changed and established (Jordan and Lenschow, 2008b: 11; Jacobs et al., 2008: 27–28). The institutionalization of integration processes for environmental policy should clarify the structure of the transition to a sustainable society.

The third point is cooperative governance by various actors, including citizens, NPOs, non-governmental organizations (NGOs) and corporations, of the formation, decision, implementation and evaluation of environmental policy, which will increase the capacity of these policies and the potential for action. Transparency in policy processes and disclosure of information are prerequisites for this. The effectiveness of participation also depends on the institutional design of policy processes. In terms of policy instruments, because there is a limit to command and control by the government, the focus has been shifting to cooperative policy instruments involving government and specific target groups (such as specific industries). For example, environmental agreements between government and industry may be executed to address climate change issues. It has been said that cooperation in these cases would produce better results, because the government and the target group can utilize knowledge and experiences—at least the ones gained through the process—as resources when holding direct discussions. This approach promotes problem solving because it establishes strong legitimacy of participation, consensus and results orientation among stakeholders. On the other hand, a concern has been raised regarding bypassing the legislative process by the Diet.

This soft, cooperative policy instrument is not something that can substitute for hard regulation. If success is not achievable by cooperative methods, there must also be a legal restraint present to play the complementary role of direct command and control. As Scharpf (1997) states, this is the soft means "in the shadow of the hierarchy (hierarchical regulations)".

In cooperative governance, participation by a diversity of actors is an important factor. Associated with this is the issue of the roles of policy experts, specifically of universities, research institutes, NPO- and NGO-affiliated and other civil think tanks. In the past, policy experts participated in committees, study groups and expert panels during the policy-making process. Whereas some of these committees and panels consist only of policy experts, others consist of stakeholders as well. During legislative sessions to discuss bills, policy experts are involved in public hearings and witness testimony. In the case of Germany, investigation committees made up of congressmen and experts (e.g., survey committees consisting of the same number of congressmen and of experts) have been established in the Bundestag (the German legislature) in order to conduct studies on policy issues such as climate change issues and the future of civic activity. In Germany, policy proposal development is an established field for policy experts. In Japan, the selection process for committees and panels limits the members to experts with specific orientations. Various problems, such as lack of transparency, have been pointed out resulting from this situation. It is necessary to create opportunities for policy experts with a broad range of opinions, as well as regular citizens, to participate through activities such as parliamentary reform.

The fourth point is multi-level governance. Environmental governance is characterized to have multi-levels of governance—global, international-regional (e.g., EU), national and municipal government levels—that are working together. This is a "plus-sum game" that can lead to better consequences through the involvement of multiple levels of government, rather than a "zero-sum game" involving competition for authority among multiple levels. Decentralization in line with the principle of subsidiary at the national level would increase the capacity of environmental policy and would facilitate flexibility in their policy implementation. Depending on the policy field—for example, more so in fields such as regional transport policy or regional energy policy—decisions by local governments are more effective. As reflected in Agenda 21 (adopted by the UN Summit at Rio de Janeiro in 1992), and in Local Agenda 21, the requirements for and provisions on involvement of local government, collaboration on the municipal, national and global levels is key.

However, even in a multi-level model, national-level policies are still the most crucial. For instance, environmental programs, environmental and carbon taxes, feed-in tariffs for renewable energy and emissions trading schemes are all innovations in environmental policy that have been led by environmental-pioneer countries with diffusive effects. In international politics, both national and local governments are essential for the formation of environmental policy. National governments serve as coordinators, or producers, and play the role of managers in the process of setting environmental goals.

In OECD countries, governmental activities are becoming more focused on environments, thanks to the expansion of various policies as well as of systems and mechanisms required for the integration of environmental policy. Here, in addition to the top-down transformation of environmental framework, bottom-up methods by the local government involve solving specific issues on-site with a unique dynamics. As many cases (e.g., regional energy policy) indicate, details of policy are driven by policy developments at the local government level for the area. Corporations (the market sector) as well as NPOs and NGOs (the civil society sector) also play an important role here. Formation of strategic alliances among various actors (e.g., alliances among NPOs, ecology-oriented corporations and the local government) will increase capacity to realize new environmental policy.

# Environmental governance strategies in Germany: Policies for promoting the withdrawal from nuclear energy and the adoption of renewable energy

## Establishment of systems for environmental governance

The establishment of systems for environmental governance in Germany has been shaped by the formulation of the German strategy plan for sustainable development.[3] There was a change of government in the German federal election of 1998. Although the formulation of a strategy for sustainable development was stipulated in the coalition agreement that year between the Social Democratic Party of Germany (SPD) and Alliance '90/The Greens, no such strategy planning would actually be initiated until March 2001. Therefore, the Bundestag (Federal Lower House of Parliament) took the lead, requesting the administration in January 2000 to formulate a strategy. This appeal was supported by the German Environment Ministers' Conference (UMK) in April of the same year. In response to this action, the Schröder administration decided to formulate a strategy for sustainable development at the federal level (Jänicke et al., 2002: 119; Wurzel, 2008: 184–186). To do so, the Committee of State Secretaries for Sustainable Development, or the "Green Cabinet", headed by the chancellor's chief of staff, and the Sustainable Development Council, consisting of up to 15 policy experts and representatives of organizations in the field of ecology, economic and social issues, were established. After conducting two major "social dialogues", the government produced "Perspectives for Germany", a strategy for sustainable development, in April 2002. This strategy meets the requirement for a national-level "Agenda 21" formulation that was imposed at the Earth Summit in Rio de Janeiro. It lists the ecological, economic and social dimensions as the three pillars of sustainable development and states that "it is necessary to design an effective economic development that would fit ecologically and socially, and successful results can be achieved when not only the government but also various actors in economic circles and society address this issue" (Die Bundesregierung, 2002: 1–4). The key entity of the system established for sustainable development is the Green Cabinet. The Federal Environmental Agency (in charge of tracking sustainability indicator data), the German Council for Sustainable Development (in charge of social dialogues to revise strategy), the Parliamentary Advisory Council on Sustainable Development, the federal states and local governments are invited to attend the conferences held by the Green Cabinet to contribute to the creation of development reports for the strategy as needed. Furthermore, since May 2009, a system to make an "assessment of the impact of laws and bills on sustainable development" has been adopted in every federal ministry, and reports have been submitted by all the ministries (Die Bundesregierung, 2008: 34).

After the 1986 nuclear accident at Chernobyl in the Soviet Union (now Ukraine), West Germany established a Federal Ministry for the Environment, Nature Conservation and Nuclear Safety (BMU). Authority over specific areas was transferred from the Federal Ministries of the Interior (environmental policy), Agriculture (conservation) and Youth, Family, and Health (radioactivity and chemicals in food). The BMU is organized by environmental areas. The Renewable Energy Agency of the Federal Ministry of Economics was transferred to the Federal Ministry for the Environment after the 2002 election. The BMU was reorganized to the following six divisions in 2007: Central; Climate Change, Renewable Energy and International Cooperation; Nuclear Safety; Water Management,

Waste Management, and Soil Conservation; Environment and Health, Air Pollution, Safety of Industrial Locations and Transportation, and Chemical Safety; and Nature Conservation. Federal Chancellor Merkel put high priority on climate change policies, and an inter-ministerial working group for the reduction of carbon dioxide was set up. Meanwhile, an office of experts in environmental policy in Germany, the Federal Environmental Agency (UBA), also exists. Unlike the BMU, the UBA has been restructured into a cross-functional organization in charge of the quality of air, water and soil in the mid-1990s. Currently, the UBA consists of the following six divisions: Central, Environmental Planning and Sustainability Strategies, Environmental Health and Protection of Ecosystems, Sustainable Production and Products and Waste Management, Chemical and Biological Safety and the German Emissions Trading Authority. Along with the UBA, established in 1974, other offices of experts include the Federal Agency for Nature Conservation and the Federal Office for Radiation Protection. The UBA has various important responsibilities, including scientific support to the federal government (e.g., the Federal Minister for the Environment) and implementation of important environmental laws (e.g., the Chemicals Act, Plant Protection Act, Emissions Trading Scheme, etc.), as well as providing information (e.g., environmental data and practical tips to deal with environmental issues) to citizens. The UBA's headquarters was relocated from Berlin to Dessau in 2005, and as of October 2011 a total of 1,500 staff members work in 13 locations (UBA, 2011).

Another important German environmental agency is the German Council of Environmental Advisors (SRU), which has played an important role in environmental policy-making since 1971 as an agency of policy experts. The SRU was established to provide academic proposals on policies, especially environmental policy, and has been engaged in many creative activities. Its legally assured independence allows the SRU, which consists only of academic policy experts, to play the role of connecting science and politics. The SRU engages in a wide variety of research-based dialogues with experts, representatives of various interests and policymakers, and provides policy recommendations. It consisted only of natural scientists during its first 20 years; however, because it was criticized as weak in analyzing political and economic determinants in environmental policy, as well as in analyzing relationships with countries in Europe and the world in the 1980s, the number of members was decreased from 12 to 7 in 1990, and it now consists of experts from a wide range of fields including toxicology/environmental toxicology, biology/regional landscape ecology, environmental engineering, environmental law, environmental economics, political science and ethics. The members are appointed by the federal government on the proposal of the BMU to serve a four-year term (Hey, 2009: 165–166).

Related to multi-level governance, preceding the formulation of the federal strategy for sustainable development, pioneering activities to formulate state- and local government-level versions of the Agenda 21 requirements have been carried out. The UMK, established to coordinate environmental policy between the state and federal governments and among states, has been held twice a year. The conference integrated sustainable development into the UMK protocol and adopted it in June 1997 as the main principle of environmental policy. At the state level, "environmental alliances" have been established to hold discussions with various actors in society, and "environmental agreements" with business organizations have been executed. It emphasizes ways of forming consensus (Jänicke et al., 2002: 130–133). Furthermore, at the EU level, the EU strategy for sustainable development was established in 2001 and was re-examined in 2005, leading to the formulation of a new strategy.

Climate change policies require a cross-functional vision. Energy efficiency improvements, energy conservation and shift to renewable energy, as well as transition to new low-carbon technologies, become important, and these are particularly relevant to energy, transportation and agricultural policies. In Germany, the Federal Ministry for the Environment is in charge of setting the national $CO_2$ reduction target, as well as planning how to achieve it and making adjustments as necessary. After the reunification of Germany, the target was set of reducing $CO_2$ by 25 per cent from 1990 levels by the year 2005. However, the program faced difficulties in implementation due to the resistance by the ministries in charge of energy and transportation; therefore, pressure from above, by means of the development of climate protection policies at the EU and global levels, was essential.

In terms of integrated environmental policy, in which environmental policy is implemented across various policy fields, the Schröder government integrated environmental and energy policies. The 1998 coalition agreement stipulates that "ecological modernization is an opportunity to protect the natural livelihood and create many job opportunities", and that the goal is to have "socially fair and ecologically adaptable development which is economically successful", meaning sustainable development (SPD und Bündnis 90/Die Grünen, 1998: 13). It emphasizes the integration of energy and environmental policies which is relevant to climate protection policies and lists efficient, environmentally adaptable transport policies and agricultural systems that encourage organic farming and food safety. For the integration of environmental and energy policies, Germany first decided to withdraw from nuclear energy by formulating a new, comprehensive energy policy based on consensus with large energy enterprises. Consensus to withdraw from nuclear energy was obtained in 2000, and the law was enacted in 2002. With this political decision, the operating lives of German nuclear power plants were set at 32 years, meaning that withdrawal from nuclear energy would be completed between 2018 and 2021. Second, Germany enacted the Renewable Energy Act (EEA), which involved feed-in tariffs for renewable energy sources, rapidly expanding wind-power generation and cogeneration systems. Third, they implemented an ecological tax reform, raising the petroleum tax in incremental steps and introducing an electricity tax. It is designed to be tax-neutral in that the revenue from the new tax is used to lower German ancillary wage costs (pension premium), with the dual goal of making lowered ancillary wage cost a force to create jobs and motivating energy conservation through taxation of energy sources. This reform suggests a shift to a new taxation structure—from traditional "labor-related taxation" to "environmental taxation". Independent policy experts played a significant role in this reform. After a report called *Ecological Tax— Impasse or a Fine Approach?* (Deutsches institute für Wirtschaftsforschung Berlin [DIW], 1994) commissioned by the NGO Greenpeace and compiled by the German Institute for Economic Research was published, actions such as a proposal by environmental organizations (Friends of the Earth Germany and the German Society for Environmental Protection) in 1994 and the submission of an energy-tax bill by the Green Party (1995) took the leading role.

The Greens has grown from diverse new social movements (e.g., the anti-nuclear movement, ecology movements, feminism movements and so on) in the 1970s. Environmental organizations have been raising environmental issues and spearheading a wide range of campaigns in Germany since the 1970s, and have become a driving force behind German environmental policy. Integral networks have formed among environmental organizations, and there are currently more than 400 environmental organizations registered in the country. Approximately 5 to 7 per cent of German citizens are members of one or more of these organizations. Friends of the Earth Germany (BUND), Greenpeace Germany, German Society for Environmental Protection (NABU) and World Wide Fund For Nature (WWF) Germany are the four largest and most influential environmental organizations in Germany.[4] Furthermore, various German research institutions, such as the Institute for Applied Ecology; the Wuppertal Institute for Climate, Environment and Energy; and the Potsdam Institute for Climate Impact retain or employ environmental policy experts. Meanwhile, ecology-oriented businesses appeared as new actors in the 1990s. Industries related to environmental protection have become important industry, increasing the number of environment-related jobs and adding to the driving force behind environmental policy.

Although the formulation of strategy for sustainable development was delayed, Germany formulated environmental governance strategies after the 1998 government change and initiated the transition to a sustainable society.

*The second political decision to accelerate the withdrawal from nuclear energy and policies to promote renewable energy*

The accident at Fukushima Daiichi nuclear power plant in Japan had a significant impact on the issues of withdrawal from nuclear energy and energy transition in Germany. On 15 March 2011, immediately after the accident, the Merkel government froze the decision to extend the operating lives of nuclear power plants, which had just been adopted in the fall of 2010, and to shut down seven old nuclear reactors in operation. Next, Merkel set up the Ethics Commission for a Safe Energy Supply on 4 April. Co-chaired by Klaus Töpfer (who had served as the minister of environment [1987–1994] during the conservative–liberal Kohl coalition [1982–1998] and played an important role in the United Nations Environment Programme [UNEP]) and Matthias Kleiner (who is the president of German Research Foundation [DFG]), the commission consists of 17 members, including policy experts, religious leaders and politicians. A public dialogue was held on 28 April, and a final report was submitted on 30 May. In the meantime, large rallies co-organized by environmental organizations such as BUND to protest against the use of nuclear energy took place in the country's four largest cities on 26 March. A total of 250,000 individuals participated in the rallies, including 40,000 each in Cologne and Munich, 50,000 in Hamburg, and 120,000 in Berlin. BUND, by the way, is a federation consisting of 2,000 district and regional groups.

What kinds of factors triggered such prompt action on the withdrawal from nuclear energy? The immediate factor was that the Baden-Württemberg state election was coming up on 27 March; it was possible for the conservative–liberal incumbent coalition to be replaced by Alliance '90/The Greens and the SPD. And indeed, as a result of the election, the Green party became the leading party in Baden-Württemberg and the country's first Green state minister-president was sworn in. More important is the fact that reports on energy transition and withdrawal from nuclear energy were submitted from government-affiliated institutes consisting of policy experts 10 years after the initial decision to withdraw was taken by the Schröder government. Among them, I review a report from the UBA and another from the SRU to exemplify the policy changes. These reports set a target for withdrawal of around 2021.

The UBA published a report, *Energy Goal for 2050: 100% Renewable Electricity Supply* in July 2010, ahead of the decision by the government in the fall to extend the operating lives of nuclear power plants. This study states that "electricity supplied entirely from renewable energies is realistic", suggesting this can be done with current technologies on the basis of the efficient use and production of electricity. To achieve this goal, political transformation was needed as soon as possible (UBA, 2010a: 4–5). Jochen Flasbarth, president of the Federal Environmental Agency, stated that "the earlier we take actions with persistence, the more time there will be for technical and social adaptation" (UBA, 2010b: 1–2). By doing so, Germany can lower their high degree of dependence on imported primary energy. The report also evaluated three scenarios (the "Regions Network", "International Large Scale Technology" and "Local Energy Autarky" scenarios) for transitioning to electricity supplied entirely from renewable energy, and selected the "Regions Network" scenario as a basis for their discussion. In this scenario, all potential renewable energy sources would be used in all parts of Germany, and electricity would be traded throughout the country while allowing only a small portion of electricity import from neighbouring countries (UBA, 2010a: 60–65). The Fraunhofer Institute for Wind Energy and Energy System Technology (IWES), a research institute commissioned to write a report on the matter by the UBA, states that it would be essential to manage the usage, storage and load of electricity generated by various renewable sources holistically so that the variability of renewable energies can be adjusted. In order to reorganize the electricity supply, it would be necessary to increase the amount of renewable energy and expand the electrical supply network and storage systems. Energy conservation is also required by improving the insulation of buildings. Because the electric power generation in Germany accounts for more than 40 per cent of the country's $CO_2$ emissions, switching to a renewable electricity supply is also essential for reducing the greenhouse gas emissions by 80 to 95 per cent (UBA, 2010a: 66–117).

In the meantime, the SRU, an independent agency that has played a unique role in environmental policy in Germany, released a report called *Pathways Towards a 100% Renewable Electricity System* on 23 February 2011 (SRU, 2011). This report indicates that a secure, affordable, 100% renewable electricity supply is possible in Germany by 2050, and outlines how this could be achieved as one of four very specific scenarios. Scenarios were developed for cases in which final electricity demand was assumed to be 500 TWh/a and 700 TWh/a, respectively, in 2050. These scenarios were one of 100 per cent self-efficiency within the country, two involving import of energy (pumped storage generation, geothermal power, and biomass) from Denmark and Norway and one in which energy (pumped storage generation, geothermal power, and biomass) would be imported from 35 countries in the EU and North Africa, up to 15 per cent of total German usage. In the self-sufficiency scenario, wind-power generation accounts for the highest percentage, as in the other scenarios, followed by solar power and biomass. The energy vision by the German government that extended the operating lives of the nuclear power plants in the fall of 2010 assumes that 22 to 31 per cent of the country's electricity will need to be imported to cover electricity demand of between 410 TWh/a and 430 TWh/a in the year 2050. In comparison, the SRU's scenarios are realistic without the use of nuclear energy, even when considering the variability of renewable energies. The SRU constructed its scenarios based on cost optimization. From that perspective, the amount of solar energy requirement was adjusted and the use of biomass was limited to 7 per cent because the land usage cost by biomass is relatively high (SRU, 2011: 31–37).

Related to the matter of renewable energy goal, the EU has set their 2020 energy goals as a part of the "Europe 2020 Targets" developed in 2008. Here, three "20" medium-term targets by 2020 are clearly specified for the EU's climate change and energy policies: the reduction of $CO_2$ emissions by 20 per cent from 1990 levels, increase of renewable energies to 20 per cent of total energy usage, and reduction of energy consumption by 20 per cent. EU member nations set their own goals in accordance with these objectives (EU, 2011). Meanwhile, in Germany, the project "100% Renewable Energy Regions" was initiated at the regional and municipal levels. The aim of the project is to support regions and municipalities attempting to supply 100 per cent of their own electricity needs with renewable energies on a mid- or long-term basis. The project is promoted with financial assistance by the BMU and specialized support is provided by the UBA. For this project, the Competence Network for Distributed Energy Technologies (deENet), in collaboration with the University of Kassel, implemented a research and development initiative between October 2007 and September 2010 in order to conduct an analysis of the factors that enable a region to supply its electricity needs entirely from renewable energy sources and communicate the results. This first phase was followed by the "transfer of knowledge and creation of regional networks", which is implemented as the second phase of the project (2010–2013). To find the pathway to sustainable energy supply, regions and municipalities need to share successful, transferable models with each other. According to the Institute for decentralised Energy-Technology (IdE), as of June 2013, there are 76 regions (including cities, towns, villages, counties and integrated regions) attempting to supply 100 per cent energy from renewable sources, 59 regions that had just started moving to a sustainability model and 3 urban cities. A total of 138 municipalities and regions are already participating, accounting for 21.6 million residents (IdE, 2013: 1).

Amid these trends, Merkel's administration looked for new grounds to withdraw from the decision to extend the operating lives of the nuclear power plants adopted in the fall of 2010 and to go back to the plan under the Schröder government. Merkel established the previously mentioned Ethics Commission for a Safe Energy Supply for this purpose. According to their final report, "it is possible to withdraw from the use of nuclear energy within the next 10 years, by using the measures proposed in this report. . . . The Ethics Commission considers that gradual withdrawal from the use of nuclear energy is a special challenge for all parties involved, and at the same time, a source of new opportunities that allow citizens to participate in decentralized decisions" (Ethik-Kommission, 2011: 4–7). In the following, I discuss some of their arguments. It is important to clearly define a target deadline for withdrawal. This deadline must be supported by a politically valid monitoring scheme (analysis, evaluation and action recommendation) based on consistent goals. To do so, the commission is proposing to establish an "independent Parliamentary Representative for the Energy Transition" in the Bundestag for evaluating the monitoring process on an annual basis. Generation of wind, solar, hydraulic, geothermal, and biomass power can adequately substitute for nuclear energy. Efficient energy generation and use is necessary, and the transformation of people's lifestyles plays an important role. The commission states that "nuclear power plants should stay in operation until nuclear power is replaced by low-risk energy supplies for ethical reasons" (Ethik-Kommission, 2011: 6). The total output of the seven old nuclear reactors already shut down and the one in Krummel is 8.5 gigawatts and has already been replaced by lower risk energy supplies. "Germany has a responsibility in playing an important role as a global pioneer in withdrawal from the use of nuclear energy" (Ethik-Kommission, 2011: 6). The permanent disposal of radioactive wastes must meet a high level of safety requirements. The commission stresses that "energy transformation is something that can be achieved collectively through all areas of politics, economy, and society" (Ethik-Kommission, 2011: 5). This concept is reflected in the title of the final report, *Germany's Energy Transition—A Collective Project for the Future*. It is stated that withdrawal from nuclear energy provides extensive opportunities for business enterprises. Science and research, from natural science and technology to social science, will play a significant role. A national forum, called the "Energy Turnaround", proposed by the commission is intended to encourage social dialogues and question "whether the time necessary for the withdrawal can be shortened" and "whether the withdrawal and energy turnaround can be effectively controlled" in cities, municipalities and business enterprises (Ethik-Kommission, 2011: 5). It also states that nuclear safety and the future energy supply are a topic of discussion concerning European politics, international politics and international cooperation (Ethik-Kommission, 2011: 7).

Responding to this final report, the Merkel government revoked the decision to extend the operating lives of the nuclear power plants and made the political decision to withdraw earlier from nuclear energy, immediately shutting down the old nuclear reactors and planning to gradually shut down the rest by 2022. In July 2011, the amendment of the Atomic Energy Act, the law mandating the withdrawal from nuclear energy, was passed in the Bundestag, where the opposition parties, the SPD and Alliance '90/The Greens voted in favour of the amendment. This put an end to the political and social split over the use of nuclear energy, which had gone on for more than 40 years.

As of October 2011, the Merkel government defined the following goals with regard to its energy policy: to reduce greenhouse gas emissions by 40 per cent by 2020, 55 per cent by 2030, 70 per cent by 2040 and 80 per cent to 95 per cent by 2050 compared with 1990 levels; to reduce primary energy consumption by 20 per cent by 2020 and 50 per cent by 2050; to increase the share of renewables in the total energy mix to 18 per cent by 2020, 30 per cent by 2030, 45 per cent by 2040 and 80 per cent by 2050; and to increase the share of renewables in the total electricity mix to at least 35 per cent by 2020, 50 per cent by 2030, 65 per cent by 2040 and 80 per cent by 2050 (BMU, 2011a).

However, environmental organizations published critical opinions and proposed policy changes related to items that should be improved. For example, Hubert Weiger (2011: 13), the chairman of BUND—who "has warned about the danger of nuclear power and opposed to it" since 1975—criticized that the decision was not a "true ecological energy transition [and that it was] too late and too dangerous". Weiger insisted further that "the government can ethically take responsibility only by immediately withdrawing from nuclear energy without hesitation", and continued that "it is technically possible to withdraw from nuclear energy by the year 2013", which is much earlier than the previously mentioned target (Weiger, 2011: 13). "With a half-hearted attitude, the government decided to withdraw from nuclear energy out of fear for compensation claims by atomic conglomerates and for reasons related to electoral strategy" (Weiger, 2011: 13).

Weiger also criticized the government by saying, it "is going to give preferential treatment to large-scale investments and promote new coal-fired power plants, instead of fruitfully supporting the indispensable 'bottom-up energy revolution' (Weiger, 2011: 13).

In this context, it is interesting that when the seven reactors were closed, one argument heard was that Germany was nevertheless complementing its energy supply by importing nuclear energy from France. However, according to data provided by AGBE, AG Energy Balance, although Germany's electricity trade surplus with neighbouring countries decreased between January and June 2011, the amount of exports was larger overall, showing that Germany is a net exporter of electricity. Electricity has been consistently imported from France, and the amount has increased compared to 2010 (AGBE, 2011: 23). However, Thorben Becker (2011: 16–17) of BUND states that "electricity from nuclear power cannot be obtained on a short-term basis in the electricity market; rather, Germany has been importing electricity generated in thermal power plants using fossil fuels, according to the Institute for Applied Ecology".

## Strategic challenges for environmental governance in Japan

### *Nuclear accident at Fukushima Daiichi nuclear power plant and policies for promoting renewable energies in Japan*

Although the Merkel government in Germany made a political decision to accelerate the withdrawal from nuclear energy in the wake of the 11 March accident at Fukushima Daiichi nuclear power plant, Japan's DPJ government has not yet taken a clear stance on shifting energy policy at the time of writing (November 2011). In this section, I describe the characteristics of Japanese climate change policies during the Hatoyama government and the re-evaluation of energy policy during the Kan government, while looking at issues in Japan's energy policies and environmental governance.

As we have seen, systems for environmental governance intended to help the nation work toward sustainable development had already been established in Germany following the 1998 change of government, starting with the integration of environmental and energy policies. In contrast, no specific intentions for establishing systems toward environmental governance have been indicated in Japan. Influenced by the Earth Summit held in Rio de Janeiro in 1992, the Japanese Basic Environment Law was enacted in 1993 and the First Basic Environment Plan was formulated in 1994 during the non-Liberal Democratic Party (LDP) government of Morihiro Hosokawa (1993–1994). The Basic Environment Law was something that had been prepared by the previous LDP administration. These developments were said to be the second turning point in the environmental policy of Japan. Although the Basic Environment Plan was endorsed by the cabinet, it does not fully ensure the integration of environmental considerations into other policy fields. Meanwhile, as seen in cases such as the city of Kawasaki, some municipalities enacted their own basic environmental ordinances before the Basic Environment Law was enacted, stipulating that the environmental policy would be the foundation of the policies of the city and need to be fully respected during policy-making. After the law was enacted, many municipalities established their own basic environmental ordinances and formulated basic municipal environment plans. Although there have been attempts to move toward integrated environmental policy and tasks such as implementation of a carbon tax as a policy instrument to integrate energy and environmental policy have been tabled, they are not yet realized.

Regarding Japanese energy policy, the Basic Act on Energy Policy was enacted in June 2002, and with a fundamental policy of "securing a stable energy supply, adapting to the environment, and utilizing market principles", the Basic Energy Plan was established in 2003 during the coalition government of Junichiro Koizumi (2001–2006) composed of the LDP and the New Komeito party. The New Basic Energy Plan was then revised in June 2011 after the DPJ government took over. The plan lists nuclear power, renewable energy, petroleum, natural gas, coal and others to be the "best mix of power sources". In terms of nuclear power, the goal of the plan was to add 9 nuclear reactors and achieve an approximately 85 per cent facility utilization rate by the year 2020, and add "at least 14 new nuclear reactors" by 2030, generating approximately 50 per cent of the nation's electricity with nuclear energy (METI, 2010). This facility utilization rate is considerably higher than the actual performance in recent years. At the time, there were both opponents and proponents of nuclear energy within the DPJ, so it did not re-evaluate nuclear policies. The goal for renewable energy was to increase the share of renewables in the primary energy supply to 10 per cent. Feed-in tariffs were listed as a measure to promote renewable energy.

After the Fukushima accident, then prime minister Kan expressed his view in May that the previously mentioned Basic Energy Plan should be reevaluated. On 6 May, Kan requested that Chubu Electric Power Company discontinue operations at the Hamaoka nuclear power plant, located in the focal area of a possible earthquake in the Tokai region of central Japan; Chubu Electric followed suit and shut their plant down. Additionally, Kan decided to conduct a stress test (tolerability evaluation) before permitting to resume operations at nuclear facilities that were offline. Although these actions imply withdrawal from dependence on nuclear energy, the direction is not yet clear as they are not grounded in an explicit political platform (cf. Energy and Environment Conference, 2011). During that period, it was pointed out that there was a structural problem with the administrative practices ensuring the safety of nuclear energy in Japan. Therefore, an independent accident-investigation board to assess the existing energy policies, including nuclear power policies, and clarify the complete picture of the accident will be required. The agencies intended to fill this role—the Nuclear and Industrial Safety Agency within the Ministry of Economy, Trade and Industry, and the Nuclear Safety Commission within the Cabinet Office—have not effectively functioned. In September 2012 the Nuclear Regulation Authority was established as the special Agency of the Ministry of the Environment, assuming the role of regulating nuclear energy currently held by the Ministry of Economy, Trade and Industry and the Cabinet Office. The fundamental transformation of Japanese nuclear energy administration is necessary, along with a comprehensive system for monitoring radioactivity and a structure for disclosing that information.

As for climate change policies, soon after taking office in October 2009, Prime Minister Hatoyama announced that "Japan [was] going to reduce greenhouse gas emissions by 25% by the year 2020, compared to 1999 levels" before the United Nations General Assembly, and submitted to the Diet the Bill of the Basic Act on Global Warming Countermeasures. However, after Hatoyama's resignation in June 2010, the bill was tentatively repealed for incomplete deliberations. Although it was resubmitted during the Kan government, it has not yet been passed due to the difficult situation in the so-called twisted Diet, in which the ruling party occupies more than half of legislative seats in the majority the House of Representatives, but the opposition party holds more than half of the legislative seats in the House of Councillors, making it difficult to pass a bill. The Bill of the Basic Act on Global Warming Countermeasures lists reduction of the nation's greenhouse gas emissions by 25 per cent from 1990 levels as a midterm target (by 2020) and reduction by 80 per cent by the year 2050. However, there was a problematic prerequisite to reach an agreement by all major countries to establish a fair and effective international framework and aggressive targets. Nonetheless, to achieve the goal, three key policies have been discussed: the establishment of domestic emissions trading schemes, implementation of an environmental tax (tax to address global warming) and implementation of feed-in tariffs for renewable energies. Of these, the feed-in tariff is the only one moving forward—it was passed as the Act on Special Measures Concerning the Procurement of Renewable Electric Energy by Operators of Electric Utilities, a law promoting renewable energy, on 26 August 2011. A Procurement Price Calculation Committee appointed by the Diet was established to determine tariff rates which was implemented in July 2012. This law mandates electric utilities be connected to renewable-energy power systems, although there is a provision in Article 5 that they can be excluded from this requirement when there is a risk that the connection may interrupt the smooth provision of electricity. Nevertheless, in order to promote renewable energy, it is essential to set prices based on type of energy source and form and scale of installation, and to prioritize connection of renewable energy sources to the power grid. Developing distributed energy supply systems by ending regional monopolies by electric utilities; separating power generation, transmission and distribution; deregulating electric utilities, enhancing regional grid networks; and implementing a smart grid remains as a future challenge. The Ministry of the Environment has already released a *Study on the Potential for the Introduction of Renewable Energy in Fiscal 2010*, which indicates that there is great potential.

Environmental organizations have played a large role in the creation of the Bill of the Basic Act on Global Warming Countermeasures. During the Koizumi coalition, environmental organizations such as the Kiko Network, the Institute for Sustainable Energy Policies and WWF Japan formed a group called the "Make the Rule: Climate Protection Act Campaign Committee", which submitted a bill for a Climate Protection Act with a midterm target of 30 per cent reduction from 1990 levels by 2020 and launched a support campaign (Make the Rule: Climate Protection Act Campaign Committee, 2008). Their activity has been one of the driving forces behind the Bill of the Basic Act on Global Warming Countermeasures under the DPJ's coalition. Additionally, in view of the post-Fukushima situation, the Kiko Network released a document titled "Three 25s Are Achievable Targets: Additional Estimation (No. 2) Multiple Scenarios of Withdrawal from Nuclear Energy" (Kiko Network, 2011) on 8 September 2011. In this report, the feasibility of "accelerating the pace to reduce the dependence on nuclear energy" and "expediting the abolition of all nuclear reactors" was examined. The report also suggests that "the reduction of greenhouse gas emissions to stop climate change, the introduction of renewable energy, and energy conservation are simultaneously achievable" (Kiko Network, 2011: 1, 8, 13). They examined two cases: that of decommissioning the reactors after 30 years of operation and that of decommissioning all the reactors by the year 2020. In both cases, they indicate that "it is possible to accelerate the withdrawal from nuclear energy and to reduce greenhouse gas emissions by 25% by the year 2020, by further encouraging replacement of fuels used for power generation by low-carbon fuels, improvement in power generation efficiency, and introduction of renewable energies" (Kiko Network, 2011: 13). They expect that energy-conservation investment associated with withdrawal from nuclear energy and other investments in renewable energy will have positive effects on the Japanese economy and on employment opportunities.

In Japan, social movements have not been very active in the past. However, there are new citizens' movements springing up against nuclear energy among a diversity of people, including the younger generation. For instance, on 19 September, six months after the nuclear accident in Fukushima, a rally called "Goodbye Nuclear Power Plants: 50,000-Assembly" was held in Tokyo. Not 50,000 but 60,000 people gathered to participate in the rally, which turned out to be the largest rally against nuclear energy in Japanese history. Since the accident, many other demonstrations have been held by citizens throughout the country. A "10,000,000-Signature Campaign" has also been initiated (Kamata et al., 2011: 60–70). Public awareness of nuclear energy has significantly changed as well. According to the Public Survey on Nuclear Power Plants and Energy conducted in June by the Japan Broadcasting Corporation (NHK; 2011a: 1), to the question of what should be done with Japanese nuclear power plants, "3.0 per cent answered they should be increased, 23.3 per cent answered they should stay as they are, 44.7 per cent answered they should be decreased, and 21.4 per cent answered they should all be shut down"; a survey in October (NHK, 2011b: 1) showed that "2.1 per cent answered they should be increased, 24.4 per cent answered they should stay as they are, 42.3 per cent answered they should be decreased, and 24.3 per cent answered they should all be shut down". Thus, approximately 67 per cent of respondents to the second survey thought it best to decrease the number of nuclear power plants or to abolish them. Similarly, according to an *Asahi Shimbun* poll in June 2011, 74 per cent of respondents agreed to the statement "the number of nuclear reactors should gradually be decreased to abolish them all in the future", indicating that public-opinion trends in Japan are headed in the direction of decreasing dependence on nuclear energy since the Fukushima accident (*Asahi Shinbun*, 2011).

Additionally, renewable energies are being promoted at the municipal level in Japan. The number of cities, towns and villages producing renewable energy in excess of demand by residents and local agricultural and fishery industries was 60 as of March 2010. If only electrical power is considered, that number jumps to 86.[5]

In this context, "nuclear export" is also a large issue. Under the DPJ governments, before the earthquake, nuclear agreements were signed with Viet Nam, Korea, Jordan and Russia and were submitted to the Diet. Even since the accident, nuclear negotiations with India have been resumed under Kan's successor Yoshihiko Noda (2011–2012). In terms of nuclear energy within the country, the decision to shut down the old nuclear reactors that have been operating since 1970s and to stop nuclear exports would be the first step towards full withdrawal from nuclear energy. However, there is no such move under discussion at this point.

On 19 September 2012, Prime Minister Noda of the Democratic Party made the decision to withdraw from nuclear energy totally within the 2030s, but after the re-implementation of a liberal-democratic–komei (LDP–Komei Party) government under Prime Minister Shinzo Abe in December 2012, the conservative coalition is aiming at changing Noda's decision.

## *Strategic challenges with environmental governance*

In this section, I discuss challenges in Japanese energy transition as well as in the formulation of environmental governance strategies.

First, the Great East Japan Earthquake, massive tsunami and accident at Fukushima raised broad, deep questions about the future trajectories of Japanese society and democracy. In addition to the issue related to regional revitalization in an aging society with a declining birth rate that they were already facing before the accident, disaster-affected areas now face tasks such as establishing new disaster prevention/reduction schemes, food safety, construction of distributed energy-supply systems and regional economic recovery through integrated development of industries, or "sixth-order industry", in which producers in agriculture, forestry and fisheries (primary industry) are directly involved in processing (secondary industry) and distribution (tertiary industry). With regard to democratic reform, the task of formulating a discussion framework for changing energy policies is not hampered by existing barriers and vested interests. To begin with, information disclosure needs to be addressed as a fundamental issue. It is essential to establish a system for regular measurement and inspection of and information disclosure on radiation-contaminated soil, farm produce, seafood and other food products.

Second, to achieve energy transition, it is necessary to pass the Bill of the Basic Act on Global Warming Countermeasures and allow feed-in tariffs for renewable energy to function, as well as to introduce a cap-and-trade emissions trading scheme and adopt an environmental tax. (In October 2012, the Tax for Global Warming Countermeasures to fossil fuel was introduced and this rate of tax will be raised over three-and-a-half years in three stages.) Regarding nuclear energy, the first step is to abolish the old nuclear reactors that went into operation in the 1970s, and the second step is to develop a new, comprehensive energy policy and make a political decision to withdraw from nuclear energy within a specified time limit, based on political and social consensus. In this context, a related issue is the deregulation of electric utilities to separate power generation, transmission and distribution.

Third, reforms of government and the Diet are interrelated requirements for the formation of proper environmental governance strategies in Japan. Under the banner of "political leadership", the DPJ administration has attempted to pave the way for "politically-initiated" policy-making by discontinuing administrative vice-ministers' inter-ministry meetings, establishing the National Policy Unit and forming a reporting structure of minister/senior vice-minister/vice-minister. However, this reorganization is still a long way from establishing a framework for utilizing the central bureaucracy in "Cabinet-initiated" policy-making. Furthermore, policy discussion between the ruling and opposition parties on bills introduced to the Diet has been somnolent. The first important task is to initiate discussions of bills with active citizen participation through holding a public hearing during the early stage of law-making to allow people like policy experts, various citizens from relevant regions and representatives of NPOs to express their opinions. Further, restructuring is needed to reform the Diet as a "forum for discussion" by having the Diet convene throughout the year, introducing a system for reading of government bills and reforming the petition system to accommodate policies suggested by citizens. It will be equally important for the Diet to exercise its administrative investigation rights to conduct an independent "democratic audit" of the executive branch. As in the case of Germany's Bundestag, this may call for the establishment of investigating committees comprising Diet members and experts in relevant areas. The planned establishment of the "nuclear accident investigation board" in the Diet by including policy experts was a new attempt in this regard.

Along with fundamental reform of the Diet, introduction of additional systems such as an assessment system to evaluate the impact of bills on sustainable development and "green budgeting" is another subject to be debated.

Fourth, in Germany, the formulation of strategies for sustainable development or of climate change policies is an established political field that is considered "chief business" and is traditionally led by the chancellor. Similarly in Japan, the formulation of systems for cabinet-initiated policy-making as well as the Basic Environment Plan and climate change policies are political fields that require the leadership of the prime minister. Many social dialogues involving various actors have been held at the federal, state and municipal levels in Germany. Meanwhile, extensive "citizen participation" has been encouraged in the development of comprehensive programs at the municipal level in Japan as well. With the prominent role of disaster-support volunteers in the Great Hanshin Earthquake of 1995, the Act to Promote Specified Nonprofit Activities or "NPO Act" was enacted in the late 1990s, establishing a system for government certification of NPOs. In June 2011 and April 2012, similarly, a new tax scheme applicable for charitable contribution and NPOs was implemented, and Japan is now carrying out an innovative reform to promote the culture of charitable contributions. With prominent deficiencies in the nation's administrative system, activities such as understanding regional needs of citizens in order to develop policy proposals based on the opinions of policy experts as well as citizens engaged in NPO activities are becoming increasingly important. On the assumption that these movements will become more active, it is Japan's challenge to further develop cooperative governance with a wide range of participants.

(*This chapter was written in November 2011 and was updated in September 2013.)

## Notes

1. In Germany, two major political parties, CDU/CSU (Christian Democrats) and SPD (Social Democratic Party), formed a grand coalition government after the election 2005. Moreover, CDU/CSU and FDP (Liberal Democratic Party) formed a conservative-liberal coalition government after the election 2009.
2. On environmental governance, please refer to Jänicke and Jörgens (2006), Jänicke and Jacob (2006, 2007), and Tsubogo (2009a, 2009b).
3. On environmental governance strategies in Germany, I referred to the following overviews of Germany from the standpoint of international comparison: Jänicke et al. (2002), Müller (2002), Wurzel (2008) and Tsubogo (2009a, 2009b, 2011).

    On the situation during the Schröder era, I referred to Tsubogo (2009a). Please also refer to Lenschow (2002), Jordan, Wurzel and Zito (2003), Jacob, Vilkery and Lenschow (2008) and Jordan and Lenschow (2008a), all of which contain research on systems and procedures for the integration of environmental policy from the standpoint of international comparison.
4. On this point I referred to websites such as www.bund.net, www.greenpeace.de, www.nabu.de and www.wwf.de.
5. These data were provided by the Research Center on Public Affairs (Kurasaka Laboratory) of Chiba University and the Institute for Sustainable Energy Policies (2010, 2011). They call these areas "100% energy-sustainable zones" and have conducted periodic assessments of them.

## REFERENCES

AGEB (2011) *Energieverbrauch in Deutschland. Daten für das 1. Quartal 2011*, available at http://www.ag-energiebilanzen.de.
*Asahi Shinbun* (2011) "Asahi Shinbun poll in June 2011", available at http://www.asahi.com/special/1005/TKY201106130401.html.
Becker, Thorben (2011) "Atomausstieg. Praxistest bestanden", *BUNDmagazin*, 3/2011, pp. 16–17.
Benz, Arthur and Yannis Papadopoulos (2006) *Governance and Democracy*, New York: Routledge.
BMU (Bundesministerium für Umwelt, naturschutz und Reaktorsicherheit) (2011a) "Das Energiekonzept und seine beschlunigte Umsetzung", available at http://www.bmu.de/themen/klima-energie/energiewende/beschluesse-und-massnahmen/.
—— (2011b) "25 Jahre Bundesministerium", available at http://www.bmu.de/chnologie/.
Die Bundesregierung (2002) *Perspektiven für Deutschland. Unsere Strategie für eine nachhaltige Entwicklung*, Berlin:Die deutsche Regierung.
—— (2008) *Perspektiven für Deutschland. Unsere Strategie für eine nachhaltige Entwicklung. Fortschrittsbericht 2008*, Berlin: Die deutsche Regierung.
DIW (Deutsches Institut für Wirtschaftsforschung Berlin) (1994) *Ökosteuer – Sackgasse oder Königsweg? Wirtschaftliche Auswirkungen einer ökologischen Steuerreform. Gutachten im Auftrag von Greenpeace e.V.*, Berlin/Hamburg: DIW.
Energy and Environment Conference (2011) "Interim Compilation of Discussion Points for the Formulation of 'Innovative Strategy for Energy and the Environment'", available at http://www.npu.go.jp/policy/policy09/pdf/20110908/20110908_02.pdf.
Ethik-Kommission (2011) *Deutschlands Energiewende—Ein Gemeinschaftswerk für die Zukunft. Ethik-Kommission Sichere Energieversorgung*, 30 May, Berlin: Publisher, available at http://www.bundesregierung.de/Content/DE/__Anlagen/2011/07/2011-07-28-abschlussbericht-ethikkommission,property=publicationFile.pdf.
EU (2011) "Europe 2020 Targets", available at http://www.ec.europa.eu/europe2020/pdf/targets_en.pdf.
Hey, Christian (2009) "35 Jahre Gutachten des SRU—Rückschau und Ausblick", in Hans-Joachim Koch and Christian Hey (eds.) *Zwischen Wissenschaft und Politik. 35 Jahre Gutachten des Sachverständigenrat für Umweltfragen*, Berlin: Erich Schmidt Verlag, pp. 161–279.
IdE (Institut dezentrale Energietechnologie) (2013) "100% Erneuerbare-Energie-Regionen", June, available at http://www.100-ee.de/index.php?id=216 (100ee-Karte-Liste_Juni_2013.pdf.
Jacob, Klaus, Peter H. Feindt, Per-Olaf Busch and Frank Biermann (2007) "Einleitung: Politik und Umwelt", in Klaus Jacob et al. (eds.) *Politik und Umwelt*. Politische Vierteljahresschrift (PVS), Sonderheft 39/2007, Wiesbaden: VS Verlag für Sozialwissenschaften, pp. 11–37.
Jacob, Klaus, Axel Vokery and Andrea Lenschow (2008) "Instruments for Environmental Policy Integration in 30 OECD Countries", in Andrew Jordan and Andrea Lenschow (eds.) *Innovation in Environmental Policy? Integrating the Environment for Sustainability*, Cheltenham: Edward Elgar, pp. 24–45.
Jänicke, Martin and Klaus Jacob (eds.) (2006) *Environmental Governance in Global Perspective. New Approaches to Ecological and Political Modernisation*, Berlin: Forschungsstelle für Umweltpolitik (FFU).

Jänicke, Martin and Helge Jörgens (2006) "New Approaches to Environmental Governance", in Martin Jänicke and Klaus Jacob (eds.) *Environmental Governance in Global Perspective. New Approaches to Ecological and Political Modernisation*, Berlin: FFU, pp. 167–209.

Jänicke, Martin, Helge Jörgens, Kirsten Jörgensen and Ralf Nordbeck (2002) "Germany", in *Governance for Sustainable Development. Five OECD Case Studies*, Paris: OECD, pp. 113–153.

Jordan, Andrew J. and Andrea Lenschow (eds.) (2008a) *Innovation in Environmental Policy? Integrating the Environment for Sustainability*, Cheltenham: Edward Elgar.

Jordan, Andrew J. and Andrea Lenschow (2008b) "Integrating the Environment for Sustainable Development: An Introduction", in Andrew J. Jordan and Andrea Lenschow (eds.) *Innovation in Environmental Policy? Integrating the Environment for Sustainability*, Cheltenham: Edward Elgar, pp. 3–23.

Jordan, Andrew, Rüdiger K. Wurzel and A. R. Zito (eds.) (2003) "'New' Instruments of Environmental Governance?", in *Environmental Politics*, Special Issue, Vol. 12 No. 1, London: Routledge.

Kamata, Satoshi and Oe Kenzaburo et al. (2011) "Document on the Good-by Nuclear Power Plants: 60,000-Assembly", in *Sekai,* November, 60–70.

Kiko Network (2011) "3 Achievable Targets of 25: Additional Estimation (No. 2) Multiple Scenarios of Withdrawal from Nuclear Energy", available at http://www.kikonet.org/research/energyshift.html#proposal.

Kooiman, Jan (2002) "Governance — A Social-Political Perspective", in Jürgen R. Gorte and Bernard Gbikpi (eds.) *Participatory Governance*, Opladen: Leske + Budrich, pp. 71–96.

Lenschow, Andrea (ed.) (2002) *Environmental Policy Integration*, London: Earthscan.

Make the Rule: Climate Protection Act Campaign Committee (2008) *Make Rules to Prevent Climate Change: A Booklet That Explains Why Laws Need to be Established Now*, available at http://www.maketherule.jp.

METI (Ministry of Economie, Trade and Industrie) (2010) "Energy Basic Plan", available at http://www.meti.go.jp/press/20100618004/20100618004-2.pdf.

Müller, Edda (2002) "Environmental Policy Integration as a Political Principle: The German and Implications of European Policy", in Andrea Lenschow (ed.) *Environmental Policy Integration*, London: Earthscan, pp. 57–77.

NHK (Japan Broadcast Corporation) (2011a) "June 2011—Public Survey on Nuclear Power Plants and Energy", available at http://www.nhk.or.jp/bunken/summary/yoron/social/pdf/110709.pdf.

—— (2011b) "October 2011—Public Survey on Nuclear Power Plants and Energy", available at http://www.nhk.or.jp/bunken/summary/yoron/social/pdf/111104.pdf.

Research Center on Public Affairs of Chiba University and Institute for Sustainable Energy Policies (2010) "2010 Report on Energy-Sustainable Zones", available at http://sustainable-zone.org/docs/Sustainable_Zone_Report_2010.pdf.

—— (2011) "About the Release of 2011 Estimation (Brief Edition) on Energy-Sustainable Zones", available at http://sustainable-zone.org/docs/111017-sustainable-zone-2011-press-release2.pdf.

Scharpf, Fritz W. (1997) *Games Real Actors Play. Actor-Centered Institutionalism in Policy Research*. Oxford: Westview Press.

SPD und Bündnis 90/Die Grünen (1998) *Aufbruch und Erneuerung – Deutschlands Weg ins 21. Jahrhundert, Koalitionsvereinbarung zwischen Sozialdemokratischen Partei Deutschlands und Bündnis 90/Grünen*, Bonn, 20 October.

SRU (Sachverständigenrat für Umweltfragen) (2011) *Wege zur 100% erneubaren Stromversorgung*, Berlin: Erich Schmidt Verlag.

Tsubogo, Minoru (2009a) *Environmental Politics: Germany and Japan*, Tokyo: Waseda University Press.

―― (2009b) "Environmental Governance and Policymaking—Arguments Over Environmental Targets and Environmental Indicators", in Yukio Adachi (ed.) *Democracy for the Sustainable Future*, Tokyo: Minerva Shobo, pp. 127–146.

―― (2011) "Environmental Governance and Integrated Environmental Policy in Germany", in Junichi Nagamine (ed.) *Comparing Environmental Governance*, Tokyo: Minerva Shobo, pp. 214–238.

UBA (Umweltbundesamt) (2010a) *Energieziel 2050: 100 Prozent Strom aus erneubaren Quellen*, Berlin: UBA, available at http://www.uba.de/uba-info-medien/3997.html.

―― (2010b) *Presse Release No. 39*. "Energy goal for 2050: 100% renewable electricity supply n", available at http://www.umweltbundesamt.de/uba-info/index.htm.

―― (2011) "Das Umweltbundesamt – Aufgaben und Oganisation", available at http://www.uba.de/.

Weiger, Hubert (2011) "Energiewende. Zu langsam, zu gefährlich", *BUNDmagazin*, 3/2011, p. 13.

Wurzel, Rüdiger K. (2008) "Germany", in Andrew J. Jordan and Andrea Lenschow (eds.) *Innovation in Environmental Policy? Integrating the Environment for Sustainability*, Cheltenham: Edward Elgar, pp. 180–201.

# 6

# Environmental governance failure and environmental metagovernance for local sustainable development: Local Agenda 21 in Japan

*Kentaro Miyanaga*

> *Amongst the laws which rule human societies there is one which seems to be more precise and clear than all others. If men are to remain civilized, or to become so, the art of associating together must grow and improve in the same ratio in which the equality of conditions is increased.*[1]
>
> Alexis de Tocqueville, *Democracy in America*

In this era of globalization, issues of global and local sustainability are becoming more and more closely connected. Hence, governing mechanisms for promoting the global sustainability dimension cannot work well without appropriate governing mechanisms of fostering the local dimension. This is one of the reasons why the concept of "Multi level Environmental Governance" is of increasing relevance.

Local Agenda 21 (LA21) is a typical and well-known approach toward local sustainability, which is based on the recognition of such global-local interrelation. In chapter 28 of Agenda 21, adopted at the Earth Summit in 1992, it is emphasized that local governments play a vital role to global sustainable development, and recommended for local governments in each country to adopt "local Agenda 21" with the involvement of various stakeholders. Later, LA21 was further defined by the International Council for Local Environmental Initiatives (ICLEI) as "a participatory, multisectoral process to achieve the goals of Agenda 21 at the local level through the preparation and implementation of a long-term, strategic action plan that addresses priority local sustainable development concerns" (ICLEI, 1997). In the last 20 years, many practical endeavours concerning LA21 have been made especially in Europe, and the approach has also been underpinned by academics (e.g., Lafferty, 2001; Lafferty and Meadowcroft, 2000; Lafferty and Eckerberg, 1998).

The main purpose of this chapter is to examine practices and institutions of LA21 in Japan through two analytical concepts: *environmental governance failure* and *environmental metagovernance*. However, this purpose involves more than introducing the lesser-known LA21 practices. First, the examination could make a new theoretical contribution to environmental governance debates. Some governance theorists applied the concept of governance failure or metagovernance (e.g., Jessop, 2000), but these have been rarely discussed or elaborated within the context of environmental governance. Second, the analysis in this chapter could shed light on one important theoretical aspect of the multilevel nature of environmental governance, because taking up the theme of metagovernance, which means "the governance of governance" (Sørensen and Torfing, 2009), could lead to an exploration of a *relationship* between environmental governance mechanisms. Third, Japanese environmental policy studies (e.g., Tsuru and Weidner, 1989; Broadbent, 2002; Schreurs, 2002) have focused mainly on various nongovernmental actors' activities or citizen movements in terms of environmental governance, whereas participatory mechanisms or institutions such as LA21 were rarely mentioned. Although there are some exceptions (e.g., Barrett and Usui, 2002; Imura, 2005a, 2005b), these studies generally do not refer to governance literature for the analysis.

The structure of this chapter is as follows: next I examine and summarize current discussions of the concept of governance and show this chapter's view of environmental governance. I then discuss the analytical framework: environmental governance failure and environmental metagovernance. I then address the issues of Japanese LA21 approaches in more detail and show the prospects. Finally, this chapter concludes by examining how the LA21 system could contribute to local sustainable development with reference to environmental governance failure and environmental metagovernance.

## The concept of governance revisited

There have been ample academic debates about the governance concept, but to date "there is no universally accepted definition of governance" (Jordan et al., 2005: 478). To make matters worse, we often have difficulties in conducting case studies of governance, partly because governance cannot "be adequately captured by laws, statutes or formal constitutions" (Chhotray and Stoker, 2009: 6). Coupled with the multidisciplinary nature of governance research, governance debates often have some confusion.

To take overall surveys of governance literatures or explore the complete definition of governance is, of course, beyond the scope of this chapter. Yet it can be boldly said that the concept of governance mainly pays attention to the growing government-society interdependencies and the highly blurred border between them. It is often noted, sometimes with enthusiasm, that government is no longer the sole actor of governing, and the main function has moved away from "rowing" to "steering" (Osborne and Gaebler, 1992). With this perspective, the governing structure would be seen to become more decentralized and pluralistic, and government as a governing actor could be characterized as a *primus inter pares* (first among equals).

In sum, one of the very essences of the governance concept is *governing actors and their diversification*. At issue here are two related problems. The first is *why* governing actors are (or in some cases should be) diversified. For example, non-government actors like voluntary groups and non-profit organizations are now increasingly involved in public decision-making processes: policy preparation, implementation, monitoring and evaluation. What lies behind the trend is that there are a growing number of complicated social problems in this contemporary world—one of them being of course the environmental problem—that no sole actor is capable to tackle and resolve on his or her own. Additionally, there is an increasing recognition that it could be an attractive means for enhancing effectiveness, legitimacy and transparency of public policies.[2] From such perspective, many researchers have also insisted that mechanisms and institutions for broad public involvement would be indispensable (e.g., Huxham, 2000; McQuaid, 2000; Brinkerhoff and Brinkerhoff, 2002).

The second question, which we have to look at more carefully, is about *relationships among governing actors*. A traditional governing mechanism is characterized by the vertical relation between governmental and non-governmental actors, principally through power and authority in terms of legislation and administration. However, more attention has been paid recently to the horizontal relation expressed by negotiation and collaboration. This is why governance often works in a less formalized way, in which relatively autonomous actors act and interact in the form of a network or a partnership. The structure and process are investigated particularly by network governance theorists (e.g. Pierre and Peters, 2000; Rhodes, 2000; Sørensen and Torfing, 2007).

## Defining environmental governance

In spite of the essence of the governance concept shown in the previous section, some important issues still remain to be explored. In terms of environmental governance for local sustainable development, further and more in-depth discussions are needed.

It is worth reconsidering whether it is analytically proper to take notice of governing actors only. Pierre and Peters (2000) aptly said, for example, that much of the governance literature has been fairly quiet on who defines the objectives of governance. Bressers and Kuks (2005) also defined five components of environmental governance: (1) administrative and other scale levels, (2) actors in the policy network, (3) policy objectives, (4) strategies and instruments, and (5) organization and resources of implementation. These notions would indicate that the structure of environmental governance could be regarded as multidimensional and that actors are only one of several components.

Following the framework of Miyanaga (2011), I consider environmental governance as having three dimensions: *policy actors*, *policy objectives* and *policy instruments*.[4] In order to explain what this consideration means, I begin with looking at the concept of sustainable development and the relationship between these three dimensions.

Sustainable development requires the simultaneous and integrative treatment of the environmental, economic and social dimensions of sustainability (e.g., Barbier, 1987; Serageldin and Steer, 1994; Serageldin, 1996; Harris et al, 2001; Morotomi, 2003). Hence, policy objectives which aim only at improving the local environment must be reconsidered in line with the idea of sustainable development.

Besides the contents of policy objectives, it is also important to consider how the process of setting policy objectives in environmental governance should be. Considering the probability that a policy objective in environmental governance for local sustainable development covers broader local issues, the process inevitably needs to be participatory. In a practice or an institutional framework of environmental governance, when dealing with an issue of policy objectives, people must inevitably think of policy actors.

Moreover, the nature of policy instruments has great significance for analyzing environmental governance. Policy instruments in the environmental policy field usually consist of "command and control" regulation, economic instruments using incentive mechanism, provision of social infrastructure like sewerage and incinerator, or all of these combined. As is shown above, however, to set policy objectives with broader public involvement per se also is becoming an important measure taken for local sustainable development.

At the same time, another policy instrument would be required for local sustainable development. One of the most essential examples is actors' capacity-building or citizen empowerment. This would indicate a new agenda of environmental policy in an age of sustainable development (Miyanaga, 2011).

## Environmental governance failure and environmental metagovernance for local sustainable development

The governance concept alone does not set the preconditions under which mechanisms such as networks and partnerships function in a satisfactory way. Involving various actors is often accompanied with high transaction costs or does not always ensure adequate and intended consequences. Moreover, although collaboration may be fruitful and effective, it can deteriorate into blame avoidance and an unwillingness to take responsibility (Chhotray and Stoker, 2009).

What causes these failures? In the context of environmental governance, the essence of which was addressed in the previous section, the background of environmental governance failure is discussed as follows:

- *Lack of skill, experience or institutional framework of deliberative process for horizontal interaction between actors.* Actors in environmental governance never operate in a vacuum. For example, the quality or outcome of deliberative processes is dependent on the extent of skill or experience. Without this, both local civil servants and citizens often have difficulties in communicating with each other.

It is also important to consider into what kind of institutional framework actors are embedded. Later in this chapter I pick up the political and administrative system in Japanese local government, under which environmental governance is put into practice.

- *Inexistence of the common policy objective.* Generally speaking, collaboration among various actors cannot work well without a shared common objective. In other words, even if there are many actors taking part in the policy process, it can still lead to fragmentation and thus does not assure success of networking or partnership.

- *Poor policy instruments to tackle problems of power weakness of nongovernmental actors or power asymmetry between actors.* An asymmetric relationship between policy actors, especially between local government and non-governmental actors, is frequently observed in environmental policy practices. It would lower the quality of participation or outcome of collaboration no matter how actors are diversified or how strongly they are involved in the policy process.

In these situations, it must be investigated how the governance failures can be overcome. In this chapter, I call the device to overcome governance failure metagovernance. Considering the preceding discussion, we should take notice of the following issues concerning environmental metagovernance:

- *Preparing practical devices or appropriate institutional arrangements for better horizontal relations between local government and nongovernment actors.* To date, many governance researchers have discussed how diversified policy actors can successfully construct networking or partnerships. For example, Niikawa (2004) stated in the Japanese local governance context that governance might undermine its merits without "working conditions", for example, monitoring, exploring, intermediating, coordinating and guideline-setting of governance as metagovernance function. Moreover, As Klijin and Edelenbos (2007: 203–206) hold, metagovernance as network management often takes the form of process management strategies for guiding stakeholder interaction, and these may be classified as follows: activation of actors and resources, creation of organizational arrangements, guidance of interaction, goal-achieving strategies, joint knowledge production and trust creation.

All these are expected to work as several devices and institutions for better horizontal relations between actors. Hence, one of the main analytical themes in the following sections is to examine whether practices and institutions of Japanese LA21 aim at providing a deliberative process for horizontal interaction between actors.
- *Setting policy objectives of local sustainable development with involvement of various actors.* In the search for environmental metagovernance, the dimension of policy objectives also should be addressed. Preparing a kind of common local vision would be indispensable for better horizontal relations between actors, especially in local sustainable development strategies. We must keep in mind, however, that not only the vision per se but also the process of constructing the vision are of great importance (Miyanaga, 2011). Providing enough space or time for setting local visions involving various actors may contribute to better networking or partnerships.
- *Implementing policy instruments for empowering actors who take initiatives for local sustainable development.* In cases where we try to tackle problems concerning power weakness of nongovernmental actors or power asymmetry between actors, appropriate policy instruments are required, which would be expected 'to re-balance power differentials by strengthening weaker forces or systems in the interests of system integration and/or social cohesion' (Jessop, 2000: 23–24). As mentioned before, capacity building and citizen empowerment are one of the approaches. Moreover, they can help to foster initiatives for local sustainable development. It will be explored in the following sections how capacity building and citizen empowerment are dealt with in Japanese LA21 systems.

## LA21 in Japan: An overview

According to a survey by the Ministry of Environment, 318 municipalities in Japan had an LA21 initiative as of 1 March 2003. However, very few practices in Japan are under the flag of LA21. As mentioned more precisely in the following sections, it is the most typical case for the Japanese LA21 approach to be in the form of Kankyo Kihon Keikaku (Basic Environmental Plan, BEP). By using the data of the survey, Nakaguchi (2002) has shown that about 70 per cent of municipalities consider their BEP as LA21.

To explore what this really means, I begin by sketching the political and administrative system in the Japanese local government.

*Political and administrative system in Japanese local government:*
*The institutional and practical context of Japanese LA21*

The Japanese local government system is two tiered; prefectures constitute the upper tier, while municipalities represent the lower tier. In this chapter, I focus on the latter, for it is at the municipality level at which Japanese LA21s, as a participatory and multi-sectoral process, are substantially put into practice. A Japanese local government consists of a legislative organ (assembly) and an executive organ; the former decides, for example, ordinances and budgets, and the latter implements administration in accordance with the former. Japanese local governments adopt a dual-representation system, in which the chief executive and members of the assembly are both elected directly by residents.

One of the prominent features in Japanese local administration can be expressed as "administration by planning", which is very unique and original from an international perspective (Matsushita, 2005; Niikawa, 1995). It should be kept in mind, however, that the word *planning* should not be confused with governing local society in the manner of a planned economy system or with governing local society based on rigid scientific future estimation. The expected function is to coordinate several policies and projects in the local government. Moreover, not only is it the administrative device but it also includes some political meanings, because various interests and actors are normally involved in its planning process. Planning as a tool of governing has been extensively used since post-war Japan (Akizuki, 2004) and now commonly prevails as the dominant approach in almost all local governments.

The most fundamental plan of a local government is Sougou Keikaku (Comprehensive Plan, CP), which covers the whole policy fields of local government, for example, agriculture, commerce, health, education, culture, social infrastructure, transport and environment. Local Autonomy Law requires all local governments to enact Kihon Koso (Basic Vision) through the assembly's consent, and it is normal that municipalities establish CP which is composed of Kihon Koso, Kihon Keikaku (Basic Plan) and Jisshi Keikaku (Implementation Plan).

*LA21 as BEP: Contents and process*

There are also plans in each policy field, including environmental policy. In Japanese local government, administration in the environmental policy field basically depends on BEP. BEP is a non-mandatory plan, but it is often the case that a local government enacts the Kankyou Kihon Jourei (Basic Environmental Ordinance, BEO) and prepares the BEP on the ground of the BEO. BEP is not required to be decided in the assembly unless there is a special reference to it in the BEO.

Although BEP is certainly a plan in the environmental policy field, it is not equivalent to city planning or land-use planning, as, for example, in developed Western countries. It aims basically to embody contents of the BEO and to coordinate various environmental policies and projects. The situation differs significantly from one local government to the other, but the BEP contains the following typical elements:
- Vision (long-term objectives of environmental policy)
- Period of the plan (normally 8–15 years)
- Basic principles of environmental policy (e.g., "collaboration and partnership", "symbiosis with nature")

- Measures and projects (taken as an action plan in some cases)
- Indicators and targets
- Management system of the plan

Principally, there are two ways in which an administrative organ prepares the BEP: doing it all alone or doing it under a contractual arrangement with a delegated consulting firm. Moreover, especially through the preparation process, some important procedures are mostly applied outside an administrative organ. Firstly, the draft version of BEP is very often explained and consulted about two or three times in a year in *Shingikai* (advisory council), which is also primarily used at the national level (e.g., Schwartz, 1998). Usually the BEO requires the local government to establish a council as an attached organ, and respect its decision. Members of the council come mainly from outside the local government and usually comprise scholars, community groups (*Jichikai* or *Chonaikai*) or various local stakeholders, such as representatives of a chamber of commerce. Second, the local government frequently provides an opportunity for ordinary residents to submit opinions on the draft; in Japan, it is called "public comment". Third, although the assembly basically does not need to decide on draft, on occasion, there is a consulting process at an environment-related standing committee, composed of some of the assembly's members. Yet it depends on the decision of the chief executive how deeply their opinions are considered.

## Environmental governance failure in BEP system

As mentioned earlier, it is the most typical feature of the Japanese LA21 approach to adopt a BEP system. In other words, LA21 initiatives in Japan are embedded deeply in the Japanese local administrative style, which causes some problems from an environmental governance failure perspective.

In analysing Japanese LA21, I shed light on the structure of environmental governance, which is seen to comprise policy actors, policy objectives and policy instruments. In each of these aspects, I deal with the following issues: *citizen participation*, *sustainable development* and *investment in social capital*.

### Inadequate citizen participation: On policy actors

The BEP system raises some issues concerning policy actors, especially non-governmental actors, such as ordinary citizens. Only two years after the 1992 Earth Summit, Agyeman and Evans (1994: 197–8) made the following relevant statement concerning citizen participation in LA21:

> Sustainability and the new environmental agenda imply more than simply providing an opportunity for citizen participation in decision-making. As the Agenda 21 agreement

makes very clear, both empowerment and capacity building are central to the environmental policy process. There has to be only a programme of education and encouragement which will prepare people for informed participation in the decision-making, but also mechanisms which will enable and assist in building the capacity to actually deliver policy and programmes in partnership with other agencies.

"Administration by planning" inevitably leads to some problems about citizen participation, because LA21 has to be more than just a general device for participation. In environmental governance failure perspective, existing BEP participation systems have a tendency of failing to meet Agyeman and Evans's (1994) demands; collaboration between actors is not always vitalized, nor are fruitful results really achieved. In the following, four issues are explored.

First, there are some people saying that *Shingikai* tends to be "composed of government-picked experts, generally meeting behind closed doors and legitimizing bureaucratically sponsored decisions" (Barrett and Usui, 2002: 50), which is critically expressed by Imura (2005a) as the "*Shingikai* method". But in this chapter's context, this is not the problem per se. In fact, citizen groups or civil organizations have also recently been appointed as *Shingikai* members, and local governments partially adopt a public advertisement system, through which normal citizens could become members. However, in essence, the *Shingikai* system has little potentiality for working as a participatory system in Agyeman and Evans' (1994) sense. The relationship between government and citizens still remains in older form of participation, namely, consulting and consulted, and far from horizontal collaborative relation. This is also true for the public comment system, which lacks an interactive and deliberative process. Furthermore, opportunities for discussing are provided only a few times in a year, which would induce participative practices to become less horizontal or deliberative.

Second, even when the horizontal relation between government and non-governmental actors are put into practice, it might not work well if it lacks a facilitator or coordinator moderating the process as a third party. In fact, scholars in *Shingikai* are most often set in position of "persons of learning and experience" (*gakushiki keikensha*) and referred to as "neutral" (*churitsu*) or "public-interest" (*koeki*) representatives (Schwarz, 1998). As a result, such individuals often become a chairperson. However, coordination of a discussion in *Shingikai* and coordination of relations between government and non-governmental actors for local sustainability are obviously other things.

Third, very few non-governmental actors would take part in the implementation process, if citizen participation in the preparation process were conducted in the previously mentioned way. The same is true for the monitoring or evaluating process of the BEP.

Fourth, however deep and deliberative citizen participation is aimed to be realized by local governments in the BEP system, it would be possible to say that BEP is essentially not a form of LA21, because it is just an administrative plan.

Takahashi (2000) concludes that BEP should not be regarded as LA21. This topic will be picked up again later.

*Sustainable development misunderstood or mishandled: On policy objectives*

In terms of policy objectives, I turn to the theme of sustainable development. In BEP, it is frequently misunderstood or mishandled.

*Tatewari-Gyosei*, which has been translated into "vertical administration" (Samuels, 1983) or "functional fragmentation" (Reed, 1986), might induce some problems concerning this theme. First, the task of BEP management institutionally belongs to the environment division of local government in the Japanese local government system; that is to say that it cannot sufficiently deal with economic and social issues. Men could rarely see local economic and social vision in BEP, except in the case that the chief executive has the special interest and exerts strong leadership in preparing BEP.

In Japanese local governments, "planning inflation" (Niikawa, 1995: 236), which means "problems arising from too many plans" and is mainly caused by the prevailing "administration by planning" system, is sometimes observed. Usually environment, economic and social divisions have their own administrative plan, which also tends to prevent actors to build networking across policy fields.

Worse is that in every environmental policy field there are respective administrative plans, for example, climate change, biodiversity and waste and recycling. The most popular one is the basic domestic waste disposal plan (*Ippan Haikibutsu Syori Keikaku*), which is mandatory, that is, designated by law. There are also a growing number of plans concerning global warming, named regional promotion plans for combating global warming (*Chikyuu Ondanka Taisaku Chiiki Suishin Keikaku*). Additionally, some local governments have their own strategy for conservation of biodiversity (*Seibutsu Tayousei Hozen Chiiki Senryaku*). In these situations, the BEP is likely to be only a nominal and abstract umbrella plan. Needless to say, it does not deserve to be regarded as LA21.

Moreover, although an important essence of LA21 is the recognition of the close relationship between local and global sustainability, BEP rarely includes policies or projects which directly deal with global issues. In European LA21 initiatives, for example, fair-trade projects involving such products as coffee or chocolate are sometimes included. Yet in Japan almost all programmes concerning the third world are conducted outside of the BEP framework.

*Low investment in social capital: On policy instruments*

In terms of policy instruments, we should focus on issues involving civil organizations. The power and influence of civil organizations in Japan is generally weak, which partly reflects the "dual civil society (many small local groups, but few large professionalized groups)" (Pekkanen, 2006). However, there is little recognition in BEP that local sustainable development needs specific policies for citizen empowerment or capacity building, which Agyeman and Evans regard as crucial elements.

In other words, the BEP approach tends to be characterized by a lack of investment in social capital. There are in fact a growing number of divisions which are in charge of citizen activities, but an integrative effort with regard to BEP management can hardly be seen in Japanese local government. In the BEP system the problem of environmental governance failure stemming from non-governmental actors' weakness or asymmetry has not been sufficiently addressed to date.[3]

## How does environmental metagovernance function? Emerging new trends and future directions

The BEP system has several defects in terms of LA21 and local sustainable development, but denying all well-meaning efforts in the BEP system could be considered as superficial. In this section I address the question, How does environmental metagovernance function? By introducing some new trends both within and without BEP, I show the prospects of Japanese LA21 and local sustainable development strategies.

### Vitalized citizen participation and capacity-building under BEP

There are some local governments in which BEP is managed substantially as more than a mere administrative plan, especially in terms of citizen participation and capacity building. If some cases, environmental governance failure problems on policy actors are appropriately tackled as follows.

Beyond the limits of the older form of participation, some BEPs try to initiate a deeper and broader public involvement, for example, in Nisshin, Minamata and Yasu.[5] In these cities, the committee for preparing the BEP, which is mainly composed of civil servants and motivated ordinary citizens, is organized separately from the Shingikai. Regular meetings are held once or twice a month and organized about a year and a half to two years in advance, which is conductive to citizen empowerment. In the process, a coordinator or facilitator with special skills sometimes mediates between citizens and civil servants and enhances the communication process or provides solutions when conflicting interests become apparent.[6]

After the preparation, the organization, which is chiefly composed of members of the committee, for implementing the BEP is established in these cities. Because citizen members have been deeply involved in the preparation process, they have strong motivations in the implementing process, too. Obviously, they are not just consulted people but become actors that promote the LA21 process with the local government.

Importantly, the organization functions also as a kind of forum, where opportunities for finding potential members or enhancing members' ability are often provided. This is the foundation of synergy effects through collaboration between local government and citizens.

*Policy integration for local sustainable development under BEP*

It could be generally said that the *Tatewari-Gyosei* ("vertical administration" or "functional fragmentation") problem partly comes from the failure of coordinating all divisions in local government under one common vision. In some cities, during the BEP preparation process, committee members have tried to build an inclusive vision for environmental, economic and social sustainability.

However, a more powerful way to coordinate policies or projects is involving as many divisions in the local government as possible in the BEP preparing process, which is seen in the case of Yasu city (Miyanaga, 2008). If successful, the coordination process between the divisions could be linked to discussions between local government and citizens in the meeting of the BEP preparing committee. In this case, the BEP is expected to function as an environmental metagovernance mechanism to "ensure the compatibility or coherence of different governance mechanisms and regimes" and "act as the primary organizer of the dialogue among policy communities" (Jessop, 2003: 108).

*LA21 and BEP: An alternative approach*

As noted earlier, it is sometimes said that the BEP system is not suitable for LA21, as long as it remains in the institutional framework of the administrative plan. At the same time, however, we cannot imagine a situation in which a LA21 initiative in Japan can develop without the BEP in the Japanese local administrative culture. Hence the question is how a practical and institutionally appropriate relationship between LA21 and BEP can be fostered.

Besides "LA21 *as* BEP" shown in this chapter, it would be possible to think of "LA21 *outside* BEP". Very few local governments such as Kyoto City and Toyonaka City, which are pioneers of Japanese LA21, have both LA21 and BEP based on the awareness of the difference between the two. However, it is difficult for ordinary citizens to understand the difference, under the situation where even the term *LA21* is not well known. In the worst case, the "LA21 *outside* BEP" system might suffer from little support from local government, which causes a severe resource shortage problem.

*LA21 as CP: Is it possible and favourable?*

In the Japanese local government system, the CP (Comprehensive Plan, Sougou Keikaku) is institutionally the most fundamental plan that covers all major policy fields. Considering this fact, LA21 *above* BEP, that is, LA21 as CP, may be a more promising approach, because the BEP basically addresses only environmental issues. In fact, there are a few local governments, such as Shinsiro City and Anjou City, where CP accommodates the issue of sustainable development.

However, several particular conditions should be required if CP is to be managed as LA21 and thus intended to exert an environmental metagovernance function. First of all, CPs in many local governments have actually only vague policy objectives, tend to be across the board, lack the ability of policy coordination and are far from thinking strategically. Additionally, the highly political character of the CP could bring about some problems. As mentioned earlier, the CP must be decided in the assembly. Because various, sometimes contradictory, interests are brought into the assembly, a radical social vision such as sustainable development is undoubtedly hard for all parties to agree on in a smooth and consensual manner. Moreover, because CP is one of the administrative plans which best reflect the political interest of the chief executive, there is a strong influence from the election cycle. Therefore, it might be in opposition to the long-term character of the LA21 approach.

## Conclusion

Asking whether the Japanese LA21 system is a good practice or negative exemplum for pursuing local sustainable development from an international comparative perspective is less meaningful. The answer is, of course, heavily dependent on contextual conditions, which include, among others, the leadership of the chief executive, understanding and ability of local civil servants, activity of citizen members and political and public awareness of sustainable development, as the analysis in this chapter has suggested.

It is also necessary that LA21 practices and institutions are conscious of factors underlying environmental governance failure and that they are equipped with environmental metagovernance functions. Furthermore, policy processes should be designed in a way in which issues concerning policy actors, policy objectives and policy instruments are comprehensively addressed in the LA21 framework.

## Notes

1. This English paragraph translated from the original French version is cited from the Project Gutenberg eBook, available at http://www.gutenberg.org/files/816/816-h/816-h.htm.
2. Of course, the diversification of governing actors per se does not ensure the improvement of the qualities of public policies. As is discussed in the later section, it requires some preconditions or adequate management.
3. In the formulation of this trichotomy, I was greatly inspired by Ueta (1996), which is a Japanese textbook of environmental economics and policy studies.

4. In fact, we can see very often projects such as environmental education, which is one of the most typical policy fields in BEP. But it is apparent that it does not directly deal with the problem of nongovernmental actors' weakness or asymmetry.
5. The case of Yasu City is analysed in Miyanaga (2008).
6. However, persons with reliable professional skills are hard to find. This could constitute a bottleneck for networking and development of partnerships (Miyanaga, 2011).

REFERENCES

Agyeman, J. and B. Evans (1994) "Viewpoint: Making Local Agenda 21 Work", *Town and Country Planning* 63(7/8), pp. 197–198.
Akizuki, K. (2004) "Local Planning at the Crossroads: NPM and Participation in Contemporary Japan", in Nakamura, A. (ed.), *Public Reform, Policy Change and New Public Management: From the Asia and Pacific Perspective*, Tokyo: EROPA Local Government Center, pp. 169–182.
Barbier, E. B. (1987) "The Concept of Sustainable Economic Development", *Environmental Conservation* 14(2), pp. 101–110.
Barrett, B. and Usui, M. (2002) "Local Agenda 21 in Japan: transforming local environmental governance", *Local Environment* 7(1), pp. 49–67.
Bressers, H. and S. M. Kuks (2003) "What Does 'Governance' Mean? From Conception to Elaboration", in H. Bressers and W. A. Rosenbaum (eds.), *Achieving Sustainable Development: The Challenge of Governance Across Social Scales*, New York, Westpoint, London: Praeger, pp. 65–88.
Brinkerhoff, J. M. and D. W. Brinkerhoff (2002) "Government-Nonprofit Relations in Comparative Perspective: Evolution, Themes and New Directions", *Public Administration and Development* 22(1), pp. 3–18.
Broadbent, J. (2002) "Japan's Environmental Regime: The Political Dynamics of Change", in D. Uday (ed.), *Environmental Politics and Policies in the Industrialized Countries*, Cambridge, MA: MIT Press, pp. 295–355.
Chhotray, V. and G. Stoker (2009) *Governance Theory and Practice: A Cross-Disciplinary Approach*, Basingstoke and New York: Palgrave Macmillan.
Harris, J. M., T. A. Wise, K. P. Gallagher and N. R. Goodwin (eds.) (2001) *A Survey of Sustainable Development: Social and Economic Dimensions*, Washington, DC: Island Press.
Huxham, C. (2000) "The Challenge of Collaborative Governance", *Public Management* 2(3), pp. 337–357.
Imura, H. (2005a) "Japan's Environmental Policy: Institutions and the Interplay of Actors", in H. Imura and M. A. Schreurs (eds.), *Environmental Policy in Japan*, Cheltenham and Northampton, ST: Edward Elgar, pp. 49–85.
―― (2005b) "Environmental Policy Instruments", in H. Imura and M. A. Schreurs (eds.), *Environmental Policy in Japan*, Cheltenham and Northampton, ST: Edward Elgar, pp. 153–184.
ICLEI (International Council for Local Environmental Initiatives) (1997) *Local Agenda 21 Survey: A Study of Responses by Local Authorities and Their National and International Associations to Agenda 21,* available at http://www.un.org/documents/ecosoc/cn17/1997/background/ecn171997-1.rpt1.htm.

Jessop, B. (2000) "Governance Failure", in G. Stoker (ed.), The New Politics of British Local Governance, London: Palgrave Macmillan, pp. 11–32.
—— (2003) "Governance and Meta-governance: On Reflexivity, Requisite Variety and Requisite Irony", in H. P. Bang (ed.), Governance as Social and Political Communication, Manchester and New York: Manchester University Press, pp. 101–116.
Jordan, A., R. K. W. Wurzel and A. Zito (2005) "The Rise of 'New' Policy Instruments in Comparative Perspective: Has Governance Eclipsed Government?", Political Studies 53(3), pp. 477–496.
Klijin, E.-H. and J. Edelenbos (2007) "Meta-Governance as Network Management", in E. Sørensen and J. Torfing (eds.), Theories of Democratic Network Governance, Basingstoke: Palgrave Macmillan, pp. 199–214.
Lafferty, W. M. (ed.) (2001) Sustainable Communities in Europe, London: Earthscan.
Lafferty, W. M. and K. Eckerberg (eds.) (1998) From the Earth Summit to Local Agenda 21: Working toward Sustainable Development, London: Earthscan.
Lafferty, W. M. and J. Meadowcroft (eds.) (2000) Implementing Sustainable Development: Strategies and Initiatives in High Consumption Societies, Oxford and New York: Oxford University Press.
Matsushita, K. (2005) Jichitai Saikouchiku (Reconstruction of Local Government), Tokyo: Koujinnotomo Sha.
McQuaid, R. M. (2000) "The Theory of Partnership: Why Have Partnerships?", in S. P. Osborne (ed.) Public-Private Partnerships: Theory and Practice in International Perspective, London: Routledge, pp. 9–35.
Miyanaga, K. (2008) "Kankyo Kihonkeikaku niokeru Sankaku to Partnership: Shigaken Yasu Shi no Kokoromi o Jirei toshite" (Preparation and Implementation of The Basic Environment Plan through Public Involvement and Partnership: A Case Study of Yasu City, Shiga Prefecture), Zaisei to Koukyo Seisaku (Public Finance and Public Policy) 30(1), pp. 89–104.
—— (2011) Kankyo Governance to NPO: JIzokukanou na Chiikishakai eno Partnership (Environmental Governance and NPO: Partnership for Local Sustainable Development), Kyoto: Showado.
Morotomi, T. (2003) Kankyo (Environment), Tokyo: Iwanami Shoten,
Nakaguchi, T. (2002) "Jizoku Kanou na Hatten Seisaku to Local Agenda 21 no Genjou to Kadai (Sustainable Development Policy and Local Agenda 21)", in K. Kawasaki, T. Nakaguchi and K. Ueta (eds.), Kankyo Management to Machizukuri (Environmental Management and Community Development), Kyoto: Gakugei Syuppansya, pp. 28–39.
Niikawa, T. (1995) "Jishitai Keikaku no Sakutei (Preparation of Local Government Planning)", in M. Nishio and M. Muramatsu, eds., Kouza Gyouseigaku—Vol. 4—Seisaku to Kanri (Lecture Series Vol. 4 Policy and Management), Tokyo: Yuhikaku, pp. 235–269.
—— (2004) "Partnership no Shippai: Governance Ron no Tenkai Kanousei (Partnership Failure: the Study of New Governance)", Nenpou Gyousei Kenkyu (The Annals of the Japanese Society for Public Administration), No. 39, pp. 26–47.
Osborne, D. and T. Gaebler (1992) Reinventing Government: How the Entrepreneurial Spirit Is Transforming the Public Sector, New York: Addison-Wesley.
Pekkanen, R. (2006) Japan's Dual Civil Society: Members without Advocates, Stanford, CA: Stanford University Press.
Pierre, J. and B. G. Peters (2000) Governance, Politics and the State, Basingstoke: Macmillan Press.

Reed, S. (1986) *Japanese Prefectures and Policy Making*, Pittsburgh, PA: Pittsburgh University Press.
Rhodes, R. A. W. (2000) "Governance and Public Administration", in J. Pierre (ed.), *Debating Governance: Authority, Steering, and Democracy*, Oxford: Oxford University Press, pp. 54–90.
Samuels, R. (1983) *The Politics of Regional Policy in Japan: Localities Incorporated?*, Princeton, NJ: Princeton University Press.
Schreurs, M. A. (2002) *Environmental Politics in Japan, Germany, and the United States*, Cambridge: Cambridge University Press.
Schwartz, F. (1998) *Advice and Consent: The Politics of Consultation in Japan*, New York: Cambridge University Press.
Serageldin, I. (1996) *Sustainability and the Wealth of Nations: First Steps in an Ongoing Journey*, Washington, DC: The World Bank.
Serageldin, I. and A. Steer (eds.) (1994) *Making Development Sustainable: From Concepts to Action*, Washington, DC: World Bank.
Sørensen, E. and J. Torfing (2009) "Making Governance Networks Effective and Democratic through Metagovernance", *Public Administration*, 87(2), pp. 234–258.
—— (eds.) (2007) *Theories of Democratic Network Governance*, Basingstoke: Palgrave Macmillan.
Takahashi, H. (2000) *Shimin Syutai no Kankyo Seisaku* (Environmental Policy Centering around Citizens), Tokyo: Kojin Sha.
Tsuru, S. and H. Weidner (eds.) (1989) *Environmental Policy in Japan*, Berlin: Edition Sigma.
Ueta, K. (1996) *Kankyo Keizaigaku* (Environmental Economics), Tokyo: Iwanami Shoten.

# 7
# Transition to sustainable urban development in Japan: A case study of an antipollution movement in Nishiyodogawa Ward, Osaka City

*Mayuko Shimizu*

A number of local communities in Japan have experienced pollution as an environmental and social crisis. It not only causes environmental deterioration resulting in health hazards but also seriously damages the very foundations of human communities. The destruction of lives and livelihoods through pollution can be considered a violation of fundamental human rights and an infringement of social justice that may spark conflicts. Because any pollution-causing economic activity could possibly end with the devastation of natural and human capital, it is very likely to cause various risks in the long term unless appropriate countermeasures are taken. Pollution indeed is a product of unsustainable development.

Movements instigated by pollution victims in Japan have put pressure on the government, companies and civil society to recognize the importance of environmental conservation as a key political and social challenge. As severe pollution damages have been revealed consecutively, public concern about these problems has been growing. Under such public pressure, a series of environmental laws were enacted. Among them was the revision of the Basic Law for Environmental Pollution Control in 1970 which is regarded as the implementation of Japan's first systematic environmental policy (Hashimoto, 1988). The enactment of the Pollution-Related Health Damage Compensation Law in 1973 is said to be among the most notable achievements of pollution victims' appeal.

According to Schreurs (2002), however, people's intense interest in and their organized movements against tremendous pollution damages failed to remain a driver for environmental policies once some judicial and political measures were taken. She holds that Japanese people did not consider environmental problems as important policy challenges until Japan came under pressure from the international community to address global environmental issues. After the oil shock in 1973, there was a regression in Japan's environmental policy called the "backlash" driven by the business world aside from the settlement of several specific cases. It can be said that no antipollution movement effectively reversed this backlash to date.

Did environmental movements by pollution victims in Japan disappear after the institutional compensation for victims and the environmental policies implementation were achieved to a certain extent because "the wind was taken out of their sails" (Schreurs, 2002: 71)? This chapter discusses a case in which a victim's movement continues to thrive in a different form. The focus is on whether the efforts made in this case go beyond simple antipollution activities and pursue sustainable urban development. Antipollution movements in Japan directly questioned the accountability of pollution-causing companies and the negligence of the government. In fact, pollution lawsuits ruled that the accused companies or the government had assumed responsibility for the damages in question at least to a certain extent. However, if one pursues the revitalization of damaged natural and social environments in the context of sustainable urban development, one has to be concerned with community governance beyond discussions as market failure and government failure.

For the case discussed in this chapter, some victims, through their long, painful struggle with pollution, came to understand that local communities needed to be strong enough to prevent pollution in the future. Since then, activist victims have hoped to establish a new framework of environmental governance based on the local community and involved new actors who had not directly participated in the past movement.

This chapter addresses the questions of how their various activities and current strategies differ from past antipollution movements and whether there is a significant crossover between the new framework and the shift to autonomous governance for sustainable urban development.

## Conceptual background

The concept of governance has different historical roots. It refers to something broader than government and is often used to describe the changing quality and role of the public sector (Kjær, 2004; Bevir, 2009). New public challenges, such as environmental issues, have made governance a major topic of debate on a system of rules under which policies are made and implemented by a network of many different actors.

Sustainable development has also been defined in many ways. Based on the extensive literature on sustainable development, the Organisation for Economic Co-operation and Development (OECD; 2008: 30) argues that "[i]t might be useful . . . to see the advent of sustainable development as a significant change in how people and governments perceive their activities." In the same book, sustainable development is interpreted also as an idea that has three aspects: a conceptual framework, a process and an end goal. Dryzek (2005) understands sustainable development as a discourse that will inspire experimentation, rather than a clearly defined target or practical guidance. According to him, various ideas about sustainable development are to be discussed in such discourse. It also entails the implementation and verification of experimental policy programs in different localities that could open new possibilities. Sustainability is largely social learning, involving exploratory and variable approaches (Dryzek, 2005: 158). Aside from whether sustainable development is a goal, process or discourse, each of them seems to accurately epitomize one aspect thereof. In this context, sustainable development can be understood both as a socially structured concept for dealing with certain dynamic changes in society and a goal to be achieved.

According to Dryzek (2005), the structure of a political system changes during the process of pursuing sustainable development with a vertical and horizontal transfer of power at different levels. He believes, therefore, that this dynamic process is most suitable for a decentralized, networked governance approach based on the participation of and interactions between various actors inside and outside the government. This is because it helps build non-hierarchical relationships between actors in a pluralistic world. Dryzek also argues that extensive involvement in the discourse on sustainable development can channel efforts for decentralized, networked governance toward sustainable development as a common good.

Such dynamic governance will hold a prominent position in the long-term view of sustainable development. In today's complex society, Loorbach (2007) advocates governance transition management in the process of structural social change toward sustainable development. The principles of such governance include multi-actor policy-making, multi-perspectivity, experimenting with various options, learning and reflexivity. Governance in the process of shifting to sustainable development is thus understood as an open process in which diverse actors repeatedly learn new ways of thinking and innovate their actions. He argues that because sustainable development is a socially constructed concept, the process of pursuing its realization fits better with networked governance than with a hierarchical one intended to achieve given objectives effectively and efficiently, at least at the starting point of the process.

This understanding of sustainable development as a dynamic process has shed more light on diverse actors and their interactions in an urban community. Rydine (2010) puts great importance on networked governance based on interactions between diverse actors and learning as a core concept for sustainable urban development. According to Rydine, learning means learning norms and values through interactions with other actors, not a one-sided infusion of knowledge from experts. She sees learning as an indispensable element for changing governance structure because it entails reframing the agendas, perceptions and even identities of actors. Furthermore, it also plays an important role in developing resistance to accepting established ways of seeing things.

Then, how can we recognize changes in governance? Van Bueren and ten Heuvelhof (2005) understand sustainable urban development not as a substance but as a process and analyse the criteria for evaluating governance arrangements focusing on inner changes of stakeholders and changes in relationships between actors about several factors. Among such factors are satisfaction of policy outcomes, interaction patterns, collective learning about the nature of sustainable urban development and social learning about the actions needed to achieve sustainable urban development.

The concept of sustainable development was created to review unsustainable, unfair development involving resource depletion and inequalities in the quality of life. The question is how governance should be designed in order to change the social structure responsible for the unsustainable reality and people's perceptions. In this way, discourses of governance for sustainable development emphasize unfixed processes that result in structural changes of specific societies. In other words, no one can define the definite goal of sustainable development. Therefore, it is difficult to "correctly" evaluate the expected outcome of a process toward sustainable development with generally accepted standards. However, it is meaningful in both a theoretical and a practical sense to discuss whether a case of governance is on a right path to sustainable development focusing on the interactions between actors and their visions.

# A case study of an antipollution movement in Nishiyodogawa Ward, City of Osaka

## Victims' movements

### Health hazards and the organization of victims

Air pollution, one of the oldest types of pollution, occurred in different locations throughout Japan soon after the modernization of the country. Many suburban areas in Japan experienced rapid urbanization and industrialization after the latter half of the nineteenth century, and air pollution became a social problem causing damages to labourers and crops. Although there were some well-known cases of victims' appeals, they were fundamentally different from victims' successful movements after World War II in terms of governance because such early efforts hardly affected the government and responsible companies. Nishiyodogawa Ward, Osaka City, originally was a farming village near Osaka, Japan's second-largest city. After the modernization, the village was transformed into an industrial area to which many labourers flocked. Residents experienced air pollution caused by smoke from steel mills and other factories. Not until after the war did pollution victims begin organizing themselves and appealing for pollution control and compensation through negotiations with governments and companies and eventually lawsuits.

The Nishiyodogawa area started suffering from air pollution again in the 1950s when Japan experienced a dramatic recovery from the war. At that time, it became one of the key areas in a major industrial zone with increasingly concentrated factories. Air pollution in Nishiyodogawa at that time was caused by different sources including smoke from machines and chemical factories within the area, smoke from thermal power plants in adjacent areas and exhaust fumes from cars driving on nearby highways. A quarter of the population suffered from chronic bronchitis, bronchial asthma and other diseases at its peak. Various burdens created by these diseases deprived them of their jobs. Although some of them moved to less polluted places, others had to remain in Nishiyodogawa for economic and therapeutic reasons. Few doctors had enough understanding of pollution-derived disease.

The antipollution movements in Nishiyodogawa began with an incident in 1969. Several people, mainly from local community associations and Parents and Teachers Associations (PTAs), lodged complaints about the high level of sulphur against the responsible factory. Because the factory managers did not listen to them, they organized a citizen group through which they disseminated information on this issue to more residents and negotiated with the factory management. Similar citizen groups were formed to address pollution problems, such as a plan to establish a new chemical factory in the ward and the designation of a neighbourhood as an industrial district in an urban planning decision. Through these experiences, residents in Nishiyodogawa became increasingly conscious of pollution issues and movements against them.

The other starting point was the establishment, in 1972, of the Nishiyodogawa Pollution Victims and Families Association (hereafter, Victims Association), one of the most important actors in the antipollution movements in the area. The background of the establishment was that YODOKYO Medical & Welfare Foundation (hereafter, YODOKYO) had contributed to the improvement of local medical services for labourers in Nishiyodogawa as part of its traditional labour movement. While calling for the establishment of a universal health care system and the improvement of social security programs and medical services for labourers, YODOKYO opened some clinics in the ward and organized a grass-roots organization in each district to provide community-based health care services. In 1970, a pollution-related-disease testing centre was established within the clinic funded by a joint project. There, people suffering from pollution-related diseases were diagnosed and certified as pollution victims to be eligible for institutional compensation. Then, this clinic became an early centre of the victim's antipollution movement in Nishiyodogawa. At the time the Victims Association was established in 1972, there were 2,600 officially certified patients in Nishiyodogawa (Nishiyodogawa Pollution Victims and Families Association, 2008).

The major drivers of the rise of the antipollution movements in Nishiyodogawa were the organized labor movements focusing on community-based health care activities and the official framework of certification and compensation of pollution patients under the Pollution-Related Health Damage Compensation Law. As discussed later in this chapter, however, the antipollution movements faced challenges that could not be solved only with institutionalized compensation.

*Political actions for compensation and pollution control*

Several pollution-related diseases became known in Japan in the late 1950s. In most cases, victims were not empowered enough to force the companies to take responsibility for health damages caused by the pollution. However, the lawsuit brought by victims of Niigata Minamata disease in 1967 said that it encouraged victims in other pollution-affected areas to pursue polluter's responsibility in court. These lawsuits triggered protest against pollution among the general public that was reflected later in the enactment of the series of pollution-related laws in 1970, and the Pollution-Related Health Damage Compensation Law (hereafter, the Compensation Law) in 1973.

Meanwhile the Victims Association in Nishiyodogawa was actively involved in political activities. The association also lobbied for the Osaka city government to establish its own compensation system for certified pollution victims in 1973. However, the 1973 Oil Shock triggered a backlash from an opposition believing environmental policy was a brake on economic growth. There were two incidents epitomizing a regression in Japan's environmental policy at that time. One was the Environment Agency's announcement of the relaxation of its environmental standards regarding nitrogen dioxide, contained within automobile gas emissions. The other was the revision of the Compensation Law in 1987 that terminated the official certification of air pollution victims.

There were also some moves to push back pollution control in Nishiyodogawa. In 1973, construction began to add a new raised highway over Route 43, a busy highway deemed to be a main source of air pollution. Additionally, in 1977, an area covering about 40 per cent of the Nishiyodogawa ward was designated a Restricted Industrial Zone by the Osaka city government. Although the designation was repealed in response to vehement opposition from local residents, there was a force aiming at further promoting the industrialization in the ward despite heavy environmental damages.

Meanwhile, the organization of pollution victims and advocacy activities for them gained momentum on a nationwide scale. In 1976, the National Liaison Council of Pollution Victims Association (NLCPVA) was formed by victims' associations across the country, and they started a nationwide campaign called the Pollution Victims Action Day. In each session of the campaign, victims made direct negotiations with and protests to the relevant governmental agencies. The Victims Association in Nishiyodogawa also actively worked with NLCPVA, particularly in the campaign against the revision of the Compensation Law, for a period of years and participated in direct actions such as sit-in protests. However, it did not succeed.

Victims involved in this nationwide campaign returned to their local activities, pledging to win their lawsuits to prove who was responsible for pollution. Then they shifted their strategy to a grass-rooted approach through which they pursued to solve problems in their local communities while continuing negotiation with the central government.

*The Nishiyodogawa Pollution Lawsuit supported by public empathy*

After the regression of environmental policy, Nishiyodogawa victims chose to take legal action mainly for two reasons. One was to get judicial judges to pressure the government to take more fundamental measures for pollution control and for compensation. The other was to have each polluting company recognize its responsibility for the damage done to the victims.

Owing to the commitment for political activities at the national level and the defendants' negative attitude, the lawsuit was protracted. Seeking an early conclusion, the plaintiffs and their legal team decided to launch a grass-roots campaign. They made visits to labour unions, consumers' cooperative societies and consumer associations in which victims themselves talked about pollution damages. These activities eventually helped increase support. In 1990, they held an event called Kyokan Hiroba (Sympathy Park) in 13 different areas in order to gain broader support for and public understanding of pollution and environmental problems. Meanwhile, the Victims Association submitted a petition with around 1,300,000 signatures collected in Osaka Prefecture appealing for the elimination of air pollution and an early settlement of all cases to the court. In fact, it was a difficult lawsuit for the plaintiffs because there is no precedent. It is said, however, that such grass-roots campaigns affected the court's decision recognizing the liability of the defendants from moral standpoint (Nishiyodogawa Pollution Victims and Families Association, 2008).

The Victims Association began reflecting an idea of rehabilitating the environment and community in Nishiyodagawa before the settlement of the lawsuit. In 1988, they organized public meetings to ask various citizen's groups or parties for their support for the lawsuit. In 1989, they held a symposium on community planning of the Nishiyodogawa area under the theme of uniting global environmental issues and community-based actions. From then on, they began to be aware not only of the responsibility of the government and companies but also of the need for community development without pollution in their activities.

In 1991, the lawsuit went in favour of the plaintiffs with respect to the liability of the accused companies. In 1995, a settlement between the plaintiffs and the defendant companies was reached in the lawsuit through their negotiations. At first, the largest of the defendant companies, an electricity company, was reluctant to make negotiations with the plaintiffs about compensation. It is notable, however, that the company was interested in accepting the plaintiffs' request to offer its cooperation for the revitalization of the community of Nishiyodogawa (Nishiyodogawa Pollution Victims and Families Association, 2008).

Because the plaintiffs showed their intention to pursue the renewal of the community without pollution, the lawsuit became something more than a simple conflict between the private interests, created a wave of empathy among the public and encouraged all concerned parties to address the pollution problem as a public issue.

## Revitalization of the community

### Establishment of the Aozora Foundation and knowledge accumulation

In 1991, the Victims Association unveiled (the preliminary draft of) the Nishiyodogawa Redevelopment Plan with the help of a group of urban policy specialists just before the first court decision on the lawsuit. The plan was repeatedly revised up to the sixth edition. It was the first community development plan proposed from pollution victims in the history of pollution in Japan. In 1995, the plaintiffs of the lawsuits won a settlement of about 40 billion yen from the defendant companies. They decided to use 1.5 billion yen of the settlement for improving the environmental health and living conditions of the plaintiffs and their neighbours and for revitalizing the local community, without distributing the money among individual plaintiffs. For this purpose, they established the Center for the Redevelopment of Pollution-damaged Areas in Japan (the Aozora Foundation). During the preparation period, they held another symposium in order to outline the basic direction for the foundation's activities. They invited a broad range of people to it including not only supporters for their activities and lawsuit but also the government, economic organizations and experts in various fields. The following is the Aozora Foundation's statement of principle:

> Redeveloping polluted areas does not merely involve rejuvenating, recreating, and preserving the natural environment. In our way of thinking such redevelopment depends on recovering and improving the health of local residents; recovering and fostering community functions lost on account of economic-first development; rebuilding relationships of trust and cooperation among standpoint, obtaining the cooperation of local authorities, businesses, and all other social entities (Charter of The Aozora Foundation, 1996).

According to the leader of the Victims Association, this idea of revitalizing the community, which was not limited to pollution control and compensation, was totally new even in the policy-making scenes at the Environment Agency and other governmental agencies.

Soon after the establishment, the foundation was operated by a committee composed mainly of urban planning and policy researchers and practitioners under which each project was carried out with the participation of a committee member and volunteers. The foundation conducted a number of research projects commissioned by the Environment Agency and other organizations, and joint research projects with academics and the Victims Associations. The issues discussed through such research projects by experts, for the purpose of building urban environments without pollution, included possible solutions to land contamination, the creation of green spaces in mixed areas of industrial and residential districts and road maintenance with less pollution. Through these projects, approaches for community revitalization from pollution were explored. They included some basic research with the participation of local residents, such as one featuring interviews with people living in Nishiyodogawa including pollution victims by student volunteers in which interviewees talked about natural surroundings and lifestyles before the pollution aggravated the area (Muneta et al., 2000). The foundation's research efforts also included a case study on the environmental reclamation of industrial areas with the participation of experts and students of urban environment policy and planning. The project members collected information on some of the most-cutting-edge examples in the world such as Groundwork's famous efforts in the United Kingdom to recover brownfields and the Internationale Bauausstellung Emscher Park project in Germany.

The Aozora Foundation, as a non-governmental organization (NGO), aims at regenerating the nature and the community through community-based activities with many experts. As discussed more in the following sections, the foundation has become an important hub for learning networks to support the transition from the recovery from pollution to sustainable urban development.

*Collaboration for urban environment improvement*

In 1998, the plaintiffs of the Nishiyodogawa Lawsuit reached a settlement with the national government following the court's decision recognizing its responsibility for the health hazards of roadside residents. Pursuant to the settlement provisions, an official forum was established for discussions between the plaintiffs and the government about measures to prevent health problems caused by exhaust fume from automobiles on the road in question. The forum is the only place where the discussions are limited to the topics covered by the settlement provisions, and the decisions are not legally binding. Thus, it is very difficult for the victims to effectively affect the government's advanced environmental policy through the deliberations in the forum. In order to eliminate causes of pollution, the role of the government as the main actor to construct and maintain roads and public transportation networks appropriately is very important. However, the government is not always keen to be involved in antipollution projects here. Furthermore, the pollution victims, a minority of the society, do not have enough opportunities to reflect their opinions directly in the decision-making processes by the government. To change urban spatial structures requires the government and other authorities to change the centralized structure of their governance.

On the other hand, the Aozora Foundation started making increasingly experimental efforts in collaboration with different stakeholders several years after its establishment. It can be understood that the foundation started using its accumulated knowledge to take actions. In 2000, the foundation unveiled two proposals. One was a more detailed version of the aforementioned community redevelopment plan by pollution victims. The other was a proposal on TDM (transport demand management) that advocated the reduction of large trucks and the promotion of the use of low-emission cars. The latter was prepared in collaboration with a group of traffic planning researchers, and copies of the reports were distributed to various organizations in the area.

These reports were important material for further discussion among various local stakeholders and the foundation. For example, an eco-driving pilot program based on the TDM proposal was launched after a series of discussions and negotiations with the national government, local economic organizations and a trucking association. As part of this program, the foundation held a series of demonstration experiments using eco-driving navigation systems from 2003 to 2005 in Nishiyodogawa with the participation of 315 trucks from 39 transportation companies. The experiments showed that eco-driving, which is a driving style that reduces fuel consumption and increases safety, indeed improved fuel efficiency and safety. They also helped improve the morale of the participants as professional drivers. The foundation now holds eco-driving classes based on the results of the experiments.

The foundation's activities also include developing tools for communication with and education of local people such as their own guidelines for making environmental diagnosis maps for local people, educational video programs and textbooks on pollution in Nishiyodogawa, and its own library with stored information and materials about pollution problems. Among its educational tools is a card game to learn the idea of "food miles", a way of assessing the environmental impact of food consumption. Developed by a group of volunteer teachers and researchers in 2006, the card game has been used in the special lectures given by the foundation at schools and organizations. The purpose of this game is to encourage people to change their way of life by recognizing the environmental impact of their own choices. By playing the game, players come to understand traffic pollution as a contemporary issue as they learn the relationship between transportation and everyday life in a very familiar context. The process of learning through this game is not a one-sided infusion of structured knowledge but more like a process of learning new norms and values through interactions with diverse actors.

These communicative learning programs do not immediately change the structure of urban environments. However, they encourage city dwellers to change the way they behave by offering them an opportunity of learning, and thus affect the governance about the use of urban space.

*Building networks inside and outside the community*

Although the Aozora Foundation is involved in a broad range of projects, each of them has developed its own network of participants. Aiming at realizing a pollution-free society, one of the foundation's important missions is to provide information on antipollution activities in Nishiyodogawa and its efforts. China and other Asian nations have recently experienced serious environmental problems as they have gone through a dramatic economic growth. In order to share its experiences of pollution with people from Asian countries, the foundation has been active in interacting with them. It has formed an extensive global network through its various activities such as study tours, training programs, international symposia and the translation of pollution-related materials.

In 2007, Nishiyodogawa was designated as an ESD (Education for Sustainable Development) model area by the Ministry of Environment, and a platform for different local organizations, called the Nishiyodogawa ESD Commission, was established. The participating organizations include schools, citizen groups, companies, NGOs, universities and administrative agencies in the area. Among diverse activities through this platform was a program to make biodiesel fuel. In this program, a group of high school students made biodiesel fuel using a filter press from used edible oil collected from households and businesses in cooperation with local volunteer groups. The fuel was later used at community events and for municipal buses.

The Nishiyodogawa ESD Commission aims at preparing for a future pollution-free sustainable urban development. Meetings under the commission are held in a workshop style in which the participants exchange their ideas and opinions about problems and goals of urban development while planning future projects. The role of the Aozora Foundation at the Nishiyodogawa ESD Commission is not to allocate specialists and volunteers but to "coordinate" collaborations between diverse actors of the local community as a hub for networks. The Aozora Foundation provides them a place where they can get together to develop ideas about how they can cast a constructive concept of sustainable urban development into shape. They are now integrated into specific processes for achieving the foundation's big goal or the creation of a pollution-free sustainable urban community. In this sense, the foundation's activities are quite different in nature from antipollution activities in the past with clear-cut goals, such as the elimination of pollution and compensation of victims.

## Discussion and conclusion

### *Shift of the focus between national and local*

The stage of the antipollution movement was local at first, moved to national, and returned to the local community again. Focusing on the local level again, the movement could be transformed into community-based activities of the foundation, not just ending with political and legal settlement.

However, these shifts imply difficulties of moving towards a society without pollution. One is about its relationship with the government. Located on the periphery of metropolitan Osaka, Nishiyodogawa was bound to be categorized as a non-residential area, as an industrial area from the beginning. In fact, the government once tried to designate the ward a restricted industrial district. The political and economic functions required for such categorization by the government contradict the functions required for the regional community as a living environment. It seems quite natural in terms of distribution and construction efficiency that arterial highways are concentrated in Nishiyodogawa from a viewpoint of industrial development. Multi-level governance is needed to reconcile such competing interests.

The governance within the community and the relationship between the community and the outside world seem to be two separate problems, though they mutually affect each other. A problem that cannot be solved in a local community could be solved at the national level. On the other hand, national-level politics sometimes has an impact at a local level when implementing policy. It is true that pollution victims associations, demanding the institutionalization of compensation of victims, have been significantly affected by national-level political conditions. For example, if a victims association receives support from a specific political party and related organizations for its political actions or lawsuits, it is very difficult to get support from those in a different political position at a local level. Governance for sustainable urban development has to be multilayered with different levels of legitimacy.

*Challenge of multilayered environmental governance*

Community-based activities of the foundation have also changed its property, from pursuing a given goal to constructing an interactive learning network. It represents the change of relational structure of relevant actors, from strongly tied members of an organization with a shared specific goal to a flexible network of local actors with various interests.

Comprehensive community regeneration entails not only the recovery of specific damages or the reclamation of environment. It includes the rehabilitation of the entire community in social and economic aspects. Thus, there are no clear definitions thereof just like sustainable development. Community regeneration and sustainable urban development can be achieved through a process of participation and learning. Many different experts and practitioners in various fields are involved in the activities of the Aozora Foundation. They work together, sometimes as volunteers, to conduct surveys and make proposals while building and expanding networks. The participation of local residents in such networks has recently become increasingly conspicuous. It seems that local residents joined in these networks not as participants of the foundation's activities. It is more likely that the foundation's projects triggered the emergence of networks involving local residents. Different networks of experts and local residents have been built for different themes. Several visible results, such as policy proposals and pilot programs, have been produced through these networks. There are even some permanent networks involved in constant activities. It seems that what Dryzek (2005: 154) describes as "decentralized dynamic networks that best suit sustainable development" have been formed around the Aozora Foundation.

*Reconstruction of the local collectivity*

Through 40 years, the focus of a series of efforts in Nishiyodogawa has changed from antipollution to making a sustainable urban community. It requires rebuilding the spatial and relational collectivity of a local community and gaining a function of coordinator of an actor's network. Regarding the former, the economic collectivity of many different factories as a source of pollution was proved in the lawsuits. A development plan to intensify such collectivity among polluting companies is very likely to prolong damages. Many different factories with spatial and economic collectivity are concentrated in Nishiyodogawa adjacent to residential structures. If this spatial structure is a fundamental factor of pollution there, it has to be redesigned.

In other words, partnership here entails not only collectivity created for economic reasons but also collectivity of local community residents based on their daily lives. The community-based activities by the plaintiffs of the lawsuits seeking an early decision of the court was not to create agitation, but to gain neighbours' understanding and support for their intention to restructure the existing collectivity causing pollution. Later, this intention was presented in the community renewal plan by them. The Aozora Foundation was established as the main actor for putting the plan into practice.

In order to turn the pollution victims' wish to build a new collectivity into a wish of the local community, the first thing that needed to be done was to clarify the defendant's responsibility for pollution damages. This was the most important prerequisite for demonstrating the significance of making structural changes in the community damaged by pollution as a public challenge. Specific processes for making such changes—what was to be done, by whom, how and why—were to be agreed on thereafter.

After the responsibility of the defendant was clarified to a certain extent through the lawsuits, activities by pollution victims in Nishiyodogawa were shifted to the Aozora Foundation based on dynamic networks of diverse actors. The staff members of the foundation have never included direct victims of pollution. Furthermore, many of them have never participated in antipollution activities. The post of chief director, however, has been filled by the former chairperson of the Victims Association and a lawyer involved in the lawsuit. One of the Victims Association's objectives, the elimination of pollution, was included in one of the goals of the Aozora Foundation in a more developed form, the construction of a local community which will cause no pollution in the future.

There is significant crossover between the renewal of polluted areas and sustainable urban development. The statement of principle of the Aozora Foundation emphasizes that the redevelopment of polluted areas entails not only the maintenance and rejuvenation of the natural environment but also various social and economic aspects such as pollution-free economic activities and the relationships of trust among diverse actors. In order to renew a polluted area, environmental, social and economic dimensions of sustainability need to be addressed. Everyone is at risk of becoming a victim of pollution. Therefore, the renewal of a polluted area means that all people can lead a healthy, fair, enriched life there. Sustainable development can be achieved if the natural and social environments allowing such a life are built and maintained, which can be passed on to the next generations.

Being an NGO aiming at sustainable urban development, the changes effectuated by the Aozora Foundation might be limited. The main challenge of environmental governance in Nishiyodogawa is turning such small changes into large, sustainable, structural changes. As urban communities in Nishiyodogawa are in the transition process to sustainable urban development, it is indispensable for them to secure the type of governance that could change the spatial, social and economic structures thereof. This is because such pollution was caused partly by such structures. Today several dynamic networks with new collectivity are being formed in Nishiyodogawa. Such networks did not exist when Nishiyodogawa was undergoing its worst period of pollution or even when the plaintiffs reached a settlement of the lawsuit. Such a relationship could be a basis of community governance in the process of transfer to sustainable urban development.

REFERENCES

Aozora Foundation (1996) Charter of the Aozora Foundation, Osaka: The Aozora Foundation.
Bevir, Mark (2009) Key Concepts in Governance, Sage Publications Ltd.
Dryzek, John S. (2005) *The Politics of the Earth: Environmental Discourses*, 2nd ed., Oxford: Oxford University Press.
Hashimoto, Michio (1988) *An Unofficial History of Environmental Administration: The Asahi Shimbun Company*, Tokyo, Asahi Shinbun-sha (in Japanese).
Kjær, Anne Mette (2004) *Governance*, Cambridge: Polity Press.
Loorbach, Derk (2007) *Transition Management: New Mode of Governance for Sustainable Development*, Utrecht: International Books.
Muneta, Yoshifumi, Kitamoto Toshio, Kanki Kiyoko and Aozora Foundation (2000) *Restoring the Natural Environment in a City: Urban Development*, Kyoto: Gakugei Publisher (in Japanese).
Nishiyodogawa Pollution Victims and Families Association (ed.) (2008) *Pollution in Nishiyodogawa*, Tokyo: Hon no Izumi Publisher (in Japanese).
OECD (2008) *Sustainable Development: Linking Economy, Society, and Environment*, Paris: OECD Publishing.
Rydin, Yvonne (2010) *Governing for Sustainable Urban Development*, London: Earthscan.
Schreurs, Millanda A. (2002) *Environmental Politics in Japan, Germany, and the United States*, Cambridge: Cambridge University Press.
Van Bueren, Ellen and Ernst ten Heuvelhof (2005) "Improving Governance Arrangements in Support of Sustainable Cities", *Environment and Planning B: Planning and Design*, 32, pp. 47–66.

# Part III
Democracy and institutional reforms for sustainable development

# 8
# Democracy in transition management for sustainable development

*Yukio Adachi*

It is sometimes asserted that an undeniable affinity or correlation exists between "sustainable development" as a norm of public policy and "democracy" as a political institution. The correlation found between sustainable development and democracy, however, is by no means strong or direct, and the gap between them cannot be ignored. Democracy does not necessarily guarantee sustainable development, nor is it an indispensable precondition of sustainable development. So, what kind of democracy is compatible with the goal of sustainable development? Under a system of democracy, and conforming to the democratic legal procedures, how is it possible to overcome the apparent democratic pathology of myopic public policy decisions being enacted one after another that ultimately hamper sustainable development? In this chapter, these concerns are fleshed out by examining institutional and policy implications of uncertainties and complexities facing transition management for the sustainable development.

It is no simple task to embed an ethical responsibility to future generations in real public policies by way of the democratic political system and the political process. Under democracy, the loudest tend to profit and those who do not fight for their rights or, as is the case with future generations, those who have no means to fight, are liable to be mistreated or ignored. Even with such apparent defects of democracy, however, it never follows that democracy is unnecessary for sustainable development, or undemocratic (authoritarian) political systems are preferable to a democratic political system for achieving sustainable development. Serious, that is, qualitative or hard, uncertainties and complexities to be adequately dealt with by decision-makers in the transition process for sustainable development make a shift "from government to governance" unavoidable,

---

*Transition management for sustainable development*, Ueta and Adachi (eds.), United Nations University Press, 2014, ISBN 978-92-808-1234-3

leading to an increasingly diffuse and cooperative style of policy-making and policy implementation.

However, even this still is not enough. What are further required in order to prevent democracy from degenerating into sheer tyranny of the myopic majority are self-restraint mechanisms built into democracy itself. Democracy is by no means, and should not be, a vehicle for negating power and leadership. No, on the contrary, we must ask ourselves the following questions: How many highly talented policy professionals have we fostered in society, and to what degree are they "utilized" in public governance and how much authority are they granted?

## What is sustainable development?

As is well known, the principle of sustainable development was originally advocated in the context of foreign aid, foreign investment and trade. It was vigorously propounded as a principle that called to the public and private sectors of developed countries for governmental development aid and private sector investment and trade that contributed to economic development and poverty reduction in line with an environmental protection model.[1]

Recently, however, the principle of sustainable development came to be recognized by international society, especially among developed countries, in the context of constitutional (institutional) transformations of governance system as well. Developed countries now find themselves pressed to conduct a full and fundamental review of their own "development" style and way of life in the light of sustainability. Without causing irreversible damage to the resilience of the developing country's ecosystem, developed countries do have the international responsibility of contributing to developing countries in accordance with the country's economic power while powerfully and doggedly promoting the transition to a sustainable society. And at the same time they should attempt to guarantee for their citizens, including future generations, a tolerable, healthy and culture-rich lifestyle more or less equivalent to that before the transition, if not a more prosperous or comfortable one. Developed countries are thus increasingly pressed to create a schedule for the transition to a more sustainable economic and social system, and to take responsibility for putting the theory into practice. In other words, governments in developed countries are now charged with the very difficult task of "guiding" the transition to a sustainable society by means of the management and control of an adaptive evolutionary process.

Sustainable development is widely recognized as a normative concept that influences long-term social change (development) and trends. In most countries, including Japan, both political and economic systems are created to address short-term and at the very least mid-term public problems, and function to this end with varying degrees of success. By contrast, very few countries have systems and policies whose mission is to formulate and manage long-term policies. Even where these exist, they rarely function to a satisfactory degree. The principle of sustainable development centres on how best to achieve long-term goals. As a result, we are faced with extremely challenging questions: What systems and frameworks are necessary for sustainable development, and how can these be established?

## Critique of the philosophy of social planning

How are long-term goals to be achieved? In the final analysis, long-term goals are achieved through implementation of appropriate measures to address the various types of pressing problems faced by the members of society, and this is the only way to achieve long-term goals. Hence, if long-term goals are to be more than just empty promises, it is necessary at every stage to introduce strict checks to determine whether public policies formulated and implemented for the purposes of solving short- and mid-term problems are not in conflict with long-term goals and whether these policies contribute to long-term goals and to what extent. At the same time, if a solution to a given problem apparently runs the risk of coming into conflict with a long-term goal, concessions and compromises may be deemed unavoidable.

Thus, achieving long-term goals is an extension of solving short- and mid-term problems. Hence, the design of public policies aimed at achieving long-term goals falls under the same constraints as the policies crafted to solve short- and mid-term problems. Contemporary advanced democracies are in general characterized by (1) determination and implementation of a policy through the democratic political process, (2) rivalry between the values of individual citizens, (3) complexities (being an elaborate system composed of a complex blend of diverse elements) and (4) a high degree of uncertainties. One must thus take on board these given preconditions and constraints and craft appropriate policies when attempting to achieve long-term goals. What we can draw from these points is that to pursue and achieve long-term goals, we require (1) the maximum possible dependence on the spontaneous order "crafted" by market mechanism (the maximum possible use of the innate self-organizing capacity of the market) and (2) the continuing process of trial and error, namely, sustained enterprise, through what is in some ways the very inefficient method of the political process in democracies.

To be emphasized in this regard is that, if public problems are in essence of "wicked" (that is, "badly structured") nature, as Rittel and Weber (1973) persuasively argued in their seminal article on policy design, we cannot expect answers to be forthcoming solely from science.[2] The domain of science is the analysis of events in all their forms. Science breaks down complex events into elementary parts, subjects each element to a precise analysis and, in so doing, forms a recognition and understanding of the event as a whole. What it does not do is make up a prescription for solving the wicked-type problems at hand. In spite of this blindingly obvious fact, many people still place great faith in science and its application in the form of technology as a means to solve public issues. The disposition towards (or ethos of) science/technology worship still binds people at large.

Without a doubt, the progress in science in recent years has brought many miracles and much good news. Much that was heretofore impossible has been brought into the realm of the possible. Even many of those things thought unchangeable, things that are our fate to be borne, subversions of which are held to be found only through prayer, are now considered just random attributes of the world that can be altered at will. We can now change our looks, even our sex, at a whim. Even the threats of nature and physical constraints that have plagued and tormented the human race for hundreds and thousands of years are now becoming malleable and manageable by human hands. How many things that were once the preposterous imaginings and dreams of the science fiction novel have become incontrovertible facts!

The philosophy of "policy design" based on the recognition that public problems to be dealt with by public policies are wicked-type problems is at the opposite pole from utopian anti-political thought which also appears in the thinking behind and practice of social planning, and is thus a form of thought that is inherently political. Here, the "philosophy of social planning" indicates a social plan for fundamental reconstruction of society through rigorous and "objective" analysis of the serious political, economic and social problems that trouble humankind, rather than a haphazard application of stopgap measures. To realize such a comprehensive plan in a forceful and organized manner, government would have to introduce measures and intervene across all aspects of citizens' lives, and public policies would be an essential tool to this end. Given that the philosophy of social planning relies heavily on the outcomes of "scientific" research, it should be clear to all that the philosophy of social planning has a definite affinity with the disposition towards science/technology worship. It can be said, thus, that philosophy of this stripe conflicts starkly with the philosophy of policy design. Indeed, the two are as different as oil and water.

The philosophy of social planning has its roots in the pioneering advocate of hedonistic utilitarianism, Jeremy Bentham. Its prototype was later largely completed by the French utopian socialists Henri de Saint-Simon and Auguste Comte. This philosophy calls for powerful state intervention in markets and social life in general. Intellectuals are divided as to whether to view the repressive political systems that wreaked havoc in the (former) socialist countries as the legitimate or illegitimate offspring of the philosophy of social planning, or even as an unconnected anomaly. Nevertheless, the philosophy of social planning joins the tide of science/technology worship mentioned previously and charms people for many years, in the Western capitalist countries and elsewhere. Highly favourable soil for the growth of this philosophy was provided by a number of experiences and events in the history of humankind. From the end of the nineteenth to the beginning of the twentieth century was great upheaval in the format of the state (from the night watchman state to the administrative, or welfare, state) in a large number of west European countries, which was accompanied by massive expansion and diversification of the function of the state. There was also the United States' massive experiment, the New Deal, with roots in the Great Depression. In addition, during the two World Wars, there was a wartime economy and corporatism as well as the formulation and implementation of large-scale post-war reconstruction plans.

It is common knowledge that the most militant critic of the philosophy of social planning is F. A. Hayek. In comparison with a spontaneous order, which is a dynamic system formed from free interpersonal interactions and is capable of automatically regulating its own internal environment, social planning, when formulated and performed without sufficient care, is far from being good news for humankind; rather, it can invite great disaster. In the eyes of Hayek (1960), the attempt, through the guidance of a powerful centralized administration—to reform society in an organized and planned way according to some blueprint for an ideal society—can but harm the smooth operation of society's innate function for self-ordering. In a similar spirit, Michael Oakeshott and many other modern conservatives place the abstract reasoning (what Hayek christened "constructive rationalism") that appears in the philosophy of social planning at odds with collective and experiential wisdom. Moreover, they have sought to protect traditions, which are the crystallization of experiential wisdom, and have sounded the alarm bell regarding the large risk posed by drastic social reforms (Oakeshott, 1962). Karl Popper (1945), the famous social philosopher and advocate of piecemeal social engineering, drew the conclusion that the philosophy of social planning is an extremely reckless form of utopian social engineering, pointing out the dangers therein.

The above criticism of the philosophy of social planning appears to be sufficiently convincing. But what exactly is wrong with the philosophy and practice of social planning? Put simply, we cannot expect policymakers and executors to have the high level of knowledge and skills required for the formulation and management of appropriate long-term social planning. Moreover, advocates of social planning either ignore or dismiss the obvious fact that policy science and the other social sciences have not developed yet the expertise and knowhow necessary for such a venture and will probably not do so in the future.

In reality, there is almost no future for any social planning or social management that neither places any trust in the social integrative function of spontaneous ordering nor makes any attempt to check itself or to adjust its trajectory from sub-governmental levels after passing through the political process. Without a centralized government in possession of great political power, it is impossible to implement a comprehensive plan in line with a predetermined schedule by silencing all opposition to the plan's execution and by effectively unmasking and preventing any attempts at sabotage. Even if one were to concede that such a plan could be executed as planned, it would be unthinkable that it would in reality bring the desired results.

## Responsibility to future generations

Although the phrase "responsibility to future generations" has become firmly established in our vocabulary, by no means can we say that we have successfully translated this responsibility into a "viable ethic" that amounts to more than mere words. Frankly, to what degree an ethics of responsibility to future generations has been achieved is extremely unclear. Nor is it clear to what degree it has been embodied in government policies that are adopted in parliament and enforced and managed by the government either directly through governmental agencies or possibly indirectly through private industry and non-profit organizations (NPOs) or non-governmental organizations (NGOs). Democracy does not necessarily guarantee sustainable development, or transition to sustainable society, though it makes an indispensable component of the transition management for sustainable development.

As is commonly known, political actors attempt to push forward a great diversity of interests in the political arena. Under democracy, organization and politicization of interests tend to plague the process, resulting in an escalation in political manoeuvrings and in more intense checks and balances among organizations. As a result, when organizations find themselves engaged in not a one-shot game but rather in an itinerated game, they will eventually come to learn that, in the long run, their best interests are served by keeping their selfish demands reasonably in check. This is the process that Charles E. Lindblom (1965) terms "partisan mutual adjustment", and the more smoothly this process works, the more certain it is that attempts at domination and flagrant abuses by privileged interests (pressure groups) will come to see significant decreases.

However, when more and more citizens become aware of and informed about political initiatives, and the more they come to participate actively in the political process through various political associations—that is, the more democracy matures—the more politicians endowed with the formal authority to make policies will come to fear accusations of being "unfair". They hope to avoid to the best of their ability being labelled as a politician in the pocket of special interests. Inevitably then, they will try to strike some kind of compromise to meet the demands of conflicting parties. Of course, although this in itself is not problematic, careful attention must be paid to the way in which this balance is achieved. By far, the easiest way for politicians to accomplish this is to secure maximum returns for their client groups whom they rely on for financial backing and votes and to give the leftovers to non-client groups, on one hand, all while charming as many voters as possible with excessive lip service, on the other. Political actors in democracies can hardly ignore the fact that support from the electorate, or rather, "popularity", is the ultimate basis for legitimizing their power, and when they deem it feasible, the vast majority of politicians will regularly resort to exploiting this tactic.

However, a direct consequence of this is that public expenditures tend to be grossly inflated. Its harm will not be so desperately overwhelming, as long as voters and politicians cling to the overarching principle of "making the main beneficiaries of public policy pay the lion's share of the cost" (making the present generation deriving the most benefit pick up the bill for the policies and not shifting the cost to future generations). Nevertheless, if this constraint should be reduced to the status of a false pledge, democracy unceremoniously lapses into "interest group liberalism" (Lowi, 1979) or "bargaining democracy" (Hayek, 1960), resulting in myopic tendencies that may lead us down a path to self-destruction. Democracy is not necessarily in agreement with sustainable development and it is unclear whether democracy can overcome its myopic tendencies. To begin with, is it even possible for democratic philosophies and institutions to come to terms with an ethics of responsibility to future generations, and if so, how can this be accomplished?

German philosopher Hans Jonas, whose ideas continue to be a beacon of inspiration for today's environmental theorists and practitioners, holds that although no other system of government compares to democracy, it is difficult to rest our hopes on the outcomes of democratic politics. He was sceptical about the compatibility of the politics of democracy with the ethics of responsibility to future generations:

> According to those principles and procedures [of representative government], only *present* interests make themselves heard and felt, and enforce their consideration. It is to them that public agencies are accountable, and this is the way in which concretely the respecting of rights comes about (as distinct from their abstract acknowledgement). But the *future* is not represented; it is not a force that can throw its weight into the scales. The nonexistence has no lobby, and the unborn are powerless. Thus accountability to them has no political reality behind it in present decision-makings, and when they can make their complaint, we, the culprits, will no longer be there. This raises to an ultimate pitch the old question of the power of the wise, or the force of ideas not allied to self-interest, in the body of politic. What force shall represent the future in the present? (Jonas, 1984: 22)

Under democracy, the political awareness (political preference) of the citizenry ultimately determines in what direction political society should move. Therefore, if we imagine that the majority of citizens take on an extremely short-sighted (present-worship) mentality in their role as voters, it follows that, realistically speaking, they are sure to support measures that attempt to improve present conditions (the assurance of a richer and more pleasant life) at a cost to future generations. What can be done to avoid arriving at this rather grave state of affairs?

## Democratic measures for correcting the myopia of democracy

As shown in the preceding arguments, it is no simple task to embed an ethical responsibility to future generations in real public policy by way of the democratic political system and the political process because democracy does not intrinsically hold the promise of sustainable development.

Generally, for developed countries that have already achieved a series of mutually related processes of industrialization, urbanization and democratization, it makes no sense to construct a frame that tries to make across-the-board comparisons between democratic political systems and authoritarian political systems. What these countries should question, and what makes more sense in the first place, is not which of the two mutually conflicting political systems, a democratic system and an authoritarian system, should be adopted; rather, how we can monitor and correct the myopia of democracy? In other words, how we can decrease the possibilities of such decisions that conflict with the long-term interest of society being adopted and implemented through legitimate democratic channels.

It may sound somewhat paradoxical but the first thing that must be done is to fully explore the possibility of making democracy more substantive and engaging. Specifically, attempts need to be made to remove, to the greatest extent possible, factors that may inhibit the proper functioning of the mechanisms of partisan mutual adjustment; and the number of opportunities for citizen participation in the policy process needs to be expanded. To this end, there is a need to promote a chain of systemic reforms that will result in more checks on the myopia of democracy such as

1. more transparency in policy-making and implementation processes;
2. promotion of more thorough information disclosure;
3. strengthening democratic control over government institutions (i.e., enhancing accountability);
4. encouraging/enhancing citizenry's participation in the policy process;
5. reviewing the rules of deliberative proceedings, thus stimulating and upgrading the policy deliberation in the parliament;
6. fostering citizenry's political/democratic literacy;
7. promoting the decentralization of authority based on the "subsidiary principle"; and
8. correcting for situations where economic disparities lead to disparities in political power or influence.

To expand citizen involvement in the process of formulating, making, evaluating and implementing policies, however, does not necessarily guarantee or enhance the possibility for the adoption and implementation of far-sighted public policies that would contribute to sustainable development. Nevertheless, to the degree that they do not actively participate in that process, its true nature will remain unknown to them, making it impossible for them to have an impact on that process in any way, nor will they be able to reflect individual preferences in policy choices. Under a democratic political system, only through active participation in democratic policy process can they acquire the knowhow—or rather the knowledge, ability and virtue expected of citizens in democracies—for reforming the circumstances of political society in accordance with democratic rules.

Second, every opportunity to "launder" the political preferences of citizens, making them more public minded, should be pursued. People's political preferences are not fixed; they do change and can be changed. If the preferences of the citizenry become the embodiment of an ethics of responsibility to future generations, and accordingly, if central political agents such as journalists, bureaucrats and politicians opt to, or are forced to, change their political preferences, then the possibility for the adoption and implementation of public policies that contribute to sustainable development will surely be increased in democracies.

Of course, given that there is probably no stronger incentive than self-interest, it is no simple matter to change people's preferences in the direction of altruism and public-mindedness. Although it is true that simply one act or incident may have a great impact on people's preferences, leading to a dramatic change in public opinion, such is rarely the case. Therefore, what is most important for both institutional and policy designers is always to bear in mind that, for the time being, people's current sense of self-interests is more or less fixed, resistant to change. In other words, institutions and policies should be designed, which are most likely to ensure people's acting in accordance to their own sense of self-interests to bring about the desired social outcome.

Nonetheless, there is also a problem with such a design strategy that attempts to make the "public use of private interests" (Schulze, 1977). To begin with, the calculation regarding what level of people's self-centredness (egoism) to assume when designing a policy or an institution is by no means a simple one. Even when applying the familiar political measures of taxation and subsidy, if the analyst miscalculates the degree of people's self-centredness when deciding the amounts of them (if the average citizen is more self-centred than the analyst estimated), there is the danger that the original intent of the policy will not be realized, because there remain a considerable number of people who would not react in the way that the analyst expected. Inversely, if the analyst tries to avoid this situation, he/she may end up sweetening the pot too much (with excessively generous tax deductions and subsidies), and despite accomplishing the immediate task at hand, it would likely lead, in the long-run, to the fostering of self-centredness and state-dependence mentality.

In line with the (somewhat stereotypical) slogan "from government to governance", which expresses the idea of a co-operative society, the ranks of people engaged in policy design have begun to swell. Now, not only politicians and bureaucrats, but also a number of policy actors in civic and market sectors have come to be involved in the process of public governance for cooperatively managing public affairs. Although it is normally a good idea for anyone who wants to be an effective policy designer to try to make the most use of the tactic of appealing to the self-interest of people, it is also important to remember at the same time to think over how it is possible to foster and strengthen the sense of enlightened self-interest (public-mindedness) of citizenry. As long as people hang on to their current lifestyle or preferences, a set of serious problems that Japan and the world now face such as the skyrocketing financial debt and global warming is unlikely to be mitigated. The increase of the number of people who are ready, willingly or grudgingly, to accept the kind of policies that are undoubtedly desirable for the society as a whole in the long run but are unlikely to lend to their own well-being, often causing drawbacks, inconveniences and unfavourable circumstances, is in this sense an indispensable precondition for establishing a multi-level environmental governance for achieving sustainable development.

In correcting the myopia of democracy, the role of public interest groups that find their mission in realizing or expanding the kind of interests to be differentiated from sheer private/special interests is decisively large. The same can also be said about lobbyists for public-interest groups, and political entrepreneurs trying to represent the voice of minority groups. Policy debates among citizens should also be much more stimulated. As people actively participate in public forums that do not allow them to justify policy measures from the point of view of sheer self-interest, they will be better able to put their self-interests in perspective; any policy assertion needs to be justifiable from a societal or public point of view in public forums, whatever its main motivating factor might be for each citizen. Hence the vital need to foster and strengthen the public mind, roughly a disposition to willingly participate in cooperative societal endeavours to resolve public affairs, and we must always pursue this as one of the most important guiding principles for institutional and policy designs.

## Non-representative measures for sustainable development

Thus far, it has been argued that correcting the myopia of democracy is an indispensable prerequisite for sustainable development, and to this end, that we should press forward in accordance with the internal logic of democracy itself; namely, by making democracy more substantial and engaging. In addition, the author has also argued that we should do so by endeavouring to foster and strengthen the public-mindedness of citizenry as well as that of major political actors. However, even this is still not enough. What is further required, lest democracy should degenerate into the sheer tyranny of myopic majority, is a set of self-restraint mechanisms built into democracy itself.

The following three seem to be of special importance in this regard:
1. To reserve untouchable holy ground immune to the process of partisan mutual adjustment. There are many things in the world that are too precious to be easily changed by a simple majority rule, among which are, to mention just a few, the constitutional guarantee of human rights, budget balance as a constitutional principle put out by Buchanan and Wagner (1977), independent courts and independent career civil servants.
2. To establish a high-quality, and therefore non-representative, second chamber with significant but secondary powers, performing occasional but strict checks,

as one of its most important institutional missions, to determine whether public policies formulated by the first chamber and implemented either by governmental agencies or by NGOs to solve pressing (or midterm at the longest) problems might not cause irreversible damage to sustainable development (that is, to the long-term societal interests in which those of future generations should tacitly constitute an integral part).
3. To institutionalize an official advisory board to support executives—be they presidents, prime ministers, cabinet ministers (secretaries), governors or mayors—thus improving their performance and strengthening their authority. As has been most persuasively argued by Yehezkel Dror of the Hebrew University of Jerusalem in his seminal book on governance, *The Capacity to Govern: A Report to the Club of Rome* (2001), the most urgent need is, notwithstanding the recent textbook knowledge and public discourse preferences which tend to concentrate on the need to control and limit the powers of executives, to improve the performance of executives because of their actual and inescapable importance both in governance and in future-building in particular.

The significance of reserving untouchable holy ground immune to the process of partisan mutual adjustment is now widely acknowledged and substantiated in liberal or constitutional democracies. Parliamentary reforms, in general, and the authority and roles to be accorded to the second chamber specifically, have been one of the most hotly contested topics in democracies with a bicameral system. In stark contrast to these, it may not be too much to say that the third element has long been under taboo in a large number of democracies. The vital need to improve the performance of executives and thus to strengthen their authority has been unsuccessful thus far, at least in Japan, in establishing itself as agenda for the public forum. Rarely has it been openly debated, presumably because there are apparent dangers as well as good news in so doing.

Executives are often required, and of course love, to launch and make an eloquent speech about their "dreams" (that is, their cherished long-term policies). To weave the future is undoubtedly their mission. Unfortunately, however, they are normally too busy in "politics" (political bargaining) and in tackling a constant stream of pressing problems to think over processes or strategies by which to translate them into reality in the face of serious uncertainties, complexities and conflicts of values among voters. They do need, and should be supported by, an advisory board composed of highly talented policy professionals, recruited mainly from career civil servants and think-tank researchers who are able and determined to help executives make long-term, integrative strategic choices and to work as discreet mentors.

It goes without saying that strengthened authority of better-informed executives should be counterbalanced with powerful legislatures and oppositions with enhanced policy literacy. "Legislatures should be better equipped with professional staff to monitor and consider policy, and oppositions should be given the means to carry out improved policy reflection. . . . Consultative councils enjoying constitutional status, and composed of outstanding individuals, should therefore be set up to engage in policy deliberation on long-term critical issues, presenting evaluations, analysis, options and recommendations, to governance and the public at large" (Dror, 2001: 165–166). In the same vein, well-known American diplomat George F. Kennan proposed setting up a permanent, non-political advisory board supported by a small but first-rate staff studying issues of major long-term importance for the fortune of the country (Kennan, 1993).

The problem in Japan is that it has not yet succeeded in rearing a sufficient number of policy professionals with deep and comprehensive knowledge and with wide and long experience who are expected to do a good job as either advisors or consultants for executives and legislatures. This, the author believes, is partly because of the lack of independent think tanks working on broad, long-term and trajectory-setting policy issues. Japanese political system and political culture, the author is afraid, "lack the prerequisites for maintaining think tanks, for letting them operate freely enough to perform well, and for feeding the results of their studies into policy-making processes on crucial issues" (Dror, 2001: 163).

## The urgent need for drastic reform of the Japanese regulatory system

The transition to a sustainable society is no easy task for any Organisation for Economic Co-operation and Development (OECD) country. In the preceding two sections, it has been argued that correcting the myopia of democracy is an indispensable prerequisite for sustainable development; and to this end, that we should introduce a bunch of non-representative measures and energetically press them forward in addition to a series of the widely acknowledged measures mentioned previously to make democracy more substantive and engaging. This, however, is not still enough. For the rest of this chapter, the urgent need of drastic reform of Japanese regulatory system, taking nuclear regulatory system as an example, is argued.

On 11 March 2011, Japan was struck by an unparalleled 9.0 magnitude earthquake and a subsequent giant tsunami, which went on to trigger a level 7 core meltdown at the Fukushima nuclear power plant. This incident arguably placed Japan in the most dire straits of any OECD country, making it prohibitively "distressful" for Japan to successfully manage the transition to a sustainable society, at least for the time being. Although it would be a challenge to solve any one of the closely interlinked problems outlined in the following, Japan now finds itself having to solve them all at once. Furthermore, by now, it has become very clear to all that in tackling possibly the worst national crisis since the end of World War II, the government and cabinet of Japan, being in the position of primary responsibility regarding chaos-settling and reconstruction activities, have been grossly and regrettably lacking in a crisis management and a problem-resolving capacity.

The major challenges Japan now faces in the transition management for sustainable development include
1. urgently needing to drastically reduce the amount of government bonds outstanding, now reaching 1,000 trillion yen, approximately two times the gross domestic product (GDP);
2. somehow securing the vast amount of funds, resources and energy necessary for earthquake recovery activities, without further deteriorating the financial situation;
3. urgently reviewing its over-dependence on nuclear power and aggressively promoting the conversion or substitution to renewable energy sources;
4. maintaining or indeed exceeding its previous efforts to curb greenhouse gas emissions, as the host country of the Kyoto Protocol;
5. re-examining, from a cost-benefit perspective, initiatives such as dam construction and land reclamation, which run the risk of causing irreversible and fatal damage to the ecosystem;
6. aggressively and urgently pushing forward effective and feasible anti-depopulation measures and the compact city concept;
7. urgently designing and implementing effective and feasible measures to combat the rapidly decreasing number of children and an aging society; and
8. fundamentally reviewing the social security systems such as the health insurance system, pension system, safety-net system and employment assistance system, somehow accomplishing a soft-landing for more sustainable ones.

Japanese nuclear policy had been implemented, up until January 2001, through two separate government offices, the Ministry of International Trade and Industry (MITI) and the Science and Technology Agency (STA). The introduction, improvement and utilization of commercial nuclear power reactors; the import of uranium; the outsourcing of uranium enrichment; and spent fuel reprocessing was under the jurisdiction of MITI. The STA, on the other hand, mainly took charge of the research and development of nuclear technologies still in experimental stages.

The Long-term Program on Nuclear Energy constitutes the core of government nuclear policy, and the Atomic Energy Commission (AEC) is in the position to draw them up. Since AEC announced the first Program in September 1956, it has regularly revised the previous one. Despite the fact that AEC had such a vital policy-making role to play, it was not equipped with its own secretariat. The secretary of STA automatically assumed the office of chairperson of the commission, STA providing secretarial work for the commission. The AEC was, as it were, a bird without wings. It is partly for this reason that AEC rarely, if ever, directed or redirected the government nuclear policy of its own accord. Its function basically remained to confirm and authorize the consensus already reached among major policy actors with vested interests in the expansion of the nuclear sector.

The administrative apparatus in charge of monitoring nuclear-related facilities to ensure citizens' safety was the Nuclear Safety Commission (NSC), until September 2012 when it was substituted by the newly established Nuclear Regulatory

Authority (NRA). NSC was modelled after the Nuclear Regulatory Commission (NRC) in the United States. Unlike the NRC, which is an independent administrative commission with strong authority, however, the NSC was little more than a sheer advisory body, all rights to permit (or cancel) nuclear facilities resting with the STA or the MITI. Furthermore, although NRC commands its own staff of more than 3,000, the NSC was without either its own secretariat or staff. The NSC depended on the STA for secretarial work. Given this fact, it is quite natural that the NSC tended to be rather hesitant about advising new safety measures, the enforcement of which was, however highly desirable in terms of nuclear safety, likely to jeopardize the long-standing government policy to expand nuclear sector.

In the 1993 general election, the Liberal Democratic Party (LDP), which had been in power for almost half a century except for a very brief period soon after the end of World War II, suffered a historical defeat. It gave birth to the anti-LDP coalition government headed by Prime Minister Hosokawa. He appointed Mr. Eda, a well-known Diet member from the Social Democratic Party, to the post of secretary of STA. As the chairperson of AEC, he took initiative in trying to boost further information disclosure and democratization of the policy-making process in nuclear-related issues. Among the measures he instituted was a public hearing on the future direction of nuclear policy, which took place in March 1994. AEC members, for the first time in Japanese nuclear history, invited and heard from a couple of radical critics of nuclear-power generation. In this sense, the hearing was an epoch-making event in spite of the fact that the great majority of invited speakers were, more or less, sympathetic with the current government policy.

The 1995 accident at the fast-breeder reactor Monju accelerated this new current. On 23 January 1996, governors of three prefectures (Niigata, Fukushima and Fukui) that had hitherto accepted in aggregate over 60 per cent of all the nuclear reactors in Japan issued a joint proposal to the Japanese government. In this proposal, they stressed, first, the need for a more cautious approach on the part of government to such controversial issues as plu-thermal plans and nuclear fuel cycle projects. Second, they proposed that the government provide more opportunities (public forums) to openly discuss nuclear-related issues. Third, they urged a prompt review of the Long-term Program of Nuclear Energy. In response to this proposal, Prime Minister Hashimoto, who had by then successfully formed the LDP-led coalition government, directed the MITI and the STA to devise improvement measures for regulating the nuclear sector. One of the ideas coined by MITI and STA was to hold the Round-table Talk on Nuclear Policy.

The goals of the Talk were, like the public hearing in 1994, to further open debate and hopefully reach consensus concerning the future direction of nuclear policies. A series of talks, 11 in total, took place from March through September 1996. In total, six moderators and 127 speakers were carefully selected, nominally by AEC but substantially by the STA. However, each time a few speakers critical of the government nuclear policy were invited, the great majority proved to be always pro-government people. The historical significance of these talks is that the principle of publicity was upheld to a considerable degree. Proceedings of each talk and the minute records are open to the public and were even accessible through the Internet. Videotapes are also available. The talks, however, were closed without any remarkable achievements, only to make public once again the existence of intense confrontation over a number of key issues. The second series of round-table talks began in September 1998, and since then, such talks became institutionalized as a vital part of the policy-making process. There is no evidence, however, that they had any effect on government nuclear policy. The Japanese government had confirmed time and again, even after the level 4 criticality accident at a uranium processing plant operated by JCO Co. Ltd on 30 September 1999, that the core of nuclear policy remained, as before, in the development of fast-breeder reactors, implementation of plu-thermal plans and promotion of nuclear fuel cycle projects.

On 3 December 1997, the Administrative Reform Committee headed by Prime Minister Hashimoto announced the basic principle for administrative reform. The new system started in January 2001. By far the most dramatic reform in the context of nuclear governance was the dismantling of the STA. The jurisdiction of the AEC and the NSC moved to the newly established Cabinet's Office. The giant Department of Economics and Industry gained control of most of the regulatory authority over the development and utilization of nuclear energy. The responsibility for the implementation of nuclear policy in general, on the other hand, became part of the Department of Education, Science and Technology, with the exception of the development and utilization of nuclear energy.[3]

In spite of this administrative reform in 2001, Japanese nuclear governance has not undergone so substantial an improvement, as revealed in a catastrophic manner by the level-7 core meltdown at Fukushima Nuclear Power Plant. The NSC undoubtedly failed to fulfil its administrative mission, notwithstanding its strengthened authority and responsibility. The long-standing and much criticized characteristic of the Japanese regulatory system, namely, that the one and same department or agency simultaneously promotes and regulates a specific policy area, has little changed. The Nuclear and Industrial Safety Agency (NISA), a newly established nuclear regulatory agency by the 2001 administrative reform, remained, together with the Agency for Natural Resources and Energy in charge of the stable supply of natural resources and energy (including nuclear energy), an agency within the Department of Economics and Industry. Herein exists one of the most critical reasons why the Japanese nuclear policy network, which is often pejoratively called the "nuclear village", was unable to prevent and effectively deal with the severe accident.[4]

## Conclusion

The principle of sustainable development, which was originally advocated in the context of governmental development aid and private sector investment and trade of developed countries vis-à-vis developing countries, has come to be widely recognized, especially in developed countries, as one of the leading guidelines for weaving the future, which requires an ingenious management of long-term transition process towards a more and more sustainable society by means of steadily transforming the economic and social systems of each country.

Given that the transition to a sustainable society as a long-term societal goal can be achieved only through deliberate and skilful handlings of successively occurring pressing problems, and measures to deal with pressing day-to-day problems are politically chosen in the context of conflict of values, complexities and uncertainties, the philosophy of social planning, that neither places any trust in the integrative function of spontaneous social and economic transactions among citizenry nor makes any attempt to check itself or adjust its trajectory from subgovernmental levels, can never hope to be a leading mode of thinking for the transition management for sustainable development.

For the successful transition management for sustainable development, not only a series of democratic measures discussed in "Democratic measures for correcting the myopia of democracy," but also three of the unrepresentative measures mentioned in "Non-representative measures for sustainable development" to fight against and contain what the author calls "myopic tendencies of democracy", should be introduced. Furthermore, fundamental review of the regulatory system that has been long dominant in Japan, in which one and the same governmental department or agency simultaneously promotes on the one hand, and regulates a specific policy area in the name of equity, efficiency, safety or even social justice, on the other, should be urgently made.

## Notes

1. The final report of the Brundtland Commission, *Our Common Future*, offered the following definition of sustainable development: "Development that meets the needs of the present without compromising the ability of future generations to meet their own needs" (The World Commission on Environment and Development, 1987). To be noted in this regard is that "[b]ecause the Brundtland Commission put much emphasis on the needs of the poor in developing countries, many observers thought its message was poverty reduction and the elements that can support it—market access for developing countries, education, and basic public health, etc. Others, principally in industrialized countries, saw the report as encompassing their own needs to sustain, from generation to generation, high living standards, including a clean environment" (Johnston, 2002).
2. Rittel and Webber (1973: 161–167) characterized "wicked" problems as follows:
    1. There is no definite formulation of a wicked problem;
    2. wicked problems have no stopping rule;
    3. solutions to wicked problems are not true-or-false, but good-or-bad;
    4. there is no immediate and ultimate test of a solution to a wicked problem;
    5. every solution to a wicked problem is a "one-shot operation";
    6. wicked problems do not have an enumerable (or an exhaustively describable) set of potential solutions, nor is there a well-described set of permissible operations that may be incorporated into the plan;

7. every wicked problem is essentially unique;
   8. every wicked problem can be considered to be a symptom of another problem;
   9. the existence of a discrepancy representing a wicked problem can be explained in numerous ways;
   10. the planner has no right to be wrong. In contrast with the scientific community which does not blame its members for postulating hypotheses that are later refuted so long as the author abides by the rules of the game, in the world of planning and wicked problems no such immunity is tolerated. Planners are liable for the consequences of the actions they generate.
3. For more details about the nuclear regulatory system and policy until the administrative reform in 2001, see Adachi (2002).
4. We have to wait to see if, and to what extent, the Nuclear Regulatory Authority, which was established in September 2012 as a regulatory organization institutionally guaranteed a high-level of independence from any governmental agency, could possibly change the Japanese long-standing regulatory "culture" without being "captured" by the very objects of regulatory administration (i.e., the so-called nuclear village), and resist political pressures, remaining politically neutral. The author wonders if the authority could continue to judge whether to give sanction to the requests, from electricity companies, of resuming or newly constructing nuclear power plants from purely scientific points of view.

## REFERENCES

Adachi, Yukio (2002) "Can the Japanese Nuclear Sector Survive?", *Seisaku-kagaku*, 9(2), pp. 1–10.

Buchanan, James M. and Richard E. Wagner (1977) *Democracy in Deficit: The Political Legacy of Lord Keynes*, New York: Academic Press.

Dror, Yehezkel (2001) *The Capacity to Govern: A Report to the Club of Rome*, London and Portland, OR: Frank Cass.

Hayek, F. A. (1960) *The Constitution of Liberty*, Chicago: University of Chicago Press.

Johnston, Donald J. (2002) "Sustainable Future: Our Common Future", *OECD Observer* No. 233.

Jonas, Hans (1984) *The Imperative of Responsibility: In Search for an Ethics for the Technological Age*, Chicago: University of Chicago Press.

Kennan, George F. (1993) *Around the Cragged Hill: A Personal and Political Philosophy*, New York: W. W. Norton.

Lindblom, Charles E. (1965) *The Intelligence of Democracy: Decision-makings through Mutual Adjustment*, New York: Free Press.

Lowi, Theodore (1979) *The End of Liberalism: The Second Republic of the United States*, New York: W. W. Norton.

Oakeshott, Michael (1962) *Rationalism in Politics and Other Essays*, London: Methuen.

Popper, Karl (1945) *The Open Society and Its Enemies*, London: George Routledge and Sons.

Rittel, Horst and Melvin Webber (1973) "Dilemmas in a General Theory of Planning", *Policy Sciences* 4(i), pp. 155–169.

Schulze, Charles L. (1977) *The Public Use of Private Interest*, Washington: The Brookings Institution Press.

The World Commission on Environment and Development (1987) *Our Common Future*, Oxford: Oxford University Press.

# 9
# Does better governance make for a better environment?

*Kosuke Oyama*

## Scope

Does better governance make for a better environment, or does the environment improve as democracy takes hold? This is an interesting question, and in this work, I analyse various aspects pertaining to it by applying quantitative methods to international comparisons. There has not been much quantitative, cross-border research conducted on the relation between governance and the environment (or even democracy and the environment), and to help address this, here we present a general overview of the relation. Clearly, if we are to attempt to examine such a relation comprehensively across more than 150 countries or regions, we had better do so quantitatively, and indeed, this chapter does have a statistical focus. For a detailed discussion of governance and environment in any specific country or region, the reader is referred to case study analyses presented in other chapters.

One reason for the paucity of quantitative research and analysis in this area is a lack of data available. There is just not much data capable of supporting meaningful comparisons across 150 countries or regions; this deficiency goes beyond the difficulty of quantifying such abstractions as "governance" and "democracy" to include the clear obstacle of a shortage of environmental data pertaining to developing countries. Here we utilize two data sets which seem to be the broadest and most reliable data sets available to date: with regards to governance, we primarily rely on Worldwide Governance Indicators (WGI) from the World Bank; and with regards to the environment, we use the Environmental Performance Index (EPI; 2008 data) from Daniel Esty and colleagues (2008).

*Transition management for sustainable development, Ueta and Adachi (eds.), United Nations University Press, 2014, ISBN 978-92-808-1234-3*

The analysis results suggest that better governance (or more democracy) could make for a better environment. Furthermore, we discover that, of the various factors influencing governance, governmental competence—that is, the government's ability to execute suitable and effectual policies as indicated by such measures as government effectiveness (GE) and regulatory quality (RQ)—is particularly effective in bringing about a good environment. This conclusion is somewhat unexpected, at least from the traditional viewpoint that emphasizes the role of the citizenry (the private sector, etc.) in good governance. This said, the paucity of data, together with the extreme simplicity of the quantitative framework used here, limits the strength and generality of the conclusions drawn. Thus, this issue should be further explored using appropriate data and a suitable methodology in the future.

## Previous research in relation to this work

Although there has not been a great deal of research into the relation between governance (or democracy) and the environment, there is nonetheless considerably more now than there used to be. We take particular note of three pioneering efforts described later. Although hastening to point out that a good number of other efforts also make valuable contributions, these three pioneering efforts are of particular relevance to the present work. The first is "Box 2.3 More democracy, better environment?" text taken from *World Resources 2002–2004: Decisions for the Earth: Balance, Voice, and Power* (United Nations Development Programme, United Nations Environment Programme, World Bank, World Resources Institute, 2003). The second is *Democracy and Development: Political Institutions and Well-Being in the World, 1950–1990*, a book by Adam Przeworski and colleagues (2000). And the third is the book chapter titled "National Environmental Performance Measurement and Determinants", by Daniel Esty and Michael Porter (2002). In the following, we present a brief overview of these works and describe what distinguishes this chapter from them.

The starting point for the present work is "Box 2.3 More democracy, better environment?" (United Nations Development Programme, United Nations Environment Programme, World Bank and World Resources Institute, 2008). It addresses these questions with relative clarity: Is there a causal connection between democracy and improved environmental quality? Is there one between political freedoms and environmental sustainability? It then goes on to assert that four factors—democratic institutions, levels of wealth, citizen demands for environmental quality and levels of consumption—influence environmental quality. It also points out that little research has been carried out to verify these relations and that, in many cases, environmental data for developing countries are missing. The piece does mention that, as an overall trend, the scope of environmental responsibility tends to broaden in line with economic development from a local focus to a global one. It adds that a transition from autocracy to democracy is often marked by a period of instability during which time the environment is particularly vulnerable to damage.

In *Democracy and Development*, Przeworski et al. (2000) broadly examine a high correlation between prosperity and democracy. We learn not only that roughly 2 per cent of the world's authoritarian regimes give way to a democratic regime on average in a typical year, but also that democracies become increasingly sustainable once per capita income rises above $4,000. Similarly, the rate of national income growth under both authoritarian and democratic regimes is roughly the same at about 4 per cent[1] but that population growth is, on average, higher under authoritarianism (2.18 per cent) than democracy (1.59 per cent). This work contains little mention of countries or regions that have fallen into the spiral of poverty and civil strife, and it contains no discussion of changes since the 1990s or of the environment, our particular area of concern. As shown in Figure 9.1, however, we do learn that both the number and the proportion of democratic regimes has risen markedly since the latter half of the 1990s following the conclusion of the cold war.

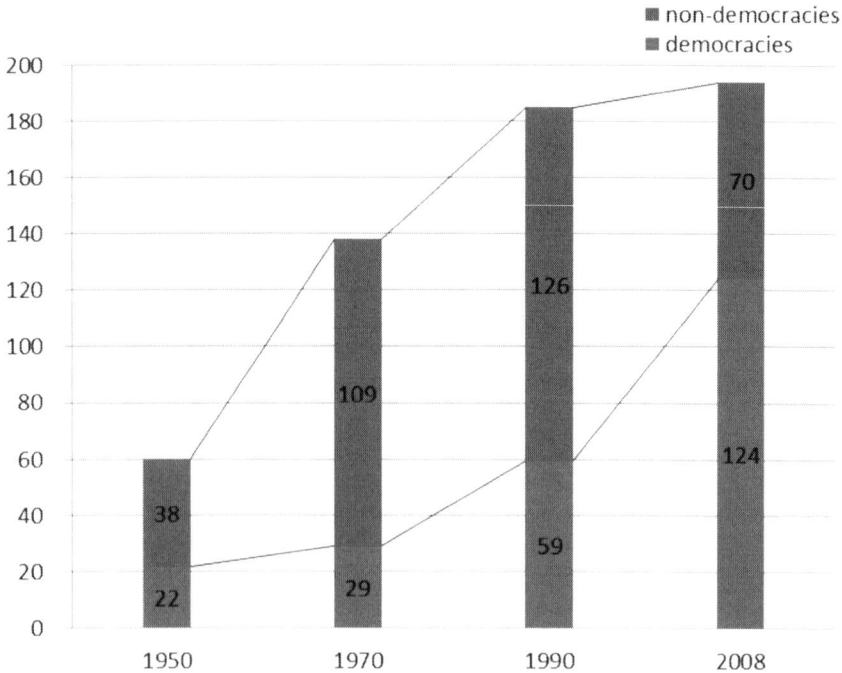

Figure 9.1 Number and proportion of democratic regimes
*Source:* Cambridge Contemporary Social International Institute (2008: 91).

"National Environmental Performance Measurement and Determinants" by Esty and Porter (2002) is particularly significant for its use of an innovative analytical framework and its reliance on data for verification. First, regarding the analytical framework, Esty and Porter consider the possibility that environmental improvements come about as a result not only of economic development or income growth but also of environmental policy. From this, they arrive at the so-called Porter hypothesis, which takes two forms. In its "soft" form, the hypothesis can be paraphrased as "environmental improvement can be obtained without impairing competitiveness" (Esty and Porter, 2002: 40); in its more rigorous, "hard" form, we have "strict environmental regulations do not inevitably hinder competitive advantage against rivals; indeed, they often enhance it" (Esty and Porter, 2002: 40) (one related implication is that measures to alleviate poverty and encourage economic growth can also be beneficial in terms of environmental improvement). In both its forms, the hypothesis propounds the utility of environmental measures; the hard form, of course, simply asserts this point more strongly.

Next, regarding the data they use to verify this hypothesis, Esty and Porter (2002) rely on the following: the Environmental Sustainability Index (ESI) for parameters relating to environmental performance (urban particulate concentration, urban sulfur dioxide [$SO_2$] concentration, etc.); the Environmental Regulatory Regime Index (ERRI) Esty and Porter developed to quantify the quality of regulation for specific countries in terms of the six determinants of stringency of standards, subsidies, regulatory enforcement, regulatory structure, information and environmental institutions; the Economic and Legal Context Index (ELCI) that is used as an index of administrative infrastructure and scientific and technological infrastructure; and a measure of economic competitiveness derived from GDP per capita data, a growth index and a current competitive index. Several issues have been pointed out in relation to Esty and Porter's data, most notably that the ERRI is procedurally complicated to calculate and perhaps is not reproducible, that environmental indices are limited by a lack of comparable data (at least relative to economic and legal indices) and that it is not always clear just how the data are processed. There is also considerable doubt about the mutual independence of the ERRI and the ELCI. Even with these issues, however, the work is highly regarded for its attempt to verify the factors behind environmental performance. Indeed, this seems to be its greatest value.

Then what differentiates the present work from the research efforts outlined earlier? First, we examine here the correlation and/or causal relation between governance and the environment not in terms of the slippery concept of "democracy", but in terms of the more objective concept of operational governance. Regarding governance, we utilize WGI data from the World Bank; for the environment, we make use of the environmental performance indices of Esty et al. (2008). These two indices appear to be the best available at present.

As a second differentiating point, we analyse the relation between economic prosperity as indexed by per capita gross domestic product (GDP) and environmental performance as indexed by EPI. This relation is essentially equivalent to the relation between economic growth and the environment, which itself is the subject of the well-known environmental Kuznets curve (EKC). The basic idea behind the EKC is that, up to a certain transitional point, economic growth is accompanied by a deterioration in environmental quality, whereas economic growth beyond that point is accompanied by an improvement in environmental quality.[2] We do not observe any EKC effect in our analysis of the relation between economic prosperity and environmental performance.

Overall, our results show some concurrence with our basic hypothesis that better governance is accompanied by a better environment.[3] However, our analysis does not extend down to such points as (1) why would the environment improve with better governance and (2) what is the cause-and-effect relation between governance (especially environmental regulation) and the environment? All we attempt to analyse in this chapter is whether our basic hypothesis holds, not why it holds or how it would hold.

## Analytical framework and hypotheses

Figure 9.2 shows the analytical framework of this research. We take three sets of variables—governance (quality), (economic) prosperity and environment (quality)—and, under three hypotheses, explore ways in which they could interrelate.

As our first hypothesis, we take measures of governance as independent variables and a measure of environmental quality as a dependent variable and consider the statement "The better the governance of the country, the higher its

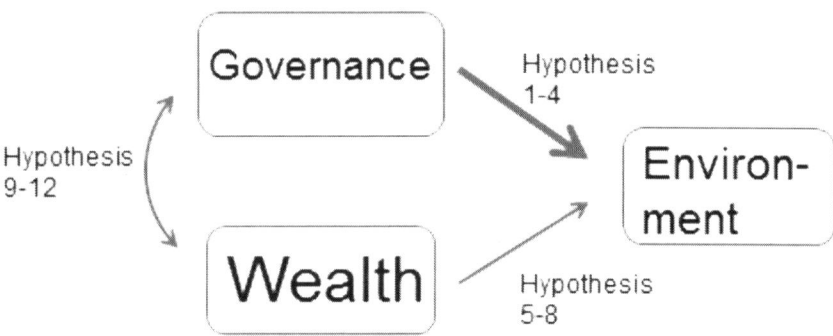

Figure 9.2 The analytical framework

environmental quality". The notion here is that as governance becomes increasingly competent, the quality of government policy-making rises in tandem with the level of public interest in the environment, acting to enhance the degree of policy oversight and of monitoring and leading to an improvement in the quality of the environment.

As our second hypothesis, we take measures of economic prosperity as independent variables and a measure of environmental quality as a dependent variable to consider the statement "The more prosperous a country, the higher its environmental quality". As also explained in relation to the environmental Kuznets curve, the notion here is that the demands of the citizenry for the economic good represented by environmental quality tend to rise once economic prosperity reaches a certain level.

It is also conceivable that governance and economic prosperity, which we assumed earlier could be represented by independent variables, are in fact interrelated. A tendency for the quality of governance to improve in step with economic prosperity is readily apparent in the development process of numerous countries, even if it is not clear which is the cause and which is the effect. This brings us to our third hypothesis, "Environmental quality improves in conjunction with an interaction between governance and economic prosperity".

In the regression analyses that follow, note that a relation is first established under the assumption that each independent variable has only a one-way causal influence on the dependent variable and this relation is then verified by seeing whether or not the null hypothesis (i.e., the hypothesis that there is no relation) holds; if it does not hold, there is a relation. Note, however, that even if we do establish that a relation exists, we cannot rule out the possibility that it has a cause-and-effect influence in the other direction. Note, however, that even if we do establish that a relation exists, we cannot rule out the possibility of a causal effect in the other direction. Thus, the use of regression analysis in itself harbours the risk of introducing a bias in cases in which, for instance, (1) there is a bidirectional cause-and-effect influence or (2) another, unidentified independent variable also inserts an influence. Here, it is important to keep in mind that our analyses do not incorporate the degree of statistical rigor necessary to correct such biases.

## The World Bank's Worldwide Governance Indicators

The World Bank's WGI were developed by Daniel Kaufmann of the Brookings Institution together with Aart Kraay and Massimo Mastruzzi of the World Bank, a team that is sometimes referred to simply as "KKZ". They indicate the quality of governance in 212 nations or regions around the world based on 35 data sources provided by 32 institutions. The data have been updated annually since 1996 and thus can usually be used for time-series analysis, with the caveat that the contents of the data (e.g., the number of countries or regions covered or the makeup of the indicators themselves) can vary somewhat from year to year.[4]

The WGI indicators comprise six dimensions of governance: (1) voice and accountability (VA), (2) political stability and absence of violence and terrorism (PS), (3) government effectiveness (GE), (4) regulatory quality (RQ), (5) rule of law (RL) and (6) control of corruption (CC). As we will mention again later, however, a fairly strong correlation is evident among these dimensions, raising doubts about their mutual independence. Indeed, one might even say that they express essentially the same thing from different aspects.[5] Furthermore, much of the KKZ data are composite and thus may include compositional errors and arbitrariness. Also, on a more basic level, some take issue with the objectivity of the survey data themselves and the lack of transparency with which data are processed.[6]

Governance is defined for the purposes of the WGI as something consisting of "the traditions and institutions by which authority in a country is exercised" (Kaufmann et al., 2009: 5) (VA and PS; see the following). The definition continues: "this includes the process by which governments are selected, monitored and replaced", which is followed by "the capacity of the government to effectively formulate and implement sound policies" (Kaufmann et al., 2009: 5) (GE and RQ) together with "the respect of citizens and the state for the institutions that govern economic and social interactions among them" (Kaufmann et al., 2009: 5) (RL and CC). The "traditions and institutions by which authority . . . is exercised" refers primarily to VA and PS. VA is given as "capturing perceptions of the extent to which a country's citizens are able to participate in selecting their government, as well as freedom of expression, freedom of association, and a free media" (Kaufmann et al., 2009: 6); PS is given as "capturing perceptions of the likelihood that the government will be destabilized or overthrown by unconstitutional or violent means, including politically motivated violence and terrorism" (Kaufmann et al., 2009: 6).

Japan is characterized by its low rating in VA relative to the other five dimensions. It is clear that Japan has more work to do with regards to assuring freedom of expression and making government more accountable. Japan ranks relatively high on PS. Other developed countries tend to rank low on the scale, particularly the Anglo-Saxon countries. Presumably this reflects a tendency in such countries for power to shift between two major political parties at fairly regular intervals under district representation systems, and it is thus quite possible that a similar tendency will emerge in Japan.

The ability to formulate and implement sound policies falls under the categories of GE and RQ. GE is given as "capturing perceptions of the quality of public services, the quality of the civil service and the degree of its independence from political pressures, the quality of policy formulation and implementation, and the credibility of the government's commitment to such policies" (Kaufmann et al., 2009: 6); and RQ is given as "capturing perceptions of the ability of the government to formulate and implement sound policies and regulations that permit and promote private sector development" (Kaufmann et al., 2009: 6).

DOES BETTER GOVERNANCE MAKE FOR A BETTER ENVIRONMENT? 161

Respect for the citizenry and the state falls under the categories of RL and CC. RL involves "capturing perceptions of the extent to which agents have confidence in and abide by the rules of society, and in particular the quality of contract enforcement, property rights, the police, and the courts, as well as the likelihood of crime and violence" (Kaufmann et al., 2009: 6); and CC involves "capturing perceptions of the extent to which public power is exercised for private gain, including both petty and grand forms of corruption, as well as 'capture' of the state by elites and private interests" (Kaufmann et al., 2009: 6).

Figure 9.3 utilizes WGI data to illustrate the state of governance in Japan. As of 2008, Japan ranked in the top 26 per cent for all six dimensions of governance.

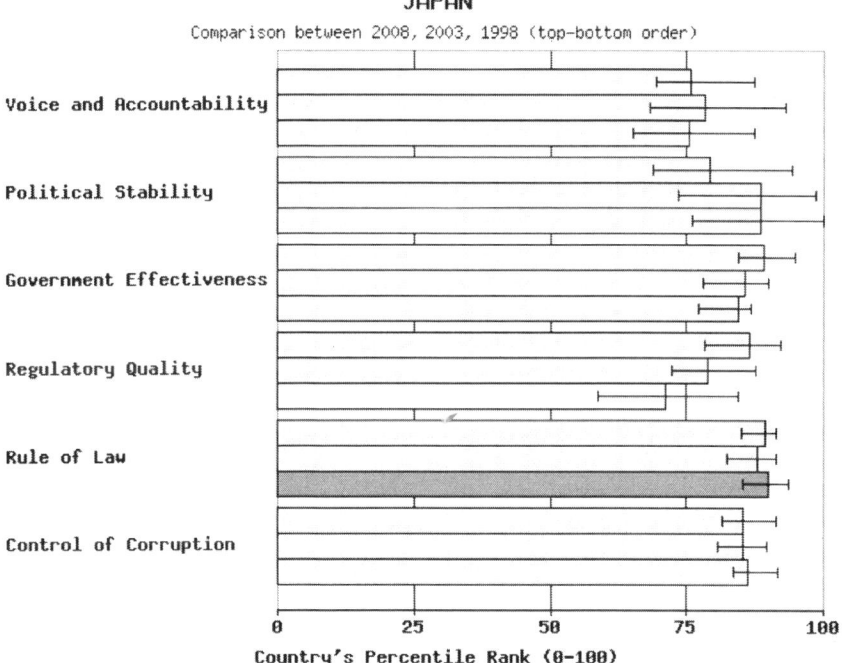

Figure 9.3 The state of Japan's governance in WGI data for 2008, 2003, 1998 (top-to bottom-order)
*Source:* The World Bank's Worldwide Governance Indicators' (WGI) website, available at http://www.govindicators.org/.
*Note:* The governance indicators presented here are aggregates of the views on the quality of governance provided by a large number of enterprise, citizen and expert survey respondents in industrial and developing countries. These data are gathered from a number of survey institutions, think tanks, non-governmental organizations and international organizations. The WGI does not reflect the official views of the World Bank, its Executive Directors or the countries they represent. The WGI are not used by the World Bank Group to allocate resources.

Of the six, the country rates strongest in RL and weakest in VA. We also note steady improvement in RQ since 1998 and see that there has been some deterioration in terms of CC.

Table 9.1 shows the sources of governance data used in the 2008 WGI update. As mentioned earlier, an increasing variety of sources is being tapped, which can be broken down into two types: expert (government, etc.) and survey. Most but not all data have been fully disclosed by the sources. We also note a high degree of variation in the broadness of coverage, with some data covering considerably more countries or regions than do others.

Table 9.2 shows the distribution of data points by type. We see that of 12,144 data points, 5,142 (42 per cent) are provided by commercial business information providers with the other sources being public-sector organizations (2,660 points; 22 per cent), non-governmental organizations (NGOs; 2,188 points; 18 per cent) and surveys of firms or households (2,124 points; 18 per cent). A breakdown by the six dimensions shows that with the exception of VA, for which NGOs account for 36 per cent of data sources, the data sources for the remaining five dimensions all centre on commercial business information providers. The distribution becomes even more skewed on weighting: commercial business information providers account for 53 per cent of total weighted shares for all indicators. Thus, it is necessary to note that five dimensions could well share the biases of their sources, that is, commercial business information providers (the exception is the VA dimension, which, as mentioned previously, relies heavily on NGOs).

## Environmental performance indices of Esty et al. (2008)

The Environmental Performance Index (EPI)[7] was developed as a comprehensive measure of environmental performance across countries by Daniel Esty of Yale University and colleagues at Columbia University in collaboration with the World Economic Forum (WEF) and the Joint Research Centre of the European Commission. It was formerly known as the Environmental Sustainability Index (ESI)[8] and was published under that name in 1999 and 2005. The EPI was positioned as a pilot index in 2002 and 2006. The latest update was released in 2008. The EPI was designed to supplement environmental targets under the United Nations Millennium Development Goals (UNMDG). However, the data do not have time-series consistency and thus cannot be readily be used for time-series analyses. Also, as we discuss in the next paragraph, EPI data tend to have little dispersion, which means that they often do not support clear distinctions across countries.

Table 9.3 shows the construction of the EPI in terms of its constituent objectives, policy categories and indicators. First, as for objectives, we have two major categories, specifically environmental health and ecosystem vitality. The environmental health objective is further broken down into the three policy categories of environmental burden of disease, water (effects on humans) and air

Table 9.1 The sources of governance data used in the 2008 World Governance Indicators (WGI) update

| | Source | Type | Public | Country Coverage | Representative | 1996 | 1998 | 2000 | 2002 | 2003 | 2004 | 2005 | 2006 | 2007 | 2008 |
|---|---|---|---|---|---|---|---|---|---|---|---|---|---|---|---|
| ADB | African Development Bank Country Policy and Institutional Assessments | Expert (GOV) | Partial | 53 | | | X | X | X | X | X | X | X | X | X |
| AEO | OECD Development Center African Economic Outlook | Expert (GOV) | Yes | 48 | | X | X | X | X | X | X | X | X | X | X |
| AFR | Afrobarometer | Survey | Yes | 19 | | | | X | X | X | X | X | X | X | X |
| ASO | Asian Development Bank Country Policy and Institutional Assessments | Expert (GOV) | Partial | 29 | | | | X | X | X | X | X | X | X | X |
| BPS | Business Enterprise Environment Survey | Survey | Yes | 27 | | | | X | X | X | X | X | X | X | X |

Table 9.1 (cont.)

| | Source | Type | Public | Country Coverage | Representative | 1996 | 1998 | 2000 | 2002 | 2003 | 2004 | 2005 | 2006 | 2007 | 2008 |
|---|---|---|---|---|---|---|---|---|---|---|---|---|---|---|---|
| BRI | Business Environment Risk Intelligence Business Risk Service/ Financial Ethics Index | Expert (CBIP) | Yes | 101 | | X | X | X | X | X | X | X | X | X | X |
| BTI | Bertelsmann Transformation Index | Expert (NGO) | Yes | 125 | | | | | X | X | X | X | X | X | X |
| CCR | Freedom House Countries at the Crossroads | Expert (NGO) | Yes | 62 | | | | | | | X | X | X | X | X |
| DRI | Global Insight Global Risk Service | Expert (CBIP) | Yes | 144 | X | X | X | X | x | X | X | X | X | X | X |
| EBR | European Bank for Reconstruction and Development Transition Report | Expert (GOV) | Yes | 29 | | X | X | X | X | X | X | X | X | X | X |

| | | | | | | | | | | | | |
|---|---|---|---|---|---|---|---|---|---|---|---|---|
| EGV | Global E-Governance Index | Expert (NGO) | Yes | 195 | | | | | X | X | X | X |
| EIU | Economist Intelligence Unit Riskwire & Democracy Index | Expert (CBIP) | Yes | 170 | X | X | X | X | X | X | X | X |
| FRH | Freedom House | Expert (NGO) | Yes | 197 | X | X | X | X | X | X | X | X |
| GAD | Cerberus Intelligence Gray Area Dynamics | Expert (CBIP) | Yes | 164 | X | | | | X | X | | X |
| GCB | Transparency International Global Corruption Barometer Survey | Survey | Yes | 80 | | | | X | X | X | X | X |
| GCS | World Economic Forum Global Competiveness Report | Survey | Yes | 134 | X | X | X | X | X | X | X | X |
| GII | Global Integrity Index | Expert (NGO) | Yes | 79 | | | | | X | X | X | X |

Table 9.1 (cont.)

| | Source | Type | Public | Country Coverage | Representative | 1996 | 1998 | 2000 | 2002 | 2003 | 2004 | 2005 | 2006 | 2007 | 2008 |
|---|---|---|---|---|---|---|---|---|---|---|---|---|---|---|---|
| GWP | Gallup World Poll | Survey | Yes | 130 | X | | | | | | | | X | X | X |
| HER | Heritage Foundation Index of Economic Freedom | Expert (NGO) | Yes | 179 | X | X | X | X | X | X | X | X | X | X | X |
| HUM | Cingranell Richards Human Rights Database and Political Terror Scale | Expert (GOV) | Yes | 192 | X | X | X | X | X | X | X | X | X | X | X |
| IFD | IFAD Rural Sector Performance Assessments | Expert (GOV) | Yet | 90 | | | | | | | X | X | X | X | X |
| IJT | IJET Country Security Risk Ratings | Expert (CBIP) | Yes | 185 | X | | | | | | X | X | X | X | X |
| IPD | Institutional Profiles Database | Expert (GOV) | Yes | 85 | X | | | | | | | | X | X | X |
| LBO | Latinobarometro | Survey | Yes | 18 | | X | X | X | X | X | X | X | X | X | X |

166

| Code | Name | Type | | N | | | | | | | | | |
|---|---|---|---|---|---|---|---|---|---|---|---|---|---|
| MIG | Merchant International Group Gray Area Dynamics | Expert (CBIP) | Yes | 156 | X | | | | | | X | X | |
| MSI | International Research and Exchanges Board Media Sustainability Index | Expert (NGO) | Yes | 76 | | | X | | X | X | X | X | X |
| CBI | International Budget Project Open Budget Index | Expert (NGO) | Yes | 85 | | | | | | X | X | X | X |
| PIA | World Bank Country Policy and Institutional Assessments | Expert (GOV) | Partial | 142 | | X | X | X | X | X | X | X | X |
| PRC | Political Economic Risk Consultancy Corruption In Asia Survey | Survey | Yes | 15 | | | X | X | X | X | X | X | X |
| PRS | Political Risk Services International Country Risk Guide | Expert (CBIP) | Yes | 140 | X | | X | X | X | X | X | X | X |

Table 9.1 (cont.)

| | Source | Type | Public | Country Coverage | Representative | 1996 | 1998 | 2000 | 2002 | 2003 | 2004 | 2005 | 2006 | 2007 | 2008 |
|---|---|---|---|---|---|---|---|---|---|---|---|---|---|---|---|
| RSF | Reporters Without Borders Press Freedom Index | Expert (NGO) | Yes | 170 | X | | | | X | X | X | X | X | X | X |
| TPR | US State Department Trafficking in People Report | Expert (GOV) | Yes | 153 | X | | | X | X | X | X | X | X | X | X |
| VAB | Vanderbilt University Americas Barometer | Survey | Yes | 23 | | | | | | | X | X | X | X | X |
| WCY | Institute for Management and Development World Competitiveness Yearbook | Survey | Yes | 55 | | X | X | X | X | X | X | X | X | X | X |
| WMO | Global Insight Business Conditions and Risk Indicators | Expert (CBIP) | Yes | 203 | X | | X | X | X | X | X | X | X | X | X |

*Source*: Kaufmann et al. (2009: 29).

Table 9.2 The distribution of data points by type in World Governance Indicators (WGI) 2008

|  | Commercial Business Information Providers | Surveys of Firms or Households | Non-Governmental Organizations | Public Sector Organizations | Total |
|---|---|---|---|---|---|
| **Number of Data Points** | | | | | |
| Voice and Accountability | 677 | 335 | 794 | 337 | 2223 |
| Political Stability/ Absence of Violence | 1087 | 139 | 0 | 327 | 1603 |
| Government Effectiveness | 738 | 3S8 | 321 | 398 | 1355 |
| Regulatory Quality | 801 | 219 | 304 | 427 | 1751 |
| Rule of Law | 920 | 420 | 474 | 743 | 2557 |
| Control of Corruption | 919 | 513 | 295 | 398 | 2125 |
| *Total* | 5142 | 2124 | 2188 | 2660 | 12114 |
| **Shares of Total for Each Indicator** | | | | | |
| Voice and Accountability | 0.30 | 0.17 | 0.36 | 0.17 | 1.00 |
| Political Stability/ Absence of Violence | 0.68 | 0.12 | 0.00 | 0.20 | 1.00 |
| Government Effectiveness | 0.40 | 0.21 | 0.17 | 0.21 | 1.00 |
| Regulatory Quality | 0.46 | 0.13 | 0.17 | 0.24 | 1.00 |
| Rule of Law | 0.36 | 0.16 | 0.19 | 0.29 | 1.00 |
| Control of Corruption | 0.43 | 0.24 | 0.14 | 0.19 | 1.00 |
| *Total* | 0.42 | 0.18 | 0.18 | 0.22 | 1.00 |

Table 9.2 (cont.)

***Weighted Shares of Total for Each Indicator***

| | | | | | |
|---|---|---|---|---|---|
| Voice and Accountability | 0.31 | 0.02 | 0.56 | 0.11 | 1.00 |
| Political Stability/ Absence of Violence | 0.78 | 0.04 | 0.00 | 0.17 | 1.00 |
| Government Effectiveness | 0.59 | 0.12 | 0.07 | 0.22 | 1.00 |
| Regulatory Quality | 0.47 | 0.06 | 0.17 | 0.29 | 1.00 |
| Rule of Law | 0.53 | 0.10 | 0.14 | 0.23 | 1.00 |
| Control of Corruption | 0.50 | 0.16 | 0.13 | 0.22 | 1.00 |
| ***Total*** | 0.53 | 0.08 | 0.13 | 0.21 | 1.00 |

*Source:* Kaufmann et al. (2009: 30).

pollution (effects on humans). Similarly, the ecosystem vitality objective is further broken down into the five policy categories of air pollution (effects on ecosystems), water, biodiversity and habitat, climate change and productive natural resources. Appended underneath each policy category are one to five concrete indicators.

Under the water (effects on humans) policy category are the two indicators of adequate sanitation and drinking water. There is another water category, under which are the two indicators of water-quality index and water stress (water stress refers to a situation in which freshwater withdrawal exceeds replenishment, as could occur as a result from drought or saltwater intrusion). Under the air pollution (effects on humans) policy category are indoor air pollution, urban particulates and local ozone; under the air pollution (effects on ecosystems) category are regional ozone and $SO_2$ emissions. The indicators under biodiversity and habitat are a conservation risk index, effective conservation, critical habitat protection and marine protected areas; those under climate change are emissions/capita, emissions/electricity generated and industrial carbon intensity; and under productive natural resources are the following: for forestry, growing stock; for fisheries, marine trophic index and trawling intensity; and, for agriculture, irrigation stress, agricultural subsidies, intensive cropland, burnt land area and pesticide regulation.

For some of these indicators, however, it is not quite clear what kinds of data were collected and how such data were used in support. Thus, as with the World Bank's WGI, there are some doubts about transparency and objectivity. Furthermore, these indicators carry various degrees of significance and are thus weighted to arrive at an overall EPI, but it is not entirely clear whether the weightings are appropriate.

Table 9.3 The Environmental Performance Index system

| Index | Objectives | Objective Weight (% of EPI) | Policy Categories | Policy Categories Weight (% of EPI) | Subcategories | Sub-category Weight (% of EPI) | Indicators | Indicator Weight in EPI % | Data Source | Target |
|---|---|---|---|---|---|---|---|---|---|---|
| EPI | Environmental Health | 50 | Environmental Health | 50 | Environmental Burden of Disease | 25 | Environmental Burden of Disease (DALYs) | 25 | WHO | 0 DALYs |
| | | | | | Water (effects on humans) | 12.5 | Adequate Sanitation | 6.25 | WHO-UNICEF Joint Monitoring Program | 100% |
| | | | | | | | Drinking Water | 6.25 | WHO-UNICEF Joint Monitoring Program | 100% |
| | | | | | Air Pollution (effects on humans) | 12.5 | Urban Particulates | 5 | World Bank, WHO | 20 ug/m$^3$ |
| | | | | | | | Indoor Air Pollution | 5 | WHO | 0% |
| | | | | | | | Local Ozone | 2.5 | MOZART II model | 0 exceedance above 85 pbb |

Table 9.3 (cont.)

| Index | Objectives | Objective Weight (% of EPI) | Policy Categories | Policy Categories Weight (% of EPI) | Subcategories | Sub-category Weight (% of EPI) | Indicators | Indicator Weight in EPI % | Data Source | Target |
|---|---|---|---|---|---|---|---|---|---|---|
| | Ecosystem Vitality | 50 | Air Pollution (effects on nature) | 2.5 | Air Pollution (effects on nature) | 2.5 | Regional Ozone | 1.25 | MOZART II model | 0 exceedance above 3000 AOT40. AOT40 is cumulative exceedance above 40 ppb during daylight summer hours |
| | | | | | | | Sulfur Dioxide Emissions | 1.25 | EDGAR/ Netherlands | 0 tons $SO_2$ / populated land |
| | | | Water (effects on nature) | 7.5 | Water (effects on nature) | 7.5 | Water Quality | 3.75 | UNEP GEUS/ Water | 100 score |
| | | | | | | | Water Stress | 3.75 | UNH Water Systems Analysis | 0% territory under water stress |
| | | | Biodiversity & Habitat | 7.5 | Biodiversity & Habitat | 7.5 | Conservation Risk Index | 7.5/ (2+AZE weight + MPAEEZ weight) | The Nature Consenancy | 0.5 ratio |

| Category | Weight | Sub-category | Weight | Indicator | Value/Formula | Source | Target |
|---|---|---|---|---|---|---|---|
| | | | | Effective Conservation | 7.5/(2+AZE weight + MPAEEZ weight) | The Nature Consenancy | 10% |
| | | | | Critical Habitat Protection* | if no AZE sites: 0; if AZE sites: 7.5/(2+AZE weight + MPAEEZ weight) | Alliance for Zero Extinction, TNC | 100% |
| | | | | Marine Protected Areas* | minimum of 7.5*EEZ area/land area and 7.5, divided by (2+AZE weight + MPAEEZ weight) | Sea Around Us Project, Fisheries Centre. UBC | 10% |
| Productive Natural Resources | 7.5 | Forestry* | 2.5 | Growing Stock Change | 25 | FAO | ratio of at least 1 |
| | | Fisheries* | 2.5 | Marine Trophic Index | 1.25 | UBC, Sea Around Us Project | no decline |
| | | | | Trawling Intensity | 1.25 | UBC, Sea Around Us Project | 0% |

Table 9.3 (cont.)

| Index | Objectives | Objective Weight (% of EPI) | Policy Categories | Policy Categories Weight (% of EPI) | Subcategories | Sub-category Weight (% of EPI) | Indicators | Indicator Weight in EPI % | Data Source | Target |
|---|---|---|---|---|---|---|---|---|---|---|
| | | | | | Agriculture* | 2.5 | Irrigation Stress* | 0.5 | CIESIN | 0% |
| | | | | | | | Agricultural Subsidies | 0.5 | World Bank, World Development Report | 0 |
| | | | | | | | Intensive Cropland | 0.5 | CIESIN | 0% |
| | | | | | | | Burnt Land Area | 0.5 | | 0% |
| | | | | | | | Pesticide Regulation | 0.5 | UNEP-Chemicals | 22 points |
| | | | Climate Change | 25 | Climate Change | 25 | Emissions Per Capita | 8.333 | IEA, CDIAC, Houghton | 2.24 Mt $CO_2$ eq. (Estimated value associated with 50% reduction in global GHG emissions by 2050, against 1990 levels) |
| | | | | | | | Emissions Per Electricity Generation | 8.333 | IEA | 0 g $CO_2$ per kWh |

174

| | | | | | | Industrial Carbon Intensity | 8.333 | IEA, WDI | .85 tons of $CO_2$ per $1000 (USD, 2005, PPP) of industrial GDP (Estimated value associated with 50% reduction in global GHG emissions by 2050. against 1990 levels) |

*Source*: "The Framework of EPI", available at http://epi.yale.edu/downloads.
* Averaged if missing data or not applicable to the country.

Also it is worth keeping in mind that the EPI is based on items that are currently measurable—specifically, air, water, soil and other such environmental media—and do not incorporate such new elements as environmental sustainability. As a result, a country such as Germany, considered to be one of the most technologically advanced nations, does not necessarily rank highly in terms of EPI, an unexpected result that has raised some criticism.[9]

There are also a good number of environmental indices other than the EPI, and Figure 9.4 illustrates how the EPI is positioned relative to them. This table is taken from the Third Environmental Basic Plan (2006) of the Japanese Ministry of Environment. We note that the EPI is synoptic (comprehensive and wide ranging) in nature. It is not so much for policy assessment (i.e., it is not policy oriented) as it is for monitoring (it is environmentally oriented).[10]

## Relations between governance, environmental indices and economic prosperity

In this section, we examine each of the three hypotheses stated earlier, namely "the better the governance of the country, the higher its environmental quality" (Hypothesis 1), "the more prosperous a country, the higher its environmental quality" (Hypothesis 2) and "environmental quality improves as result of the combined effect of governance and economic prosperity" (hypothesis 3).[11]

*Verification of relation between governance and environmental quality (Hypothesis 1)*

To examine the relation between governance and environmental quality, we begin by calculating the correlation coefficients of the six dimensions comprising the WGI (VA, PS, GE, RQ, RL and CC) and EPI. We arrive at 0.60 as the correlation coefficient for VA, 0.53 for PS, 0.68 for GE, 0.67 for RQ, 0.63 for RL and 0.63 for CC, with all dimensions being significant at the 1 per cent level. We also calculate the correlation coefficient between the average for these six dimensions (WGIAV) and EPI, obtaining a value of 0.66 (1 per cent significance). Note that this result suggests that there also exists some sort of cause-and-effect relation among the variables.

A look at the correlation coefficients for the six governance indices (i.e., dimensions) and EPI reveals that GE and RQ have relatively high values, suggesting that effective and appropriate environmental policies might contribute to an improvement in environmental quality. Note that there is also a high degree of correlation among the six dimensions, which raises the issue of independence or, more precisely, lack of it. Some might even say that each of the dimensions simply express essentially the same thing from a different aspect. Even so, it is

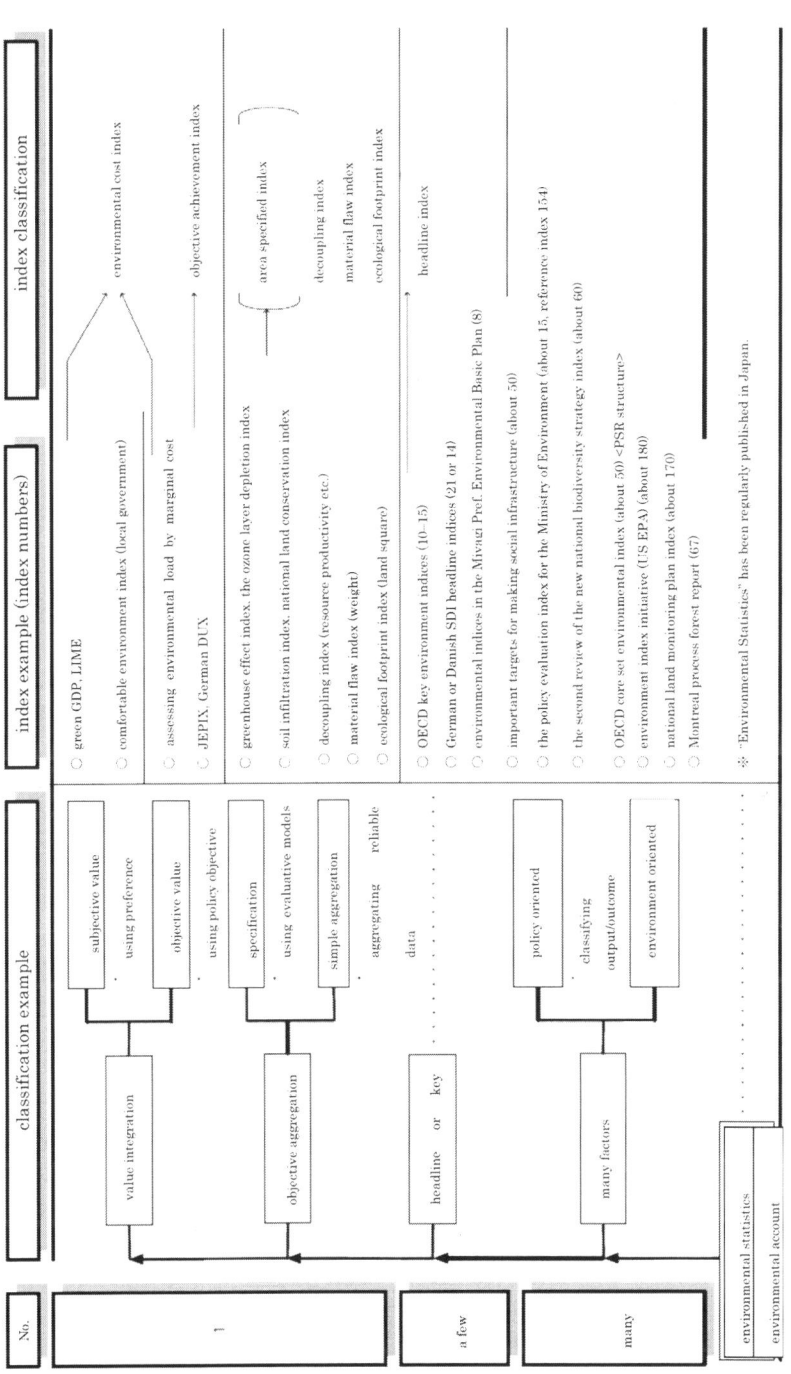

Figure 9.4 The Comprehensive Environmental Indices in the Third Environmental Basic Plan by the Ministry of Environment

*Source*: Selected translation of "Sougou-teki Kankyou Shihyou ni tsuite" ("About Comprehensive Environmental Indices"), the document used by the deliberation council, available at http://www.env.go.jp/policy/kihon_keikaku/thirdplan_sihyou.pdf, p. 3 or 5.

*Note*: JEPIX = Japan Environmental Policy Index; DUX = Deutsher Umweltindex (German Environment Index); OECD = Organisation for Economic Co-operation and Development; SDI = Sustainable Development Indicators; PSR = Pressure-State-Response; US EPA = United States Environmental Protection Agency.

fairly easy to accept from a commonsense standpoint that GE and RQ would have a stronger correlation with environmental quality than would, say PS.

Figure 9.5 is a plot of average WGI and EPI values for each country. The resulting distribution could be taken as demonstrating that, generally speaking, environmental quality is high in countries with good governance. We also see that the right side of the distribution (i.e., countries with good governance and high environmental quality) has relatively little dispersion, whereas the left side (countries with poor governance and poor environmental quality) has considerably more.

We next conduct linear regressions with each of the six dimensions of the WGI, together with a simple average of them (WGIAV), as our independent variables and EPI as our dependent variable. The resulting equation can be generally expressed as Equation (1) (with subscript i representing each specific country):

$$EPI_i = \alpha + \beta_1 AV_i + \beta_2 VA_i + \beta_3 PS_i + \beta_4 GE_i + \beta_5 RQ_i + \beta_6 RL_i + \beta_7 CC_i + \beta_8 WGIAV_i + \varepsilon_i \quad (1)$$

Our numerical results are presented in Table 9.4. Just as expected, the six explanatory variables turn out to be highly correlated with each other.[12] We thus

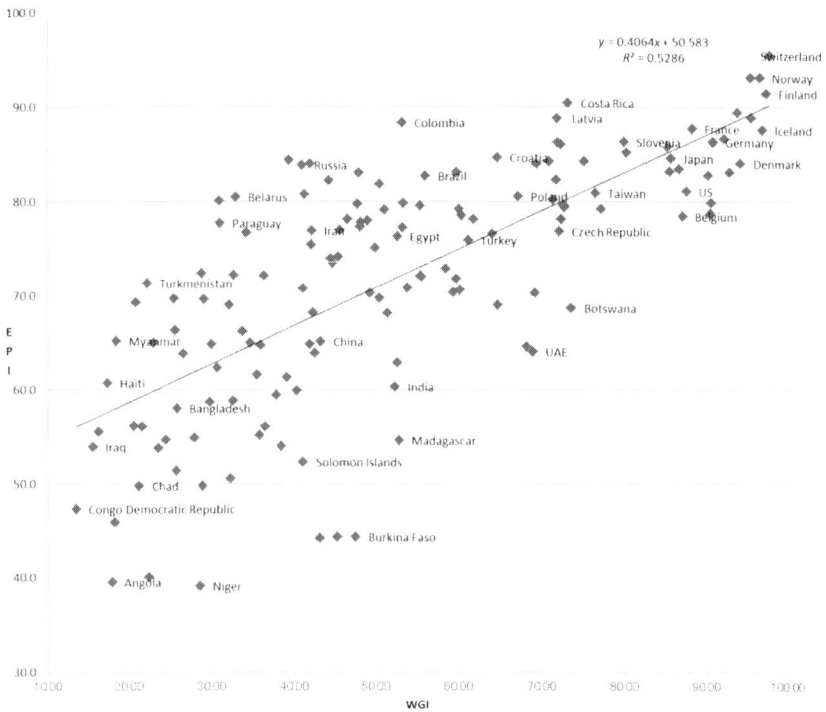

Figure 9.5 Worldwide Governance Indicators (WGI) and Environmental Performance Index (EPI)

Table 9.4 The numerical results: Environmental Performance Index (EPI) and World Governance Indicators (WGI)

| Case | (1) | (2) | (3) | (4) | (5) | (6) | (7) | (8) |
|---|---|---|---|---|---|---|---|---|
| Constant | 57.24*** (34.5) | 59.39*** (36.7) | 61.06*** (35.5) | 57.65*** (38.5) | 57.54*** (37.6) | 59.19*** (38.3) | 58.75*** (37.0) | 57.3*** (36.3) |
| VA (Voice and Accountability) | 0.014 (0.23) | 0.265*** (9.10) | | | | | | |
| PS (Political Stability) | −0.020 (−0.34) | | 0.264*** (7.47) | | | | | |
| GE (Government Effectiveness) | 0.262** (2.03) | | | 0.298*** (11.2) | | | | |
| RQ (Regulatory Quality) | 0.124 (1.18) | | | | 0.299*** (10.9) | | | |
| RL (Rule of Law) | −0.097 (−0.79) | | | | | 0.283*** (9.79) | | |
| CC (Control of Corruption) | 0.016 (0.16) | | | | | | 0.281*** (9.69) | |
| WGIAV (Average of above 6 variables) | | | | | | | | 0.317*** (10.7) |
| Adj $R^2$ | 0.441 | 0.359 | 0.273 | 0.456 | 0.447 | 0.394 | 0.387 | 0.436 |
| F-value | 20.08 | 82.77 | 55.79 | 124.4 | 119.6 | 95.88 | 93.81 | 114.5 |

Note: T-values are presented in parentheses.
***$p < 0.01$, **$p < 0.05$, *$p < 0.1$.

infer (1) a case in which we simultaneously treat all six explanatory variables and, on account of the multi-collinearity among them, (2) cases in which we treat each of the six separately.

In case (1), we simultaneously consider all six variables but find that only one, GE, is significant. It is possible that because the correlations among the variables are so high, their explanatory power was simply expressed by GE as a sort of proxy for the rest of them. A simple interpretation of these results, however, would simply be that of the six, GE has the most influence and, accordingly, is the most effective in terms of environmental quality. Note that the GE variable alone accounts for approximately one half of the EPI scatter from one country to the next ($R^2 = 0.456$).

Next, in cases (2) through (7), we consider each explanatory variable one at a time. We find that the relation is significant at the 1 per cent level in each case. We also conduct case (8) in which we take WGIAV as our explanatory variable. We obtain similar results in this case as well.

The preceding results could be taken as supporting (i.e., not refuting) Hypothesis 1: "the better the governance of the country, the higher its environmental quality". That said, we cannot discard the possibility that all six governance dimensions have some influence on the environment. From the separate comparisons of cases (2) through (7), we note that GE and RQ have relatively more significance ($t$-value) and explanatory power ($R^2$) than the other explanatory variables. However, correlations among the explanatory variables prevent us from making any further identifications, including a determination of just which governance factors have a true effect on environmental improvement and which just have a superficial correlation. It becomes necessary here to closely examine the contents of the WGI indicators themselves.

Similarly, the next question would be why a country with good governance also tends to have a good environment. One conceivable possibility is that a well-governed country tends to be economically prosperous, which promotes a transcendence beyond materialistic values and a consideration of what is beneficial for the next generation, in turn leading to increasing tolerance of environmental regulation. Such a discussion, however, is beyond the scope of this chapter.

*Verification of the relation between economic prosperity and environmental quality (Hypothesis 2)*

We next examine the relation between economic prosperity and environmental quality. We find the correlation between GDP per capita (GDPPC, which we take as our indicator of economic prosperity) and EPI to be 0.529.[13] Conducting a linear regression with EPI as the dependent variable and the log of GDP per capita as the independent variable, we arrive at Equation (2):

$$\text{EPI} = 23.386 + 5.921 \times \log(\text{GDPPC}),$$
$$(6.57)\ (13.9) \tag{2}$$

where adj $R^2 = 0.577$, $F = 193.678$, and $n = 144$.
Note: $T$-values are presented in parentheses.

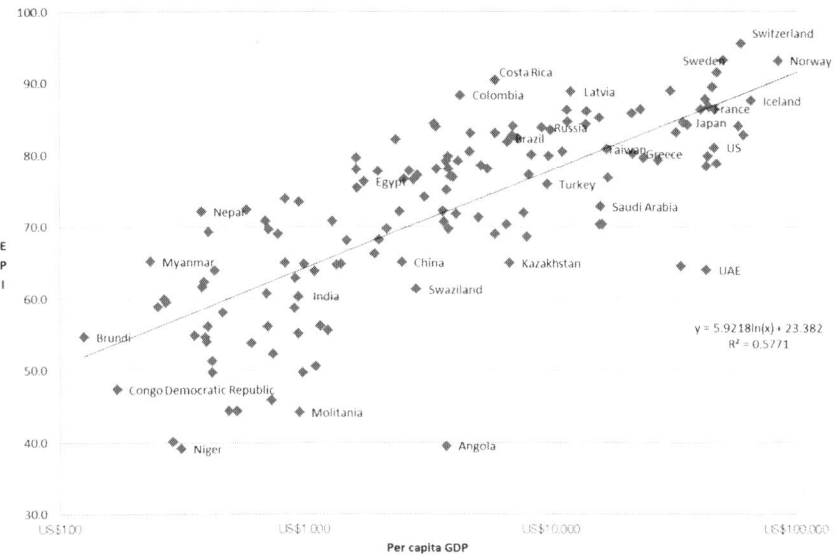

Figure 9.6 Per capita gross domestic product (GDP) and Environmental Performance Index (EPI)

Figure 9.6 is a plot with log of GDP per capita on the horizontal axis and EPI on the vertical axis. Also shown is the regression line for that distribution.

We can discern the following trends from the plot. First, on a general level, we see that EPI tends to rise with GDP per capita (logarithmic). We also note, however, that there is considerable variation in the EPI level at the lower end of the GDP per capita scale (less than $2,000–3,000), even at the same level of income, whereas above that $2,000–3,000 point, the variation diminishes to leave us with a fairly clear positive correlation. It is interesting to note that one of the assertions underlying the environmental Kuznets curve is that the turning point between environmental degradation and environmental improvement is generally around a per capita income of $3,000. Here, too, we could have a turning point near that amount. Second, from Equation (2), we see that for each 1 per cent increase in GDP per capita, the EPI for that country improves by 5.9. Thus, to support a continual improvement in environmental indicators it is necessary not only to have a simple increase in the level of income but also to maintain a certain rate of economic growth.

From the previous discussion, we were able to confirm that, generally, the more economically prosperous a country is, the better its environment. There are, however, a variety of hypotheses relating to such questions as (1) what kind of cause-and-effect relation exists between economic prosperity and environmental quality, and (2) do some other factors also have an influence? Here, we can envision a mechanism by which economic prosperity contributes to an improvement in economic quality through improving the structure of governance.

We next examine how governance and economic prosperity could synergistically act to improve environmental quality.

*Verification of the relation between governance/economic prosperity and environmental quality (Hypothesis 3)*

We conclude our verifications by examining the simultaneous influence of two variables, governance and economic prosperity, on a third, environmental quality. More specifically, we carry out a regression of environmental quality (EPI) versus the WGIAV and GDPPC. The regression takes a form of Equation (3), where $i$ indicates country:

$$EPI_i = \alpha + \beta_1 AV_i + \beta_2 VA_i + \beta_3 PS_i + \beta_4 GE_i + \beta_5 RQ_i + \beta_6 RL_i + \beta_7 CC_i + \beta_8 WGIAV_i + \beta_9 GDPPC_i + \varepsilon_i \qquad (3)$$

Differentiating this from our previous regression analyses is an expected correlation between explanatory variables. In Equation (1), we found EPI and WGIAV to be positively correlated. Similarly, in Equation (2), we found EPI and GDPPC to be positively correlated. We would thus expect at least a positive correlation between WGI and GDPPC, if not a cause-and-effect relation. We also note that the findings of Przeworski et al. (2000) suggest a correlation between economic prosperity and democracy. On calculating the correlation coefficients among the three factors of EPI, WGI and GDPPC, we find the strongest correlation to be between WGIAV and GDPPC.[14] This points not only to the issue of multicollinearity in linear regressions but also to the need to analyse the relation between governance and economic prosperity.

With the above results and with the understanding that this is a first approximation, we conduct a regression in the form of Equation (3), which is the same as Equation (1) with the simple addition of the GDPPC term.

The numerical results are presented as Table 9.5. The addition of GDPCC does act to increase the overall explanatory power, raising $R^2$ to approximately 0.4. However, in no case is GDPCC statistically significant, and thus, we are unable to verify any direct relation with EPI. Statistically speaking, governance appears to be more closely tied to environmental quality than economic prosperity does.

The results could conceivably be interpreted to mean that the economic prosperity of a country and various governance factors interact in a synergistic manner to bring about an improvement in the environment. Note, however, that among these variables exist a variety of superficial interrelations and that there are limits to our ability to unravel cause-and-effect relations with a simple regression analysis alone. As a next step, it would be necessary to conduct a detailed analysis of the causal relation between economic prosperity and the structure of governance.

Table 9.5 The numerical results: Environmental Performance Index (EPI), World Governance Indicators (WGI) and per capita gross domestic product (GDP)

|  | (1)' | (2)' | (3)' | (4)' | (5)' | (6)' | (7)' | (8)' |
|---|---|---|---|---|---|---|---|---|
| Constant | 57.46*** (30.5) | 60.21*** (34.6) | 62.90*** (35.7) | 57.66*** (34.0) | 57.37*** (33.2) | 59.31*** (33.7) | 59.77*** (32.8) | 57.31*** (30.8) |
| VA (Voice and Accountability) | 0.027 (0.46) | 0.211*** (5.26) | | | | | | |
| PS (Political Stability) | −0.053 (−0.90) | | 0.157*** (3.37) | | | | | |
| GE (Government Effectiveness) | 0.250** (1.94) | | | 0.288*** (7.08) | | | | |
| RQ (Regulatory Quality) | 0.149 (1.42) | | | | 0.291*** (7.07) | | | |
| RL (Rule of Law) | −0.028 (−0.22) | | | | | 0.264*** (5.72) | | |
| CC (Control of Corruption) | −0.068 (−0.67) | | | | | | 0.236*** (5.17) | |
| WGIAV (Average of above 6 variables) | | | | | | | | 0.310*** (6.49) |
| GDPPC (per capita GDP) | 0.424 (0.54) | 0.000*** (2.21) | 0.000*** (3.35) | 0.308 (0.48) | 0.356 (0.56) | 0.507 (0.71) | 0.885 (1.25) | 0.205 (0.30) |
| Adj $R^2$ | 0.459 | 0.386 | 0.321 | 0.458 | 0.458 | 0.404 | 0.387 | 0.435 |
| F-value | 18.30 | 46.02 | 35.08 | 61.91 | 61.82 | 49.89 | 93.81 | 56.39 |

*Note*: T-values are presented in parentheses.
***$p < 0.01$, **$p < 0.05$, per cent. *$p < 0.1$.

## Responses to expected criticisms

We have examined several hypotheses that centre around the basic contention that as governance improves so does the environment. There are, of course, problems with and limitations to the present analyses, and a few potential points of criticism are addressed.

First, can it really be said that good governance acts to improve environmental quality? Might not some other factor common to them both act to improve governance *and* the environment? For example, we can easily conceive of a situation in which the citizens of a country take on increasingly non-materialistic values in step with socio-economic advancement. Would that not act to improve both governance and the environment?

As a response, in the sense that the quality of both governance and environmental protection is something that is determined by people, sometimes for better and sometimes for worse, one could probably find sufficient support for the idea that the citizenry of a country, once advanced beyond a simple materialistic view of life, would adopt an attitude more amenable to efforts to improve both governance and the environment. If, however, we instead take "governance" to primarily mean just government effectiveness and regulatory quality, then it is clear that better governance (which would simply mean effective regulation in this case) alone would be enough to improve environmental quality. This leads to another question: What types of policies (e.g., an environmental tax) would be effective in improving the environment? We would have to study the issue further before being able to provide a suitable answer. We do not currently have access to data sufficient to withstand international comparison and, thus, in order to fully explore this question, we would probably have to supplement our analyses with case studies.

Some criticism would be expected on the point that the World Bank's WGI data lean heavily toward corporate information. There is more to public governance than simply corporate governance with a public slant. That is, a government cannot be considered a sort of board of directors under the monitoring and control of citizens and other stakeholders, but rather is an entity intended to resolve public issues through public policy in partnership with the citizenry. Here, one might say that the World Bank's indices, with their emphasis on corporate governance, downplay this aspect of partnership.

The first issue in public governance is how best to establish a system or framework by which the citizenry can monitor and check the manner in which government executes its power, and particularly important here is a shift in focus from "government" to "governance". That is, if one is simply seeking to forge a partnership between the citizenry and the government, then there is no need to drag out "governance"; "government" is good enough. The term *governance* has come to be used to refer to the formation of partnerships with the citizenry to resolve issues (such as environmental issues) unresolvable by the government alone. However, this term has the connotation of resolving an environmental problem not through some government fiat but rather through democratic means including the monitoring and participation of the citizenry.

## Summary and issues for further study

Although many commentators have implied that there is some cause-and-effect relation between democracy (or prosperity) and the environment, surprisingly few studies have been carried out to verify that contention. Here, we approached this issue by examining the WGI from the World Bank and the EPI developed by Esty et al. (2008) to determine relationships among them.

Our findings include that (1) there is a close correlation between world governance and environmental performance indicators; (2) GE and RQ, two dimensions within the governance indices, showed the strongest statistical link to environmental performance indicators; (3) the strongest correlation is between GDPPC and the EPI; and (4) there is also a strong correlation between GDPPC and the WGI, hinting that there may be some cause-and-effect relation between them. The results might have been more interesting (from, at least, the standpoint of the importance of democracy in good governance) if governance dimensions pertaining to "the traditions and institutions by which authority in a country is exercised", such as VA and PS, were shown to have a particularly strong effect on environmental performance. Although the results do not necessarily negate the influence of those factors, we find instead that traditional governance dimensions related to (perceptions of) policy-making performance and executional competence, such as GE and RQ, do express themselves strongly.

Having obtained these results, moving to the next step would involve an examination of the question of why good governance is accompanied by a good environment. One hypothesis we would examine here would be "when a society becomes more prosperous, it becomes more tolerant of environmental regulation and more willing to act in the benefit of future generations" (e.g., by transcending traditional materialistic values or becoming more aware of one's true self-interest). Another question worth exploring would be what kind of environmental policy measures (e.g., an environment tax) best contribute to environmental performance. We leave such issues for study at a later date.

## Acknowledgements

This paper is based on (1) the second meeting of a research group studying democratic ideals and systems for supporting environmental governance (the so-called democracy group, under the direction of Professor Yukio Adachi of Kansai University), conducted at the Umeda campus of Kwansei Gakuin University on 28 August 2009 in conjunction with a project relating to multi-level environmental governance for sustainable development being carried out under a Grant-in-Aid for Scientific Research from the Ministry of Education, Culture, Sports, Science and Technology of Japan and (2) "Yori minshuka suru to kankyou mo yoku naru no ka" (Does more democracy lead to a better environment?), a report presented within Session 2 (Democracy in Environmental Governance: Determination of Issues) of a symposium held jointly by the democracy group and the so-called fundamental theory group (a group studying fundamental theory relating to environmental governance for sustainable development and under the direction of Professor Kazuhiro Ueta of Kyoto University) at the Graduate School of Human and Environmental Studies, Kyoto University on 15 November 2008. The author, who had never before used quantitative analysis techniques, received helpful comments and patient explanations from Professors Adachi and Ueta at the previously mentioned meeting and symposium, and, in the editing of this chapter, from Professor Junichi Nagamine of Kwansei Gakuin University. Also of assistance were Tomoyuki Kano and Yuuki Oda, currently in the doctorate program at Keio University, who checked the statistical methods used in this chapter. The author expresses his appreciation to all. Naturally, any errors in this chapter are the sole responsibility of the author.

## Notes

1. National income growth under authoritarian regimes, at 4.4 per cent, is found to actually be somewhat higher than that under democratic regimes, at 3.9 per cent.
2. Here we thank Professor Kazuo Matsushita of Kyoto University for information on the environmental Kuznets curve. The existence of an environmental Kuznets curve was first asserted at the 1992 World Development Report of the World Bank. The original Kuznets curve was applied to economic growth and income inequality, the relationship between which is said to describe an upside-down $U$-shape. Similar relations were said to exist for the environment, leading to the concept of the environmental Kuznets curve. Note, however, that in a 1998 study by Matsuoka et al., such a relationship was observed for sulphur oxides ($SO_x$) but not for nitrogen oxides ($NO_x$), carbon dioxide ($CO_2$), access to safe water or sanitary facilities or rate of forest diminution. Those researchers thus conclude that the environmental Kuznets curve cannot be said to have general applicability. They also assert that the relationship between economic development and environmental quality cannot be gauged on economic factors alone, but also requires consideration of the social and natural (geomorphic, etc.) mechanisms behind the occurrence of environmental problems together with an understanding of environmental problems together with an understanding of environmental regulatory mechanisms within a context of information disclosure, environmental education and popular movements. Here, we believe that environmental regulatory mechanisms could be considered as an aspect of environmental governance.
3. Esty et al. (2008: 34–40) analyse factors that are effective in improving EPI performance. They call these "EPI drivers", of which they list six: (1) GDP per capita, (2) corruption, (3) government effectiveness, (4) voice and accountability, (5) competitiveness and (6) comparison between environmental health and ecosystem vitality scores. Although Esty et al.'s paper shares the concerns of this chapter and analyses data in a similar manner, the factors within it are analysed in parallel, and it is not always clear which factors are particularly effective.
4. WGI data are available online at http://www.govindicators.org. The data are scaled from 0 per cent to 100 per cent, with a higher percentage being indicative of higher-quality governance.

These data must be interpreted with care, however, because it is taken from a variety of sources and furthermore is synthesized in a manner described in the following paragraph. For a detailed listing of these sources (survey purport, contents, etc.), the reader is referred to the appendices of Kaufmann et al. (2009).

5. This issue is pointed out in Inoue (2004). The six dimensions of the WGI can be broken down into two general groups: those relating to the citizenry (VA and PS) and those primarily relating to the government (GE, RQ, RL and CC). Considering the importance of the citizenry for governance, one might expect the focus to be on VA and PS. However, analysis results suggest that GE and RQ — two indicators of (perceptions of) governmental policy-making and executional competence — actually rank higher as factors behind an improvement in environmental quality.
6. Arndt and Oman (2006). Also Hood et al. (2008), although not dealing directly with governance, assess rankings of public service performance.
7. EPI is used in this chapter as an abbreviation for Environmental Performance Index, although in other chapters it sometimes refers to environmental policy integration. EPI data for 2008 are available online at http://epi.yale.edu. As of 27 August 2011, EPI 2010 appeared to be uploaded. The data are scaled from 0 per cent to 100 per cent, with a higher percentage indicative of higher-quality environmental quality. However, as described in the following, the data sets are fairly narrow, pertaining to only 30 countries or regions at most. For a detailed listing of these sources (survey purport, contents, etc.), the reader is referred to the appendices of Kaufmann et al. (2009).
8. The ESI, which Esty and Porter (2002) cite for their data, is the predecessor of the EPI.
9. This was pointed out to the author by Professor Minoru Tsubugo of Waseda University. Professor Tsubugo propounds three types of environmental indicators: current, target and result. The EPI would presumably be the current or result type.
10. Dr. Esty once worked for the U.S. Environmental Protection Agency (EPA), so there may be some relationship between the EPI and the EPA's Environmental Indicators Initiative.
11. For statistical analysis, we used Excel 2007 and SPSS version 16 (Statistical Package for Social Science).
12. Correlation coefficients among the exploratory variables are shown in the following table. all are significant at the 1 per cent level. Correlations are particularly strong (0.90 or above) for GE–RQ, GE–RL, GE–CC, RQ–RL, RQ–CC and RL–CC. It thus seems likely that GE, RQ, RL and CC follow the same trend. The issue here would then be which aspect of governance does each express.

Table N.1

|  | VA | PS | GE | RQ | RL | CC | AV | GDPPC |
|---|---|---|---|---|---|---|---|---|
| VA (Voice and Accountability) | 1.00 | 0.72 | 0.77 | 0.79 | 0.78 | 0.76 | 0.87 | 0.58 |
| PS (Political Stability) |  | 1.00 | 0.73 | 0.72 | 0.82 | 0.76 | 0.85 | 0.58 |
| GE (Government Effectiveness) |  |  | 1.00 | 0.96 | 0.92 | 0.93 | 0.95 | 0.71 |
| RQ (Regulatory Quality) |  |  |  | 1.00 | 0.90 | 0.90 | 0.95 | 0.71 |
| RL (Rule of Law) |  |  |  |  | 1.00 | 0.94 | 0.97 | 0.72 |
| CC (Control of Corruption) |  |  |  |  |  | 1.00 | 0.95 | 0.72 |
| AV (Average of above 6 variables) |  |  |  |  |  |  | 1.00 | 0.72 |
| GDPPC (per capita GDP) |  |  |  |  |  |  |  | 1.00 |

13. For GDP per capita, we utilize data from the World Economic Outlook Database of the International Monetary Fund from October 2008, available at http://www.imf.org/external/pubs/ft/weo/2008/02/weodata/index.aspx.

14. Correlation coefficients among the three variables are shown in the following table.

Table N.2

|  | 1. Environment | 2. Governance | 3. Wealth |
|---|---|---|---|
| 1. Environment: EPI | – | | |
| 2. Governance: WGI(GE) | 0.678*** | – | |
| 3. Wealth: GDP(PC) | 0.528*** | 0.711*** | – |

\*\*\* $p < .01$.

## REFERENCES

Arndt, Christiane and Charles Oman (2006) *Uses and Abuses of Governance Indicators*, Paris: OECD.

Cambridge Contemporary Social International Institute (ed.) (2008) *Contemporary World*, Tokyo: Hara Shobo (in Japanese).

Esty, Daniel C. and Michael Porter (2002) "National Environmental Performance Measurement and Determinants", in Daniel Esty and Peter K. Cornelius (eds.) *Environmental Performance Measurement: The Global Report 2001–2002*, New York: Oxford University Press, pp. 24–42.

Esty, Daniel C. et al. (2008) "Environmental Performance Index", Yale Centre for Environmental Law & Policy, Yale University, June 16, available at http://www.yale.edu/epi/files/2008EPI_Text.pdf.

Hood, Christopher and Ruth Dixon with Craig Beeston (2008) "Rating the Rankings: Assessing International Rankings of Public Service Performance", *International Public Management Journal*, 11(3), pp. 298–328.

Inoue, Hisashi (2004) "Globalization no keizaiteki sokumen (2)—governance no kokusai hikaku" [Economic Aspects of Globalization (2)—An International Comparison of Governance], *Keizaigaku-Kenkyu (Hokkaido University)*, 54(3), pp. 23–45.

Kaufmann, Daniel, Aart Kraay and Massimo Mastruzzi (2009) "Governance Matters VIII: Aggregate and Individual Governance Indicators, 1996-2008", Policy Research Working Paper 4978, World Bank, available at http://papers.ssrn.com/sol3/papers.cfm?abstract_id=1424591#/.

Matsuoka, Shunji, Reiji Matsumoto and Ikuho Kochi (1998) "Tojoukoku no keizai seichou to kankyou mondai—kankyou Kuznets kyokusen ha seiritsu suru ka" [Economic Growth and Environmental Issues in Developing Countries—Is the Kuznets Curve Valid?], *Kankyou kagakukai shi*, 11(4), pp. 349–362.

Przeworski, Adam et al. (2000) *Democracy and Development: Political Institutions and Well-Being in the World, 1950–1990*, Cambridge: Cambridge University Press.

United Nations Development Programme, United Nations Environment Programme, World Bank and World Resources Institute (eds.) (2003) "Box 2.3 More Democracy, Better Environment?", in *World Resources 2002–2004: Decisions for the Earth: Balance, Voice, and Power*, Washington, DC: World Resources Institute, pp. 32–33, available at http://www.wri.org/sites/default/files/pdf/wr2002fulltxt_023-046_chap02.pdf.

# 10

# Deliberation, expertise and sustainability

*Makoto Usami*

## The problem

Since John Dewey published *The Public and Its Problems* (Dewey, 1927), the relationship between citizens and experts in democracy has been an issue of concern and controversy. Given ordinary people's increasing dependence on scientists, Dewey sought a way for citizens to become involved in public discussion and decision-making. The long-standing issue of citizen–expert relations has recently intensified as large-scale environmental problems, such as global climate change, deforestation and biodiversity diminution, have attained higher priority on the national and international political agenda. When considering technical policy issues for far-reaching environmental problems, citizens appear to have no choice but to rely on the natural and social scientists who provide special knowledge about natural phenomena and their causes as well as economic, political and social conditions.

During the last two decades, the movement of post-positivism has garnered widespread support among policy researchers. Proponents of this movement launched a criticism of two closely connected orthodoxies: the positivist method of policy analysis and the technocratic model of policy processes. The post-positivist policy theorists who criticized these orthodoxies (e.g., Fischer, 1990), however, found it a more difficult task to offer an alternative model of policy process. To meet this challenge, these theorists introduced deliberative democratic theory into policy studies. Since the so-called deliberative turn of the early 1990s, a growing number of policy thinkers have invoked the idea of deliberative democracy—or

*Transition management for sustainable development, Ueta and Adachi (eds.), United Nations University Press, 2014, ISBN 978-92-808-1234-3*

the slightly different notion of discursive democracy—in studying public policy and its process in general (e.g., Dryzek, 1990: 111–148; Hajer and Wagenaar, 2003) and in discussing environmental policy in particular (Smith, 2003).

Nevertheless, deliberative democratic theory in its current form might be incapable of adequately answering the question of the role of experts in the policy-making process. This is because advocates of this theory are inclined to focus on the discourse of reason-giving among lay citizens, while depreciating that of special knowledge. The two leading proponents of deliberative democracy, Amy Gutmann and Dennis Thompson (2004: 14–15) contrast the deliberative conception of democracy with the aggregative one and consider the expert-centred view as one version of the latter. True, they note the possibility that a citizen expands her knowledge through the process of reason exchange with others (Guttman and Thompson, 2004: 12), but their concern is largely about moral conflicts between competing values, not epistemic conflicts between different views on empirical data (Gutmann and Thompson, 1996).

What is more, the deliberative view has encountered moral objections, two of which are particularly relevant to the purpose of this chapter. First, some critics complain that this view tends to leave racial, cultural and political minorities and women at a disadvantage in the process of public discussion. In the contexts of environmental politics, antiglobalization movements and the like, it is argued that deliberative norms are unjustifiably critical of the tactics of political activism, where inequalities in political power and economic resources exist between activists and the establishment.

The second charge against deliberative democracy that I want to single out concerns its feasibility in real politics. A frequently raised objection is that this position remains highly idealistic, if not utopian, because it stresses the ideal conditions of discourse, the participants' inclination towards the public interest and the possibility of an emerging agreement among them (e.g., Blaug, 1999). However, the feasibility objection seems to be weakened by a great variety of experiments in citizens' deliberation assisted by experts. These experiments include Citizens Jury, Planungszelle (Planning Cell), Consensus Conference and Deliberative Polling, all of which are described below. Some political philosophers advocating deliberative democracy pin their hopes on these mechanisms. Robert Goodin and John Dryzek (2006), for example, explore the ways in which small-scale deliberative forums—what they call mini-publics—have impacts on larger policy-making processes. In the post-positivist trend in policy studies, Frank Fischer (2009) discusses the prospects of citizens' collaboration with experts by referring to innovative democratic techniques.

It is true that the results of experimental schemes for citizen–expert collaboration support some claims of deliberative democracy by illustrating ordinary citizens' potential to understand and judge technical issues—a potentiality that deliberative thinkers presuppose. And yet these schemes suffer from several problems and paradoxes, as I argue in the following at length. First, they in fact incorporate the central tenet of positivism, against which post-positivist policy researchers have struggled. Second, some institutional characteristics of deliberative forums might give rise to objectionable environmental policy recommendations. These difficulties cast doubts on the expectation that mini-publics will provide empirical grounds for the non-positivist deliberative model of the environmental policy process.

If my assessment of experiments in citizens' deliberation coupled with experts' facility is correct, then we have to study, from the post-positivist perspective, the roles professional experts can play in experimental deliberation and in the real policy process. To this end, I discuss how experts can help citizen deliberation bring about justifiable environmental policy outcomes. In so doing, I intend to offer a new vision of citizen–expert relationships in the post-positivist environmental policy process.

Before exploring the subject of this chapter, however, notes on basic concepts and terms are in order. Throughout the following discussion, I employ a distinction between citizens and experts. Note that the term "experts" refers to a different group of individuals in each context. Meteorologists may not have any expertise in the field of geology; geologists may lack technical knowledge in the area of zoology. Therefore, meteorologists fall into the category of citizens with respect to geology, and geologists do so with regard to zoology. Another note concerns "sustainability" as used in the title of this chapter, which broadly refers to the goal of environmental conservation.

In the following sections, I begin by illustrating some major types of experimental expert-assisted citizen deliberation, with special reference to experiences in East Asia. Next, the virtues and limits of these types of deliberation are identified from the theoretical and moral points of view. Then, I try to advance an alternative post-positivist vision of the multifaceted relationship between laypeople and specialists in the environmental policy process. I also defend the presuppositions and proposals of my view against several possible objections. This chapter concludes by suggesting the implication that my proposed form of citizen–expert collaboration might have on the concept of deliberation.

## Experiments in expert-assisted citizen deliberation

The experiments in expert-assisted citizen deliberation that have been conducted to date include a great variety of forms and their variations, only four of which I briefly describe here. The first is the Citizens Jury process devised by Ned Crosby in the United States in the early 1970s (Crosby, 1995; Crosby and Nethercut, 2005). In this process, a randomly selected and demographically representative panel of citizens, usually consisting of 18 to 24 individuals, meets for four or five days to examine an issue of social relevance. After hearing a variety of expert witnesses and deliberating together on the issue, the jury members present their recommendations to policymakers and the public. The Jefferson Center for New Democratic Processes founded by Crosby has implemented more than 30 projects at the local, regional, state and national levels. Among the topics tackled by juries are national health-care reform, budget priorities and environmental issues. Juries of this kind have also been formed in Australia, Britain, Canada, Denmark, Germany and Spain.

The second form of deliberative forum is the Planning Cell mechanism proposed by Peter Dienel in Germany at the beginning of the 1970s (Dienel and Renn, 1995; Hendriks, 2005). This mechanism typically includes six to nine replicating planning cells, each of which contains about 25 randomly selected citizens, resulting in the involvement of hundreds of citizens at multiple venues. Over four to five days, participants in a planning cell work on a specific issue determined in advance by the commissioning body. They have the opportunity to hear scientists, stakeholders and interest-group representatives and then discuss the issue in groups of five people. Facilitated by a male and a female process escort, citizens in each cell produce outputs, which are finally synthesized into the project report. The report is distributed to the presenters, policymakers and relevant associations.

In the early days, Planning Cell projects tended to focus on urban infrastructure problems, but later policy issues discussed have ranged over waste management, energy, gene technology and information technology. To date, the vast majority of these projects have been carried out in Germany, but interest has been growing in other countries, with similar events occurring in Austria, Switzerland and the United States. A notable variation of planning cells found in East Asia is the Citizen Deliberation Meeting process in Japan. In this process, for one or two days randomly selected citizens discuss the issue in groups of five to six people after they hear experts and local government officials. The first meeting was held in Tokyo in 2005, and since then, approximately 200 meetings have taken place around the country. The topics debated in these meetings include community building, local security and child care, among others.

The third category singled out is the Consensus Conference scheme, which the Danish Board of Technology developed in the mid-1980s by drastically amending the arrangements of the consensus development conference, an expertise-based forum for technology assessment devised in the United States in the late 1970s (Danish Board of Technology, 2006). The Danish model is a three-stage process involving a project management team, a steering committee, a citizen panel and an expert panel. At the first stage, the management team frames the topic, appoints the steering committee to oversee the following stages and chooses a moderator to facilitate the citizen panel discussion. Between 10 and 30 (usually about 15) citizens with neither prior knowledge of nor partisan interest in the topic are selected in such a way that the panel demographically represents the population of the affected community or the nation as a whole. At the second stage, the first preparatory meeting is held, in which members of the citizen panel gather to discuss a background paper and to formulate key questions for experts. Based on these questions, the management team draws up a list of candidates for members of the expert panel, which is then approved by the citizen panel at the second preparatory meeting. The appointed experts prepare their answers to the questions, using language comprehensible to laypeople. The third stage involves a four-day conference in which the scientists respond to the key questions and the citizen panel members cross-examine the presenters. After deliberating in small groups, members of the citizen panel prepare a report that summarizes their points of agreement and disagreement. The expert panel has the opportunity to correct factual misstatements in the report but does not otherwise comment on it. The report is presented at a press conference and later published.

Between 1987 and 2003, the Danish Board of Technology organized 22 conferences on a number of issues including genetically modified food, human genome mapping and environmental issues (Loka Institute, 2007). Variations of the Danish model have been used in Argentina, Australia, Belgium, Britain, Canada, the Netherlands, New Zealand, Switzerland and the United States. I focus here on some experiences in East Asia. In Japan in 1998, a group of researchers in the field of science, technology and society launched the first pilot Consensus Conference project examining the issue of gene therapy. The following year, this group conducted a second pilot to discuss information technology (Wakamatsu, 2010). The first full-fledged conference, in which citizens tackled the issue of genetically modified food, was sponsored by the Ministry of Agriculture, Forestry and Fisheries in 2001 (Kobayashi, 2003). This nationwide event was followed by two concise conferences held in Hokkaido in 2007 and 2008. In South Korea, the Korean National Commission for the UN Educational, Scientific and Cultural Organization (UNESCO) held conferences in 1998 and 1999, dealing with the issues of genetically modified food and cloning, respectively. In Taiwan, a technique of this type, combined with the Delphi method and a questionnaire survey, was employed in 2005–2006 to revise the code of ethics for nurses.

The last category of mini-publics that I want to discuss is the Deliberative Polling procedure innovated by James Fishkin at the end of the 1980s (Fishkin, 1991, 1997: 161–228; Center for Deliberative Democracy, 2011). This procedure begins with polling a representative random sample on the targeted issues. Next, respondents of the poll are invited to gather for a weekend to discuss these issues. The participants engage in a dialogue with experts and political leaders, drawing on questions developed in small-group discussions. After these events, the sample is again asked the original questions. The resulting changes in opinion that are revealed in the survey are considered, by theorists and practitioners of the deliberative poll, to represent the conclusions the public would reach if they had an opportunity to become better informed about and more engaged in the issues.

Dozens of deliberative opinion polls have been conducted in the United States since the beginning of the 1990s. Debated topics cover electric utilities, public education and local economic policy. Other countries where polls of this kind have been held include Australia (on reconciliation with Aborigines), Brazil (on public official career reform), Britain (on crimes, the monarchy and democratic reforms, among others), Denmark (on Danish participation in the European Union), Greece (on mayoral candidates) and Italy (on immigrants' right to vote). In East Asia, the most noticeable experience to date may be the 2005 Deliberative Polling conducted in China (Fishkin et al., 2010), a country where a full-fledged democracy has not been established in terms of a multiparty system or free speech. The polling, conducted in a township of a city in southern China, allowed a sample of residents to deliberate on which infrastructure projects would be funded in the coming year. After the discussion, the participants' policy choices had changed considerably, and their level of knowledge on the issue was enhanced. In Japan, two concise polls discussing the future of a city were trialled in 2010, and the first full-scale and nationwide deliberative poll on the issue of public pensions took place in 2011.

## The promise and peril of experimental deliberation

The experiences with citizen–expert collaboration of the four types described in the previous section—and of many others—seem to support claims of the deliberative conception of democracy. Deliberative theories fall into three non-exclusive categories. The first is what I call the procedure-focused theory, which explores the counterfactual conditions of public discourse under which deliberated conclusions would appear. Inspired by John Rawls (1971), Joshua Cohen (1989) advocates one version of this theory; Seyla Benhabib (1996) develops another under the influence of Jürgen Habermas (1981). Cohen, Benhabib and other proceduralists have faced the objection that such conditions are too idealistic, if not utopian, to be realized in real-world settings. The achievements of democratic forums, however, supply actual cases in which these conditions are almost met.

The second argument for deliberation is the transformation-focused theory advanced by Bernard Manin (1987) and James Bohman (1996), among others. They stress the prospect that citizens' political desires based on their private interests may be transformed, through the process of mutual reason-giving, into judgements founded on their concern for the public interest. The Deliberative Polling procedure is intended to illustrate such transformation of individual opinions, and many outcomes of other forms of innovative democratic forums more or less indicate it.

The last category of the deliberative view is the precommitment-focused theory, a typical example of which is Jon Elster's (1998) reading of the U.S. Constitution as a framework for political deliberation. One proposed institution of deliberative precommitment in relation to mini-publics is that of Deliberation Day addressed by Bruce Ackerman and James Fishkin (2004). They propose

Deliberative Polling on a national scale conducted on the weekend before the election of members of Congress.

Notwithstanding the various forms of powerful support they offer to the deliberative conception of democracy, experiments in expert-assisted citizens' dialogue seem to have some paradoxes and pitfalls. From a theoretical perspective, it is doubtful that projects of civic deliberation can lay empirical foundations for the post-positivist model of policy process. This is because such projects presuppose the separation of the realms of facts and values, which is a positivistic premise against which post-positivist policy thinkers have long struggled. In the Citizens Jury process, for instance, scientist witnesses are invited to provide a citizen jury with knowledge of the relevant facts. After expert hearings are held, members of the jury are supposed to amalgamate their competing value judgements and form a set of policy recommendations. In this setting, informants holding scientific knowledge are located in the domain of facts and the final judges lacking such knowledge are in the domain of values. This is also the case with the Planning Cell, Consensus Conference and Deliberative Polling mechanisms. From the neo-Kantian schools to logical positivism, a clear discrimination between fact and value has been the central tenet of the positivist tradition. The fact/value dichotomy shared by traditional policy analysts has been the very target of post-positivist movements during the past three decades. Therefore, deliberative experiments based on this dichotomy fail to supply empirical grounds for the post-positivist perspective on policy process.

The moral worry regarding programs of civic deliberation concerns the strict exclusion of experts from discussion on public values, which is connected with the aforementioned separation of fact and value. In a consensus conference, a citizen panel prepares a report, taking into account experts' responses to key questions on relevant facts. The expert panel is permitted to correct factual misstatements in the report but otherwise makes no comment on it. Experts are also prohibited from entering into normative discourse on moral values in the schemes of citizen juries and deliberative polls, although they do play some role in planning cells.

The circumstances in which a deliberation on values leads to a morally contestable policy recommendation might arise from two causes. One cause is what might be called the scope problem, which means that the impacts of the public policies and private actions in question go beyond the limited range of many citizens' interests and imagination. The scope problem frequently appears in the context of large-scale environmental problems. A paradigm case is global warming, which will admittedly have adverse impacts on people in many parts of the world and on their remote descendants. Other ecological problems with far-reaching effects include deforestation, desertification and biodiversity diminution. Nevertheless, it is difficult, although not impossible, for most people to be seriously concerned about the well-being of those living in other countries and at distant temporal points.

The other cause of objectionable policy proposals due to the exclusion of experts is what I call the soundness problem. The soundness problem refers to situations in which opinions shared by the majority of citizens are unfair to some members of society. The majority might simply be uninterested in racial, cultural and political minorities, or it might be biased against these minorities because of its prejudices. The soundness problem has been recognized and addressed in some past deliberative experiments. In the Deliberative Polling project conducted in Australia in 2001, which dealt with the issue of reconciliation with Aborigines, an oversample of Indigenous Australians was invited into the poll and assigned to some of the discussion groups.[1] Although such a practical remedy to the problem seems reasonable as such, it is in tension with the project's basic principle of representative random sampling.

It is noteworthy that the deliberative conception of democracy has been criticized for its negative attitude towards minorities and radical opponents. Referring to empirical findings on racial and gender biases found in jury discussions in the judicial process, Lynn Sanders (1997) objects that this conception may leave minorities and women at a disadvantage in political discussion. While partly acknowledging its significance, Iris Marion Young (1996) notes that deliberative theory rests on the dispassionate and disembodied discourse of white middle-class men, excluding several other forms of communication that characterize women and racial minorities. She also argues that deliberative norms are not justified in being critical of the strategies of political activism, such as street marches, sit-ins and boycotts, when structural inequalities exist between the activists and the majority (Young 2001).

In the context of environmental politics in particular, it is controversial whether deliberative theory adequately respects the ideal of environmental justice developed in the United States. The definition by the US Environmental Protection Agency (2012) reads, "Environmental Justice is the fair treatment and meaningful involvement of all people regardless of race, color, national origin, or income with respect to the development, implementation, and enforcement of environmental laws, regulations, and policies." In the last two decades, the environmental justice movement has spread through the political and legal struggles against environmental policies discriminative against communities of African Americans, Latinos, Native Americans and low socio-economic status groups. If deliberative theory suffers from its racial and class biases, as critics note, then it is far from clear how this theory can protect these communities from discriminatory laws and policies.

Moreover, some authors complain that deliberative democratic theory does not permit the cost-levying tactics employed by environmental protesters, such as the recurrent breaking of a targeted company's windows, even when it is substantially difficult for the protesters to participate in the reason-giving discourse because of underlying inequalities in political power and economic resources (Humphrey, 2007: 94–113). True, it is illegal and—in my view—morally indefensible for environmentalists to break the windows of a company they oppose.

Nonetheless, the problem of inequality in the political and economic domains remains, regardless of the legal and moral assessment of activists' strategies, and so deliberative democrats must respond to it.

## Experts in citizen deliberation

In the previous section, I sought to identify the theoretical and moral difficulties of experiments in a combination of citizen discussion with expert knowledge, while noting their merits from the viewpoint of deliberative democracy. The question then arises: How can we circumvent these difficulties? To answer this question, I outline the theory of how expert deliberation can enhance and improve citizen deliberation.

The theoretical concern mentioned earlier is the paradox that deliberative mechanisms, while being expected to provide empirical cornerstones for the post-positivist model of policy process, in fact postulate the positivistic separation of fact and value. A moral risk related to this paradox is that excluding experts from the debate on moral values may lead to objectionable policy recommendations. To remedy these problems, we need to expand the range of expertise used in deliberative experiments and the policy-making process more broadly.

Forms of expertise that can serve citizen deliberation fall into two categories: substantive and procedural. In the settings of the mini-publics depicted above, expert witnesses who offer substantive knowledge at hearings are natural scientists and, to a lesser degree, social scientists. Their testimonies, at times accompanied by the testimonies of stakeholders and interest-group leaders, are taken to be the fact-regarding stuff on which citizens base their value judgements about the policy issue.[2] Furthermore, such specialists of procedural knowledge as process escorts in planning cells and moderators in consensus conferences play important roles in facilitating discussion among citizens. What these experimental arrangements seem to lack is participation by experts in types of substantive knowledge other than the natural and social sciences. Moral, legal and political philosophers, who devote themselves to the analysis of and controversy over moral concepts and ideas, have so far occupied no place in most settings of citizen deliberation.

The normative knowledge held by social philosophers seems to be more relevant to environmental policy issues than traditionally supposed. Take, as an example, the issue of intergenerational justice embedded in global climate change. The massive discharge of greenhouse gases by the present generation admittedly has greater adverse effects on future generations than on this generation. In addition, the more distant our successors are from us in temporal terms, the more serious the impact of the current gas emissions they will suffer. It is a basic principle widely accepted, however, that the primary task of our government is to serve us, not others—including those living decades or centuries later. These conflicting facts pose questions about the idea of intergenerational justice: Should our government concern itself with our descendants at the cost of current citizens?

If so, why should it do so? What ought we to sacrifice for the sake of our remote successors? These and other moral issues have been tackled by many scholars of moral, legal and political philosophy during the last four decades (e.g., Sikora and Barry, 1978; Partridge, 1981; Laslett and Fishkin, 1992; Dobson, 1999; Gosseries and Meyer, 2009).

On the other hand, most citizens presumably have scant interest in their relationship with their distant descendants. True, environmental non-governmental organization leaders and supporters, ecological activists and green consumers are interested in the sustainability of the natural environment and the well-being of future individuals. Nevertheless, they do not seem ready to justify their convictions and feelings in clear and rigorous language. To make a sound policy choice, therefore, citizens need not only scientific knowledge on natural and social phenomena and the causal links therewith but also philosophical devices exploring the question of intergenerational justice. It is thus advisable to have social philosophers participate in the process of citizen deliberation over the ethical issues underlying a policy proposal affecting future people. These philosophers are also expected to take part in the processes both of official policy-making and of public opinion formation.

Let us turn to the issues surrounding the disadvantaged in reference to environmental problems. The environmental justice movement in the United States has challenged the state and national policies that leave members of racial minorities and low socio-economic status groups at a disadvantage in terms of safety and health. Such policies are also found in many other countries, even in established democracies where basic human rights are protected and equality under the law is respected. On the other hand, supporters and sympathizers of green activism pose the question of how deliberative norms can reduce the inequality in political power between green protesters and other citizens.

The first step in tackling these problems of inequality may be to make a distinction between the two roles that experts can play in deliberative processes. One is the information-providing role. In the existing arrangements of democratic experiments, scientists perform this role by answering questions raised by a citizen panel. Social philosophers should also undertake this role in discussions on moral values, as I argued. The other task experts can shoulder is the influence-promoting role, which requires specialists to enhance the political voice of a specific group of disadvantaged individuals by giving, on their behalf, a set of the reasons why the government should satisfy their claims. People with expertise who engage in augmenting the influence of the disadvantaged can be called representative experts. Representative experts might well include natural and social scientists, social philosophers, physicians and lawyers.

Each group of racial, cultural and political minorities as well as women may be supported by its own team of representative experts; however, the conflict and compromise of the groups' requirements and requests might result in the politics of unprincipled bargaining that characterizes an interest-group democracy.

The deliberative conception of democracy, or a convincing version of it, does not deny the possibility of political bargaining, but it assesses the justifiability of bargaining against the criterion of deliberation (Gutmann and Thompson, 2004: 56). Political bargaining cannot be a substitute for deliberation because the former accepts the current distribution of power and resources as a baseline from which negotiations begin (Gutmann and Thompson, 2004: 114). How can one then coordinate the competing demands of numerous groups assisted by different representative expert teams? This question leads us to the second stage of the deliberative expert theory.

In representative democracy, the primary agents in charge of coordinating conflicting group claims are to be the political representatives. However, leaving the coordinative tasks exclusively to members of the legislative and executive branches would engender some risks. The major goal of politicians is to be re-elected, and they tend to rely on votes and financial support from special interest groups in order to achieve that goal. Politicians are equipped with skills of persuasion and negotiation, but their knowledge on policy issues may be limited at times. For these and other reasons, the political process of making different groups' demands compatible requires assistance from experts. Let us call those who help legislators and executives coordinate political claims responsive experts. Responsive experts assist the political representatives as members of consultative committees of the legislature, the president, the cabinet or a ministry, appointed government officials and personal advisers of a politician. These experts play the information-providing role for policymakers in political processes. Of course, an expert is a person who lays claim to a single area of specialty, whatever technical knowledge she also has in neighbouring fields. It stems from this nature of expertise that a responsive expert's advice is frequently a recommendation made from a single perspective. Therefore, good policy advice will come from deliberation among competing responsive experts in a variety of disciplines related to the issue.

## Objections and responses

Several objections might be raised against the argument I made in the previous sections. Some critics may focus on the starting point of my discussion—a distinction between citizen and expert. Others may argue against its terminal point— the proposed active roles of experts in deliberation on environmental policy. I begin by responding to the former group of criticisms.

Possible arguments against the citizen/expert distinction include the following two: the first emphasizes the fact that there are borderline cases—an enthusiastic fossil hunter who did not major in palaeontology in his university days, for example. Of course, many cases exist near the line between citizens and experts because the difference between the two groups depends on the quality and quantity of special knowledge and thus is in part a matter of degree. The existence of controversial near-boundary cases, however, does not imply that a conceptual distinction is impossible or insignificant. We have countless ambiguous cases in the colour gradation between green and yellow, but no one denies the possibility or significance of the green/yellow discrimination.

The second criticism argues that we cannot draw a clear line between experts and laypeople in the days of mass higher education and information affluence. The fact that a citizen panel or a demographically representative sample could, in a great number of mini-public cases, understand scientist witnesses and debate with them, the argument proceeds, demonstrates the capabilities of laypeople to acquire technical knowledge. Moreover, an expert who holds a single area of specialty is not suited to tackling such multifaceted affairs as environmental problems that can be grasped only in a multidisciplinary way. This criticism is misguided in two respects. First, it is one thing to comprehend scientific observations when they are presented in simple, non-technical language; it is quite another to research, analyse and interpret these observations. The ability to carry out the latter, unlike the ability to do the former, requires systematic academic training. Second, the critics miss the point of a multidisciplinary approach. This approach does not make academic techniques in each field useless; on the contrary, it connects and integrates techniques in different fields. Therefore, multidisciplinary approaches can be taken only by a team or network of well-trained specialists.

My proposal of expanding the range of expertise used in deliberation will also meet with objections. The first objection notes that an expert, just like a layperson, is fallible in collecting, analysing and reading empirical data and might be biased by her own vocational interest. Given these unavoidable limitations of experts, my suggestion of active experts loses its force because it assumes an infallible and non-biased specialist. This objection misconstrues my discussion. I never suppose that any human being is infallible, no matter what knowledge she has. As to bias in judgement, I have no idea whether the average expert is more biased than the average layperson is because of her self-interest, prejudice or whatever else. Perhaps the answer varies from person to person. What is noteworthy here is that, in ordinary life, we do rely on the special knowledge of other people even when we recognize that they might be biased. When you buy a coat, you presumably consult a salesperson even though you know he might recommend a relatively expensive one. The government's policy choice produces much broader and more serious impacts than your coat choice, and therefore in a policy decision it is a fortiori advisable to consult those holding special knowledge.

The second charge is that the academic approach to environmental issues is in an inevitable and intense confrontation with environmental populist visions. It is observed, for instance, that US economists and policy analysts are mostly concerned with measuring the performance of agents and agencies and setting priorities among goals, whereas activists of the environmental justice movement seek the effective involvement and equitable treatment of communities of minorities and low-income groups (Foreman, 2002: 152). There are indeed differences between academic method and activist objective, but it would be too early to conclude that the two are unbridgeable. Take the case of a manufacturer's air pollution as an example. On one hand, measuring the emissions is a crucial step in protecting the security and health of affected neighbours. On the other hand, equitable treatment of disadvantaged groups counts in defining policy goal priorities. In my view, representative experts who enhance the voice of disadvantaged groups and isolated protesters are expected to couple academic tools with popular goals.

## Conclusion

In the previous sections, I endeavoured to grapple with the old question many political theorists have asked since Dewey's celebrated book was published: What is the desirable relationship between citizens and experts in democracy? I examined this question in relation to environmental problems, which require laypeople to rely on technicalities even more than many other public issues.

To begin with, I described and illustrated the four major mechanisms of expert-assisted citizen deliberation—Citizens Jury, Planning Cell, Consensus Conference and Deliberative Polling—on which post-positivist policy thinkers have pinned their hopes. Next, it was noted that these mechanisms support theories of deliberative democracy by offering real examples of ideal discourse situations, by indicating the transformation of citizens' opinions and by suggesting institutions of precommitment for deliberation. At the same time, I tried to show that democratic forums paradoxically involve the positivist separation of fact and value. Moreover, excluding experts from discussions about values, it was argued, might result in objectionable policy recommendations because of the scope problem and the soundness problem.

To tackle these paradoxes and pitfalls, I outlined a new vision of citizen–expert relationships in mini-publics and policy processes more broadly. Both the positivist fact/value dichotomy and the scope problem can be resolved by the input of special knowledge on moral values through the involvement of social philosophers in civic discussion both within and outside of deliberative forums. The soundness problem, which is connected to the unequal distribution of power and resources among citizens, can be reduced by the juxtaposition of influence-promotion by representative experts and information-provision by responsive experts. After sketching my vision of citizen–expert relations, I responded to possible criticisms of my basic distinction between citizen and expert. I also defended my proposal to expand the expertise used in deliberative policy processes against some objections.

Deliberation is one of those concepts whose meaning and connotation have drastically changed throughout the history of thought. At the end of the fourteenth century, the term "deliberate" derived from the Latin word "*librare*" (to weigh), which in turn came from "*libra*" (scales). By the eighteenth century, deliberation had come to refer to discussion within a small and exclusive group of political rulers or elites. In his 1774 "Speech to the Electors of Bristol", Edmund Burke (1999: 11) announced that "Parliament is a *deliberative* Assembly of *one* Nation, with *one* Interest, that of the whole". The elitist conception of deliberation illustrated by Burke's words was, in the 1980s, thoroughly substituted by a populist one, which demands the wide and effective involvement of ordinary people in public discussion. Based on the latter conception, experimental democratic forums aim to facilitate deliberation by dividing citizen participants into small groups and by having expert witnesses provide the participants with technical knowledge. These innovative forums, however, suffer from the paradoxes and pitfalls previously identified. To overcome these problems, we need to advance expert deliberation in various forms and to combine it with citizen deliberation. This might add a new page to the history of the meanings of deliberation.

## Acknowledgement

I am grateful to Yukio Adachi, Jun Iio, Kazuo Matsushita, Tatsuro Niikawa, Wataru Sano and Kazuhiro Ueta for their helpful comments on an earlier version of this chapter.

## Notes

1. An oversample means a deliberately selected group of individuals of a rare type that is intended to obtain reasonably precise estimates of the properties of the type. It follows from the sampling of a much higher proportion of this type than of the rest of the population.
2. By contrast, testimonies of stakeholders and interest-group leaders belong to the realm of values but are treated as a portion of the data that presumably serve citizens' final value judgements.

## REFERENCES

Ackerman, Bruce and James S. Fishkin (2004) *Deliberation Day*, New Haven, CT: Yale University Press.
Benhabib, Seyla (1996) "Toward a Deliberative Model of Democratic Legitimacy", in Seyla Benhabib (ed.) *Democracy and Difference: Contesting the Boundaries of the Political*, Princeton, NJ: Princeton University Press, pp. 67–94.
Blaug, Ricardo (1999) *Democracy, Real and Ideal: Discourse Ethics and Radical Politics*, Albany: State University of New York Press.
Bohman, James (1996) *Public Deliberation: Pluralism, Complexity, and Democracy*, Cambridge, MA: MIT Press.
Burke, Edmund (1999) *Select Works of Edmund Burke, Vol. 4 Miscellaneous Writings*, comp. Francis Canavan, Indianapolis, IN: Liberty Fund.

Center for Deliberative Democracy (2011) "Deliberative Polling: Toward a Better-Informed Democracy", available at http://cdd.stanford.edu/polls/docs/summary/.

Cohen, Joshua (1989) "Deliberation and Democratic Legitimacy", in Alan Hamlin and Phillip Petit (eds.) *The Good Polity: Normative Analysis of the State*, Oxford: Blackwell, pp. 17–34.

Crosby, Ned (1995) "Citizens Juries: One Solution for Difficult Environmental Questions", in Ortwin Renn, Thomas Webler and Peter Wiedemann (eds.) *Fairness and Competence in Citizen Participation: Evaluating Models for Environmental Discourse*, Dordrecht: Kluwer Academic, pp. 157–174.

Crosby, Ned and Doug Nethercut (2005) "Citizens Juries: Creating a Trustworthy Voice of the People", in John Gastil and Peter Levine (eds.) *The Deliberative Democracy Handbook: Strategies for Effective Civic Engagement in the Twenty-First Century*, San Francisco: Jossey-Bass, pp. 111–119.

Danish Board of Technology (2006) "The Consensus Conference", available at http://www.tekno.dk/subpage.php3?article=468&toppic=kategori12&language=uk.

Dewey, John (1927) *The Public and Its Problems*, Denver: Alan Swallow.

Dienel, Peter C. and Ortwin Renn (1995) "Planing Cells: A Gate to 'Fractal' Mediation", in Ortwin Renn, Thomas Webler and Peter Wiedemann (eds.) *Fairness and Competence in Citizen Participation: Evaluating Models for Environmental Discourse*, Dordrecht: Kluwer Academic, pp. 117–140.

Dobson, Andrew (ed.) (1999) *Fairness and Futurity: Essays on Environmental Sustainability and Social Justice*, Oxford: Oxford University Press.

Dryzek, John S. (1990) *Discursive Democracy: Politics, Policy, and Political Science*, Cambridge: Cambridge University Press.

Elster, Jon (1998) "Deliberation and Constitution Making", in John Elster (ed.) *Deliberative Democracy*, Cambridge: Cambridge University Press, pp. 97–122.

Fischer, Frank (1990) *Technocracy and the Politics of Expertise*, Newbury Park, CA: Sage.

—— (2009) *Democracy and Expertise: Reorienting Policy Inquiry*, New York: Oxford University Press.

Fishkin, James S. (1991) *Democracy and Deliberation: New Directions for Democratic Reform*, New Haven, CT: Yale University Press.

—— (1997) *The Voice of the People: Public Opinion and Democracy*, New Haven, CT: Yale University Press.

Fishkin, James S., Baogang He, Robert C. Luskin and Alice Siu (2010) "Deliberative Democracy in an Unlikely Place: Deliberative Polling in China", *British Journal of Political Science* 40(2), pp. 435–448.

Foreman, Christopher H., Jr. (2002) "The Civic Sustainability of Reform", in Donald F. Kettl (ed.) *Environmental Governance: A Report on the Next Generation of Environmental Policy*, Washington, D.C.: Brookings Institution Press, pp. 146–176.

Goodin, Robert E. and John S. Dryzek (2006) "Deliberative Impacts: The Macro-Political Uptake of Mini-Publics", *Politics and Society* 34(2), pp. 219–244.

Gosseries, Axel and Lukas H. Meyer (eds.) (2009) *Intergenerational Justice*, Oxford: Oxford University Press.

Gutmann, Amy and Dennis Thompson (1996) *Democracy and Disagreement*, Cambridge, MA: Harvard University Press.

—— (2004) *Why Deliberative Democracy?* Princeton, NJ: Princeton University Press.

Habermas, Jürgen (1981) *Theorie des kommunikativen Handelns*, Frankfurt am Main: Suhrkamp.

Hajer, Maarten A. and Hendrik Wagenaar (eds.) (2003) *Deliberative Policy Analysis: Understanding Governance in the Network Society*, New York: Cambridge University Press.

Hendriks, Carolyn M. (2005) "Consensus Conferences and Planning Cells: Lay Citizen Deliberations", in John Gastil and Peter Levine (eds.) *The Deliberative Democracy Handbook: Strategies for Effective Civic Engagement in the Twenty-First Century*, San Francisco: Jossey-Bass, pp. 80–110.

Humphrey, Mathew (2007) *Ecological Politics and Democratic Theory: The Challenge to the Deliberative Ideal*, London: Routledge.

Kobayashi, Tadashi (2003) *Who Should Think About Science and Technology? Experiments in Consensus Conference*, Nagoya: Nagoya University Press (in Japanese).

Laslett, Peter and James S. Fishkin (eds.) (1992) *Philosophy, Politics, and Society, Sixth Series: Justice Between Age Groups and Generations*, New Haven, CT: Yale University Press.

Loka Institute (2007) "Danish-Style, Citizen-Based Deliberative Consensus Conferences on Science & Technology Policy Worldwide", available at http://www.loka.org/TrackingConsensus.html.

Manin, Bernard (1987) "On Legitimacy and Political Deliberation", *Political Theory* 15(3), pp. 338–368.

Partridge, Ernest (ed.) (1981) *Responsibilities to Future Generations: Environmental Ethics*, Buffalo, NY: Prometheus Books.

Rawls, John (1971) *A Theory of Justice*, Cambridge, MA: Harvard University Press.

Sanders, Lynn M. (1997) "Against Deliberation", *Political Theory* 25(3), pp. 347–376.

Sikora, R. I. and Brian Barry (eds.) (1978) *Obligations to Future Generations*, Philadelphia: Temple University Press.

Smith, Graham (2003) *Deliberative Democracy and the Environment*, London: Routledge.

United States Environmental Protection Agency (2012) "Environmental Justice", available at http://www.epa.gov/environmentaljustice/.

Wakamatsu, Yukio (2010) *How Can the Voice of Citizens Reach the Policy of Science and Technology? Consensus Conference, Scenario Workshop and Deep Dialogue*, Tokyo: Tokyo Denki University Press (in Japanese).

Young, Iris Marion (1996) "Communication and the Other: Beyond Deliberative Democracy", in Seyla Benhabib (ed.) *Democracy and Difference: Contesting the Boundaries of the Political*, Princeton, NJ: Princeton University Press, pp. 120–135.

―――― (2001) "Activist Challenges to Deliberative Democracy", *Political Theory* 29(5), pp. 670–690.

# 11

# The restructuring of society around environmental education: From education for economic development to education for sustainable development

*Wataru Sano*

Environmental education is generally understood to be a form of education for children (and sometimes adults) that imparts a range of knowledge on the environment (e.g., the history of environmental issues, current issues, how ecosystems work, etc.) and provides opportunities to interact with and become close to nature, thus cultivating a connection with and an interest in nature and, furthermore, an understanding of the significance and importance of environmental conservation. This general understanding of environmental education is not in itself inaccurate, and there is little doubt that such education is important. Only in recent years in Japan has the importance of environmental education come to be realized, and many elementary and middle schools are providing environmental education as part of their "integrated study" curriculum. It should also be noted that, for the most part, this education is administered along the lines of the common understanding of the subject as presented earlier.

While recognizing the importance of such endeavours and efforts, in this chapter I wish to assert that a more engaged system of environmental education should be established—one which we might call "education for sustainable development". This is not to say that conventional modes of environmental education should be completely dismissed, merely that they have deficiencies and alone are not enough.

In what follows, I go into the reasons for this conclusion in more detail, but here I wish to outline the main issues. Simply put, conventional environmental education is merely the result of adding some environmental topics to existing educational curricula and systems. In other words, it consisted of an ad hoc "tack-on" approach. This approach, however, is utterly insufficient if anything close to sustainable development is to be achieved. Environmental education should be administered in conjunction with sweeping attempts to effect the kind of restructuring of society as a whole that would lead to sustainable development. Unless such attempts are made, environmental education will result in nothing more than a few increased efforts at "environmental action" (conserving energy, separating trash, etc.) built on the societal status quo. It should go without saying that I consider such environmental action far from meritless. Nevertheless, one point that the proponents of ecological modernization make is that even if the levels of such ordinary environmental activities were to increase to some extent, we would still in all likelihood be unable to resolve the serious and widespread environmental issues that we are facing. Sustainable development is impossible without a sustainable society. It is therefore incumbent on us to change modern society itself.

In fact, from my perspective, most people have acquired substantial knowledge of environmental issues, and more and more people are either working (or wish to work) to protect the environment. These people and activities certainly do contribute to a certain extent to the resolution of environmental issues, but many experts are in agreement that globally, environmental problems are becoming ever more serious and that the burden placed on the environment has not substantially declined. Needless to say, one reason is that the causes of environmental issues do not lie exclusively with individuals and how they go about their daily lives; rather, the causes can be traced to the structure of society itself. Granted, the case may be that drastic changes to consumer behaviour could lead to some improvements in—or even the resolution of—environmental problems. In most cases, however, such efforts not only fail to fundamentally resolve the problem, they are incapable of even slowing its escalation. There are fundamental limits to any system of environmental education that is predicated on current socio-economic structures. Therefore, in my mind, for any regimen of environmental education to have the desired effect, it must be administered in conjunction with programs to restructure the fabric of society. More precisely, as a condition of achieving such a restructuring, it is not only necessary to carry out environmental education but also to devise modes of environmental education that aim to realize just such a social restructuring. We must educate the people who will shoulder the new society. Getting people to learn facts about the environment without changing how society operates is simply not very effective.

Due to the preceding concerns, in this chapter I wish to take a fresh look at potential modes of environmental education based on the following positions. Specifically, future environmental education must be "education for sustainable development", rather than "education for economic development". In recent years, environmental policy is becoming less and less just one area of public policy among many, a trend which is especially evident in Europe. Instead, it is becoming an integral aspect of all sorts of policy areas, and is in effect taking on the character of a fundamental "meta-policy" that sets the tone for the way society develops as a whole. Similarly, environmental education must evolve beyond what it is now so that it mirrors the restructuring of the social fabric overall. This is precisely what the transformation from education for economic development to education for sustainable development would entail.

## Education for economic development

To begin, I wish to note that since the modernization of Japan, education has been "education for economic development" and to explore the ways in which education as such is now gradually faltering. Education is one of the chief ways in which the existing social structure is reproduced. Education is even expected to serve that function. In fact, not just in Japan, but also in most countries throughout the world, education is foremost seen as a vehicle for economic development. As I see it, environmental education to this point has been nothing more than the addition of environmental components to educational curricula that has a chief purpose of economic development. I examine this in further detail next.

### *The rapid economic development model*

Since at least the nineteenth century, many countries, including Japan, gradually came to recognize education as being critically important for achieving economic growth. The primary goals of public education in particular—official positions aside—have in reality been the economic growth achieved through it. Although things such as the cultivation of individuality, the perfection of character, the instilling of a sense of civic responsibility and so on have often been touted as the underlying principles, in reality, and especially in Japan, greater stress and emphasis have been placed on facets of education that lead to economic growth, as exemplified by the intense competition among Japanese students during entrance exams. There have, of course, been frequent disagreements over just what sort of education would be conducive to economic growth, and historically speaking, many methods have been tested. Notably, with the transition from Fordism to post-Fordism, the nature of education for economic development (EED) seems to be changing dramatically. At the same time, amidst such developments, the aim of conventional environmental education has been to mitigate environmental concerns, which are themselves the unwanted by-products of economic growth, while seeking to maintain that economic growth (and the social fabric that has made such growth possible).

As many critics have noted, during the era of Fordism, the single most important goal of a nation was economic growth through industrial development, and education was thought of as a means for achieving that goal. Japanese public education was expected not only to equip the citizenry with basic skills such as reading, writing and arithmetic, but also to offer structured, systematic and efficient learning systems through which citizens could gain basic knowledge of a variety of subjects, in addition to teaching them how to function in a disciplined manner while working in cooperation with others within organizations. To train workers en masse to have a common skill set that would allow them to go anywhere in the country and gain employment in the mass production of industrial goods, it was necessary to impart on most members of the public a universally applicable education, to teach them the discipline necessary to work as a member of a group and to ensure they were accustomed to such conditions. In Japan, there were those that opposed and resisted this style of education as early as the beginning of the twentieth century. These opponents instead advocated styles of learning based more on experience or that had stronger connections to local cultures. Such movements, however, were consistently subject to repression. At the same time, people were taught—both at school and in the home—that as long as they acquired the knowledge and discipline described above, they would be able to find stable employment that provided liveable wages and be able to purchase all sorts of consumer products with that income, and as a result would be able to live (relatively) comfortably and happy lives. Under this educational system, Japanese people were expected from a young age to excel in a highly competitive field. They were taught that the higher they rose in that competition, the better their lives would be. It is through this educational process that the Japanese people were steeped in the capitalist ethos. Furthermore, the belief has prevailed throughout society that the more thorough this education was, the larger the economic growth would become, and by following this formula, the negative consequences of that economic growth (pollution and such) could be resolved. Simply put, the generally accepted belief became that as long as EED is administered properly, not only will the economy grow, but the people will also be able to achieve happiness as well. In addition to the notion that individual happiness is guaranteed by the development of the economy, it became a commonly held belief that education plays a critically important role in that growth. In point of fact, such notions have not been merely myths. At least in Japan, until quite recently, they have been very convincing beliefs for much of the population.

*Doubts about the rapid economic development model*

Naturally, once the economy reaches a certain stage of development, models such as the one just described become less applicable. First, it becomes increasingly difficult to achieve economic growth with human resources trained under the conventional educational model. Second, the very act of realizing the leaps of economic growth the country achieved in the past becomes more difficult. Third, no matter how much the economy grows, doubts will arise among large segments of the population about whether happiness can be achieved in this manner.

Many critics have argued that in developed nations, as the economy grows, the underpinnings evolve from those of Fordism to post-Fordism and that traditional educational systems gradually become incapable of training the kind of human resources that will bring about further economic growth. On top of the decline in blue-collar jobs, there is a shift on the qualities valued in the white-collar labour force, one that is characterized by an emphasis on creativity, planning ability and communication skills above the ability to do routine work accurately and efficiently[1]. As such, the conventional modes of education that stress discipline and rote memorization cease to be useful. In fact, there is now a growing trend in which, even if students are able to excel in their competitive exams, without these newly valued skills, they have no guarantee that they will be able to gain employment at a prestigious company, and even if they do get a job, given the current global nature of competition, they may lose their job at any time. In Japan, at least, the same exam-centred mode of education continues to be the norm at nearly all schools. This form of education is no longer able to contribute to economic growth. Not only that, but for most of the country's citizens, receiving such education does not offer a guarantee of financial stability, much less one of happiness in life.

Another factor makes this situation all the more serious. As economies mature more and more with the advent of globalization, in many developed countries, including Japan, not only is achieving the kind of drastic economic growth seen in the past difficult, even if economic growth were achieved, translating that into higher levels of happiness is also becoming harder.[2] It should go without saying that the recent global recession has forced many people to look for stable jobs or an otherwise steady source of income, but even when this is taken into account it does not necessarily mean that these people are motivated by the desire to help the economy grow or that they even wish to participate in the further consumer spending that such growth would make possible. On the contrary, as it stands now, even in Japan, there are sentiments shared by growing numbers of people that traditional economic growth (i.e., mass consumption) is by no measure a road to happiness and that the goal now should be to achieve alternative lifestyles or, even further, alternative societies. Given these circumstances, it is this author's view that the current modes of education should be rethought from the ground up and that simply adding to or lengthening the environmental components in the traditional educational system is in no way a viable option.

*From burgeoning environmental education to fundamental environmental education*

If we work on the assumption that not just Japan but many nations face the circumstances outlined earlier, we can conclude that this is an opportune time to rethink methods of EED. As I argue in the following section, doubts over the overriding emphasis on economic growth are gradually prompting people to explore new ways in which society might operate. What is more is that such endeavours will inevitably have an effect on educational systems. Nevertheless, in many countries, including Japan, conventional EED methods remain the norm;

however, recently we have finally seen a broad recognition of the importance of environmental education, which in many places has just been instituted. Below is a brief review of the history of environmental education with a particular focus on Japan.

First, it is worth noting that the seeds of environmental education have been around for quite a long time. In Japan, beginning around the middle of the twentieth century, there were people pressing the importance of "nature education" and "regional studies". In addition, once serious pollution problems came to the forefront of public attention in the 1960s, there was a surge in education on pollution issues. These trends not only contained the seeds of environmental education; in retrospect, they actually offered clues as to how to go beyond the limits of what we now think of as conventional environmental education as well. For example, nature education sought to go beyond "classroom learning" in that it stressed actual interaction between students and nature and the importance of the myriad of discoveries that would result. Regional studies required that students investigate the communities in which they lived, thereby encouraging students to acquire knowledge of subjects through pragmatic means. Either of these examples can be seen as forerunners of the "education in the environment" currently advocated in environmental education, while at the same time having elements that would lead to education for sustainable development (ESD), which is explored later, in the sense that they promoted the acquisition of the knowledge to improve one's livelihood from the world around oneself through actual experience and the formation of supporting elements of communities. Nevertheless, the advocates of such educational methods were drowned out by the overwhelming voices championing the kind of structured and systematic education described earlier, and unfortunately, such educational practices became the exception. For pollution education, as the complexity of the problem increased, it was considered a priority matter that students were not only educated in the basics of science needed to understand the chemical substances and other underlying causes of pollution but were also instructed in topics related to the socio-economic mechanisms behind pollution, not to mention equipping them with the legal and political insight needed to fight pollution. The government, however, adopted certain policies with regard to pollution, and because the problem was mitigated to a certain extent, these educational programs fell by the wayside. These burgeoning forms of environmental education proved to be the seeds of later, more serious attempts at environmental education. They also offer us hints as to how to overcome the shortcomings of existing systems of environmental education, although in their time, they were relegated to irrelevance and their potential was never realized.

Subsequently, at least by the 1990s, people in Japan gradually began to note the importance of environmental education. Environmental education was eventually to be incorporated into school education, but at a basic level; it was treated as something to be "tacked on" to conventional school curricula. It goes without saying that this educational component was not devised with a view to re-envisioning the very fabric of society. Still, as I stated earlier, if we as a society are to aim for sustainable development, this kind of environmental education is utterly insufficient. Although this is a point that I have already made, I cannot stress enough the fact that ESD can never be achieved merely by adding environmental components to EED.

## Education for sustainable development

It is now incumbent upon us to ask what form ESD should ideally take and what we mean here by "sustainable development". A full discussion of the concept of sustainable development is beyond the scope of this examination. Ultimately, however, it is not the pursuit of sustainable economic growth; rather, for the present purposes, it could be better characterized as that which through sustainable means establishes a society in which as many people as possible can realize their potential or that which aims for as many people as possible to realize happiness. This is not to deny or diminish the importance of development per se. Instead, this view acknowledges that development is not just of the economic kind, but in fact places a greater emphasis on human development. The following questions then remain. What is the ideal role of education in realizing such a society? What form should that education take?

### *A sustainable society*

As the other chapters of this volume make clear, many conditions must be present to achieve sustainable development. These include, for example, the development of new technologies and productions systems that decrease environmental load, public policies which encourage such developments (e.g., policies dealing with regulations, taxation, grants, etc.) and the cultivation of political and administrative systems responsible for the integrated implementation of such policies. Each of these conditions is important and should be exhaustively explored. At the same time, many in the field of late have noted the importance of a "bottom-up" approach to achieving sustainable development over the kind of "top-down" schema noted previously. The mode of society that facilitates sustainable development becomes extremely important over the long term. There is no doubt that over the short term, given the conventional societal systems, it will be necessary to reduce the burden on the environment using the power of the government and private corporations, as well as science and technology. Nevertheless, just as ecological modernization theorists have noted, over the long term, it will be necessary to change the very fabric of society. It is true that not enough has been done to create models for what a sustainable society might look like, but at least at the present stage, we can assume that something like the following is being envisaged.

First, such a society would be decentralized, not just politically and economically, but in terms of energy and the environment as well. This does not simply mean that the authority of the central government would be delegated to lover levels of government. For example, with regard to energy, rather than using large concentrated systems such as nuclear power plants, there would be distributed systems utilizing renewable energy. As for food, that society would be characterized by high levels of local production and local consumption, enabling the recycling of local resources at the local level. Economically, it would be important to ensure that the funds of a community cycled through that community, and for the home and the workplace to be as geographically proximate as possible. Self-government in the community and the mechanisms and human resources needed to support it would be critical to establishing such a decentralized society.[3]

We can predict that if decentralization in the above sense became a reality, a richly diverse society would result. This would be a good thing not just ecologically. We could also expect a high degree of sustainability in the face of sudden and unpredictable natural disasters and such. Naturally, once a uniform system is plunged into a crisis, the entirety of that system is placed at risk of collapsing simultaneously. In fact, if the environmental problems we now face continue to escalate at their current pace, we will be in more danger of unpredictable natural disasters, but even in the face of such disasters, a society that is diversified in the above sense would be more resilient. Globalization and commercialization tend to result in social structures that are common to the whole country (and even to the world), but if decentralization were to progress, social and economic structures would arise that fit the characteristics and features of each local area. Societies rich in diversity would contribute to sustainable development from this perspective as well.

The second condition that must be fulfilled to achieve a sustainable society is that people live simple lifestyles. There is no question that it should be up to the individual to choose what kind of lifestyle he or she wishes to lead, but if a sustainable society is to be realized, then most people have to live within certain environmental constraints. This is because, barring the development of revolutionary new technologies, if constraints on resources are to be imposed, it would be impossible for every person in the world to live, for example, the "American way of life", materially speaking. Generally, people would have to live close to their places of work and in compact cities, would use bicycles rather than motor vehicles, would use light-rail and other efficient forms of transit for medium distances and would spend their free time cycling, trekking, or engaged in other environmentally friendly activities. Of course, such changes to lifestyles should not be forced on people by the government, but there is no denying that it is imperative that more and more people choose such lifestyles. Furthermore, it will be increasingly necessary to think of these lifestyle issues not only as a matter of personal choice, but also as public issues, that is, choices to be made collectively by entire communities. In fact, many communities—and not just well-known examples of environmentally friendly urban areas such as Freiburg—are already collectively making such choices as a matter of public policy rooted in a broadly held consensus among the population. They are choosing environmentally friendly lifestyles as communities, even if it does mean enduring some inconvenience.

As I reiterate later, ESD must get more people to recognize that the kind of simple lifestyles described above are more conducive to happier lives, and must alter people's values to reflect this attitude. Sustainable development cannot be achieved as long as most people cling to the belief that "happiness can only be realized by working more, making more money and consuming more". We must all come to the realization that it is possible to lead a rich life without material wealth and more consumption. Recently, throughout the world, more attention has been given to happiness as opposed to wealth, and this change in values has been gradually taking place.

Third, mutual assistance, cooperation and social participation of all kinds will be important to making such a society a reality. The relationships between people, moral standards, patterns of behaviour, etiquette and other forms of what is referred to as "social capital" must be an integral part of communities. There are numerous studies on the relationship between social capital and the environment, although the nature of the correlation between the two has not been definitively established. Nevertheless, there is little doubt that social capital or something very similar to it is needed for a sustainable society to be possible. The reasons are as follows. First, without social capital, communities could not govern themselves properly, and establishing the kind of decentralized society that does not rely wholly on corporations or the central government would be impossible. Second, as I mentioned earlier, social capital is a must if people are to enjoy the kind of simple lifestyles that do not depend on economic consumption or commercial entertainment. Third, as is often pointed out, shared ownership and the lending and borrowing of things will be more important than individual ownership in a sustainable society, and social capital will likely play an important role in making lifestyles based on these practices possible. Naturally, ESD should serve to cultivate social capital.

## *Education for the establishment of a sustainable society*

Let us now examine just what sort of education would be necessary to achieve a sustainable society. We can safely assume that it will be entirely different from the conventional system of education that has made economic growth possible.

First, as I stated earlier, although the particulars of EED has changed over time, at its most fundamental level it is a mode of education designed to serve the national goal of economic affluence and, at least implicitly, to guarantee a blissful life. A sustainable society, on the other hand, seeks to provide happiness and human development rather than economic development. These goals must be shared by society as a whole, especially because their fulfilment is vital if people are to share to some extent in the burden associated with the simple lifestyles described previously. ESD must therefore first promote the sharing of those basic values.[4] Of course, as many have noted, there are dangers involved with using the education system to instil specific values, and this fact has been pointed out with regard to environmental education as well. The argument revolves around whether it is acceptable to imprint on children's minds while they are still impressionable that the environment is important or whether doing so is in itself a violation of the principles of education. Unlike brainwashing, education is supposed to encourage young people to doubt things that are taken for granted, to think for themselves and to act upon their own judgment. Critics therefore argue that inculcating specific values goes against those principles (Jickling and Spork, 1998; Sanera and Shaw, 1996).

That said, as many other experts have noted, there is a counterargument for these criticisms (cf. Rossen, 1995; Shiokawa and Imamura, 2005). To begin with, it is possible through the educational system to get young people to question whether it is right to place overriding emphasis on economic growth, and whether increased levels of spending leads to happiness in life, before instilling in them the principles and values of a sustainable society. It can be argued that the very act of encouraging children to challenge those assumptions is desirable according to the ideals of education described earlier. In order to get people to alter their ever-persistent faith in the importance of economic growth above all other matters, it is vitally important to get children to think critically and to judge for themselves whether entering the most prestigious university they can, joining the biggest company they can, earning as much as they can and gaining the ability to spend as consumers as much money as they want is a truly desirable path to pursue. Moreover, children should be taught about matters of happiness and human development. It should also be noted that the attainment of these values is not necessarily at odds with the purpose behind teaching young people to think for themselves. If anything, as Nussbaum has pointed out, it is highly likely that being able to think for oneself that makes true independence possible and leads to happiness and human development (Nussbaum, 2000). If this is the case, then is it not possible to teach the values of happiness and human development without diminishing the value of education? What is more, if we are to teach the role that the environment plays (or is capable of playing) in the attainment of happiness and human development, it should also be possible to have ESD that is fundamentally different from brainwashing or advocacy (cf. Uzzell et al., 1995; Scott and Oulton, 1998).[5] In fact, the brand of environmental education practiced in many countries where children are taught simply to take pro-environmental action, without any particular consideration to critical thought, is far more out of step with the ideals of education (cf. Robottom and Hart, 1995). Likewise, efforts to raise awareness of the environment using quasi-religious language and imagery such as "Mother Earth" and the idealization of pre-modern cultures as exemplars of harmony with the environment may actually become obstacles to independent thought.

Second, to achieve regional independence through cooperation, collaboration and dialogue under decentralized political and economic systems, it will be necessary to train people capable of doing those things, and for this ESD will undoubtedly play an important role. The skills required of such human resources are not the same as those required for economic development. Instead, they must have civic virtue and civic competence. More specifically, they must have the ability to patiently carry on dialogues with people of differing opinions while working in cooperation with them to get things done. They must also be willing and eager to solve problems themselves rather than rushing to enlist the help of the government, experts and so on. Many countries in the West have long held the position that civic virtue and competence should be actively taught through programs of citizenship education, which has taken many forms. In Japan, however, not only are such programs still very underdeveloped; there is also a general lack of proper recognition that this sort of education is necessary for the establishment of a sustainable society. Before, when pollution education was at its height, children were taught about the importance of their rights as citizens, but that aspect is quite diluted in today's environmental education. In addition, even when children were taught about their rights as citizens over the course of pollution education, the subject of their duties as citizens was rarely or barely touched upon. However, to facilitate the evolution of environmental education into ESD, these components of citizen education will require much more emphasis. It should also be noted that such education will be all the more important in the interest of developing the types of social capital mentioned earlier.

Third, ESD must cultivate the practical wisdom needed for problem-solving. When and if the goal of "economic development = mass consumption = happiness" is dispensed with, the next set of goals will involve finding balanced solutions that take into account a broad range of values. In an era in which one needs only to pursue economic growth and material wealth as objectives, one only has to choose the most efficient means of doing things. This means one needs only to develop one sort of "computational skill". However, an entirely different type of problem-solving ability will be necessary to find appropriate solutions while maintaining a reasonable balance among multiple values and interests, including material affluence.[6] The term *problems* here does not refer to problems of the sort in the field of mathematics where logically there is a single solution to be found. It refers instead to the sort of problems in which there are no unique solutions—in other words, problems for which there are no right answers, only reasonable solutions.[7] Simple means-to-an-end–type thinking is not enough to find solutions to these kinds of problems. They require practical wisdom and practical skills. However, these things are difficult to learn in a classroom environment. Rather, they likely fall under the category of knowledge and skills that can only be acquired through real-world experience in solving problems. With problems such as how to achieve economic growth and how to boost company sales, it is logically possible to arrive at a single right answer, and logically it is possible to develop the ability to come up with the right answers through academic study, or so-called book learning. Yet when it comes to, for example, arriving at a suitable pension system, the answers are not nearly as simple, and there is no single correct solution. That said, not all solutions are equal. Some are better than others. In order to "solve" such problems, it is more important to possess a special kind of wisdom that is rooted in context- and situation-specific decisions than to have generalized and replicable knowledge. In no way does this mean that acquiring knowledge in the classroom is unimportant; merely that what is learned in the classroom alone is not enough. In this respect, in recent years, many countries have placed increased priority on the acquisition of applied knowledge, and it is important to take note of attempts such as the Program for International Student Assessment (PISA) to measure this kind of skill, the increase in supporters for "education in place", and other developments indicative of a marked awareness of the importance of cultivating context-specific problem-solving skills and the importance of using experience to internalize knowledge (i.e., not knowledge kept as mere information but something more visceral).[8]

If environmental education is to be understood in the manner described earlier and put into practice, it would not be merely a matter of piling more information on the environment onto the existing system. Instead, it would be coupled with real changes in the way society operates.[9] Sustainable development cannot be achieved with the "end-of-pipeline" environmental policies of the past. As many have previously noted, it will be impossible to achieve without a radical change to the very inner workings of our society. At the same time, environmental education must not be coupled to conventional societal models. Instead, it must not only adapt to societal changes, but also be a force behind those changes. A sustainable society cannot be established through education alone. A myriad of other reforms to the social fabric must also be instituted. Nevertheless, no matter what kinds of systems are put in place, a need will arise for human resources to run those systems, and these human resources will not always spring out of the woodwork spontaneously. For these reasons, we must conclude that the role of public education in general, and compulsory education in particular, will be of great importance in this regard.

*Expected difficulties and how to overcome them*

At least in principle, I believe that most people would agree with the positions taken above concerning environmental education. In fact, the "United Nations Decade of Education for Sustainable Development" began in 2005, and efforts to implement this kind of environmental education are underway in countries throughout the world, including Japan. At the same time, however, more than a few critics are pessimistic about the achievements of the program. Although I am unable to offer a detailed assessment of this UN program here, I will say that the arguments of the critics who view it in a poor light do not appear baseless.

The root causes likely have to do with the sheer number of obstacles and barriers to instituting an ideal ESD program.[10]

First, as many educators have noted, education is an institution that is expected (at least tacitly) to replicate the characteristics of a given society, so it is extremely difficult to implement reforms to education that would bring about social change. Not only does the content of education serve to justify existing social institutions and systems, the behaviours, values and self-awareness of students are also determined by educational methods, the overall educational system and even (although most often tacitly) by the value systems of the teachers. Schools constitute a social order in and of themselves. Students must obey the rules of that order, and especially in Japan, a uniform set of values tends to be drilled into students not through the curriculum, but through the teaching methods and the approach taken to education itself, such as becoming accustomed to functioning gregariously, managing time as group and being ranked through competitive tasks. Hence, for education to practically function for sustainable development, it is necessary to change this school-specific social order and educational approach. Not surprisingly, there is considerable resistance to these kinds of changes, particularly from within the system.[11] Accordingly, if the ideal mode of ESD is to be implemented, it is necessary to rethink the way schools are socially ordered, but making changes requires a great of power (i.e., political leadership backed by popular mandate).

The second point also relates to the issues raised earlier. Even if an ideal ESD system is put into place, when the recipients of that education become contributing members of society, if there is too large a gap between the real world and what they have learned, then that education will ultimately be seen as a token nod to the issue or as just a form of idealism and will be discarded as such. Indeed, much progress has been made in Japan in the way of gender equality in schools, but one often hears of stories involving recent graduates who try to find work and are taken aback for the first time at the blunt reality of gender discrimination. The same thing could happen with ESD.[12] In education, there is always interdependency between cause and effect, and as is often pointed out, one must change society itself before the education system can be overhauled, but at the same time, education must be changed in order to overhaul society. For recipients of ESD to be able to play meaningful roles in society and at the same time live fulfilling lives, the nature of the society around them must be conducive to their contributions. In reality, however, there is no guarantee that consistently following the path toward that ideal will result in its attainment. For this reason, it may also be necessary to consider measures that will help people get through those difficult transitional phases. It may also be the case that making gradual and simultaneous changes in the direction of sustainable development to both educational and social systems may result in a smoother and more effective transition than making sweeping changes to the educational system that are not accompanied by parallel changes to societal structures (or, even worse, a reversion thereof). Moreover, it is possible that small examples of successful change could serve as examples to follow, which might in turn lead to more aggressive moves to change both educational and social structures.

The important thing in overcoming the difficulties associated with the type of transitional period described earlier is for students to have rich opportunities to learn and re-educate themselves even after they reach adulthood. First of all, teachers need to be re-educated in order to institute the kind of in-school social order and curricula conducive to ESD. Second, during the transition period to a sustainable society, it is necessary to ensure that the majority of people are able to receive the kind of adult education necessary to meet the needs of the changing society. As I previously described, if both educational and social changes are to be implemented in parallel incrementally, there will inevitably be a period in which even graduates will need opportunities for adult education. The skills and knowledge required of people in a sustainable society will in all likelihood be very different from those demanded of workers in a growth-oriented society. If this proves to be true, it follows that educational systems for minors and adults alike must be in place to aid in developing new skills and to facilitate a reassessment of values.

## ESD as citizen education

There are many debates ongoing among researchers in Japan over the subject of environmental education, and every point made in these debates is important to consider. For example, there is the question of whether to establish environmental studies as a separate subject to be taught within the curricula or to incorporate environmental issues broadly across a range of subjects; the question of whether environmental education should focus on knowledge that can be taught in classrooms or on "hands-on", experience-based learning; and so on. I have not argued the individual points of these issues here, but given the nature of these debates, the directions which environmental education should take will become clear as a natural matter of course. What is most important here has to do with the fundamental problem of what the majority of these traditional debates expect of schools. Finally, I would like to conclude this examination by touching on the subject of what forms education should ideally take in a universal sense.

There has recently been a developing trend that is not just evident in Japan but also throughout the world in which education has become a service offered as part of the service industry for individuals wishing to advance their careers. If formal education were to remain such a service, the contributions that could be made by ESD would be minimal. In recent years, there has in fact been a growing body of opinion in Japan suggesting that the role of formal education as occupational education deserves renewed attention. Formal education, however, is not simply meant to merely provide private goods. It is also expected to play a role as citizenship education. Education for the purpose of career advancement and vocational training is ultimately the purview of the service sector. If the view were to be adopted that schools as well should serve only this purpose, it would naturally mean the privatization of education. Citizenship education, however, is something that by its very nature cannot be privatized, and it can be considered that this is where the role of public education lies. In this regard, ESD should be viewed as either a form of citizenship education or development-oriented education.

Nevertheless, it goes without saying that even ESD is not lacking components of career education. On the contrary, ESD curricula should seek to actively offer forms of career education. As we saw earlier, if ESD is to encourage people to rethink the relative value of economic growth and material wealth, it will be necessary to rethink the reasons for which we work, and it will be necessary to know what kinds of jobs are available in the world, what the everyday conditions and attitudes are of people are like in different occupations and so on. In Japan in particular, as the number of households in which the primary earner is a salaried worker has increased, the harder it has become for many to imagine anything other than certain established livelihoods and lifestyles. In that regard, young people should be told as a matter of career education that there are a variety of forms of work and lifestyles in the world and that "getting a good job" does not necessarily mean getting into prestigious universities and becoming a salaried employee at a prestigious company. Hence, in this sense, career education should also be included in ESD, but it should only be viewed as such insofar as it is a part of citizenship education. The people who will shoulder the responsibility for the coming society will not appear spontaneously as if moved by the power of some "invisible hand". Rather, it is the role of public education to train people capable of taking on that responsibility.

Notes

1. Certain educators in Japan view this new emphasis on such skills in a highly negative light, calling it "hyper-meritocracy". Regardless, such skills are not just necessary for future economic development; they will also doubtlessly play an important role in attaining sustainable growth. Hence, the development of post-Fordist economic models has the potential to work in a positive direction in bringing about sustainable development.
2. Many recent studies on happiness have pointed out that economic growth beyond a certain level no longer contributes to increased levels of happiness.
3. Needless to say, the promotion of decentralization in this sense does not mean renouncing international partnerships, divisions of labour or free trade. Rather, these could be critical to realizing sustainable development.
4. It has long been thought by many—and not only with regard to environmental education—that if people are equipped with accurate knowledge, they will act properly. Recent studies, however, have shown that this is not always the case (cf. Jensen, 2002). For this reason, a certain amount of "values education" is unavoidable.
5. Naturally, there is no guarantee that critical thinking will always contribute to sustainable development. Hence, it is not enough for ESD to merely cultivate critical thinking skills. Rather, the

education that is administered must be rooted in certain values. In any case, it is unlikely that there is such a thing as wholly value-neutral education to begin with (cf. Saylan and Blumstein, 2011).
6. It should go without saying that although material wealth will cease to be a value of the highest priority, it will continue to be an important value. In developing countries in particular, in the interests of both sustainable development and human development, economic growth is a must. Even in developed countries, it is impossible to discard material wealth as a concern. The view advanced by some extreme environmentalists, that the natural environment should be our only matter of concern and that all other things should be subordinate, is actually counterproductive to sustainable development.
7. Pragmatism is historically one school of philosophy that addressed the importance of practical wisdom. Pragmatism enjoyed considerable influence in the United States and Japan, but as education became more formalized and systematic, philosophies such as pragmatism were turned to less and less. Nevertheless, for the purposes of ESD at least, it would be worthy, if not necessary, to look at the theories of education inherent in the school of pragmatism.
8. In this respect, certain circles of debate assert that environmental education should be seen as a kind of capstone. There is little doubt that a variety of knowledge in the natural and social sciences and in humanities, in addition to practical problem-solving skills, will play a major role in addressing and resolving environmental issues (cf. Robottom and Hart, 1993; Disinger, 2001).
9. Generally, proposals for ESD include not only these components, but also address the North–South problem, gender issues and matters of peace. I am unable to address each of these in the present chapter, but in terms of perspective, this chapter is, for the most part, in agreement with other arguments which do encompass these topics.
10. Shiokawa and Imamura (2005) expand on the work of Fien (1993) and Ham and Sewing (1988) and identify the following four barriers to environmental education: conceptual barriers, logistical barriers, educational barriers and attitudinal barriers (Shiokawa and Imamura, 2005). I am unable to cover these barriers exhaustively (e.g., concerning administrative and budgetary assistance), but they are nonetheless important points.
11. On this point, especially in countries such as Japan, where the ministry responsible for the environment is in charge of environmental education, that ministry has no direct say over what happens in classrooms, so it is not uncommon to encounter situations in which there is no effective way to advance environmental education. In such situations, it is also difficult to formulate uniform national standards or to implement systems to check their effectiveness. These problems are commonly cited in relation to many countries, not just Japan. I was not able to address these administrative obstacles in any detail here, but such issues have the potential to become the biggest problems in implementing ESD in the future.
12. In the Republic of Korea, for example, there is the problem that, even if one completes the teacher training course for environmental education, there are no actual environmental education teaching positions.

## REFERENCES

Disinger, John F. (2001) "K-12 Education and the Environment: Perspectives, Expectations, and Practice", *Journal of Environmental Education*, 33(1), pp. 4–11.

Fien, John (1993) *Education for the Environment: Critical Curriculum Theorising and Environmental Education*, Geelong, Australia: Deakin University.

Ham, S. and D. Sewing (1988) "Barriers to Environmental Education," *The Journal of Environmental Education*, 19(2), pp. 17–24.

Imamura, Mitsuaki (2009) *Kankyo Kyoiku to iu Kabe: Syakai Henkaku to Saiseisan no Daburubaindo wo Koete* (The Barrier of Environmental Education: Beyond the Double Bind *Between* Social Change and Reproduction) [in Japanese], Kyoto: Syowado.

Jensen, B. B. (2002) "Knowledge, Action and Pro-Environmental Behaviour", *Environmental Education Research*, 8(3), pp. 325–334.

Jickling, B. and H. Spork (1998) "Education for the Environment: A Critique", *Environmental Education Research*, 4(3), pp. 309–327.

Nussbaum, Martha C. (2000) *Women and Human Development: The Capabilities Approach*, Cambridge University Press.

Robottom, Ian and Paul Hart (1993) *Research in Environmental Education: Engaging the Debate*, Geelong, Australia: Deakin University Press.

—— (1995) "Behaviorist EE Research: Environmentalism as Individualism", *The Journal of Environmental Education*, 26(2), pp. 5–9.

Rossen, J. van (1995) "Conceptual Analysis in Environmental Education: Why I Want My Children to Be Educated for Sustainable Development", *The Australian Journal of Environmental Education*, 11(i), pp. 73–81.

Sanera, Michael and Jane S. Shaw (1996) *Facts, Not Fear: A Parent's Guide to Teaching Children About the Environment*, Washington, DC: Regnery.

Saylan, Charles and Daniel T. Blumstein (2011) *The Failure of Environmental Education (And How We Can Fix It)*, Berkeley: University of California Press.

Scott, William and Scott Oulton (1998) "Environmental Values Education: An Exploration of Its Role in the School Curriculum", *Journal of Moral Education*, 27(2), pp. 209–224.

Shiokawa, Tetsuo and Mitsuaki Imamura (2005) "Jizokukanosei ni mukete no Kyoiku wo Habamu Shoheki wo Norikoeru tameni (For Crossing the Barrier to 'Education for Sustainability')" [in Japanese] in Mitsuaki Imamura (ed.), *Jizokukanosei ni mukete no Kankyo Kyoiku* (Environmental Education for Sustainability)[in Japanese], Kyoto: Showado.

Uzzell, David L., Allison Rutland and Dan Whistance (1995) "Questioning Values in Environmental Education", in Yvonne Guerrier et al. (eds.) *Values and the Environment: A Social Science Perspective*, Chichester: John Wiley, pp. 171–182.

# 12
# Is contemporary capitalism sustainable?

*Satoshi Niioka*

Contemporary capitalism faces two major constraints. One involves society, and the other concerns nature. If we fail to recognize and then deal with the two constraints, contemporary capitalism will inevitably run into tremendous difficulties and become unsustainable.

The first of these constraints discussed in this chapter—social constraint—refers to the limitation of the self-regulating market. Since the 1980s, neoliberalism has had a dominant influence in the economic and social domains, and policies based on this ideology have become prevalent worldwide in the form of marketization, privatization and deregulation. As a result, economic gaps have widened, and global-scale financial and economic crises have occurred.

The second constraint—natural constraint—refers to the limitation of the natural environment. Economic growth was pursued as a goal by many countries after the end of World War II, and as growth-oriented policies have spread from advanced countries to emerging countries, these policies have caused environmental degradation, including global warming, because they entail enormous energy consumption. It is widely known that there are strong doubts about the sustainability of the current economic system from an environmental standpoint.

Based on an examination of various studies analysing these two constraints, this chapter discusses what form a new public policy framework should take.

## The limitation of the self-regulating market

### Polanyi's argument

Fred Block (2001) holds that Polanyi's *The Great Transformation* of 1944 is indispensable for understanding the dilemma facing global society at the beginning of the twenty-first century. Modern capitalism is currently facing economic and social crises, and many scholars and politicians want to understand the origin of these crises and resolve them. To help us do this, we must heed Polanyi's arguments.

Polanyi (2001: 3) believed that the origins of such problems stem from the utopian endeavour of economic liberalism to set up a self-regulating market system. He insisted that the classical economists wanted to create a society in which the economy had been effectively disembedded and that they encouraged politicians to pursue this objective; however, they did not and could not achieve this goal. In fact, Polanyi repeatedly said that the goal of a disembedded, fully self-regulating market economy is a utopian project; it is something that cannot exist. The efforts of free market theorists to disembed the economy from society are doomed to fail. He argued that market societies are constituted by two opposing movements (double movements): the laissez-faire movement to expand the scope of the market, and the protective countermovement that emerges to resist the disembedding of the economy.

This argument can be summarized in the historical context as follows: nineteenth-century civilization rested on four institutions, namely, the self-regulating market, the liberal state, the international gold standard and the balance-of-power system. The self-regulating market was the fount and matrix of the system; the liberal state was a creation of the self-regulating market; the gold standard was an attempt to extend the domestic market system to the international sphere; and the balance-of-power system was a superstructure erected upon and working through the gold standard.

Market society originated in England, and a market economy, free trade and the gold standard were English inventions. The expansion of the market system in the nineteenth century was synonymous with the simultaneous spreading of international free trade, a competitive labour market and the gold standard. There was nothing natural about laissez-faire; it was enforced by the state.

The 1920s saw the prestige of economic liberalism at its height. It was hoped that a gold bug would restore the pre-World War I global liberal system. The restoration of the gold standard became the supreme aim of all organized efforts in the economic field. Many countries returned to the gold standard system in order to restore the self-regulating market. The gold standard was intended to create an integrated global marketplace that reduced the role of the national government, but its consequences were exactly the opposite. Efforts to realize these dreams through the gold standard produced two horrific world wars. The simple rules of the gold standard imposed economic costs that were literally unbearable. In the 1930s, labour movements reacted against the exigencies of the market and demanded state action to mitigate the market's effects by embedding liberalism. Fascism, socialism and the New Deal appeared to put to bed the self-regulating market. Polanyi (2001) argued that human beings should use the instruments of democratic governance to control and direct the economy to meet individual and collective needs.

The self-regulating market has been succeeded by neo-liberalism or market-fundamentalism.

## Neo-liberalism and embedding the self-regulating market

Policy-makers in advanced countries adopted Keynesian economic policy with big government until the end of the 1970s. Such a policy had created the golden age of the 1960s. But it ultimately brought economic deadlock and stagflation and fell out of favour. It was replaced by neoclassical economic policy, characterized by small government. As is well known, small government means pinning importance on the self-regulating market.

This concept of the self-regulating market links with two other concepts: neo-liberalism and the global economy. The self-regulating market is supported by neo-liberalism willing to create a global economy. The global economy is characterized not only by the free trade of goods and services but even more by the free movement of capital as well. These three principles then — the self-regulating market, neo-liberalism and global economy — form a trinity. In greater detail, neo-liberal economic policy seeks to eliminate government deficits and inflation, sharply cut back on government spending, deregulate the labour and financial markets and open national economies to free trade and multinational capital investment.

Events that occurred after the collapse of Lehman Brothers in 2008 raise questions about the function of the self-regulating market. Neo-liberal economic policy has led to widening economic gaps, financial and economic crises, and other kinds of societal discordance. As a consequence, various alternatives to the self-regulating market have been proposed.

I now turn to the research on global governance by Held and McGrew (2002). With regard to ideal governance in today's globalized society, they consider six schools of thought: neo-liberals, liberal internationalists, institutional reformers, global transformers, statists/protectionists and radicals.

Neo-liberals advocate a mode of governance that relies on the self-adjustment capability of the market. Since becoming influential in the 1980s, they have strongly favoured enhanced globalization. An opposite position is held by radicals who criticize the destructive potential of the market (producing bubbles and busts, widening economic gaps, etc.) and argue that governance should centre on the community as opposed to the market. The radicals' argument assumes the existence of humans who emphasize collaboration and cooperation, rather than individuals taking actions for profit based on economic rationality. The two schools of thought thus have diametrically opposed views. Positioned between them are the liberal internationalists, institutional reformers, global transformers and statists/protectionists.

Liberal internationalists (Keohane, 1984) and statists (Gilpin, 2001) advance different arguments in the field of international political economy: the former advocate arguments that are based on complex mutual dependence theory or neo-liberal institutionalism, whereas the latter support arguments that are based on hegemonic stability theory or neorealism. Also, the former find means to stabilize the international community in the international regime, while the latter find such means in the power of the hegemon. It should be noted, however, that both schools of thought have played a role in defending US interests in the post-World War II world.

Institutional reformers attribute current political and economic problems to global public goods not being provided in a form appropriate to advance globalization. Their argument emphasizes international cooperation in, among other actions, poverty reduction and environmental protection, as can be inferred from the fact that the argument is advocated by researchers from the United Nations Development Program (UNDP, 1994), which has proposed new concepts such as human security and the human development index. As for global transformers, many of them are political scientists, and they see hopes in the development and strengthening of multilayered democracy spanning the local, national, regional and global levels (Held and McGrew, 2002).

As discussed earlier, various ideas have been proposed for governance of the global community. These ideas should be assessed from the standpoint of, for example, whether the self-regulating market should be left untouched or should be complemented with additional mechanisms or whether the act of governance involves reincorporation of markets into society.

## Economic growth and the limitation of the environment

### Daly's approach

The unleashed power of the market system is not the only factor threatening the sustainability of contemporary capitalism. Environmental impacts, a major example of which is global warming, also raise questions about the sustainability of contemporary capitalism.

In the field of economics, Daly (1996) has analysed such environmental constraints. According to him, the central problem of contemporary economic theory is that today's economic policy leads to wasteful use of resources that goes beyond the regenerative capacity of the earth and thus to their eventual destruction. The economy is a subsystem of the natural environment in the first place. However, dominant economic models behave as if the ecosystem was its subsystem. At the core of such an economy are policies emphasizing the supremacy of economic growth. In response, Daly turns to the concept of sustainable development (advocated by the Brundtland Commission) as an alternative to dominant economic models. Sustainable development discussed here is defined as "meeting the needs of the present without compromising the ability of future generations to meet their own needs" (World Commission on Environment and Development [WCED], 1987: 43). Although this definition is somewhat vague, Daly appreciates the fact that it potentially contributes to a shift in a basis of the economic norm from quantitative expansion (growth) to qualitative improvement (development). Such a shift gives rise to the economics of development without growth or the economics of development beyond growth.

To deepen his view, Daly (1996: 3) revisits research by J. S. Mill. Using the concept of steady state, Mill (1973) tried to show a situation in which technology and ethics would consistently improve even with zero growth in population and capital stock. According to him, the steady state is by no means static but describes a society experiencing continuous renewals and qualitative improvement in the stock of capital. Although many classical economists feared situations where no economic growth would occur, Mill rather welcomed such situations. Whereas Mill's concept of the steady state has largely been forgotten with the rise of neoclassical economics and focus on economic growth, Daly sees it as being revived today in the new concept of sustainable development. As the Industrial Revolution occurred, researchers' attention shifted from classical economics, which studied labour and resources, to neoclassical economics, which considered utility, exchange and market efficiency. As the transition from an economy with unrestricted input and output to an economy where limitations are imposed on input and output due to environmental constraints has become inevitable, Daly considers that the concept of steady state has been revived in the concept of sustainable development.

Daly (1996: 159–160) also refers to the notion of allocation, distribution and scale. According to him, neoclassical economics excessively emphasizes the allocation of resources from the standpoint of efficiency, but only supplementarily deals with issues associated with the distribution of resources that is intended to realize fairness and equity. He then points out that neoclassical economics does not deal with issues involving scale which are closely related with sustainability and that even if such issues are handled, it is inappropriately done as part of allocation-related issues. Establishing a vision of sustainable development entails the setting of problems involving allocation, distribution and scale as central issues facing society. The problems involving scale are decisively important especially from the standpoint of environmental issues.

In addition, to realize sustainable development, Daly (1996: 147) proposes compensatory tariffs be introduced in the face of free trade and globalization. Contrasting with trade policy instruments for protecting inefficient domestic industries, compensatory tariffs are considered to protect domestic policies that internalize environmental and social costs from harmful effects of competition with countries that disregard such costs. Daly's vision of the international economy is summarized in the following statement: "Globalism does not serve world community—it is just individualism writ large. We can either leave transnational capital free of community constraint, or create an international government capable of controlling it, or renationalize capital and put it back under control of national community. I favor the last alternative" (Daly, 1996: 148).

*Environmental problems and global theory*

Let us now examine the challenges facing the existing global theory that are raised by environmental problems.

The well-known scenario of destabilization of the international economy put forth by hegemonic stability theory (Gilpin, 2001) can be described simply as follows: free riders exist in international society, and the hegemon thus loses its ability and willingness to keep providing international public goods sufficiently. Insufficient supply of international public goods results and leads to destabilization of the international economy. What is then sought is reconstruction of the hegemon's leadership. According to hegemonic stability theory, global governance must be restructured with the United States, the hegemonic country, at the centre.

For their arguments, hegemonic stability theorists assume that international public goods include a free-trade system, an international monetary system and international security. As obvious from their creation process, international public goods include international systems that strongly reflect the interests of the United States. Such international public goods were created based on the country's post-war pursuit of excessive capital and production, dominantly superior international competitiveness, establishment of the US dollar as the key currency and anti-socialism. Therefore, in hegemonic stability theory, the term *free riders* refers to countries other than the United States.

Today's global warming problem, however, has been at odds with US interests from its beginning. The energy-wasting system of mass production, mass consumption and mass waste disposal that is built into US society is in disagreement with international efforts to curb global warming. The United States, which emits 20 per cent of the $CO_2$ emitted worldwide, is a free rider of the global environment (international public goods or global public goods), and significant changes in production systems and in lifestyle are necessary for the country to stop being such a free rider. If the global environment is regarded as a public good for human beings, the view on free riders must be changed entirely. The problem becomes that, contrary to the traditional view, the United States, the hegemonic country, is a free rider in environmental issues. One can thus draw the conclusion that under the status quo, the United States cannot continue being the leader in global governance because it cannot fulfil relevant responsibility.

In contrast with the hegemonic stability theorists, regimists have focused on elimination, or at least mitigation, of dilemmas, which arise from collective actions, by regimes. Regimists do not limit the actors in international relations to nations and appreciate the role of various entities such as multinational firms, international organizations and non-governmental organizations (NGOs). Young (2001) supports the validity of the regimist view, arguing that there are many examples in which regimes were successfully created in certain conflict domains even if the hegemonic country played a small role or even if, in a more limited sense, no single actor played a dominant role. More specifically, the United States persistently acted passively in the Earth Summit in 1992, COP-3 in 1997 and COP-6 in 2000 and rejected ratification of the Kyoto Protocol in 2001. The Kyoto Protocol therefore provides an example of successful formation of a regime without the presence of a hegemonic country (Young, 2001).

The refusal by the United States to ratify the Kyoto Protocol also shows a limitation of the regimist view. There are certainly situations where regimists' claims are valid. This is true in domains that hegemonic stability theorists have not sufficiently examined. However, the regimist approach also has weaknesses. As Young (2001) admits, regime theorists have mainly analysed individual regimes with a focused scope. Examples include the whaling regime, the biodiversity protection regime and the international insurance regime. As seen in these examples, regime theory provides influential analysis for individual regimes that are not of central importance to a hegemonic country. For regimes of central importance (e.g., those involving free trade, international monetary issues and security), the hegemonic stability approach remains effective. Therefore, in explaining actual events or situations, hegemonic stability theory and regime theory should mutually complement each other.

A weakness of regime theory can thus be found in the fact that its analysis focuses on individual governance systems or in its lack of a comprehensive view on global governance. What regime theory needs to perform is in-depth analysis of not only peripheral regimes but also core regimes. Today, environmental regimes belong to the core regimes along with the international trade, international monetary and security regimes. As environmental problems become mainstream issues, it is necessary to reconsider the theoretical framework of both hegemonic stability theory and regime theory, which have been developed mainly in US academia.

The aforementioned claim by a UNDP group that the supply of global public goods is insufficient can be regarded as an attempt to understand the reality described earlier. In this context, cooperation between advanced countries and developing countries should be at the centre of discussions. In other words, although all countries should cooperatively reduce $CO_2$ emissions, it is inevitable that differences arise in the approach taken between advanced countries, which have both funds and technology, and developing countries, which lack them. The approach taken by the United Nations Framework Convention on Climate Change—"common but differentiated responsibility"—thus becomes important.

## Quest for global governance

### Global civil society

As discussed earlier, various governance models have been proposed out of discussions on global governance. Many schools of thought refer to the existence of civil society, although the degree of emphasis may be different. The concept of civil society is considered to have emerged due to the rise of neo-liberalism and the end of the Cold War. According to Harvey (2005: 78), "[t]he period in which the neo-liberal state has become hegemonic has also been the period in which the concept of civil society—often cast as an entity in opposition to state power—has become central to the formulation of oppositional politics." According to Kaldor (2003: 77), "[t]he 1989 revolutions legitimated the concept of civil society and consequently permitted the emergence of global politics—the engagement of social movements, NGOs and networks in the process of constructing global governance." Also, Kaul et al. (1999) makes the following statement:

> [C]ivil society and the private sector have formed transnational alliances far beyond the reach of national governments. Similarly, their actions sometimes determine policy outcomes far more than government actions. Since effective solutions to pressing global problems are unlikely to emerge from forums that exclude these important actors, a new tripartism is recommended, involving government, business, and civil society.

What our society should establish are connections among a "new trio"—government, firms and civil society—in the face of globalization, instead of the links among the "traditional trio"—government, firms and labour, which are strongly regulated in the national domain. The traditional trio has played its role in countries with Keynesian policies and has been disbanded due to neo-liberalism, which has led to tremendous instability in the economy and society. Therefore, despite being in unchartered territory, establishment of this new trio to face globalization is a challenge to be tackled today.

Sadako Ogata understands that governance is a combination of control of others and autonomy (Matsushita, 2002). If this is true, attention should be paid to the role of civil society which is closely related with autonomy. There is, however, a problem to be solved. It involves the vagueness of the concept of civil society. What does the concept of civil society represent? Many people understand it through images of civil movements led by NGOs and non-profit organizations (NPOs). It is possible to consider that the concept of social capital put forth by Putnam (1993, 2000) actually points to civil society itself. The image of civil society that can be drawn from research such as his is a public domain that is based on people's voluntary activities. But the vagueness of the concept of civil society still remains. Clarification of this concept and research into the new trio are undertakings that cannot be avoided when considering the actors who reintegrate the market into society.

*New public policy*

New public policy in the global era is often explained as follows:

> States suffer a further diminution in power because the expansion of transnational forces reduces the control individual governments can exercise over the activities of their citizens and other peoples. For example, the increased mobility of capital, induced by the development of global financial markets, shifts the balance of power between markets and states and generates powerful pressures on states to develop market-friendly policies, including restricted public deficits and curbs on expenditure, especially on social goods; lower levels of direct taxation that are internationally competitive; privatization and labour market deregulation. . . . In effect, the autonomy of states is compromised as governments find it increasingly difficult to pursue their domestic agendas without cooperating with other agencies, political and economic, above and beyond the state.
> (Held and McGrew, 2002: 22–23)

Although care should be taken in asserting that the power of national governments in governing the economy has declined, there is no doubt that various issues that must be dealt with globally have emerged as policy issues. The problem concerning the market and the environment is exactly one such issue. Dealing with global issues requires implementing international policy coordination, which in turn requires a shift in values and principles that support the policies.

As has been the case in any era, new social values need to be shown in establishing new public policy. Such new values are not created in a vacuum, but emerge from basic values in society and combinations among them. Human society has accepted the four basic values of security, wealth, freedom and justice, and it can be said that public policy has historically changed due to changes in these four basic values and new combinations among them (Strange, 1988). Figure 12.1 characterizes post-war public policy based on combinations of these four social values.

| Keynesianism | Security | Wealth, Justice | Freedom |
| Neoliberalism | Security | Wealth, Freedom | Justice |
| New public policy | | Security, Wealth, Justice | Freedom |

Figure 12.1 Post-war public policy characterized by combinations of the four basic social values

Regarding public policy in the era of Keynesianism, advanced countries placed certain levels of emphasis on the combination of wealth and justice even though differences existed among the countries, and growth policy was linked with employment policy under government responsibility. These countries have been commonly called welfare states. There were significant differences among them regarding freedom, and freedom was subject to social and economic regulation even in the United States that attaches greater importance to freedom. The rationale and structure of security were formulated during the Cold War era.

As to public policy in the era of neo-liberalism, which started in the 1980s, wealth and justice were considered separately, and a strong connection was formed between wealth and freedom and became a significant force. Deregulation, privatization and liberalization were at the centre of policies, global market fundamentalism became rampant, and justice, on which a certain level of emphasis had been placed, was confined to playing a minor role. As a result, the gap between the rich and the poor widened in many countries. As details of security changed due to the collapse of socialism, new concepts such as comprehensive security and common security were proposed (Porter and Brown 1996).

What kind of combination of values should we then pursue in the era of new public policy? Here, we must take into account the fact that environmental problems are among the central issues of public policy. Also, it is necessary to consider what kinds of effects environmental problems have on each of the four values and then to examine combinations of these values.

First, with regard to wealth, wealth based on the energy-consuming system of mass production, mass consumption and mass waste disposal is not sustainable today or in the future. Wealth certainly has different meanings in advanced, emerging and developing countries, but the concept of wealth in a growth-centric ideology must be changed when the sustainability of the global environment is considered. Proposals for a steady-state economy are being made in advanced countries, and there is call for the role of production and consumption of wealth to change. The position of wealth in society must be reconsidered, with new interpretations attached to the concept of wealth.

Second, as to justice, it should be re-emphasized following its trivialization in the era of neo-liberalism that began in the 1980s. The reason is that it is necessary, more than anything else, to narrow the gap between the rich and poor, which had widened in the neo-liberal era. Also, problems involving the sustainability of the global environment have made clear that justice should be conceptualized not only for the current generation but also for future generations. In other words, a broader concept of justice with intergenerational consideration must be introduced. This calls for restoring the emphasis on justice.

Third, as for freedom, the global market, which expanded with deregulation under neo-liberal ideologies, has repeatedly experienced bubbles and busts in various countries since the 1980s. Moreover, the expansion of freedom associated with old wealth has made environmental problems more serious and globalized.

The recent economic events have shown that an excessive connection between wealth and freedom has caused serious social problems (a bubble economy and its collapse, global warming, etc.). To avoid damaging the value of freedom, it should be connected with justice so it can play its social role.

Fourth, security is being redefined. Strange (1996: 33) makes the following statement:

> But once the security is redefined . . . as those arrangements providing people with security not just from attack and injury or death at the hands of forces from another state but with security from all sorts of other risks—of long-term environmental degradation, of hunger, of shortages oil or electricity, of unemployment and penury and even perhaps of preventable disease—then the central role of the state crumbles.

In other words, the traditional security structure is being redefined due to increased risks associated with environmental destruction, widening gaps between the rich and poor, economic collapse, diseases spreading with global transportation of goods and people, and globalization. Therefore, security today needs to be redefined, not as national security, which was a dominant factor in the Cold War era, but as comprehensive security, common security and human security, which can adapt to the global era (UNDP, 1994).

Based on the preceding discussions, the combination of security, wealth and justice is the proper combination of social values that is going to support new public policy. With the redefinition and new combination of these values that centre on environmental problems, the concept of freedom would also be redefined in the context of an expanding public domain. The four social values and their combinations, which have changed as described earlier, define new public policy. A system of global governance that is capable of incorporating the global market into society will emerge from new actors and a new combination of social values.

## REFERENCES

Block, Fred (2001) Introduction in Karl Polanyi's *The Great Transformation: The Political and Economic Origins of Our Time*, Boston: Beacon Press.

Daly, Herman E. (1996) *Beyond Growth: The Economics of Sustainable Development*, Boston: Beacon Press.

Gilpin, Robert (2001) *Global Political Economy: Understanding the International Economic Order,* Princeton, NJ, and Oxford: Princeton University Press.

Harvey, David (2005) *A Brief History of Neoliberalism*, Oxford, New York: Oxford University Press.

Held, David and Anthony McGrew (2002) *Globalization/Anti-Globalization*, Cambridge: Polity Press.

Kaldor, Mary (2003) *Global Civil Society: An Answer to War*, Cambridge and Malden, MA: Polity Press.

Kaul, Inge, Isabelle Grunberg and Marc A. Stern (eds.) (1999) *Global Public Goods: International Cooperation in the 21st Century*, New York and Oxford: Oxford University Press.
Keohane, Robert O. (1984) *After Hegemony: Cooperation and Discord in the World Political Economy*, Princeton, NJ: Princeton University Press.
Matsushita, Kazo (2002) *Kankyo Gabanansu* (Environmental Governance), Tokyo: Iwanami Shoten.
Mill, John Stuart (1973) *Principles of Political Economy*, edited by William Ashby, Clifton, NJ: Kelly.
Polanyi, Karl (2001) *The Great Transformation: The Political and Economic Origins of Our Time*, foreword by Joseph Stiglitz and introduction by Fred Block, Boston: Beacon Press.
Porter, Gareth and Janet Welsh Brown (1996) *Global Environmental Politics*, Boulder, CO: Westview Press.
Putnam, Robert D. (1993) *Making Democracy Work: Civic Traditions in Modern Italy*, Princeton, NJ: Princeton University Press.
—— (2000) *Bowling Alone: The Collapse and Revival of American Community*, New York: Simons & Schuster.
Strange, Susan (1988) *States and Markets: An Introduction to International Political Economy*, London: Pinter Publishers.
—— (1996) *The Retreat of the State: The Diffusion of Power in the World Economy*, Cambridge: Cambridge University Press.
UNDP (1994) *Human Development Report 1994*, New York and Oxford: Oxford University Press.
World Bank (2010) *World Development Report 2010: Development and Climate Change*, Washington, DC: The World Bank.
World Commission on Environment and Development (Brundtland Commission) (1987) *Our Common Future*, New York: Oxford University Press.
Young, Oran. R. (2001) "The Theory of Global Governance", in Akio Watanabe and Jitsuo Tsuchiyama (eds.) *Gurobaru Gabanansu* (Global Governance: In Search of Order without Government), Tokyo: University of Tokyo Press, pp. 18–44.

# 13
# Decentralization and local governance for sustainable development

*Katsutaka Shiraishi*

## Local government towards sustainability

This chapter aims to clarify the significance of decentralization to realize sustainable development. Decentralization is a complex and multifaceted concept. In this chapter, the concept of decentralization is defined as the transfer of authority and responsibility for public functions from the central government to subordinate or quasi-independent government organizations. As for the transfer to the private sector, the concept refers not to privatization, but to public private partnership.

Strengthening activities at the local level, which interacts very directly with people's lives, can enhance people's engagement in realizing sustainable development. By promoting the policy shift at the local level, the premises for the transition to sustainable society are to be revealed.

The Charter of European Cities and Towns towards Sustainability,[1] also known as the Aalborg Charter, says

> We are convinced that sustainable human life on this globe cannot be achieved without sustainable local communities. Local government is close to where environmental problems are perceived and closest to the citizens and shares responsibility with governments at all levels for the well-being of humankind and nature. Therefore, cities and towns are key players in the process of changing lifestyles, production, consumption and spatial patterns.

In cities, towns and villages, each local government is unable to change lifestyles, production, consumption and spatial patterns by itself. Therefore, it is necessary for local people, local businesses or local activists to get involved. The knowledge of experts outside is also necessary. For making such changes, various stakeholders must be involved.

The role of local government is imperative in order to change the lifestyles, production, consumption and spatial patterns. However, in order for local government to play the expected roles, it is necessary for local government to undergo reform. Specifically, local government should undertake the following efforts:

a. To understand and empathize with the significant meanings of deliberative democracy in the development process at the local level
b. To design policies which demand public involvement and public–private partnership
c. To foster the ability in the problem-solving approach through public–private partnership taken by governmental officials as well as local assembly members

Needless to say, local reform is largely determined by the policies of central government as well their laws. However, achievements at the local level can influence the policies and laws of central governments. In order to realize sustainable development with citizens' participation, it is necessary to decentralize in such a way to promote local governmental reform. From such a perspective, the Aalborg Charter insisted on decentralization.

By decentralization, the efforts to realize sustainable development will link to local governments and citizens. As a result, local government and citizens can take approaches that differ from those employed by the central government as well as by other sovereign states.

*Relativity between the social system and the ecosystem*

In terms of the goals of governance for realizing sustainable development, it is essential to clarify what conditions can ensure improving people's livelihoods in a sustainable way. From the perspective of the relativity between the social system and the ecosystem, these conditions are to be examined.

The social system is a system directly related to the regeneration of human society. The social system, in a broad sense, includes economies, public administration and the built environment. The ecosystem is a system that is related to the conservation of natural environment and biodiversity. The human being as a living creature is also a part of the ecosystem. The conceptual relativity of the social system and the ecosystem was categorized into three types according to Marten (2001), as shown in Figure 13.1.[2]

First, the separate type is the image that many of us have had in our modern society. Although attention has been paid to social society in our daily lives, attention has hardly been paid to the ecosystem. Of course, nature must be protected from development activities for human beings. The conservations of the ecosystem there are the ones like in natural reserves as well as national parks.

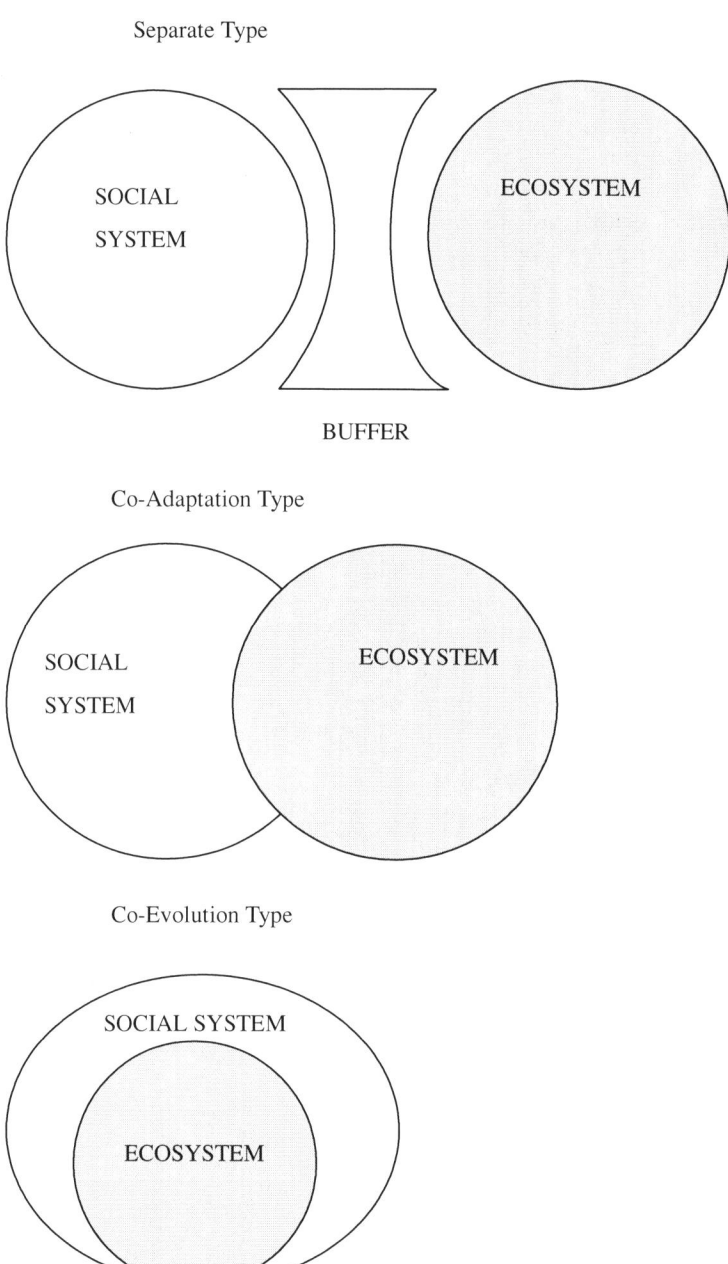

Figure 13.1 Conceptual relativity of the social system and the ecosystem
*Note:* Original concept and figures come from Marten (2001: chap. 7). The author has modified and simplified them.

Such conservation based on the separate type do not help to reconsider the lifestyles of the people.

Second, the co-adaptation type is indicated in the image of Figure 13.1 in which the ecosystem and the social system are mutually independent and partially overlap. In this type, people consider the amenities gained from the ecosystem. The ecosystem is imagined as if it were independent from the social system; therefore, people's approaches to the ecosystem are limited.

Third, the co-evolution type is represented in the third image of Figure 13.1 in which the ecosystem is subordinate to the social system. In this type, the social system is decisively influential on the ecosystem. As the consequences of human activities, destruction of the global environment, loss of biodiversities and/or global warming are caused. Under the conditions of such destruction of the ecosystem, reproducing the social system will be harder. If the reconstruction of the social system in which conserving the ecosystem is not achievable, it implies that the human existence as a living creature is threatened.

From the viewpoint of emphasizing sustainability when thinking about local policies, it is necessary to reconstruct the social system that is based on the co-evolution type. The local governments can play a leading role in such reconstruction processes, as the Aalborg Charter describes.

## Local government reforms and deliberative platforms

When determining a goal of local government and a path to it, deliberative democracy is more suitable than is liberal democracy, in which the majority make the decisions. In order for deliberative democracy to work effectively, creating the policy formation and implementation system with open style at the local level is key.

Deliberative democracy attempts to include all actors potentially influenced by certain decisions. For example, Eckersley (2004) perceives the wider range of participants in the deliberative processes. Therefore, it widens not only to children, but also to future generations as well as other species than human beings (Eckersley, 2004). The purpose here is not to discuss issues of environment and justice. Rather, I suggest that deliberative democracy will lead to a change in thinking about local government reforms.

The roles of the government sector can take various forms. The local governments that play vital roles in sustainable development change their style of government. They do not solely make decisions or implement them in a top-down manner; they involve many stakeholders in the local policy-making process through partnership and participation. By adopting the partnership approach that involves various actors in local policy processes, the focal point will shift from the decentralization process in which power is devolved from the central government to local governments, to a process whereby local governments shift responsibilities to non-governmental organizations within the regions.

The local government must play the role of ensuring the existence of deliberative platforms. Such platforms may differ in size or scale to best fit to each primary subject of policies.

For example, in the case of policies at the local level regarding watercourses, the suitable size will exceed the one of the realm of a single local government. Regarding economic activities, for policies at the local level, the size of suitable trade areas and industrial clusters will show an overlap among numerous local governments. In a case of interpersonal public services important for people's lives, the size of suitable policies at the local level are considered to be small neighbouring communities.

As the policies for sustainable development at the local level evolve, various platforms of partnership will be created with the sizes that are best suited for each subject matter, not by the boundaries of local governments. Hence, horizontal networks among local governments will be required. At the same time, it will be necessary to connect each platform.

The Local Strategic Partnership (LSP), which Britain's former Labour government under then prime minister Tony Blair developed, aimed to create partnership platforms for each subject matter. It was a scheme to achieve the midterm objectives for local governments in collaboration with each platform. The partnership platforms were designed in such a way that economic policies were of larger scale, whereas the social issues were scaled with consideration of the sizes of neighbouring communities.

In the United States, under the government of then President Bill Clinton, so-called empowerment zones were adopted. Selected local governments explored overall and comprehensive solutions based on a partnership approach.

The challenges towards modifying policy decisions and implementation processes at the local level are in the trial-and-error stage. They have not established yet. From the context of realization of local governance, it might be possible to develop a scenario as follows: formal and best-fitting partnerships will be organized according to each subject matter with participation of local governments, local governmental agencies and private organizations, as well as local organizations.

At the local level, putting sustainable development in perspective, decentralization process does not merely mean constructing smaller local governments. A more complex decentralization process is therefore necessary.

## Trends of decentralization reform

### The two types of reform of the Keynesian welfare state

Why is decentralization an issue in the context of developed countries? By considering the critical factors confronted by the Keynesian welfare state, eliciting the two genealogies of decentralization reform is possible. The three interlinked factors forced changes to the Keynesian welfare state. The first factor is the crisis of Fordism, the second factor is intensifying globalization and the third factor is the rise of neo-liberalism.

Regulation theory, as an interpretive model in macroeconomics, describes the mechanism of combining mass production and mass consumption as the Fordist Development Pattern (Lipietz, 1985, 1987; Boyer, 1986, 1990). The capital allows wage growth and the burden of indirect wages such as social welfare to secure mass consumption. Regulation theory describes it as a "Fordist compromise". Under a capitalist economy, labour power is commoditized in the labour market. The Fordist compromise enabled the Keynesian welfare state to develop social policies for decommoditizing labour power.

The capital began to escape from the Fordist compromise in the early 1970s. This meant that the capital refused its burden of the wage costs including indirect wages. The phrase "escape from the Fordist Compromise" implies intensifying globalization.

Regulation theory describes the Keynesian welfare state from the perspective of the nation state and the national economy. The continuation of the Fordist Development Pattern will face difficulties resulting from globalization. It will be more difficult for a state to finance policies that sufficiently protect people from life risks.

Neo-liberalism is a theory that positively explains such circumstances. Neo-liberalism declares that smaller government fits the market-driven economy and globalization. It also denies the Keynesian welfare state. This helped conceptualize the framework of post-Fordism.

Needless to say, the Keynesian welfare state was criticized from the market-oriented perspective. Under the concept of deregulation, the extension of market competitiveness, namely, the control through the market, was required. The redistribution policies by a state were criticized as big government. This led to the creation of an approach aimed at downsizing a state through decentralization.

Additionally, the Keynesian welfare state was criticized from the civil society perspective. As a prominent view, there is a criticism of "decolonization of life-world" by capital and a state. People-related strategic decisions will be transferred to the market as well as to professional administrative bureaucrats. Habermas (1985) described it not as communications and deliberations, but as one feature of a late capitalistic society for its control by market economies and its administrations. This had led to the creation of a new approach to enhance the independency of civil society through decentralization.

Today's discussions towards decentralization overlap with the two reform initiatives of the Keynesian welfare state: market-based reform and civil society-based reform.

It is considered that there are two perspectives to discuss on decentralization from a central government to local ones. One is authorizational decentralization, and the other is deprivational decentralization by local governments.

Is it possible to understand the actual dynamics of today's decentralization? As an analogy to authorizational decentralization, it can be explained that in order to downsize the central government, authorization is for local governments. As an analogy to deprivational decentralization, it can be explained that starting from the collaboration between local government and its citizens, the role of a central government needs to be re-examined. From the point of view of autonomous solutions of local agendas and the development of citizens' participation, there are calls to strengthen the functions and mandates of local governments. This is what the Aalborg Charter aims to do.

*The context to the theories of governance*

Recent history suggests that in seeking the post-Keynesian welfare state the reformative initiative took the lead.

Commodifying every action targeted at the environment is difficult. Commodifying everything that is meaningful to human lives is also inconceivable. In other words, the responses to the crisis of the sustainability of the ecosystem and social system cannot be achieved in the way where capital and markets lead. Therefore, the roles of the market-driven reforms to be played for realizing sustainable development must be limited.

In this regard, the work of Polanyi has gained currency again. Polanyi (1957) characterizes labour, land and currencies as "fictitious commodities". Polanyi questioned how it was possible to reintegrate the protruded marketized economies into the societies.

Based on Polanyi, Esping-Andersen (1990) asserted that there must be a premise that decommodification is to be achieved in some way, in order for labour as a fictitious commodity to prevail against commodity. The indicator of such decommodification was first introduced by Esping-Andersen to typify welfare regimes. Since then, despite its criticism, it has been used as an imperative indicator to typify the welfare regimes.

Human beings can only "survive" by participating as labour power commodities in the markets as well as maintaining the lives at certain standards even though one cannot participate in the markets. The Keynesian welfare state developed the social policies for decommodification to accept people excluded from the commodification of their labor powers because of sickness, old age and/or unemployment.

Under the social system, the environment is widely defined as including the built environment. Environmental conservation includes issues such as natural resources, natural resources management, infrastructure management of houses and water-supply systems necessary for social lives, as well as adequate waste disposals, amongst others.

The excessive dependency on the government had been seen particularly in relation to the maintenance of the built environment necessary for the policies of decommodification as well as social lives. Such dependency on the government was obviously seen not only at the national level, but also at the local level.

In Habermas's analysis of the late capitalist society, he suggested two types of social existence composing the modern society. These are the "lifeworld" and the "system". For him, the lifeworld represents the informal unmarketized realm. He divided the system into two subsystems, which were money and power.

Habermas explains that money and power are "steering media" for capitalist market economies as well as national administration and its relevant institutions, respectively. The steering media such as money and power will be separated from the lifeworld, and strategic decisions relating to people will be relegated to the markets as well as professional administrative bureaucrats. Habermas not only explains the phenomena that people's survival is increasingly dependent on the market economies and public administration, but also attempts to find the modern society's pathological causes in the fact that the system was replacing such a lifeworld and consequently eroding it.

Applying a scheme such as Habermas's to affairs at the local level, some implications can be deduced by using the explanations of the history of rural areas in Japan. Historically, in rural areas of Japan, citizens have played significant roles in maintaining the social-ecological system. For example, regarding the use and management of regional resources, such as forests, water sources and rivers, amongst others, as well as the operation of the mechanism of sustainable material cycles, the non-market, non-administrative social relationships have been important to a large extent.

In Japan, since the mid-1960s, the management of the social-ecological system has been the responsibility of the national and the local governments. During the 1970s, subsidy policies towards agricultural products had regressed. Instead, the targets of the governments were income redistribution toward local governments through civil engineering works, such as land improvement for agricultural lands and building infrastructures. Thus, the governmental operations had a pervasive impact on rural societies. Markets and governments had taken firm root in the lives in rural societies.

The population concentration in urban cities brought by the subsequent rapid economic growth, the pervasiveness of lifestyles based on large-scale production and consumption and the recession of competitiveness of agriculture and forestry combined with a strong yen and globalization brought various difficulties to the disadvantaged areas.

The attempts to maintain and reconstruct the agricultural societies were made mostly by public administration through its public projects aiming to modernize rural life as well as to improve agricultural productivity. In the process, the agricultural communities' issues were regarded as base economic issues. In Japan, modernizing such agricultural communities led to the decline of communality and of autonomy in these rural societies, which resulted in the deepening dependency on public administration.

Habermas's writing is considered a contemporary analysis to explain the characteristics of Fordist welfare states from the perspectives of anti-capitalism and anti-nationalism. Restoring and reconstructing the lifeworld mean realizing the style of new social integration and policy integration, which are neither excessively controlled by public administration nor excessively marketized. This perspective leads to the theories of governance.

As to the maintenance of infrastructures necessary for the decommodification policies and lives, it has been excessively dependent on governments. The difficulties of sustainability of the social system had increased in the era of the post-Keynesian welfare states. In the United States, in the eurozone countries and in Japan, the cash-strapped states of public finance can already be seen, and there are increasing concerns that such situations may lead to national financial defaults, at worst. Given these circumstances, governments are likely to become a risk factor with regard to maintaining a viable social system. Therefore, interest in theories of governance has gained momentum.

*Local governance and decentralization*

As mentioned earlier, there are two mainstream reform perspectives addressing criticism of the Keynesian welfare states. One is about market-oriented reform; the other is about civil society-oriented reform. The discussions on governance are ideologically linked to these.

Jessop (2007) insists that if the interests in Fordism are focusing on the relationship between states and markets, the present agenda should be related to governance and network. Jessop explains that there are largely two perspectives, society-centred governance and state-centred governance. This overlaps with the discussions on post-Keynesian welfare states. Whichever perspective one takes, using the term *governance* implies that certain attention has been paid to governance without government. Consequently, the concept of "from government to governance" has been created.

Pierre and Stoker (2000) organized the discussions on governance from following two perspectives: the first perspective focuses on governance as formal or informal processes. It asserts that a "self-governance network" is playing a dominant role in such processes. The second perspective focuses on governance from the state-centric viewpoint. States remain to be central in governance by making use of their huge resources.

Bakir (2009) analyzed network governance by categorizing it into two types. The first type is governance with government, and the second is governance without government.

Theories of governance are discussions on the role of a state in political science. In putting the realization of ecological sustainability into the discussions, these theories will confront additional problems.

This point of views shares some similarity with Eckersley's questions. With regard to states, Eckersley (2004) claims few social institutions can match the same degree of capacity and potential legitimacy that states have.

In order to realize sustainable development, reviewing the potential of a state is necessary. The discussions in this chapter, which place a high value on the roles and functions of local governments, are also made in such a context. The discussions here are based on the approach of state-centric governance.

However, thinking in such a way, the significance of the third sector as a social actor (non-state actor) is emphasized rather paradoxically. It is considered that governance through the horizontal interactions between state actors and social actors is necessary, not a governance through hierarchy (Bell and Hindmoor, 2009). The self-governance network is essential in terms of social actors' playing the roles.

Governance will be understood as an actual concept, not as a normative concept or as an analysis concept. Only when the governing structure and the governing process horizontally interact, will governance be realistically envisaged and realized. This means that governance requires a governing structure and a governing process. Local governance has the highest potential for realizing governance as an actual concept.

By demonstrating the feasibility of local governance, governance is developed from a normative concept into a fact. In order to realize local governance, it is necessary to achieve decentralization from a central government to local governments. At the same time, decentralization within regions is necessary. This is because it is key to realizing sustainable development in which an open policy-making and implementation system is established at the local level and deliberative democracy functions well. In other words, establishing a form of local public–private partnership able to perceive the problems and solve them is closely related to the realization of sustainable development.

## Decentralization for sustainable development

### Embedment of sustainable development

From the sustainability perspective, good governance is deemed necessary. In Japan, regarding this respect and approaching from a governance perspective, sustainability is treated as one of a group of policy issues but is not discussed as an essential element. I contend that it is necessary to embed sustainable development in the society.

As for the difficulties of sustainability of the ecosystem, market economies and human lives are considered to be the triggers, from the perspective of deep ecology. This is to say that the market economy and human activities are threatening ecosystems.

This is the primary root of difficulties in achieving sustainability. Regardless of whether changes to a radical economic society are desired, economic and other human activities need to be conducted within the boundaries set by the environmental capacity, and a low-carbon society must be realized by effectively reducing greenhouse gases.

The life of a human being as a biological existence is ensured by the social system. When the natural ecosystem is broken, the social system will face the risk of collapse. The social system will also face crisis when the ecosystem is difficult to maintain.

The social system is related to the way in which human society is reproduced. The modern human society is to be largely influenced by the performance of administrative authorities. It is a significant element for the life of a human being whether a social system is inclusive or exclusive.

What does it mean to embed sustainable development in societies? It is to realize it by combining people's basic social needs and essential social infrastructures with environmental issues. Conclusively, it means making an effort to overcome the difficulties of achieving sustainability of both the ecosystem and the social system.

People prefer simultaneous actions for sustainable development by accepting such a code of conduct as social and global citizenship together with integrating environmental issues. In order to attain a new code of conduct, it will be helpful to expand the capacities and roles of the civil society sector. Such people's behaviours will relate to a way of thinking that regards market economies and the status of an administrative state as relational.

If governance is envisaged as the one that includes decommodification policies for maintaining a social system, the aim will be to realize social inclusion and social equity. If governance is envisaged as a post-Keynesian welfare state model, efforts will be directed at converting the roles and functions of a government.

Based on such understandings, the process of embedding sustainable development into a society is considered one of preparing to create an orientation towards people's governance.

The concept of embedment of sustainable development into a society may sound ambiguous as well as idealistic. At the local level, this concept may sound somewhat more realistic. It originates not from the territorial smallness, but from the concreteness of the issues.

An insatiable economic globalization and the difficulties of governmental finance have caused numerous problems in local societies. At the same time, efforts are made in order to approach their self-sustaining solutions toward local problems including local economies. The important point regarding problem-solving approaches is participatory development through public–private partnership as well as restructuring local economies.

Restructuring local economies under globalization is, for one thing, for enhancing the economic activities that are competitive in the global economy. Another thing is to pursue the possibility of economies that do not prioritize profit-making. It may be possible to envision the possibilities for a quasi-market economy in contemporary society based on the activities of non-profit organizations, local community organizations and social enterprises.

Some face-to-face services and basic goods are provided at the local level through quasi-market economy or social exchanges. In addition, the conservation of the natural environment and the utilization and control of local resources from the viewpoint of ecology must be achieved at the local level. These are achieved not only as governmental activities but also as economic activities.

Participatory development through public–private partnership will enhance the roles of local governments. The coexistence of quasi-market economies and market economies will enhance local economies. Such phenomena can be explained as embedment of sustainable development in local societies.

*Impacts of local governments*

Embedding sustainable development in local societies is not simultaneously carried out in all local governments. Some local governments will be established as beacons, and they will have an impact on other local governments. As such interactive actions are disseminated, the networks among local governments will expand.

In order to solve ecological issues, the resources for desirable social changes through strengthening the environmental regulation by states must be used. From the perspective of non-state-centric governance, the role of central government is considered redundant. Despite decentralization, local governments should accept the regulatory role of state in terms of environmental protection.

By advancing decentralization, the mutual process that includes the tensions between local and central governments will be created. With regard to environmental regulations, energy policies and nature conservation policies, local governments, rather than the central government, will be able to adopt ecological policies. As for the roles of local governments, it will be possible to choose the model to enhance the institutional capacities of local governments, rather than the kind of withdrawal model in which they "open up various services to the private sector" by downsizing themselves. Advancing policy changes at the local level will result in motivating local governments to make policy preferences that are different from the central government.

Concrete cases show how networks of local governments can have an impact on the central government.

In response to the Bush administration's rejection of the Kyoto Protocol, networks of state governments exercised their own policy initiatives. In the northeastern United States, the emissions trading system of cap and trade, named the "Regional Greenhouse Gas Initiative" (RGGI), which targeted $CO_2$ emissions from electric power plants, was initiated. Following the initiatives by these northeastern states, Western Climate Initiative (WCI) was initiated in by western states as well as by Canadian states. In midwestern states, as well as in Canadian states, the Midwestern Greenhouse Gas Reduction Accord (MGGA) was initiated. The WCI and MGGA are regional emissions trading systems of cap and trade which cover various types of businesses.

In Japan, in order to reduce the particle materials (PM) emitted from diesel engines of automobiles, local governments in the capital region collaborated to reduce them. The four local governments of Tokyo, Chiba, Saitama and Kanagawa prohibited new automobiles (except passenger cars) that did not fulfil the standards to run in their areas. As for new cars with diesel engines, they requested to move up the scale and implement the future standards set by the central government. In addition, they requested necessary measures against existing diesel engine automobiles. The impacts of the regulations in the capital region entailing numerous logistic issues were not only visible at the local level. Automobile manufacturers quickly improved their diesel engines to satisfy the prescribed standards. The transportation companies using diesel engine automobiles took additional measures to improve their engines.

Beyond the impact on individual policies, local governmental networks can also have an impact on the orientations of governments and international society by suggesting comprehensive policy goals. Typical examples include Local Agenda 21 and, recently, the notion of "resilience". International organizations such as the Organisation for Economic Co-operation and Development (OECD) as well as the International Council for Local Environmental Initiatives (ICLEI) have come to use the term *resilience* as a conceptual term for local polices including adaptation to climate change (OECD, 2010; ICLEI, 2011).

The term *resilience* is an umbrella term. Based on the understanding that the idea adapting climate change is its origin, it needs to be a broad policy goal. First, by the various plans such as spatial planning or construction planning, it is necessary to enhance resilience of the built environment against various types of disasters caused by climate change. Second, by preserving and restoring the natural capital, it is necessary to maintain and improve the resilience of ecosystems. Third, by increasing social capital and human capital, the resilience of the social system is ensured as a result of economic and social changes.

The policies aiming to realize three pillars of resilience need to be developed at the local level. Despite decentralization, local governments should accept governmental policies and measures for achieving resilience.

## Concluding remarks

The concept of sustainable development is the one that largely includes uncertain factors in the meaning of its goals and in the paths to its realization. Social experimental challenges at the local level have large impacts on the conceptualization of sustainable development. In order to suggest the orientation of policy changes, as well as to induce the conditions necessary for the transition toward a sustainable society, the achievements and lessons learned at the local level are essential.

Decentralization for sustainable development is a condition to enrich the achievement at the local level as well as a process. If it is possible to regard local governance as an actual concept by decentralization for sustainable development, local governance can be converted from a purpose to a means. The realization of local governance and the challenges toward sustainable development at the local level will be pursued simultaneously and synergistically, under the decentralization for sustainable development.

## Notes

1. The "Aalborg Charter", which European local governments adopted and signed, was promulgated at the first European Sustainable Cities and Towns, hosted in Aalborg, Denmark, in May 1994. By signing the charter, local governments committed themselves to initiate activities under the Local Agenda 21 program, as well as to make commitments to develop their long-term plans for sustainability and their implementations. This quotation is quoted from the chapter I-7 of the Aalborg Charter.
2. The positional relationships of social system and ecosystem and their names are those of Marten (2001). The predication on the relativity of these two systems is solely due to the author.

## REFERENCES

Bakir, Caner (2009) "The Governance of Financial Regulatory Reform: The Australian Experience", *Public Administration*, 87(4), pp. 910–922.

Bell, Stephen and Andrew Hindmoor (2009) *Rethinking Governance: The Centrality of the State in Modern Society*, New York: Cambridge University Press.

Boyer, Robert (1990) *The Regulation School: A Critical Introduction*, translated by C. Charney, New York: Columbia University Press.

Eckersley, Robyn (2004) *The Green State: Rethinking Democracy and Sovereignty*, Cambridge, MA: MIT Press.

Esping-Andersen, Gøsta (1990) *The Three Worlds of Welfare Capitalism*, Cambridge: Polity Press.

Habermas, Jürgen (1985) *The Theory of Communicative Action, Volume 2: Lifeworld and System: A Critique of Functional Reason*, translated by T. McCarthy, Boston, MA: Beacon Press.

International Council for Local Environmental Initiatives (ICLE I) (2011) *The Resilient City: A Demand Driven Approach to Development, Disaster Risk Reduction and Climate Adaptation: An ICLEI White Paper, ICLEI Global Report*, Bonn: ICLEI.

Jessop, Bob (2007) *State Power: A Strategic-Relational Approach*, Cambridge: Polity Press.

Lipietz, Alain (1987) *Mirages and Miracles: Crisis in Global Fordism*, translated by David A. J. Macey, New York: Verso Books.
Marten, Gerald G. (2001) *Human Ecology: Basic Concepts for Sustainable Development*, London: Earthscan Publications.
Organisation for Economic Co-operation and Development (OECD) (2010) *Integrating Climate Change Adaptation into Development Co-operation: Policy Guidance*, Paris: OECD.
Pierre, Jon and Gerry Stoker (2000) "Towards Multi-Level Governance", in P. Dunleavy et al. (eds.) *Developments in British Politics 6*, Basingstoke: Palgrave Macmillan, pp. 29–44.
Polanyi, Karl (1957) *The Great Transformation: The Political and Economic Origins of Our Time*, 2nd edition, Boston: Beacon Press.

# Part IV
# Social movements and social learning in transition management for sustainable development

# 14
## Anti-nuclear movements in Japan: Before and after the Fukushima nuclear disaster

*Koichi Hasegawa*

The accident at the Fukushima Daiichi Nuclear Power Plant triggered by the Great East Japan Earthquake and Tsunami on 11 March 2011 significantly changed anti-nuclear movements in Japan. To grasp the nature of this change requires an understanding of the history and main characteristics of anti-nuclear movements in Japan from the beginning.

The first questions this chapter addresses are what kind of history does the anti-nuclear movements in Japan have and what are their main characteristics. These movements in Japan have a long history, a fact not necessarily well known to European countries or the United States. Despite its long history, the social and political influence of anti-nuclear movements in Japan has been limited compared to countries such as Germany. Moreover, prior to the Fukushima nuclear accident, the greatest number of people mobilized was 20,000, recorded in April 1988, two years after the Chernobyl nuclear accident, and the movement lost momentum in the more than 20 years since. The next question this chapter addresses is what Japan's anti-nuclear movements have achieved despite their limited influence and ability to mobilize people prior to the Fukushima nuclear accident. The movements' achievements are examined in terms of legislative and judicial results and referendum outcomes. Another question addressed is the kinds of changes that have occurred in the anti-nuclear movements or in their protests since the Fukushima nuclear accident and the characteristics of the newly emerged movements. The final question addressed concerns what challenges the anti-nuclear movements in Japan face in their quest to realize a shift in the country's nuclear policy. This chapter provides answers to these questions from the standpoint of social movement theory.

*Transition management for sustainable development, Ueta and Adachi (eds.), United Nations University Press, 2014, ISBN 978-92-808-1234-3*

## The state of affairs before the Fukushima nuclear accident

The promotion of a "nuclear renaissance" started worldwide in 2001, the year George W. Bush became president of the United States. As Table 14.1 shows, as of the end of 2010, the number of nuclear reactors under construction in Western Europe and the United States was as few as three.[1] The construction of the reactor in the United States actually began in 1973 but had been suspended for a lengthy period. In 15 years, the number of reactors in operation in Western Europe and the United States decreased by 29 from 280 in 1995 to 251 in 2010. In contrast, the number of reactors in operation in Asia increased by 35, and the number of reactors under construction is as many as 42. Of the 64 reactors under construction worldwide, 65.6 per cent are in Asia; in particular, 37 reactors are in East Asia. Thus, there is a sharp contrast between East Asia, whose dependence on nuclear power has rapidly increased due to economic growth and a jump in energy demand, and European countries and the Unites States, where nuclear power generation has declined as societies have matured.

Table 14.1 Number of nuclear reactors (1995 and 2010)

| Countries | End of 1995 | | End of 2010 | |
|---|---|---|---|---|
| | Number of reactors in operation | Number of reactors under construction | Number of reactors in operation | Number of reactors under construction |
| **Western Europe** | | | | |
| France | 56 | 4 | 58 | 1 |
| Germany | 20 | | 17 | |
| United Kingdom | 35 | | 19 | |
| Sweden | 12 | | 10 | |
| Spain | 9 | | 8 | |
| Belgium | 7 | | 7 | |
| Switzerland | 5 | | 5 | |
| Finland | 4 | | 4 | 1 |
| Netherlands | 2 | | 1 | |
| Subtotal | 150 | 4 | 129 | 2 |
| **North America** | | | | |
| United States | 109 | 1 | 104 | 1 |
| Canada | 21 | | 18 | |
| Subtotal | 130 | 1 | 122 | 1 |
| **Asia** | | | | |
| Japan | 51 | 3 | 54 | 2 |
| South Korea | 11 | 5 | 21 | 5 |

Table 14.1 (cont.)

| | | | | |
|---|---|---|---|---|
| Taiwan | 6 | | 6 | 2 |
| India | 10 | 4 | 20 | 5 |
| China | 3 | | 13 | 27 |
| Pakistan | 1 | 1 | 3 | |
| Iran | | 2 | | 1 |
| Subtotal | 82 | 15 | 117 | 42 |
| **Eastern Europe** | | | | |
| Russia | 29 | 4 | 32 | 11 |
| Ukraine | 16 | 5 | 15 | 2 |
| Lithuania | 2 | | 0 | |
| Kazakhstan | 1 | | 0 | |
| Armenia | 1 | | 1 | |
| Bulgaria | 6 | | 2 | 2 |
| Hungary | 4 | | 4 | 2 |
| Czech | 4 | 2 | 6 | |
| Slovakia | 4 | 4 | 4 | |
| Slovenia | 1 | | 1 | |
| Romania | | 2 | 2 | |
| Subtotal | 68 | 17 | 67 | 17 |
| **Latin America** | | | | |
| Argentina | 2 | 1 | 2 | 1 |
| Mexico | 2 | | 2 | |
| Brazil | 1 | 1 | 2 | 1 |
| Subtotal | 5 | 2 | 6 | 2 |
| **Africa** | | | | |
| South Africa | 2 | | 2 | |
| Subtotal | 2 | | 2 | |
| Total | 437 | 7 | 443 | 5 |
| Total amount (MW) | 346,743 | | 375,374 | |

Source: IAEA, Nuclear Power Reactors in the World 2011 Edition, available at http://www-pub.iaea.org/books/IAEABooks/8752/Nuclear-Power-Reactors-in-the-World-2011-Edition.

The difference is usually explained by economic growth and increased demand for energy, but this explanation is insufficient because it merely reduces the issue for discussions on economic growth and determinants of energy demand. What is interesting from a sociological perspective is the influence of the political establishment and civil society on energy policy.

The three East Asian countries and Taiwan have lacked a change of ruling party under a lasting regime controlled by one dominant party. China is still under the one-party rule of the Communist Party. In Japan, conservative government lasted for a long time until a Democratic Party administration started in September 2009, with the exception of two 10-month periods under the Katayama cabinet from May 1947 to March 1948, the Hosokawa cabinet from August 1993 to June 1994 and the subsequent Hata cabinet. In South Korea, too, conservative government has been long lasting, except in the period between February 1998 and February 2008 under the Kim Dae-jun and Roh Moo-hyun administrations. In Taiwan, conservative government lasted except for the period from May 2000 to May 2008 under the Chen Shui-bian administration. With the lack of opportunities for a regime change, the stability and consistency of long-term policies, such as energy policy, in particular, become stronger. The political regimes in East Asia are centralized compared to Germany and the United States where a change in ruling party often occurs under a decentralized federal system. In fact, in Taiwan and South Korea an authoritarian political regime continued to exist until the mid-1980s, and the three East Asian countries and Taiwan lacked a tradition of civil society.

In recent years, South Korea has emerged as a rival to Japan in the export of nuclear equipment and technology to developing countries. In December 2009, outdoing Japan and France, South Korea succeeded in winning a contract for exporting nuclear equipment to the United Arab Emirates through a sales promotion by President Lee Myung-bak himself. South Korea is aiming to export 80 nuclear reactors by 2030. China also clearly intends to actively pursue exports of nuclear equipment, as can be seen from the order it received for a pressure vessel for a nuclear power plant in Pakistan in 2004. It was expected that Japan, South Korea and China would become rivals not only in economic growth, but also in the export of nuclear equipment. The nuclear reprocessing policy of Japan stimulated that of South Korea, and South Korea has been in negotiation with the United States since October 2010 to revise the nuclear agreement between the two countries and to gain consent for commercial nuclear reprocessing.

The nuclear power industry of the world is currently led by Japan and France. In 2005, Toshiba bought Westinghouse (WH). In response to this, Hitachi merged its nuclear power business with that of GE, and Mitsubishi Heavy Industries reached an agreement for business cooperation with Areva, a statutory corporation of France. These three pairings—Toshiba–WH, Hitachi–GE and Mitsubishi–Areva—are the major players. As mentioned earlier, Japan's pro-nuclear policy led to the acceleration of South Korea and China's pro-nuclear policies, triggered a nuclear renaissance in European countries and the United States, and stimulated developing countries' interest in building nuclear power plants. In public lectures and in a previous paper, the author posed the question of whether we would need another nuclear accident like Chernobyl to change Japan's pro-nuclear energy policy (Hasegawa, 1999). Unfortunately, my warning from 15 years ago finally became a reality with the Fukushima nuclear accident.

## An analysis based on social movement theory

This chapter analyses the questions mentioned earlier from the standpoint of social movement theory. Among the models in social movement theory, the most general and comprehensive model used is what the author refers to as the triangular model of social movement (TRIM). The model is based on the work of McAdam (1996) and includes three representative theoretical frameworks on social movements—collective behaviour theory, resource mobilization theory and new social movement theory—as depicted in Figure 14.1. More specifically, focus is placed on three factors: the structure of political opportunity, mobilized resources and cultural framing. The history of Japan's anti-nuclear movements are explained from the standpoint of how these three factors have changed (see also Hasegawa, 2004: chap. 4; 2011).

The anti-nuclear movements in Japan can be divided into five periods according to points of issue and organizers.[2] The first period (1954–1973) is the period of movements for the abolition of nuclear weapons. The second period (1973–1986) is the period of movements against the construction of nuclear power plants. The Chernobyl nuclear accident in 1986 greatly energized the anti-nuclear movements in Japan and started a change in their nature. The third period (1986–1992) is the

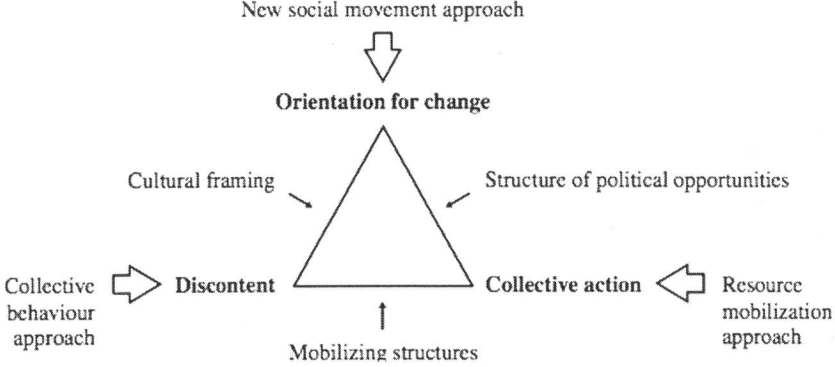

Figure 14.1 The triangular structure of social movement analysis

period when grass-roots activities in metropolitan areas became active. It was at the end of this period, in 1992, when the uranium enrichment plant in the nuclear fuel recycling facilities in Rokkasho Village became fully operational. This led to the fourth period (1992–March 2011), a period of anti-plutonium movements. The fifth period is the post-Fukushima period when again the anti-nuclear movements have been energized after the nuclear accident. In this latest period, radioactive contamination has become a real problem and has posed a threat to people's daily lives.

The years 1973, 1986 and 1992 roughly correspond to significant transitions in the Japanese economy. In 1973, an oil crisis occurred and rapid economic growth ended. The period 1986–1992 approximately corresponds to Japan's bubble economy that followed a low interest rate policy resulting from the Plaza Accord in September 1985. The period of movements pressing for the abolition of nuclear weapons corresponds to the period of rapid economic growth, the period of movements against construction of nuclear power plants to the period of stable economic growth, the period of grass-roots protests in metropolitan areas to the bubble economy period and the period of anti-plutonium movements to the post-bubble-economy period.

*First period: the period of movement for the abolition of nuclear weapons (1954–1973)*

In his address to the United Nations General Assembly in December 1953, the then US president Eisenhower proposed "Atoms for Peace". The speech contained the country's intention not only to sell licenses and nuclear fuel to capitalist allies but also to block nuclear militarization through a nuclear agreement, during the Cold War period.

Since the Fukushima nuclear accident, foreign scholars have frequently asked me why Japan has built as many as 54 reactors in its small territory even though it was attacked with nuclear bombs and knows of actual nuclear damage. Ulrich Beck, a sociologist known for his risk society theory, poses the same question (Beck et al., 2011). The first answer to this question is that having been attacked by nuclear bombs, Japan would serve as a convenient showcase for the United States in demonstrating the peaceful use of nuclear power to the international community. Second, as a country defeated in war and lacking natural resources, Japan had a strong desire to excel in science and technology. Having been defeated and having lost its colonies, Japan sought affluence through economic growth based on the cutting-edge technology of nuclear power. By accepting US strategies, Japan chose a path to becoming a major economically developed country excelling in science and technology based on the promotion of nuclear power while distinguishing between military use and peaceful use of nuclear power.

Third, it has been found in a classified document of the Ministry of Foreign Affairs that, from the beginning, Japan had a motive to secure technological capabilities for developing nuclear weapons through the development of nuclear technologies, although this fact was hidden behind a proclaimed goal of peaceful use of nuclear power, was not reported by the media and was not explicitly regarded as a problem by the Diet.[3] Former prime minister Yasuhiro Nakasone was an advocate of nuclear militarization and was a key player in Japan's nuclear energy policy. In March 1954, a budget associated with nuclear power was approved for the first time, and one of the proposers of the budget was Nakasone, a young 35-year-old member of the Diet at the time. When the system of subsidies for power plant siting was implemented in 1974, he was the head of the Ministry of International Trade and Industry, which oversaw the system. Also, he was prime minister when the US–Japan Civil Nuclear Agreement was revised in 1988 and included comprehensive approval by the United States for nuclear reprocessing.

As a budget associated with nuclear power generation was approved in 1954, the history of nuclear power development in Japan started. Anti-nuclear movements in Japan date back to March of that year when the crew of a tuna trawler, the *Daigo Fukuryu Maru*, was exposed to radiation from the testing of a hydrogen bomb by the United States in Bikini Atoll. One crew member ultimately died. In response to this incident, women from Suginami Ward, Tokyo, started a movement for the abolition of atomic and hydrogen bombs. However, until the first half of the 1960s, protests at nuclear power plant sites lacked organization; in the latter half, such protests became active. Anti-nuclear movements in the early days were like peace movements, were supported by the Socialist and Communist Parties and the labour unions and were not clearly separated from movements for elimination of nuclear weapons. However, in 1965, the movement for eliminating nuclear weapons backed by the Socialist Party, which opposed the possession of nuclear weapons by any country, was separated from the movement backed by the Communist Party, which tolerated possession of nuclear weapons by socialist countries.

Thus, the anti-nuclear movements in the first period were characterized by their close connection with movements pressing for the elimination of nuclear weapons in terms of cultural framing, by support (resources) from left-wing political parties and labor unions and by activities under a Cold War–period political opportunity structure (POS), namely, left-wing politics.

## *Second period: The period of movements against the construction of nuclear power plants (1973–1986)*

In the 1970s, movements against construction of nuclear power plants spread due to the influence of the debate on nuclear safety in the United States, which started in 1969; the influence of anti-pollution movements in Japan; and a series of malfunctions and failures at operating nuclear power plants. In terms of resources, the protests of farmers and fishermen at nuclear power plant construction sites were a distinctive characteristic of anti-nuclear movements in Japan. Landowners and fishermen can effectively exercise a veto against a plan to construct a nuclear power plant by refusing to sell land for such construction and by opposing the transfer of fishing rights, respectively. Because the construction of nuclear power plants was conducted under national policy and, in most cases, with the support of the prefectures where they were to be constructed, the only effective way to oppose the construction was to claim property rights, such as land and fishing rights.

From the 1960s, a period of rapid economic growth, the influence of the Socialist Party of Japan started to wane and the party suffered a major loss in the 1969 general election because they clung to Marxism-Leninism and showed its support for the Soviet Union's military intervention in Czechoslovakia in 1968. The Communist Party also suffered a loss in the 1976 general election. Therefore, a mood of disappointment in socialism spread, and the influence of the left-wing parties declined gradually as multiple political parties emerged for POS.

As for cultural framing, under these circumstances, the anti-nuclear movements shifted away from ideological opposition to actual attempts to stop construction of nuclear power plants one site at a time. Farmers and fishermen in particular tried to defend their property rights and feared decreases in the prices of agricultural and marine products caused by actual radiation leakage and negative rumours. A clear example is the lawsuit against the construction of Ikata Nuclear Power Plant initiated by local residents in August 1973. Lawsuits involving the Tokai Daini Nuclear Power Plant, the Fukushima Daini Nuclear Power Plant and the Kashiwazaki-Kariwa Nuclear Power Plant were filed in October 1973, January 1975 and July 1979, respectively, were regarded as the pioneering lawsuits in Japan against nuclear power plants (Kaido, 2011). The four lawsuits took the form of administrative litigation in which the defendant was the national government (Minister of International Trade and Industry), which had permitted the construction of the nuclear power plants, and cancellation of the permission was sought.

In August 1975, the first national anti-nuclear conference was held in Kyoto, and the All Japan Anti-Nuclear Liaison Association was born. In September, the Citizens' Nuclear Information Center was started under the leadership of Jinzaburo Takagi. After his death in October 2000, the Liaison Association and the Information Center have continued to function as the hub of the anti-nuclear movements in Japan. Around 1975, an organizational system for anti-nuclear movements was created in which protests at plant construction sites were backed by support groups located at regional hub cities such as capital cities of prefectures, whereas the Liaison Association and the Information Center served as national-level information centres.

As for the government side, the system of subsidies for power plant siting was implemented under Prime Minister Kakuei Tanaka in June 1974 as a countermeasure to rising protests. The system was intended to suppress protests through the payment of "nuisance fees" to municipalities that had a nuclear power plant and its surrounding municipalities, and it has proved to be an effective measure for dealing with local opposition. The system encompasses all types of power plants but is particularly intended to promote the construction of nuclear power plants. The amount of subsidies provided for a nuclear power plant is more than twice that for a fossil-fuel-fired or hydropower plant of equivalent size. As for the financing of the subsidies, close to 2 per cent of household electricity bills is automatically collected from consumers as an earmarked tax already included in the bill. In other words, the consumers of electric power in Japan have been paying this Electric Power Development Tax, which amounts to 1,350 yen per year (assuming that the annual amount of electricity used by a household is 3,600 kWh), without noticing it because it is not listed in the breakdown of the electricity bill. In the government budget proposal for 2010, approximately 179 billion yen were allocated as subsidies for power plant siting.

*Third period: the period of grass-roots protests in major urban areas (1986–1992)*

The Three Mile Island nuclear accident that occurred in the United States in March 1979 and the Chernobyl nuclear accident that occurred in the Soviet Union in April 1986 greatly shocked the world and cast serious doubts on the safety of nuclear power plants. With regard to the POS, the Chernobyl nuclear accident, in which a nuclear reactor exploded, resulted in a substantial amount of fallout, made a vast area uninhabitable due to radioactive contamination and stirred fears about, for example, food contamination among the people of Europe.

In the wake of these accidents and especially that at Chernobyl, the Japanese government and electric companies announced that a similar accident could not occur in Japan, pointing out differences in reactor type and safety regulations. However, for resources, people living in major cities, particularly housewives with small children, started to oppose nuclear power generation because these two massive accidents involving nuclear meltdowns had occurred in short succession in the world's two superpowers—the United States and the Soviet Union. Protests in Japan in the first and second periods, be it by farmers and fishermen at the plant sites or by political parties and labour unions, had been conducted mainly by men, with female participants limited to members of the Japan Teachers' Union. Also, in many protest activities, the participants were organizationally mobilized, and they were less like citizens' movements in which individuals would participate at their own will. A network structure for the anti-nuclear movements, which included person-to-person networks, was created, as shown in Figure 14.2.

A book titled *Kiken na hanashi: Cherunobuiri to nihon no unmei* (*On the Risk of Nuclear Power Stations: Chernobyl and Japan's Fate*) by nonfiction writer Takashi Hirose (1987) became a best seller. Hirose starts out by telling stories from his own viewpoint as a father of two daughters. His message that efforts to stop nuclear power generation are made to protect the lives of the children resonated greatly with housewives who were concerned about the safety of imported food products. The anti-nuclear movements reached their height with two

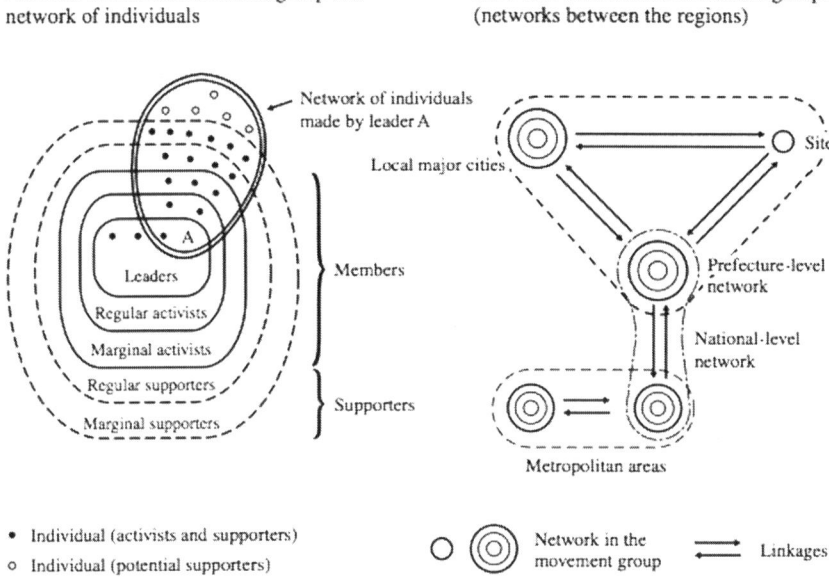

Figure 14.2 Network structure of anti-nuclear energy movements

events: the gathering of 3,000 people in front of the headquarters of the Shikoku Electric Power Company in Takamatsu City when an output adjustment experiment was conducted at the Ikata Nuclear Power Plant in February 1988, and the participation of 20,000 people (twice the number expected by the organizers) in a rally held at Hibiya Park in Tokyo in April 1988 to commemorate the two-year anniversary of the Chernobyl nuclear accident.

What is characteristic of these movements is a tendency toward self-expression and defence of self-determination by individuals. This is represented by a comment made by a female leader who called for a protest against the output adjustment experiment at the Ikata Nuclear Power Plant in February 1988: "It is imperative to regain control of the will of oneself and the belief of oneself and to stop nuclear power generation by expression of the will of oneself by any means necessary" (Obara, 1988: 22). The term *oneself* appears as many as three times in this short statement. In a straightforward yet naive manner, the comment directly relates one's self to a modern civilization supporting the existence of nuclear power plants. Regarding cultural framing, a style of movements that would match the participants' feeling and sense of daily life was explored with emphasis placed on songs and dance. These tendencies can be seen in the naming of groups such as the Apple Flower Club (Aomori Prefecture) and the Grape Club against Nuclear Power (Miyagi Prefecture), as well as in slogans in local dialects such as "kakunen maine" (which expresses opposition to construction of a nuclear fuel processing plant in the Tsugaru dialect) and "odazu nayo genpatsu zosetsu" (expressing the disgust of an extension built to an nuclear power plant).

Anti-nuclear movements in Japan after the Chernobyl nuclear accident became active mainly among well-educated women in major urban areas and became a typical example of individual-identity-oriented new social movements. However, due to a lack of strategic ideas and a sense of political effectiveness, these movements rapidly lost momentum as the impact of the Chernobyl nuclear accident faded away.[4]

*Fourth period: the period of anti-plutonium movements (1992–2011)*

At the nuclear power plants in Japan, 20 reactors started operating in the 1970s and 16 started operating in the 1980s. In other words, around two reactors began operating per year. However, a series of functional failures and accidents occurred at nuclear facilities in Japan in the 1990s. The major incidents included a fire at FBR Monju in December 1995 due to sodium leakage, a fire and an explosion at the bitumen solidification facility in the PNC Tokai Reprocessing Plant in March 1997 and a nuclear criticality accident that occurred in September 1999 at the JCO nuclear fuel plant located in a residential area in Tokai Village.

In the JCO accident, two workers died and one worker became seriously ill following exposure to strong radiation. Three firefighters were also exposed: they had been called in for the rescue operations but had not been informed of it being a nuclear criticality accident, and thus were not protected against radiation. The criticality condition lasted for around 20 hours. Approximately 150 residents living within a 350-metre radius were advised to evacuate the area, and about 310,000 residents living within a 10-kilometre radius were advised to stay inside. As many as 667 people, including JCO employees and neighbourhood residents, were certified by the accident investigation committee as victims of radiation exposure.[5]

In August 2002, a cover-up of functional failures at the Fukushima Daiichi Nuclear Power Plant operated by the Tokyo Electric Power Company was exposed, which led to temporary stoppage of operations at all 17 nuclear reactors owned by the company. A pipe breakage occurred at the Mihama No. 3 Unit operated by the Kansai Electric Power Company, leaving five workers dead and six with burns. Through a series of such accidents, citizens lost trust in the government's execution of nuclear policy.

Functional failures frequently occurred at a fast breeder reactor and nuclear fuel cycle facilities overseen by the Science and Technology Agency. The most serious bottleneck for nuclear power plants is the treatment of spent nuclear fuel (back-end measures). Since the beginning of the nuclear energy project, Japan has chosen to reprocess spent nuclear fuel: mixing the remaining uranium and plutonium extracted and reusing them as nuclear fuel. An alternative approach to handling the spent fuel is disposal of it, carried out by the United States, where no reprocessing is conducted and nuclear fuel is used only once. An increasing number of countries have shifted to disposal because of high reprocessing costs and significant delays in putting fast breeder reactors, which burn reprocessed plutonium, into practical use. In contrast, countries sticking to the reprocessing approach include Japan, France, Russia and China. Because Germany has now abandoned reprocessing, Japan is currently the only country among the non-nuclear weapon countries that is allowed to reprocess spent nuclear fuel.

Nuclear fuel recycling facilities consist of a uranium enrichment plant, a low-level radioactive waste storage facility, a temporary storage and monitoring facility for high-level radioactive waste and a spent fuel reprocessing plant. A basic construction agreement was reached in April 1985, and it was decided that these four types of facility would be built in Rokkasho Village, Aomori Prefecture (Funabashi et al., 2012). It was in 1992 when, among the four types of facilities, a uranium enrichment plant became the first to begin full operation, and the path to the use of plutonium actually started. In January 1993, a Japanese ship, the Akatsuki Maru, which was transporting 1.5 tons of plutonium extracted in France through the reprocessing of spent nuclear fuel from Japanese nuclear power plants, arrived in Tokai Village. However, because the plutonium was being transported from France, many countries expressed their strong alarm and opposition.

As Japan's nuclear policy was faced with the difficult problem of how spent nuclear fuel would be treated, the policy came to a standstill. At the same time, the anti-nuclear movements could not come up with effective strategies or tactics in response to the accidents and functional failures occurring at the nuclear power plants. Many Diet members left the Liberal Democratic Party, new political parties such as the New Frontier Party were formed and the election system for the House of Representatives shifted to a single-seat constituency system in 1996. In such a new environment, the number of Diet members from the Social Democratic Party (formerly the Socialist Party) and the Communist Party decreased, beset by rivalry between the Liberal Democratic Party and the Democratic Party of Japan. With regard to the POS, due to the 1989 unification of the labour front, the Japanese Trade Union Confederation supporting the Socialist Party merged with the Japanese Confederation of Labor supporting the Democratic Socialist Party. This weakened the labour unions' influence, and they gradually stopped supporting the anti-nuclear movements. It became difficult to find new groups of people who would drive the movements as housewives in major urban areas had done after the Chernobyl nuclear accident. In the movements in various areas, the members became old, and the size of the movements declined. As for resources, the frequency of media coverage of anti-nuclear movements gradually decreased, and the coverage itself lessened except in periods immediately after major accidents or functional failures. With regard to cultural framing, a certain level of support among young people was invoked by the Stop Rokkasho project, in which an internationally well-known composer Ryuichi Sakamoto and others asked musicians worldwide to offer their music for the cause, and by movies like Miyuki Kamanaka's *Rokkasho Rhapsody*.

## How nuclear power generation could have been stopped

What then could have stopped the construction of nuclear facilities prior to the Fukushima nuclear accident? Was a shift away from pro-nuclear national policy possible?

Let us look at what was possible in each of the three arenas—legislation, administration and judicature. Taking legislation first, one possibility was enactment of a denuclearization law like that enacted in Germany in 2002 following a denuclearization agreement in June 2000. Actually, in Japan in response to rising national-level anti-nuclear movements after the 1986 Chernobyl accident, there was a movement to collect signatures in order to demand enactment of a denuclearization law. Although 2.51 million signatures were collected nationwide, the movement ended when the list of signatures was submitted to the Diet in April 1990. The possibility that the law would be enacted by the Diet essentially evaporated as the Liberal Democratic Party won the House of Representatives election held in February 1990. As more efforts were directed toward the signature-collecting campaign, the anti-nuclear movements rapidly lost momentum after reaching their height in 1988, and consequently there was a sense of defeat in the movements (Takagi, 1999). As long as there was one-party dominance of politics and as long as the Liberal Democratic Party and the Ministry of International Trade and Industry strongly continued a pro-nuclear policy, the legislative and administrative arenas were in effect closed to the anti-nuclear movements.

### Lawsuits against nuclear power plants

Although there is currently limited possibility of exerting political influence over the legislative and administrative branches, the courts are the arena where social movements may win and achieve certain goals. In fact, in Germany and France, this route provides important opportunities for the closure of nuclear power plants or facilities.

In Japan, there have been a total of about 20 lawsuits against nuclear power plants, but the plaintiffs lost in all of them before the Fukushima accident. There were only two cases of wins in the lower courts. In January 2003, in a landmark decision for the second trial in an administrative litigation, in which the invalidity of the permission to construct Monju was sought, the Kanazawa branch of the Nagoya High Court decided that there had been errors and omissions in the safety review process that could not be overlooked—a definitive win for the plaintiff.[6] In Japan, this was the first lawsuit against a nuclear power plant won by the plaintiff. The decision took into account the sodium leakage that had occurred in December 1995. However, the decision in the Supreme Court trial held in May 2005 in response to an appeal by the government recognized the government's discretion over the safety review of the basic design and stated that the construction permission was not illegal, and thus reversed the previous decision and marked a loss for the plaintiff.

On 24 March 2006, immediately after Unit No. 2 at the Shika Nuclear Power Plant started operations on 15 March, the Kanazawa District Court made a landmark decision (for a civil lawsuit filed in August 1999) that the old review guidelines for earthquake-resistant design, which was being revised at that time, were not adequately appropriate in light of the Great Hanshin Earthquake. The court ordered the Hokuriku Electric Power Company, the defendant, to stop the reactor operation. This is the first, and so far the only, decision to have ordered an operating light water reactor be stopped due mainly to insufficient anti-earthquake measures in design. However, in this case too, in March 2009 the plaintiff eventually lost as the Kanazawa branch of the Nagoya High Court rejected the decision of the first trial, positively viewing the new guidelines for earthquake-resistant design issued in September 2006. The Supreme Court rejected the plaintiff's appeal in October 2009, upholding the High Court's decision (Kaido, 2011).

There have been many lawsuits asking the courts to stop the construction or operation of large-scale public facilities and infrastructure, including fossil-fuel-fired power plants, the Shinkansen bullet train, highways, airports, military bases, dams and industrial waste disposal sites in addition to nuclear facilities. However, the only court decisions that approved a cease-and-desist order are a district court decision (1973, partial cease and desist) and a high court decision (1975, complete cease and desist) for a lawsuit involving the noise from and around Osaka Airport. Since the Supreme Court rejected in December 1981 a petition for a cease-and-desist order for the same lawsuit (which was settled in 1984), for 20 years there had been no court decision approving a cease-and-desist order. Subsequently, a partial cease-and-desist order was approved at the first trial for a lawsuit involving air pollution from roads in Amagasaki (January 2000) and in the first trial for a lawsuit involving air pollution in southern Nagoya (November 2000) caused by a combination of automobile exhaust gas and smoke from factories. Both lawsuits were settled during the appeal trials.

Aside from the aforementioned decisions by the Kanazawa branch of the Nagoya High Court in the lawsuit involving Monju and by the Kanazawa District Court in the lawsuit against the Shika Nuclear Power Plant, other major court decisions approving a complete cease-and-desist order as demanded by plaintiff residents include only the first trial for a lawsuit involving cancellation of the approval of the Odakyu Line railway overpass project (October 2001) and the first trial for a lawsuit involving a high-rise condominium in Kunitachi in which the removal of the part of the building exceeding 20 meters above ground was ordered (December 2002). In these two lawsuits, both plaintiffs lost in the higher courts, and the decisions were subsequently upheld by the Supreme Court.

These lawsuits constitute a new type of lawsuit called policy-oriented lawsuits in that the points in dispute not only include simple compensation for and prevention of the damage suffered by the plaintiff, but also include basic choice of public policy (Hasegawa, 2004). However, the judicial authorities, especially the higher courts and Supreme Court, are not in favour of an increasing number of such policy-oriented lawsuits and their social influences. The first reason is that they are concerned about and wary of approval of a cease-and-desist order setting a precedent that would result in the increase of policy-oriented, cease-and-desist lawsuits filed against public projects and public policy in general and would induce decisions in favour of plaintiffs. The second reason is the judicial authorities' resistance to a potential situation where, with frequent cease-and-desist court orders against public projects or facilities, judges would have the authority to make a policy-based judgment or an ultimate de facto veto on issues such as whether construction of a nuclear facility should be allowed.

The judicial branch has been controlled by extremely passive views on its role, with no sufficient consideration being given to questions such as to what extent it is allowed to make policy-based decisions under current conditions (including superficial division of powers due to increased administrative power, slow legislative and administrative response and stubborn administration of energy policies), how its pseudo-policy-making functions should be considered and whether there are effective problem resolution mechanisms that could replace the court system (Hasegawa, 2004).

*Referendum*

Faced with the closedness of all arenas—legislation, administration and judicature—at the national level, it was as if anti-nuclear movements had been thoroughly hemmed in. In such circumstances, a referendum on the construction of a nuclear power plant held in August 1996 in Maki Town, Niigata Prefecture (presently Nishikan Ward, Niigata City), showed that rejecting such construction through the efforts of local residents was in fact possible. This was the first official referendum in Japan based on local ordinances. The voter turnout was 88.3 per cent, and 60.9 per cent of the voters opposed the construction. Although the voting result was not legally binding, in December 2003, the Tohoku Electric Power Company ultimately gave up its plan to construct the nuclear power plant in Maki Town. The referendum had a significant impact on local disputes in various regions across Japan that involved not only nuclear issues but also American bases and construction of industrial waste disposals. Nationwide, Maki's referendum triggered movements seeking referendums. Within the next five years, there were 12 official referendums held in Japan, reflecting an upsurge in people's interest in them.

There are two other examples of referendums on nuclear power plants. One referendum was held in Kariwa Village, Niigata Prefecture, in May 2001 and voters were asked whether they would allow a "plutonium-thermal" project (plutonium burned in an existing reactor). The other was held in Miyama Town, Mie Prefecture, in November 2001 and voters were asked whether they would support soliciting the construction of a nuclear power plant. In the case of Kariwa Village, 53.6 per cent of the valid votes were against the plutonium-thermal project, and thus, the implementation of the project plan at the Kashiwazaki-Kariwa Nuclear Power Plant became suspended. In the case of Miyama Town, the referendum was actually proposed by the pro-nuclear power plant group consisting mainly of people from the commerce and industry who were worried about a decline in the fishing and forestry industries. However, the town mayor announced that the town would give up the solicitation because 67.5 per cent of the valid votes were against it.

Referendums reflect people's longing for self-determination—their desire to decide the fate of their home area by themselves. They provide a way for voters to directly express their choice on a given issue of dispute, as opposed to representative democracy in which voters choose leaders and representatives. Referendums, which are open equally to all voters, provide opportunities for the most straightforward form of civil participation.

Due to a decline in labour movements and groups supportive of the Social Democratic Party and the Communist Party, it has become difficult to conduct strategies with mobilization of the public based on existing organizations or to organize movements for direct negotiation backed by such strategies. For this reason, attention has been attracted to referendums in which participation and self-decision are the part of the framework. Referendums bring issues directly to individuals' attention. Aiming to hold a referendum is significantly meaningful for both social movements and anti-nuclear movements. First, short-term goals and strategies, schedules and issues to be dealt with are clear. The step for stopping nuclear power generation can thus be clearly shown. Second, unification of a wide range of people and formation of a majority are key to realizing and winning a referendum. In other words, it is necessary to unite people (including conservatives and people in the "silent majority") beyond existing political parties and factions, political views and conflicts of interests in order to realize a referendum and to form and maintain a majority. The possibility of holding a referendum stimulates social movements to mature. Third, the process of conducting a referendum also provides people with opportunities to learn about issues. The process toward voting has an effect on people's learning in that their exposure to information increases; their interest in issues becomes stronger; and they talk about the issues with family members, friends and acquaintances.

Criticisms against referendums point out their incompatibility with representative democracy, their ineffectiveness due to the fact that they are not legally binding, "regional egoism" such as NIMBY (not in my backyard) and the possibility that national policies can be affected by the results of referendums held in certain regions. However, it is necessary in Japan to enact a local ordinance in order to hold a referendum, and enactment of a local ordinance requires majority support in the local assembly. Because a referendum cannot be held without assembly approval, it is not at odds with representative democracy. In most cases, a referendum is not held because the assembly does not give approval even if the majority of voters want it. In reality, it is often the case that conservative representatives hold a majority in the assembly of a municipality where a nuclear power plant is (or will be) located. With resistance from them, no referendum regarding a nuclear power plant has been held except for the aforementioned three municipalities.

The background and result of the referendum held in Maki Town have been analysed by Hasegawa (2004: chap. 9) with focus placed on (1) changes in the POS at the town level, that is, the declining influence of powerful conservative politicians, who had influenced town politics for a long time, because of an exodus of Diet members from the Liberal Democratic Party (July 1993); (2) rich human resources resulting from the town's nature as a central place of activities and a neighbour of the prefectural capital city (mobilized resources); and (3) the framing of a referendum as self-determination of the region's fate.

## Changes observed after the Fukushima nuclear accident

The accident at the Fukushima Daiichi Nuclear Power Plant, which began on 11 March 2011, fundamentally changed the aforementioned unfavourable conditions. A station blackout over a long period, whose risk had long been pointed out by the anti-nuclear movements and which had been assumed would not occur in Japan, led to the loss of cooling systems at four nuclear reactors and then to significant damage to reactor buildings due to hydrogen explosions, reactor core meltdown at three reactors and discharge of an enormous amount of radioactive substances into the atmosphere. On 22 April, the Japanese government provisionally assessed that the severity of the accident was level 7 on the International Nuclear Event Scale (INES), the same level that was used to describe the Chernobyl nuclear accident.

Important characteristics of the accident that are different from those of the Three Mile Island and Chernobyl nuclear accidents and are unique to the case of the Fukushima nuclear power plant include the following: (1) the Fukushima accident is the world's first severe nuclear accident caused by natural disaster, a massive earthquake (magnitude 9.0) and a subsequent tsunami; (2) for the first time in history, four nuclear reactors (no. 1 unit through no. 4 unit) almost simultaneously fell into a critical state; (3) the critical state of the reactors and the discharge of radioactive substances continued for more than nine months; and (4) due to the plant's location on a coastline, marine contamination resulted from both leakage and intentional discharge of an enormous amount of radioactively contaminated water.

As of March 2012 (one year after the accident), approximately 160,000 people of Fukushima Prefecture were being forced to live outside the evacuation zone. Radioactive contamination has been detected in drinking water, soil, fish and shellfish and agricultural products such as beef, tea and rice. Radioactive contamination has become a reality. The rest of the country as well as East Japan must be facing this for another 100 years or so, because the half-life of cesium-137 is about 30 years.

Except for a period right after the Chernobyl nuclear accident and except for the areas surrounding a nuclear power plant, the number of people in Japan who have expressed concerns about nuclear power plants actively and publicly has been extremely limited, even though many have internally felt such concerns. After the Fukushima accident, it took a while until protests criticizing Tokyo Electric Power Company and the government started to emerge. Protests that attracted attention included that held in Koenji on 10 April and another held in Shibuya on 7 May, each of which was attended by about 15,000 people, and the protest held in Shinjuku three months after the accident, on 11 June, at which 20,000 people gathered (these numbers were provided by the organizers). It was the first time in the 23 years since the 1988 protest at Hibiya Park that 20,000 people had participated in a protest. In response to calls for protests, 140 protests were held nationwide on 11 June. Even in Sendai, central city in Tohoku area, which is located 100 kilometres north from the Fukushima Daiichi Plant, about 400 people participated in a protest; before the Fukushima nuclear accident, it had been rare to see an anti-nuclear protest with more than 40 participants in Sendai.

The largest protest was called for by Nobel Prize author Kenzaburo Oe and others and was titled *sayonara genpatsu goman nin shukai* (50,000-person protest for denuclearization). The event was held in Meiji Park, Tokyo. The number of participants was 65,000, which exceeded the 50,000 targeted and expected by the organizer, and was the largest since the protest held in front of the Diet building on 15 June 1960 during the period of anti-Japan and the US Security Treaty protests in 1960. It was a freestyle "sound-based protest" which would be seen in protests in Europe and the United States, and few political messages except for criticisms against nuclear power were presented. Its style is similar to that of anti-nuclear new-wave protests, which gained momentum around 1987 and 1988 after the Chernobyl nuclear accident, in terms of apparent self-expression, festive performances and radical denial of a controlled protest, but its political messages were weaker. The protest depended on people's anger toward the Fukushima nuclear accident, people's anger and distrust toward the responses of the electric power company and the government and participants' own feelings and sense of daily life. In an interview conducted by the Asahi Shimbun, Hajime Matsumoto, an organizer, commented that it is okay to be festive; that it is desirable to have discussions on politics as a normal part of daily life; that opinions should be expressed by musicians through music, by craftsmen through their creations and by dancers through dance; and that this type of protest would not last if it was not fun (Asahi Shimbun, 16 June, 2011). This protest and the Arab Spring share a common characteristic whereby new word-of-mouth communication tools such as Twitter and Facebook were utilized to mobilize people widely.

Yuko Hirabayashi (2013) conducted surveys on 11 June and 11 September by distributing questionnaires to about 150 participants at each of six protests held at the Shiba, Hibiya, Yoyogi and Shinjuku Chuo parks in Tokyo. She lists the following three groups as typical participants. The first consists of people aged 50 or older who are interested in protecting the Constitution and peace issues and who lean toward leftist ideas. The second group mainly consists of women in their 30s and 40s who, as mothers, are interested in a shift toward renewable energies. The third group consists of people aged between 20 and 35 who are interested in anti-poverty activities and job-hopper issues as well as nuclear problems. Participants in the protests hold the attitude that they do not trust the existing media and try to turn themselves into a medium of information without criticizing it. Hirabayashi calls such an attitude "media activism".

## Outlook: What are the strategies of the post-Fukushima movements?

What are the strategies of the anti-nuclear movements after the Fukushima nuclear accident? The most serious problem is that there is no concrete political program or agenda for the period after protests. Questions to be posed include where the energy shared by the protesters should be directed, how anti-nuclear movements should be organized toward new directions, what the next step should be and who their political partners are.

A movement for denuclearization and renewable-energy-based society titled *sayonara genpatsu issenman nin shomei* (10 million signatures for denuclearization) was called for by Kenzaburo Oe similarly to the case of the 50,000-people protest held on 19 September. It started on 15 June 2011. As of December 21, six months later, about 3.2 million signatures had been collected (see http://sayonara-nukes.org). The strategy is to put social pressure on the government with the collected signatures, but this strategy will result in the same failure as the one experienced by the 1990 movement that collected signatures to demand enactment of a denuclearization law.

Nuclear power will not be discussed as one of the central issues in the next general election. Nuclear policies of the Democratic Party of Japan (the ruling party), the Liberal Democratic Party (the largest opposing party) and the Komei Party (the third-largest party) are all vague, and it is expected that these three parties will avoid making nuclear policy an election issue in the general election. Although the Communist Party, the Social Democratic Party and the "Your Party" are explicitly supporting denuclearization, the number of seats in the House of Representatives for each party is currently single digit.

As of 5 May 2012, all of the nuclear reactors in Japan had closed operations. In Japan, due to regular inspection, no reactor can operate continuously for more than 13 months. The Noda administration is planning that based on the result of stress tests to confirm the safety of nuclear power plants, relevant Ministers will decide whether the operation of nuclear reactors can be resumed. However, at the time of writing (6 May 2012), the outlook for resumed operations is unclear. In many cases, a provision in the safety agreement requires consent from the head of the prefecture or the municipality before operation is resumed. Therefore, the heads of the prefectures and municipalities with a nuclear power plant have a de facto veto on resumption. Also, the EPZ around a nuclear power plant designated for priority measures for disaster prevention used to be a 10-kilometre-radius area before the Fukushima nuclear accident, but it has been enlarged to a 30-kilometre-radius area after the accident. If all local governments located within a 30-kilometre-radius area want to establish a safety agreement, the number of leaders with the de facto veto will increase. A major focus will be on how each nuclear power plant should be allowed to resume operation.

As time passes, anti-nuclear movements without effective political strategies will lose their influence to mobilize people. A major challenge is how the movement energy can be maintained at high levels. At the international level, highly specialized, large-scale professional environmental non-governmental organizations (NGOs) such as the WWF (World Wide Fund for Nature), Friends of the Earth, Greenpeace, the World Information Service on Energy and the Union of Concerned Scientists are leading anti-nuclear movements. It is necessary to improve the ability of NGOs and anti-nuclear movements to make policy proposals concerning the promotion of renewable energy and efficient use of energy, with collaboration with scholars through a re-examination of the separation of electricity distribution from electricity generation, liberalization of the electricity market, integration of climate change policy and energy policy, regulation for nuclear safety and reviewing of the nuclear fuel recycling policy.

## Notes

1. In the United States, licensing for new construction and operation of a total of four nuclear reactors at two sites in Georgia and South Carolina were approved in February and March 2012. This is the first such approval in 34 years, since 1978. The operation is planned to begin in the second half of the 2010s, but whether the construction will progress as scheduled is unclear.
2. Yoshioka (2011), a historian of science who has studied nuclear power issues, divides the development process for constructing and utilizing nuclear power plants in Japan into six periods, the first of which includes the pre-war period: 1939–1953, 1954–1965, 1966–1979, 1980–1994, 1995–2010 and a period from 2011. The number of periods since 1954 is five, as is the case in this chapter.
3. *The outline of Japan's foreign policy* (Japanese Ministry of Foreign Affairs (1969)), which was a top-secret document dated 29 September 1969 that was declassified in November 2010, reveals

that Japan had a policy not to possess nuclear weapons for the time regardless of its participation/ non-participation in the NPT (Nuclear Proliferation Treaty), but had the intention to always maintain its technological and economic potential for manufacturing nuclear weapons and to avoid any foreign interference with these efforts (p. 67).
4. Hasegawa (2004: chap. 8) conducts a detailed analysis of the anti-nuclear movements in Japan right after the Chernobyl nuclear accident.
5. In February 2000, the author conducted a survey of Tokai Village residents regarding the effects of the JCO accident on their health and daily life, using a drop-off and pickup procedure. See Hasegawa and Takubo (2001).
6. The lawsuit was filed in September 1985, but at first it was immediately rejected with the reason that the plaintiffs were not qualified for administrative litigation. Therefore, no actual trial was held. The Supreme Court recognized the qualification of all members of the plaintiffs in September 1992 and the lawsuit was sent to the Fukui District Court where the actual trial began.
7. In an interview conducted by the Asahi Shimbun after the Fukushima nuclear accident, the judge who gave the decision described the psychological pressure felt over giving the decision to stop the reactor, saying that he would sweat profusely in bed in winter when he was thinking about the influence of the decision and could not sleep (Interview with a former judge, Ido Ken'ichi, Asahi Shimbun, 2 June 2011).

# REFERENCES

Beck, Ulrich et al. (eds.) (2011) *Risukuka suru nihon shakai: Ulrich Beck tono taiwa* (Japanese Society as a Risk Society: Dialogue with Ulrich Beck), Tokyo: Iwanami Shoten.

Funabashi, Harutoshi, Koichi Hasegawa and Nobuko Iijima (2012) *Kaku nenryo saikuru shisetsu no shakaigaku: aomori ken rokkasho mura* (Sociology of the Nuclear Fuel Cycle: Aomori-ken Rokkasho-mura), Tokyo: Yuhikaku Publishing.

Hasegawa, Koichi (1999) "Genshiryoku hatsuden o meguru nihon no seiji keizai shakai" (Japanese Politics, Economics and Society on Nuclear Energy), in Yoshikazu Sakamoto (ed.) *Kaku to ningen I: kaku to taiketsu suru nijuseiki* (Confronting Nuclearism, Vol. 1: The 20th Century World in Crisis), Tokyo: Iwanami Shoten, pp. 281–337.

―― (2004) *Constructing Civil Society in Japan: Voices of Environmental Movements*. Montreal: Trans Pacific Press.

―― (2011) "A Comparative Study of Social Movements for a Post-Nuclear Energy Era in Japan and the U.S.", in Jeffrey Broadbent and Vickey Brockman (eds.) *East Asian Social Movements: Power, Protest and Change in a Dynamic Region*, New York: Springer, pp. 63–79.

Hasegawa, Koichi and Yuko Takubo (2001) *JCO Criticality Accident and Local Residents: Damages, Symptoms and Changing Attitudes; Data and Analysis of the Results of a Field Survey of Tokai-mura and Naka-machi Residents*, Tokyo: Citizens' Nuclear Information Center.

Hirabayashi, Yuko (2013) "Nani ga "demo no aru shakai" wo tsukurunoka (Japanese society turned into a society with frequent anti-government demonstrations)", in Tanaka Shigeyoshi, Funabashi Harutoshi and Masamura Toshiuki eds, *Higashi Nihon Daishinsai to Shakaigaku: Daisaigai wo umidashita shakai* (The Great Eastern Japan Earthquake and Japanese Sociology: How a Country Brought Disaster Upon Itself), Kyoto: Minerva Shobo, pp. 163–195.

Hirose, Takashi (1987) *Kiken na hanashi: cherunobuiri to nihon no unmei* (On the Risk of Nuclear Power Stations: Chernobyl and Japan's Fate), Tokyo: Hachigatsu Shokan.

Japanese Ministry of Foreign Affairs (1969) *Wagakuni gaiko seisaku taiko* (The outline of Japan's foreign policy) available at http://www.mofa.go.jp/mofaj/gaiko/kaku_hokoku/pdfs/kaku_hokoku02.pdf.

Kaido, Yuichi (2011) *Genpatsu sosho* (Legal Actions against a Nuclear Power Plant), Tokyo: Iwanami Shoten.

McAdam, Doug (1996) "Conceptual Origins, Current Problems, Future Directions", in Doug McAdam, John D. McCarthy and Mayer N. Zald (eds.) *Comparative Perspectives on Social Movements: Political Opportunities, Mobilizing Structures and Cultural Framings*, Cambridge: Cambridge University Press, pp. 23–40.

Obara, Ryoko (1988) Genpatsu yori mo inochi ga daiji (Life Is More Important than Nuclear Power), *Kuritiku (Critique)*, 12, pp. 21–30.

Takagi, Junzaburo (1999) *Shimin kagakusha toshite ikiru* (My Life as a Citizen Scientist), Tokyo: Iwanami Shoten.

Yoshioka, Hitoshi (2011) *Shinban genshiryoku no shakaishi* (Social History of Nuclear Power, rev. ed.), Tokyo: Asahi Shimbunsha.

# 15

# Social learning for endogenous development and sustainable world: From the viewpoint of experiences and discussions in Japan

*Takayuki Ota*

There have been numerous studies on the meaning of sustainable development and sustainable society, and many approaches for sustainable development and society under various regional and local conditions have been discussed (Atkinson et al., 2007). In these discussions, we have come to a common understanding that social learning is one of the key actions for realizing sustainable development and society and a transition from the present development approaches and economic models toward sustainable ones (Loorbach, 2007; Wals, 2007; Grin et al., 2010).

Why is social learning important for achieving sustainable development and society? One reason is that we can generate essential discussions by people and induce consensus formation to realize sustainable development and society from local levels to the global level. Hence, social learning is one of the significant mediating actions for realizing sustainable development and society through a trans-disciplinary approach (Wals, 2007).

Under such discussions on social learning and its relations to sustainable development and society, some critical issues have been raised by scholars from various disciplinary backgrounds. One of the main issues is how we can stimulate substantive social learning that is able to realize sustainable development and society.

Very few discussions reflect on the unique Japanese experiences with social learning and its relation to sustainable development and society at the local and regional level. In this chapter, I try to extract implications from Japanese experiences and discussions with a main focus on the multiple-loop learning model, which is one of the most notable models of social learning.

*Transition management for sustainable development, Ueta and Adachi (eds.), United Nations University Press, 2014, ISBN 978-92-808-1234-3*

In the following, I focus on two objectives. First, I reflect on the Japanese experiences and approaches to social learning for sustainable development and society, drawing on a case study that will help to extract some implications for social learning. Second, I establish the link between the discussions of social learning for sustainable development and society and Japanese experiences and discussions about regional and local developments from a viewpoint of social learning.

## Social learning, regional and local development in Japan

### Social learning for sustainable development and society

What is social learning? Glasser (2007) surveys various disciplines focusing on social learning, and provides a comprehensive overview of the discussions and definitions about social learning from many disciplines. Glasser understands social learning from four angles, namely, (1) a form of learning for the purpose of personal and social adaptation, (2) a process of understanding the environmental circumstances by organism, (3) a key mechanism for arriving at a more desirable future by interdependent stakeholders' shared learning with system thinking and (4) adaptive management. He also states that social learning consists of passive social learning and active social learning. The former rests on prior learning from others and learning from various sources such as reading newspapers, listening to the radio and watching movies and other media. The latter is communicative learning and conscious interactive and dialogical learning among actors which he considers more effective in creating innovations and in widely diffusing novel behaviours. He notes that active social learning has three types: "co-learning" based on collaboration, trust and full participation by people, which is most desirable for achieving sustainable development and society.

As mentioned in the introduction of this chapter, social learning is one of the key factors in the transition to a sustainable development and society. When reflecting on social learning in the regional or local sphere, Glasser (2007) draws on the concept of "regional survey" by Mumford (1970) as a model of social learning, especially co-learning for sustainable world.

Mumford (1970) presented the concept of regional survey to protect local government from fascism and as a method for autonomous local government. He said that regional livelihoods are mirrors to environments and histories and that these were the source of the regional autonomy and the resistance to fascism.

Although Glasser (2007) holds that this regional survey was abstract and broader, he tries to pick up hints for the way of social learning. Although one of the main concerns of Mumford (1970) is how to prevent fascism politics, I agree with his appreciation of Mumford regional survey and treat this as an ideal model of social learning in the region or local areas.

*Regional and local development and social learning in Japan*

In Japan, we have unique experiences and discussions about regional and local development. One approach to development is called "endogenous development" (Miyamoto, 2007). This model for regional and local development does not only focus on economic development but also on environmental conservation and social revitalization. Another unique element is that local residents' and citizens' movements and social learning based on these movements are necessary conditions for endogenous development and realizing a sustainable world.

After World War II, Japan experienced not only rapid economic growth but also a period of regional and local development. Regional economic disparities have been reduced through the regional and local development. On the other hand, however, the country had to face some serious environmental problems (*Kogai*) caused by industrial firms,[1] so there is a need to reconsider the method of regional development and the concept of regional affluence and alternative ways of regional development.

To deal with pollution problems caused by industrial development, local residents and citizens campaigned persistently against industrial firms and governments to improve or eliminate *Kogai* problems. They sometimes achieved the abandonment of such unwanted industrial developments. In some cases, they studied the knowledge of environmental science, medicine and so on and researched the cause of environmental pollutions by themselves. They have reflected on the outcomes of these learnings on their movements. Their attitudes and insistences could receive sympathies from other regional and local actors, so their movements spread to the region or local area. Of course, every local movement did not succeed, because consensus-building in region or local areas often proved very difficult; hence, some movements failed to have their ideas realized. However, whether these movements succeeded or failed, they stimulated discussions and studies on environmental problems and on the directions of regional and local development. These processes have contributed to the learning process on how to develop regional and local areas in Japan.

Miyamoto (2007) surveyed some cases viewed as endogenous development, and extracted commonalities from these. He organized these commonalities and posed the principles of endogenous development, as shown in Box 15.1. The principles of endogenous development have linked to sustainable development and society in Japan.

In principle 1 in Box 15.1, social learning by the people has been one of the main features of the regional and local movements in Japan. In some cases, the people studied and learned not only the knowledge of some disciplines but also

> Box 15.1 Principles of endogenous development by Miyamoto (2007)
>
> 1. We should develop our region not through external big business enterprises or big public work projects, but based on inherent techniques or industries or culture there. In doing so, we have to target markets in there firstly. The key factor is that the central players in these activities are local residents or regional actors. These actors should study and learn, plan and manage to develop their area.
>
>    But these activities are not based on a narrow-minded regionalism and localism. We collaborate with other urban areas or the central government actively. What is important is that central actors of the regional and local development are local residents and regional actors.
> 2. We have to conserve environmental resources firstly and develop our region under environmental conservation. We should have amenities conservation as the central idea and sustain nature and beautiful sceneries and landscapes too. Besides, in regional development, we should have comprehensive ideas, for example, building and strengthening human rights of local residences to promote our welfares and cultures.
> 3. We have to develop industries not only within particular businesses but with a broad range of industries. We may set out to achieve intricate webs of ties between local and regional industries and to gain added values to the various levels of the region and local area.
> 4. We should institutionalize residents' and citizens' participation in public plans and works. Through these institutions, we make our local government as representing the local will. We set out to have the autonomy to be able to control movement of capital and land use and so on.
>
> *Source:* Miyamoto (2007: pp. 316–323).

discussed and searched for an alternative for regional development. In cases when they rejected locations of industrial firms or big public-works projects, so-called exogenous development, they have found another way of development, which is endogenous development through many studies and discussions for a long time. So, social learning has been the basic activities of the regional and local developments.

## The multiple-loop learning model

Social learning has attracted attention from various disciplines, and there are many discussions and models on social learning. In this chapter, I focus particularly on the "multiple-loop learning model". The basic ideas and concepts of this model are presented by Argyris and Schön (1996), scholars from the organizational science field. Keen et al. (2005) expand this model from the viewpoint of environmental management and governance for sustainable development. In the following, I provide a brief overview of this model.

Argyris and Schön (1996) focus on an organization as one of the learning actors because of various interactions about information, knowledge, strategies and so on. They study dynamic changes of an organization under changing environments from some case studies and found that it was by learning activities that an organization could adapt to the changes.

Argyris and Schön (1996) model learning in an organization as systematic feedback loops. This model mainly consists of two loops of learning. One is single-loop learning. This loop learning changes daily actions or strategies of action, but this does not change actors' values of theories in use or their assumptions about actual states that basically support their actions or strategies. So, this loop learning leads to changing the actions to respond to the changing realities and this change is only incremental. Another type is double-loop learning. This changes the values and norms of theories in use or the understanding of assumptions or conditions about actual states for actors. These elements are governing actors' recognition, so this loop learning leads to fundamental and radical changes in an organization. They discuss loop learning first from individuals and then expand it to an organizational level.

Currently this multiple-loop learning model has been applied not only to business firms but also to governments, non-governmental organizations, schools, regions and so on for an adaptation to dramatic changes in their organizational setup. Keen et al. (2005) reassemble this feedback loop model and expand it to a triple-loop model as illustrated in Figure 15.1.

About the loop learning, Keen et al. (2005) also see the feedback loop model in the process of participation and engagement. But not all actors or all members reflect on (or can reflect on) their actions through these feedback loops. For example, Wenger et al. (2002) classify memberships of communities as core groups, active groups and peripheral groups. The core group commits more than the latter groups, and the peripheral group commits less than the former. But that does not mean the peripheral group does nothing; members of this group fill their own roles by doing what they can and contributing to an organization. Members of the core group could reflect on their actions through the learning loops more than do those in the active group and the peripheral group.

The appeal of this model is its systematic build-up from the individual level to the social level which consists of multi-actors. But the question is how we can support this multiple-loop learning process. Grin et al. (2010) discuss three important conditions for double-loop learning. First, they state that negative surprises might induce this loop learning. They note also that exogenous events, such as terrorism or economic crisis, and global trends, such as the

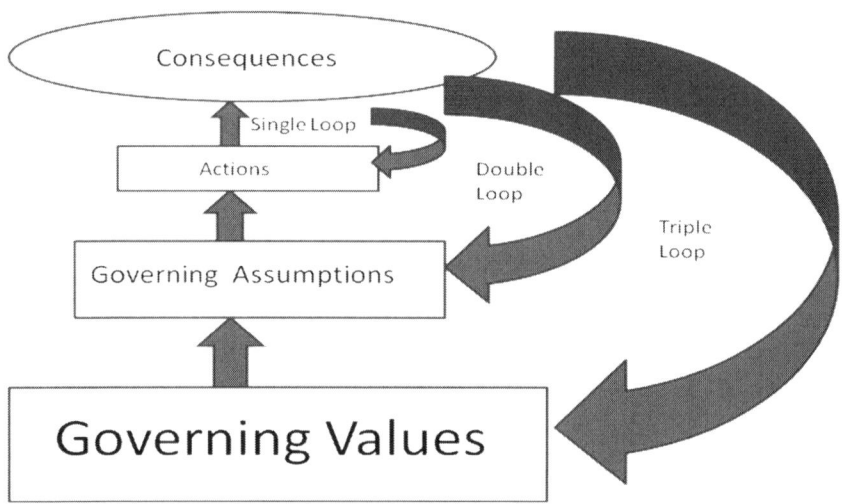

Figure 15.1 Multiple-loop learning
Sources: Argyris and Schön (1996) and Keen et al. (2005).

increasing geopolitical role of emerging economies, could induce this learning. Second, when actors are confronted with novel external views and ideas, this loop learning becomes more likely. Third, they indicate the importance of safe spaces. Actors may review their own precepts such as theories in use when they can do so without giving up the possibility to resort to their previous strategies.

In the following section, I focus on multiple-loop learning through a case study of Japanese discussions about social learning, regional and local development and about sustainable development and sustainable society. The process and factors for multiple-loop learning, and the catalyst for producing double loop learning, are examined.

## Water pollution in Yahagi River and the association against pollution

### Water pollution in Yahagi River

The Yahagi River basin in Aichi Prefecture presents an interesting case of social learning for endogenous development. In this river basin, industrialization and urbanization reached a peak in 1955, and water pollution became severe in connection with these trends. The causes of pollution were multifactorial. One of the main causes of pollution was industrial activities. At the time, pit-gravel extractions were prosperous in the upstream and mainly machine industry pulled the local economy along the midstream and downstream.[2] In addition, local governments did not invest in sewerage management adequately, so waste water from households was another cause of pollution. Besides, there were many large-scale development projects such as golf links in the 1980s. All of these triggered serious pollution problems along the river (Yahagi River Base Water Quality Preservation Association [YWPA], 1999). Local residents, especially farmers and fishermen, suffered most from this water pollution. Damages reached about 640 million yen in 1970, and fishermen suffered losses of about 1 billion yen in 1984 because of pollution (YWPA, 1999). Other residents in this basin were affected too. An association was established aiming at water-quality management and pressuring national and local governments and polluter firms for maintaining effective water-quality governance.

## Setting up the association of Yahagi River and features of this association

Farmers and fishermen who suffered from water pollution had organized themselves into an association involving local governments and developed activities for water pollution prevention. When farmers and fishermen realized that water pollution was a major problem in 1962, they asked local governments to implement anti-pollution policies but could not achieve any results. Therefore, they decided to organize themselves and to make a large association to cope with pollutions effectively. They persuaded other agrarian and fishery organizations who suffered from water pollution to get involved. In addition, they also requested local municipalities, especially their waterworks department, using water from Yahagi River as tap water to participate. As a result, in 1969, they succeeded in organizing the Yahagi River Basin Water Quality Preservation Association (YWPA). At the beginning, it included six agrarian organizations, seven fishery organizations and seven local governments (Yahagi River Coterie, 1979), but later on more fishery organizations and local governments got involved with the YWPA. In 1987, this association had grown to include all 26 local governments of the basin, 4 agrarian organizations and 20 fishery organizations, thereby covering the entire basin.

There are some interesting points in the process of formation of the YWPA. First, farmers and fishermen could set up the YWPA with the participation of local governments, which had the authority to conserve water quality by regulations and policies. Second, they could also organize YWPA with the participation of organizations upstream on the Yahagi River. In 1977, a local government upstream joined the YWPA, and 12 organizations had become members of the YWPA by 1987. These organizations were not industrial organizations but

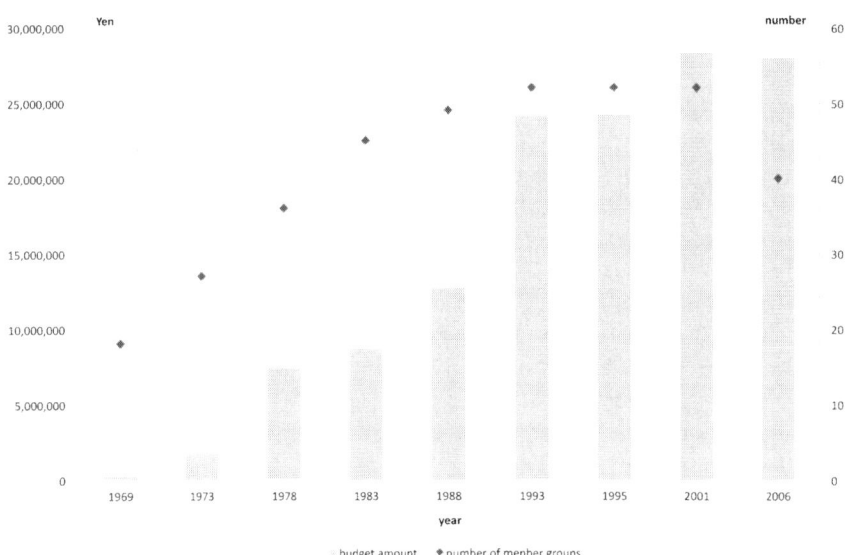

Figure 15.2 Number of organizations involved in YWPA and the YWPA's budget
*Source:* Data from materials made available during an interview with Hiroshi Amano, the executive officer of the YWPA.

agrarian organizations, fishery organizations and local governments. Hence, their interests were partly similar with farmers and fishermen, who suffered from water pollution, whereas some of the interests of upstream organizations conflicted with the farmers and fishermen in the midstream and downstream parts of Yahagi River because they also earned their livings from the industries which polluted the water in the upstream area.

Figure 15.2 shows the expansion of involved organizations in the YWPA and its budget.[3] The member organizations of the YWPA pay a membership fee which is a source for the YWPA's budget. The budget is utilized for paying staff working for the YWPA. In addition, general meetings are held for consensus building once a year to decide on annual plans of activities and expenses.

## Activities for water quality preservation of YWPA

The YWPA has mainly engaged in (1) monitoring water quality, (2) developing the Yahagi River Method and (3) approaching upstream organizations. These activities are discussed in detail next.

## Area-wide monitoring

The YWPA has put a lot of effort into this activity. Monitoring is composed of patrols and observations of the entire basin by all members, and these activities have been the basic elements of their local movement for water-quality conservation.

Farmers and fishermen started patrols respectively around 1962 (Yahagi River Coterie, 1979). Beginning with the basin patrols, they studied and learned about water pollution, such as indicators of water pollution and conservation criteria for water quality, with the help of local governments and the research institute in this basin.

Farmers and fishermen started full-scale patrols in the entire basin after organizing the YWPA. They collected evidence on pollution through patrols and submitted them when they petitioned the central government and the local government of Aichi Prefecture (Naito, 1988, 1999). Hence, patrolling is considered a complement to their movements. The Water Pollution Control Law with punitive clauses came into force in 1971, providing legal support for patrollers to make accusations against violators.

The staff in the bureau of the YWPA mainly went on patrols in the Yahagi River and continued to monitor business activity. Through these patrols, they had evidence of pollution and violations, and they made accusations against businesses that violated water quality standards at least eight times between 1972 and 1983 (YWPA, 1999). Such accusations based on patrols changed the behaviour of businesses that had previously polluted water in this basin. Polluting businesses started to take measures to gradually stop pollution (Yahagi River Fishery Cooperative Editorial Committee, 2003).

Staff in the bureau reported actual conditions such as information that complied with water quality standards and development of business in the entire basin at a general meeting of the YWPA. Staff reported more details about potential polluting cases. Through these reports, members could identify almost all developments and business activities in this basin and determine whether businesses were complying with the standards. Besides, the members could observe potential polluting cases and make requests to local government in the area for taking strong measures against such potential business.

Interestingly, the members of YWPA not only found violators of the water-quality standards but also identified industrial firms which had no knowledge and skills to prevent water pollution (Naito, 1999). YWPA developed techniques for water quality conservation with an external research institute (Yahagi River Association on Environmental Technology, 1994). Sometimes they developed knowledge and skills with polluting industries in the upstream and midstream of the Yahagi River. These techniques were not expensive to conserve water quality for these industries. They also disseminated the techniques and ideas for water-quality conservation through holding a seminar of water-quality management and providing these techniques when they patrolled. Through this process of patrolling and information dissemination, the YWPA has successfully monitored the entire Yahagi River basin for about 40 years.

*The Yahagi River Method*

In Aichi Prefecture, there are rules that businesses have to consult, and they undergo reviews with the prefecture before they start to develop or carry out economic activities in the river basin. In the Yahagi River, the YWPA is able to be involved in the process of this prior consultation and review between the prefecture and businesses, and consult with businesses from its own point of view. This procedure of involvement with YWPA in prior consultations and review by the prefecture is called the Yahagi River Method. This has been realized as a de facto rule in this basin.

The Yahagi River Method consists of two types of consultations. One is a consultation for large-scale developments (greater than one hectare). Another is for small-scale developments and economic activities draining pollution into the Yahagi River. Figure 15.3 shows the consultation and review process of the first type.

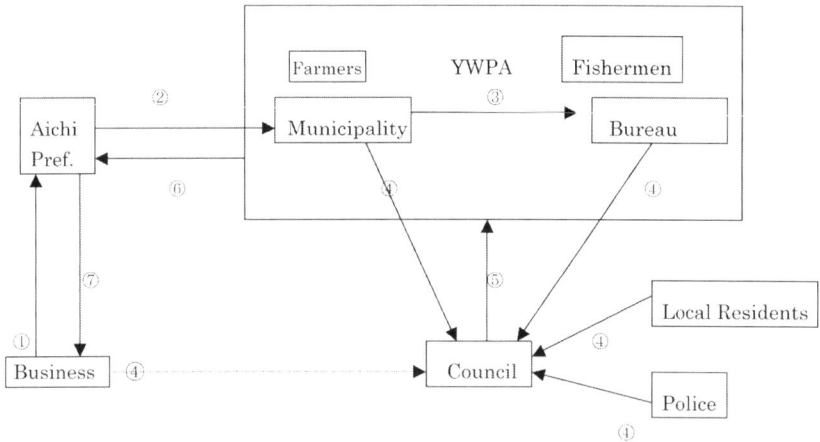

①:application ②③:notice ④: participation ⑤: notice of results
⑥: notice of agreement or not   ⑦: notice of permission or not

Figure 15.3 The Yahagi River Method for large-scale developments
*Source*: Mainichi Newspaper Company (1980).

The Yahagi River Method of large-scale developments proceeds as follows: when a company decides to develop economic activities in this basin, it applies to the prefecture directly or via local municipality. The prefecture receives the application and forwards it to the YWPA. The prefecture also asks the company to consult with the YWPA (see step ①→②→③ in Figure 15.3). When a company consults with the YWPA, the YWPA holds a council meeting with representatives from local residents, police, neighbouring municipalities and agrarian and fishery organizations (see step ④ in Figure 15.3). The company also participates in this council meeting (see step ④ in Figure 15.3). During the meeting, participants check the business plan, which includes information on the quantity and quality of waste-water discharge to the Yahagi River and an environmental impact assessment. If this plan and the result from the environmental impact assessment are acceptable, participants will review the next measures and techniques to prevent water pollution. If they consider these measures and techniques appropriate, the council meeting is concluded. If a company does not present an appropriate plan to the council, results from environmental assessment and/or measures for preventing water pollution, the YWPA and the participants will conduct regular assessments of the company's activities and will continue to consult with the company.

After the council meeting, the company conducts additional consultations with the YWPA and receives the approval (see step ⑤ in Figure 15.3). Next, it is reviewed by authorities from the prefecture (see step ⑥ in Figure 15.3). The prefecture examines its plan, judges these processes comprehensively and determines whether the company should be given the official permission or not (see step ⑦ in Figure 15.3).

As explained previously, the second type the Yahagi River Method addresses is small-scale developments (less than one hectare) and economic activities with water drainage (from 10 tonnes to 20 tonnes per day). This type is almost the same as the preceding type, with only some differences. In this type, a company consults with the YWPA, but the YWPA does not without conducting a formal council meeting. Therefore, local residents and police are not involved in the consultation and reviews; only agrarian and fishery organizations are involved.

The companies have to bear the costs of measures for water pollution and environmental assessment in the Yahagi River Method.[4] The YWPA targets not only developments by private companies but also public developments by central and local governments.

The Yahagi River Method is limited in that the process has no legal foundation.[5] In spite of this limitation, the approach functions well in this basin because it is very convenient for the YWPA members. For example, sometimes business plans are problematic from the viewpoint of local conditions but pose no problems from the legal perspective. In these cases, local municipalities as governments have to give the permissions. Nevertheless, the municipalities are entitled to require companies to modify plans as members of YWPA.[6] Figure 15.4 shows the total number of consultations and total area of business developments and activities reviewed under the Yahagi River Method in the past. The number of consultations peaked in 1990 and stabilized at about 250 consultations per year by the mid-1990s.

The Yahagi River Method can be described as a sort of watershed management with participation of local residents, and the YWPA have achieved water-quality management based on local residents' participation through their eager patrols in the basin and through movements for water-quality conservation. This approach also works as a regulation of land use in the basin. The YWPA consults businesses with the object of water-pollution prevention from economic activities in this basin. If the YWPA regards business plans and results from environmental assessment as inadequate, it requires companies to rethink plans, to take measures to prevent pollution and to conduct a new environmental assessment. If businesses are not able to gain approval by the YWPA, they cannot continue with their activities because the YWPA process is completed *prior* to the consultation. Therefore, the Yahagi River Methods regulates land use in addition to managing water quality.

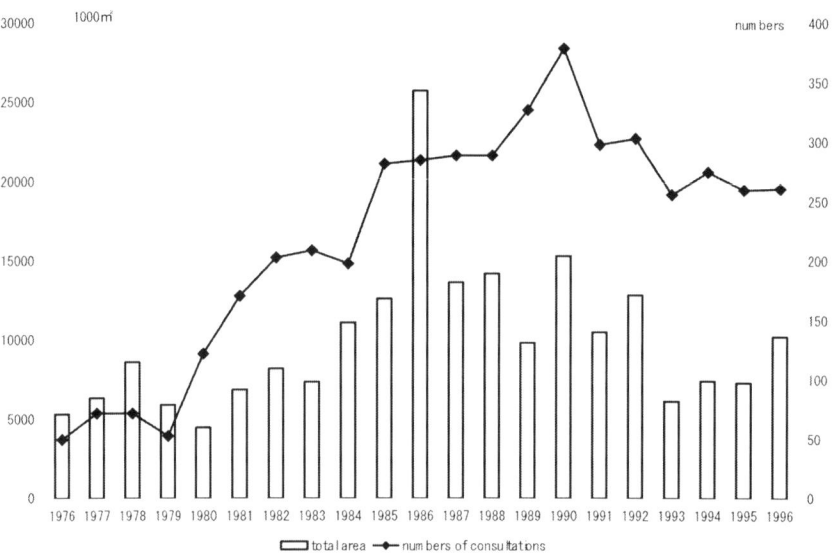

Figure 15.4 Total number and area of prior consultations under the Yahagi River Method
*Source:* Data from materials made available during an interview with Hiroshi Amano, the executive officer of the YWPA.

## Approaches to the upstream organizations

For YWPA it was important to be able to integrate upstream organizations along the Yahagi River. Thus, they have been able to manage water quality at the watershed scale.

As noted earlier, the people upstream earned their livings from industries which were having a negative impact on the water quality. This resulted in conflicts between the people of the upstream area and farmers and fishermen in the midstream and downstream parts of the basin.

The reason the upstream organizations joined the YWPA was that they could contribute to mutual understanding among all stakeholders. Through their movement, the core members of the YWPA learned and knew that upstream people depended on industrial and manufacturing activities, which polluted water, for their living and that the YWPA could not count on these people's understanding about their movement intended to preserve the water quality (Mainichi Newspaper Company, 1980). Hence, based on these insights, the YWPA changed their approach and strategies in two ways.

First, the YWPA started new activities to engage with upstream people. For example, they began to interact with the people through selling fish to them at low prices from the downstream part of the river. They also started inviting children from the upstream part of the river to the seaside, where the river drains into the ocean. For both of these activities, they secured the cooperation from members engaged in fisheries. Through these activities, they tried to gain understanding from the upstream people about their movement and their situation. In addition, they tried to encourage these upstream actors to join the YWPA and to conserve water quality on the watershed scale.

These interactions raised the upstream people's awareness about the negative impact of water pollution on downstream areas and their understanding of the YWPA movements. As a result, they joined the YWPA and conserved water quality in cooperation with it. Thus, the YWPA succeeded to accomplish its objectives.

## Effects of YWPA activities for water-quality preservation

What are the effects that the YWPA activities have brought about until now? With respect to water quality in the Yahagi River, Figures 15.5 and 15.6 show changes of biochemical oxygen demand (BOD) and suspended solid (SS) levels in the Yahagi River, respectively, from the 1970s to the beginning of the 2000s. The data suggest that BOD levels fluctuated within a range of 0.5 to 2.5 milligrams per litre and did not worsen. The SS levels were worse in the 1970s but gradually improved from then on. These improvements not only indicate a restoration of

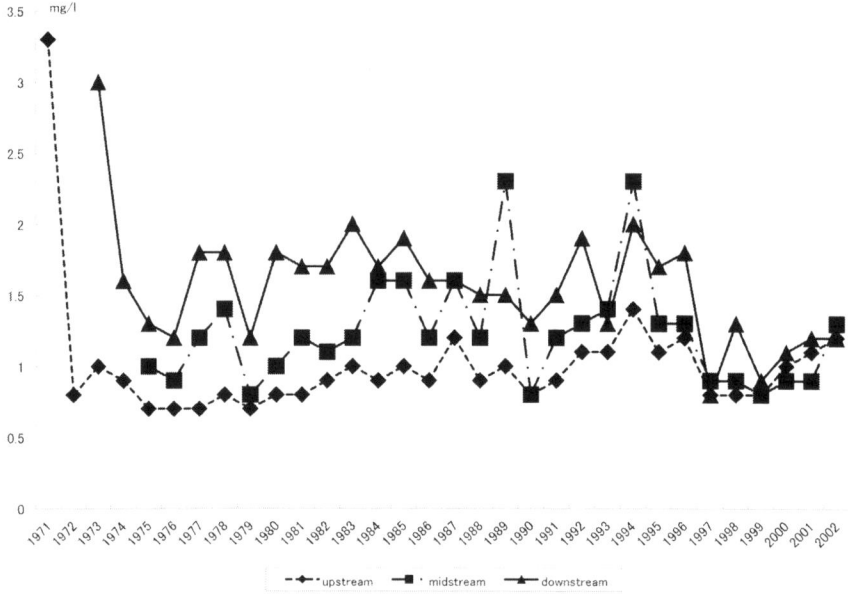

Figure 15.5 Biochemical oxygen demand shift, 1971–2002
*Source:* Data from *Annual Reports of Water Quality Survey* by Environment Department of Aichi Prefecture.

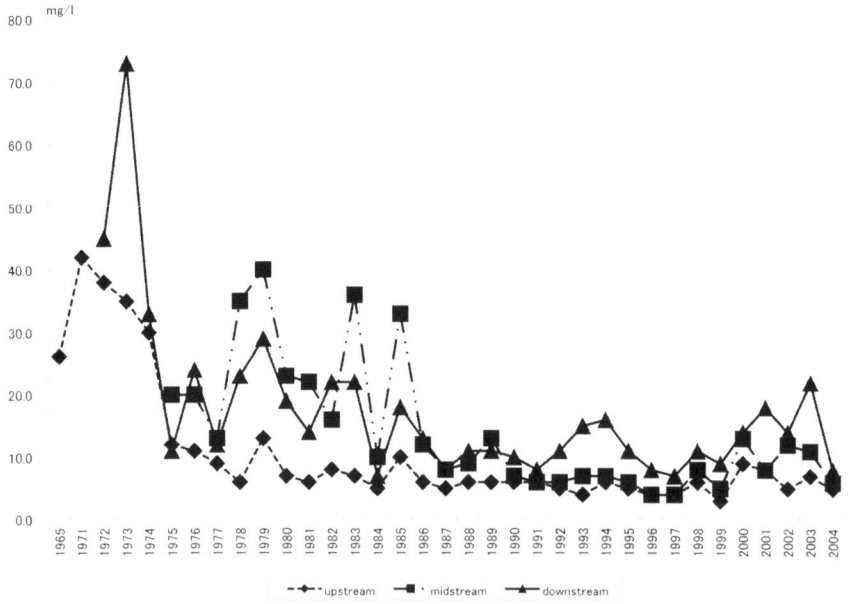

Figure 15.6 Suspended solid shift, 1965–2004
*Source:* Data from *Annual Reports of Water Quality Survey* by Environment Department of Aichi Prefecture.

water resources, but also that the improvements contributed to the recovery of the Yahagi River environment.[7]

It would appear that various factors cause these water-quality shifts aside from YWPA activities, for example, changes in industrial structures in this basin, measures for pollution prevention by firms, and so on. But as we explained, the YWPA prevented water pollution through their movements, particularly through monitoring and the Yahagi River Method. The YWPA checked many business developments and economic activities as shown in Figure 15.4. In summary, the YWPA has contributed significantly to the improvement of water quality in the Yahagi River.

## Discussion

This chapter focused on the case of water-quality management in the Yahagi River. This case took root in the development in the Yahagi River basin and thus can inform discussions of environmental problems and of regional and local endogenous development in Japan. It provides evidence that it was the movements based on social learning that enabled the YWPA to manage water quality in the Yahagi River basin by the Yahagi River Method. This approach is congruent with the principles of endogenous development.

From the viewpoint of social learning, we can extract two types from this case. First, as noted earlier, farmers and fishermen systematically collected information about water pollution and water-quality conservation, supported by local governments and research institutes. Using this knowledge, they campaigned against industrial firms and local governments, and patrolled in this basin. Collecting information not only was about gaining knowledge of water quality but also helped in reflecting on strategies for their movements and other activities.

Patrolling the basin and diffusing information on the development situation in this basin at the conference from these patrols are also elements of social learning. As described earlier in the chapter, these activities have supported water-quality management by the YWPA, and the members of the YWPA could come to a common understanding of the development situation in this basin. These social learning processes are based on their own interests and the aim of water resource conservation for farm and fishery.

Second, social learning can be observed at the point of interaction and mutual understanding between people in the upstream area of the basin and the members of YWPA. As noted earlier, these actors previously had conflicting interests; therefore, by 1977, the YWPA only consisted of local governments and agrarian organizations and fishery organizations in the midstream and downstream parts. There were almost no understanding of their movements in the upstream, but through movements and negotiations to the upstream, the core members of the

YWPA recognized that people's livelihoods partly depended on the industries which polluted water. They understood the actual situation of the upstream people, so they changed their policy and strategies and tried to establish trust and understand their mutual situation. In this learning process, we can find the feature of double-loop learning.

These activities can be interpreted as attempts for collaborating in terms of water-quality conservation, but the fact that organizations from the upstream area have become members of the YWPA also suggests a deeper involvement. One of the apparent reasons is that they have recognized the importance of local industries in the upstream area for the people living there. The YWPA members did not deny the significance of these local industries and have provided knowledge and skills for water-quality conservation to these industries, as outlined earlier. Moreover, they have shown their recognition of industries because of developing good skills for protecting water pollution or achieving performances in terms of water-quality conservation. Presumably these recognitions and activities were behind their joining the upstream organizations in the YWPA. These social learning processes are based on comprehensive and commonly defined aims and not only their own interests in the aim of water resource conservation for farm and fishery.

We can argue that social learning found in the YWPA and the Yahagi River basin is the type of active social learning emphasized by Glasser (2007). Besides, the activities of the YWPA also show similarities with the concept of regional survey by Mumford (1970). Identifying conflicts and enhancing these interactions are based on knowing and understanding the situations of this basin, so these are social learning processes based on the regional survey concept.

We can also find the conditions of surprise and outside views in the case of the Yahagi River, which corresponds with the conditions for feedback loops as outlined by Grin et al. (2010). In terms of surprise, the farmers and fishermen were forced to face and tackle water pollution by industries in the basin. They could not depend on local governments because there were few institutions for water-quality conservation at that time. These were negative surprises for them because they found local governments, which they thought did something about water pollution, were ineffective regarding water-quality conservation. In these situations, they organized the YWPA and campaigned and educated upstream and manufacturing industries and the central and local governments with their studying and learning.

Regarding the outside view, this is reflected in the conflicts and interactions between people from the upstream area and the members of the YWPA. In the movement and monitoring, the YWPA understood and learned gradually the actual situation of people upstream being dependent on industries for a living, so they began to interact with these people to understand mutual situations in the movement. Their learning from these situations was reflected in the movements and led to changes and interactions in and among the movements. For example, the YWPA sold fish to upstream people and invited upstream children to the seaside among the movement and monitoring of the Yahagi River. This learning was double-loop learning for the YWPA because they changed the movement from a conflict type against the upstream to the interact type in the watershed. Besides, the upstream organizations also produced double-loop learning because they changed their attitudes to the YWPA and joined the organization.

From the viewpoint of the conditions for double-loop learning, we can note these features about the case of Yahagi River. But, in this case, there is another important point for double-loop learning: the movement based on social learning by its members led to producing double-loop learning. In Japan, local residents' and citizens' movements are considered a key to change the way of regional and local development and transition for sustainable development and society. At the Yahagi River basin, we can find the same feature. In sum, local movements are one of the conditions for double-loop learning and social learning for a sustainable world from Japanese experiences and discussions.

Finally, the YWPA has formed the community of practice in terms of water-quality conservation in the Yahagi River.

From the viewpoint of Wenger et al. (2002), the members of the YWPA, especially farmers and fishermen, were the *core members* of water-quality conservation because they managed water quality through patrols and the Yahagi River Method. Local governments can be considered as *active actors* of water-quality conservation due to their contributions to conserve water quality using their authority and regulations. Industries were *peripheral actors*. They did not become members of the YWPA, but they have protected water pollution by using skills and knowledge provided by the YWPA, and their efforts were sometimes honoured by the YWPA.

## Conclusion

In this chapter, social learning was discussed from the viewpoint of Japanese experiences and discussions for regional and local developments. More specifically, I examined the condition of social learning, especially double-loop learning, for good regional and local development. In Japan, local residents' and citizens' movements against industrial and urban development are one of the important elements and are the catalyst of social learning for endogenous development. These points are important in realizing sustainable development and society based on social learning. The Japanese experiences and discussions about local movements for sustainable development are exemplary from the viewpoint of social learning, especially the multiple-loop learning model.

Some research issues are left for our study. We have to shift the analysis of the case in the Yahagi River from social learning to societal learning. Social learning has been distinguished from societal learning by Bawden et al. (2007). They hold that the former is a simplistic group-based learning and that the latter is more learning oriented in the way society needs to tackle important issues towards a sustainable world. They think that societal learning is related directly to the capacity of the civil society and is able to lead to improvements of the lives of marginalized groups and poverty groups. Hence, societal learning concerns our civil society more broadly and is key to achieving sustainable development and sustainable society.

As noted previously, some local residents' and citizens' movements with elements of social learning were able to change policies or policy stances from industry-favoured ones to more environment-friendly ones. In this process, policy-makers have sometimes engaged in the learning process with local residents and citizens through mutual negotiations, alignment of previously conflicting interests and acceptance of their opinions. These processes can be described as a policy-learning process following Grin and Loeber (2006). To conclude, there are two types of learning processes in the regional or local areas when we face problems of regional development. One is the learning process as experienced by local residents and citizens about environmental pollution and regional and local development problems in their movements. Another is the administrative policy learning through responses to these movements. The relationship between these two learning processes needs to be more closely examined in future research.

## Notes

1. See Tsuru and Weitner (1989) for a discussion of the details.
2. There are cities, for example, Toyota and Okazaki, with famous companies, such as Toyota, along the midstream of the Yahagi River.
3. Figure 15.2 shows a sharp decline in number of members from 2001 to 2006. This is because there were some municipal mergers during these years.
4. Based on the Yahagi River Association on Environmental Technology (1994), the total cost borne by companies is within 2 to 7 per cent of the total project costs, which is a relatively modest share.
5. In particular, local municipalities realize this limit in hearings.
6. See Mainichi Newspaper Company (1980).
7. At that time, when water quality was very bad, children could not play in and around this river. However, as water quality was gradually restored, children were able to play in the water again (YWPA, 1999).

# REFERENCES

Argyris, C. and D. A. Schön (1996) *Organizational Learning: Theory, Method, and Practice*, Reading, MA: Addison-Wesley.

Atkinson, G., S. Dietz and E. Neumayer (eds.) (2007) *Handbook of Sustainable Development*, Cheltenham: E. Elgar.

Bawden, R., I. Gujit and J. Woodhill (2007) "The Critical Role of Civil Society in Fostering Societal Learning for a Sustainable World", in A. E. J. Wals (ed.) *Social Learning: Towards a Sustainable World*, Wageningen: Wageningen Academic Publishers, pp. 133–147.

Glasser, H. (2007) "Minding the Gap: The Role of Social Learning in Linking Our Stated Desire for a More Sustainable World to Our Everyday Actions and Policies", in A. E. J. Wals (ed.) *Social Learning: Towards a Sustainable World*, Wageningen: Wageningen Academic Publishers, pp. 35–61.

Grin, J. and A. Loeber (2006) "Theories of Policy Learning: Agency, Structure and Change", in F. Fisher, G. Miller and M. Sidney (eds.) *Handbook of Public Policy Analysis: Theory, Politics, and Methods*, London: Taylor and Francis, pp. 201–219.

Grin, J., J. Rotmans and J. Shot (eds.) (2010) *Transitions to Sustainable Development: New Directions in the Study of Long Term Transformative Change*, New York: Routledge.

Keen, M., V. A. Brown and R. Dyball (eds.) (2005) *Social Learning in Environmental Management: Towards a Sustainable Future*, London: Earthscan.

Loorbach, L. (2007) *Transition Management: New Mode of Governance for Sustainable Development*, Utrecht: International Books.

Mainichi Newspaper Company (1980) *Meiji Yosui*, Nagoya: Mainichi Newspaper Company (in Japanese).

Meiji Irrigation System Editorial Committee (1979) *History of 100 Years of the Meiji Irrigation System*, Anjo: Meiji Irrigation and Land Improvement District (in Japanese).

Miyamoto, K. (2007) *Environmental Economics*, Tokyo: Iwanami Shoten (in Japanese).

Mumford, L. (1970) *The Cultures of Cities*, New York: Harcourt, Brace, Jovanovich.

Naito, R. (1988) "To Make Polluted Yahagi River Limpid Stream", in Naito Renzo (ed.) *Water Is Living*, Nagoya: Fubaisya, pp. 13–31 (in Japanese).

—— (1999) "30-Years Battle Through Movements for Water Quality Preservation", *River*, 634, pp. 44–47 (in Japanese).

Tsuru, S. and H. Weidner (eds) (1989) *Environmental Policy in Japan*, Berlin: Edition Sigma.

Wals, A. E. J. (ed.) (2007) *Social Learning: Towards a Sustainable World*, Wageningen: Wageningen Academic Publishers.

Wenger, E., R. McDermott and W. M. Snyder (2002) *Cultivating Communities of Practice: A Guide to Managing Knowledge*, Boston: Harvard Business School Press.

Yahagi River Association on Environmental Technology (1994) *Monitoring System and Construction Technologies considering the Water Environment: Practice of the Yahagi River Method with Large-Scale Construction Project*, Nagoya: Chunichi Publishing Company (in Japanese).

Yahagi River Basin Water Quality Preservation Association (YWPA) (1999) *Books of 30-Years News Report of Movement for Water Quality Preservation*, Anjo: Yahagi River Basin Water Quality Preservation Association (in Japanese).

Yahagi River Coterie (1979) "For 10 Years Battling Water Pollution", *Monthly Yahagi River*, 28, pp. 6–15 (in Japanese).

Yahagi River Fishery Cooperative Editorial Committee (2003) *Declaration of Fishery Cooperative for Environment Preservation: History of 100 Years of the Yahagi River Fishery Cooperative*, Nagoya: Fubaisya (in Japanese).

# 16

# Undesirable facility siting and democracy: A comparative analysis of radioactive waste repository siting in Japan, South Korea and France[1]

*Shunsaku Komatsuzaki*

Radioactive waste repository siting has been one of the most difficult "not in my back yard" (NIMBY) problems in the world and remains unsolved in most nations. Radioactive waste needs to be safely stored, or disposed of, for a long period until its radioactive isotopes decay to a safe level. High-level radioactive waste (HLW) requires more than 10,000 or even 100,000 years for this decay process to be completed, and it is currently assumed by international experts that deep underground disposal is the best available method to manage HLW. Every nation that produces radioactive waste has been trying to determine a radioactive waste repository site, especially one for HLW, within its territory following the International Atomic Energy Agency (IAEA) Joint Convention on the Safety of Spent Fuel Management and on the Safety of Radioactive Waste Management (IAEA, 1997) and/or its national law. Only Finland and Sweden, however, have determined final disposal sites for HLW, while the United States has withdrawn the siting policy of the Yucca Mountain repository. The need for repository siting is becoming more pressing in nations that have not yet determined a site for radioactive waste repository, such as Japan, France and the United Kingdom, because their short- and mid-term storage facilities are approaching capacity after around 50 years of nuclear power generation and because of additional waste from the upcoming planned decommissioning of old nuclear power reactors. Radioactive waste repository siting is thus an urgent problem to be analysed as every nation with nuclear reactors needs to determine sites that comply with international, national and local agreements. This article examines three past contrasting cases regarding radioactive waste management in Japan, South Korea and France and analyses critical factors affecting people's attitudes in each case.

*Transition management for sustainable development, Ueta and Adachi (eds.), United Nations University Press, 2014, ISBN 978-92-808-1234-3*

This chapter first provides an analytical framework consisting of two steps for synthesizing the attitude formation process and examining decisive factors affecting this process. By splitting the process into two steps, Emotional Judgement and Reasoned Negotiation, this framework clearly illustrates reasons of past failures in radioactive waste disposal siting, for instance, why a policy which increases compensation often fails to acquire people's acceptance. The chapter then offers three contrasting case studies of radioactive waste management in Japan, South Korea and France that show three common factors in the attitudinal formation process, despite the differences in sociopolitical conditions and the objects of siting between the cases. First, political leadership to set a national agenda and initiate a fundamental review of the problem would play an important role in creating a fair and democratic process of site selection, authorizing processes and increasing trust in policy. Second, trust would be the most important factor in people's attitude formation, as people refuse negotiation when there is a lack of trust. Third, a fair, transparent and democratic process of site selection is important, but direct democracy, such as in the form of a referendum, may not always be necessary to overcome the Emotional Judgement step. In the following section, the attitude formation process and the decisive factors affecting it are analysed and discussed in detail.

## Methodology and analytical framework

There have been two basic approaches to analysing the radioactive waste repository siting process: (1) analysing factors that affect local acceptance or decision-making, for instance, by covariance structure analysis or by policy attitude modelling based mainly on quantitative data (Kunreuther et al., 1990; Sjöberg, 2004; Chung and Kim, 2009), and (2) analysing decisive and substantial factors that influence, or even control, a policy or a dispute process based on methods of policy analysis (Gerrard, 1994; Dawson and Darst, 2006; Pescatore and Vári, 2006; Vandenbosch and Vandenbosch, 2007; Johnson, 2008; Sherman, 2008). I employ interpretive policy analysis based on the post-empiricist, or social constructionist, perspective in order to shape social explanation and understanding of the dispute/policy process (Fischer, 2003).

The dispute process in Japan is described based on a review of the literature regarding the Toyo-cho dispute (Harada, 2007; Masano, 2007; Tashima, 2008; Geki, 2006; Hirota, 2007), newspaper reviews (*Kochi Shimbun*; *Asahi Shimbun*) and interview surveys with residents in Toyo-cho and others concerned with the dispute. The interview surveys were carried out in August 2008 in Toyo-cho and November 2008 in Tokyo, and the interviewees were the then mayor Yasuoki Tashima; two town council members; a director of the planning, commerce and industry division of Toyo-cho; six influential or core residents of both opposing and promoting groups (including a past chair of the town council); two ordinary citizens; a local newspaper reporter (the head of the *Kochi Shimbun*'s Muroto city branch); and a director-general of the Siting Public Relations Department of the Nuclear Waste Management Organization of Japan (NUMO). The interviews were based on a semi-structured interview method and took about one to two-and-a-half hours each.

South Korea's policy process up until 2005 is described based on reviews of the literature regarding the decision analysis in Gyeongju (Chung et al., 2008; Chung and Kim, 2009) and interview surveys with the public officials and specialists concerned, the media, opposing activists and residents in Gyeongju. The interview surveys were carried out in Seoul and Gyeongju in July, August and October 2009, and the interviewees were three former commissioners (a social scientist, a nuclear engineer and a public official) of the Site Selection Committee, a former public official in the Nuclear Plant Project Support Group in the Ministry of Commerce, Industry and Energy (MoCIE), the president of the Korea Radioactive Waste Management Corporation (KRMC), an editor of a national newspaper, an opposing activist of a national-level environmental organization, the general manager in South Korea of an international PR consulting company concerned with the project, the publisher of a local newspaper in Gyeongju, a professor of geotechnical engineering in Gyeongju University and three influential leaders of local residents' organizations in Gyeongju. The interviews were based on a semi-structured interview method and took about one to two hours each.

The policy process in France from the 1980s to 1998 is described based on reviews of the literature regarding radioactive waste management in France (Barthe and Mays, 2001; Barthe, 2009) and interview surveys with MP Claude Birraux, the mayor of Bure, the director of Groupement d'Intérêt Public (Public Interest Group; GIP)[3] Meuse, members of Comité Local d'Information et de Suivi (Local Information and Oversight Committee; CLIS),[4] specialists in Agence nationale pour la gestion des déchets radioactifs (ANDRA), a member of Commission nationale du Débat Public (National Commission for Public Debate, CNDP),[5] a member of an environmental non-profit organization (NPO), local opposing activists in Bar-le-Duc and a social scientist at the Centre de Sociologie de l'Innovation, École des Mines de Paris who has been studying radioactive waste management in France. The interview surveys were based on the semi-structured interview method and were carried out in Paris, Bure and Bar-le-Duc in July and September 2009; each took about one to three hours.

Based on the analysis of the dispute/policy process in each case, the residents' attitude formation process and the factors that influence it are then analyzed. A two-step framework consisting of Emotional Judgement and Reasoned Negotiation (see Figure 16.1) is used to understand the picture of attitude formation in each case. This framework was created based on our study of the French case (Onga et al., 2011), referring to the dual-process theories of persuasion (Chaiken and Trope, 1999), for instance, the Elaboration Likelihood Model (Petty et al., 1983; Petty and Cacioppo, 1986) and Heuristic-Systematic Model

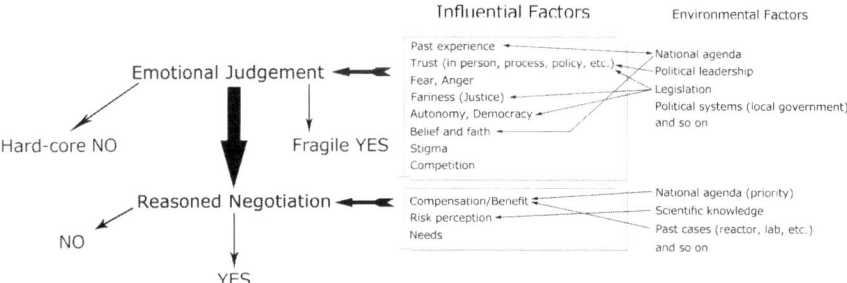

Figure 16.1 A two-step framework of attitude formation

(Chaiken, 1980) and recent attention to the role of emotion[6] in attitude formation in neuroscience (Damasio, 1994), attitude theory (e.g., Cacioppo and Gardner, 1999; Petty et al., 2001) and policy analysis (e.g., Marcus, 2002; Fischer, 2009). At the Emotional Judgement step, the attitude of the local resident is influenced by various factors such as trust, fear (risk perception), fairness, justice and belief. When residents had a common positive emotion about a project, they would agree to discuss whether to accept a facility; otherwise, they would absolutely refuse negotiation whatever compensation was proposed ("hard-core no"[7]). At the Reasoned Negotiation step, the attitude of the local resident is influenced by some amount of compensation, a cost-benefit perception and a risk perception. When residents' needs are fulfilled, the facility would be accepted.

## Attitude formation analysis of three contrasting cases and decisive factors

### Radioactive waste management in Japan, South Korea and France

Based on the Designated Radioactive Waste Final Disposal Act enacted in May 2000, Japan adopted the "application-based" (voluntary) siting policy regarding HLW management and the four-step repository siting process, which consists of (1) the literature survey[8] (2 years), (2) the preliminary investigation (4 years), (3) the detailed investigation (15 years) and (4) the site selection for repository construction. NUMO, which was established in October 2000 as a result of the Designated Radioactive Waste Final Disposal Act and operates the nation's radioactive waste management, has since 2002 invited applications from mayors of municipalities[9] for the literature survey. Applying municipalities, known as "candidates", will receive grants for development of areas locating electric power stations; the grants will amount to about 2 billion yen (1 billion per year) for the literature survey and at most 7 billion yen (2 billion per year) for the preliminary investigation. (The amount of the grant after the Detailed Investigation will be determined by law in the future.) Funds for the grants and the HLW final disposal, provided by the electric power companies, are to be administered by the Radioactive Waste Management Funding and Research Center (RWMC), and the RWMC reimburses the funds based on NUMO's requirements with the approval of the government. Although some municipalities have considered applications for the literature survey since 2002, either in municipal councils or at mayors' discretion, the first applications were not submitted to NUMO until 2007.

In January 2007, Toyo-cho, Kochi Prefecture, became the first—and to date the only—municipality to apply for the literature survey. The application and subsequent dispute, however, resulted in serious antagonism among residents, a strong opposition campaign to collect signatures, the mayor's resignation and, finally, the withdrawal of the application by the new mayor. The dispute made the residents enthusiastic to deliberate the issue and eventually caused a chasm that divided the local community, which has not been resolved yet. Lessons about decisive factors influencing dispute regarding HLW repository siting should be learned from this case so that similar antagonism and problems can be avoided by municipalities applying in the future.

Radioactive waste is classified into two categories in South Korea: spent nuclear fuel (SNF) and low- and intermediate-level radioactive waste (LILW).[10] LILW includes anything worn by nuclear power plant workers (e.g., gloves, cover shoes and clothes) as well as all machine parts replaced as part of maintenance procedures. Because of the Joint Declaration of the Denuclearization of the Korean Peninsula, the Democratic People's Republic of Korea (DPRK) and the Republic of Korea (ROK), in 1992, South Korea cannot currently reprocess SNF, and HLW, therefore, often includes SNF in South Korea. Since the basic policy of radioactive waste management was established in 1984, the South Korean government tried nine times between 1986 and 2004 to determine a site for LILW disposal and interim SNF storage, failing each time. As part of that long effort, the voluntary ("local application-based") system and the increase of economic benefits were considered and had sometimes been applied. However, all attempts ended with strong opposition by residents near the candidate sites.

After the severe conflict[11] in Buan-gun, Jeollabuk-do in 2003 and 2004, the government, and in particular some political leaders and specialists, thoroughly reviewed the past "failures" and determined some drastic policy changes that were institutionalized as "Special Law for the Hosting Regions of LILW Disposal Facilities"; for instance, the uncoupling of the LILW disposal site from the SNF interim storage site and the institutionalization of compulsory referendum. Finally, in 2005, four municipalities that voluntarily applied to the LILW disposal site selection held referenda at the same time, and Gyeongju-si, Gyeongsangbuk-do "won" at 89.5 per cent acceptance.[12] Lessons about decisive factors, especially in policy-making and democracy, could be learned from the experiences in South Korea.

France, which reprocesses SNF,[13] had already selected the LILW repositories, the SNF/HLW midterm storage sites and the underground research laboratory for HLW management in Bure (Meuse), and an HLW repository is under consideration to be sited near Bure by 2025. After decades of hard effort by politicians, the French government and local residents, France finally enacted the Law of 28 June 2006 on the sustainable management of radioactive materials and waste, which also indicated that the final repository would be built somewhere within a 250-square-kilometre zone around Bure.

Four sites had been selected as HLW repository candidate sites by ANDRA, the agency responsible for the management of radioactive waste in France between 1988 and 1989, but public opposition at the four sites and across the nation became so strong that in 1990, the then prime minister, Michel Rocard, suspended the project for at least a year. During the one-year moratorium, Christian Bataille, a member of the Parliament of France and the Office Parlementaire d'Évaluation des Choix Scientifiques et Technologiques (The Parliamentary Office for Evaluation of Scientific Technological Options, OPECST), was asked across party lines to conduct a thorough survey and review of the reasons for the public opposition, and the 1991 Waste Act (Loi Bataille, Bataille Law) was enacted based on his report. The Bataille Law required nationwide transparent communication, which was led by MP Bataille, an open and transparent democratic process of decision-making, and a step-by-step policy-making process that fixed a 15-year period (1991–2006) for research and review and prescribed that a new law for radioactive waste management be legislated in 2006. After eight years of consultation and communication, Bure and surrounding communes in Meuse and Haute-Marne Department mostly agreed with the HLW underground laboratory project under the condition of the reversibility concept[14] in 1998, although alternative site selection was cancelled due to problematic procedure and management. In 2006, the Law of 28 June 2006 on radioactive waste management, which had been initiated by Claude Birraux, a member of the Parliament of France and the OPECST, was enacted.

*The case in Japan (Toyo-cho, Kochi Prefecture)*

In the dispute in Toyo-cho, most residents admitted that they did not deliberate at all, instead forming their attitude at the "Emotional Judgement" step (Figure 16.2). All opposing residents interviewed mentioned angrily that they would never consider the application for the literature survey, whatever amount of compensation would be given, quoting then governor Daijiro Hashimoto's (2006) criticism that "[t]he national government is slapping the cheeks of rural and disadvantaged people with a wad of bills". In addition, responding to Mayor Tashima's request, Akira Amari, the then minister of economy, trade and industry, and Toru Yamaji, the president of NUMO, confirmed in writing that a municipality applying for the literature survey can reverse the application at any point,

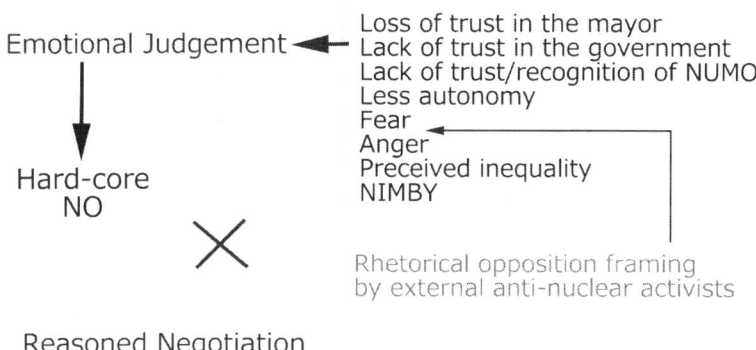

Figure 16.2 The residents' attitude formation throughout the dispute in Toyo-cho

as noted in the *Kochi Shimbun* on 23 December 2006. Opposing residents did not, however, believe such agreements of politicians, nor did they trust politicians and/or administrators at all. Some opposing residents even said, "It is dishonest and unacceptable to withdraw the literature survey after receiving compensation for a few years", although they had no intention of considering the application in the first place. Eventually, the residents reluctantly accepted Yasutaro Sawayama as a new mayor only in order to stop the application, saying, "The withdrawal was a top priority. Otherwise we never would have accepted such an awful person as a mayor".

An analysis of the interview texts reveals four decisive factors that resulted in the "hard-core" opposition: (1) loss or lack of public trust in politicians, governments and NUMO; (2) fear and anger strongly framed by anti-nuclear activists from outside the local community; (3) unfair law/process of decision-making; and (4) NIMBYism and perceived inequality. On the first point, the residents lost, or, to begin with, did not have, trust in local and national politicians and governments and in NUMO. Mayor Yasuoki Tashima had not publicly stated that he would apply for the literature survey, but his "confidential" attempt at applying in March 2006 was exposed by a newspaper in January 2007. Before that public disclosure, residents understood that the then mayor strongly favoured applying for the literature survey, despite his "keep studying the project" statements. The residents felt that Tashima was hiding his true intentions from the public, and thus, they began to lose trust in him, although previously they had re-elected him twice. At the same time, a few trusted residents in the community joined the opposing party, and public opinion of Mayor Tashima fell further. The residents finally lost trust in him when his "confidential" attempt at application was exposed. Although he repeatedly claims that his motivation for applying was to find a solution to the severe condition of the town, especially in terms of the rapidly aging residents (populace) and shrinking economy[15] (Tashima, 2008; interview), clearly he did not adequately understand how sensitive the HLW and nuclear issues were for residents. Only the deputy mayor, the director of the planning, commerce and industry division of Toyo-cho, the application agent, NUMO and the mayor himself knew about that first application attempt, and Tashima did not take prompt action to deal with the rapidly growing opposing signature campaign, which finally influenced the attitude of town councillors and prompted his own ouster. The local politicians (town councillors) also kept saying to the residents, "keep studying", because they had made an agreement with the mayor not to make any decision but to keep studying the project. The residents would have liked the councillors, who had been elected as leaders, to take the initiative in making decisions, but they lost trust in them when it was apparent that they had adhered to their private agreement with Tashima rather than answering the residents honestly. Moreover, because residents could not depend on their local politicians, the opposition group of residents was able to unite, and with some reluctance accepted Yasutaro Sawayama, an outside activist, as a candidate for mayor so that he could represent them with national-level authorities. In addition to those local authorities, residents did not trust either NUMO or the national government. The interviewees in Toyo-cho said that they had heard about NUMO only as a result of the dispute. Residents considered the national government their "opponent", although NUMO is not a public agency but a private organization instituted by the power companies under the supervision of the Ministry of Economy, Trade and Industry. Supporting residents had directly communicated with staff of NUMO and understood its nature, but they criticized NUMO's ability to manage the dispute, and therefore, NUMO lost the trust not only of opposing residents but also of residents who supported the endeavour.[16] The residents also did not trust the national government, as the example of the negotiation about reversibility earlier shows.

The second factor contributing to hard-core opposition was that residents' fear and anger was strongly framed by anti-nuclear activists from the outside and prevented them from being able to deliberate the issue calmly. The rhetorical expression "40,000 vitrified wastes, each of which equals 30 Hiroshima-type a-bombs, will be buried under the ground", which Mr. Baku Nishio of the Citizens' Nuclear Information Center used,[17] was so widely and deeply propagated among residents that almost all interviewees in Toyo-cho mentioned it. Governor Hashimoto's phrase about "slapping cheeks with a wad of bills" was also widely propagated and became a dominant phrase for opposing residents to criticize the promoting stakeholders. As Lau and Schlesinger (2005) mention in the context of "cognitive frame" and "policy metaphor", most residents had framed their understanding of the HLW's risk by the cheek-slapping metaphor and thereafter never trusted explanations of the HLW's safety by NUMO or experts. The residents had a vague fear of "unknown material" (HLW) from the beginning, and that metaphor effectively met their needs to understand, or frame, the fear. Explanations of the safety could not satisfy such needs, and once their recognition was framed, no words of safety could convince them otherwise. Governor Hashimoto's metaphor also met the residents' needs to frame their potential fear of and anger against the national government. The particular residents of the opposing group in Toyo-cho worked as a receptor and a propagator; for instance, residents who had worked with anti-nuclear activists and/or had some experiences of social movements contacted outside anti-nuclear activists as receptors, and others who have close relationships with receptors and are well trusted by residents organized the opposing movement as propagators. Based on Benford and Snow (2000), it can be said that a "strategic fitting" type of social movement diffusion process[18] took place in Toyo-cho. The transmitters (propagators) actively and effectively tailored and fitted the frame and the practices to the context of Toyo-cho by gaining support from potential adopters (receptors). The framing of the residents' fear and anger by rhetorical expressions and the effective collaboration of opposing activists both in the town and from outside, thus, strongly affected the dispute process. In addition, some interviewees mentioned the potential risk of earthquakes in Toyo-cho. Because many older residents had experienced the Showa-Nankai Earthquake in 1946 and media and experts repeatedly reported the growing risk in the near future, the residents feared that such an earthquake would cause a serious disaster at an underground nuclear waste disposal facility, a fear that contributed to driving them into opposition.

A third factor contributing to hard-core opposition was that the residents thought the laws and the process of repository siting were unfair and undemocratic. The law allows mayors of municipalities to apply for the literature survey without the agreement of governors of prefectures and residents. NUMO (and the Ministry of Economy, Trade and Industry) in fact rejected Mayor Tashima's "confidential" application for the literature survey in March 2006 on the grounds that the application had not been made based on an understanding with the residents, but the residents nevertheless felt that the process of decision-making was unfair and undemocratic because the law itself permitted such an application. Interviewees also maintained that they understood they had chosen the mayor through democratic election but that they did not know that the mayor had such a strong authority to make a serious decision without their agreement. The opposing groups in Toyo-cho tried to take measures of direct democracy to express their opposition and to stand against the "tyrannical" mayor and the national government. They started with a signature campaign for a local ordinance to ban bringing nuclear waste into the town, and when that failed to overturn the process, they initiated a recall campaign against Mayor Tashima.[19]

A fourth factor contributing to hard-core opposition was that the residents' NIMBYism drove them into opposition, and their perception of inequality further strengthened NIMBYism. The opposition group indeed recognized that since Japan has been developed rapidly by using a large amount of electricity, a significant part of which is produced by nuclear power generation, nuclear waste must then be managed in Japan, but NIMBYism influenced their opposition. They felt that rural areas, such as Toyo-cho, had been left behind by advancing urban cities. One interviewee said,

> Considering our economic development and current global warming, it might be true that nuclear power generation is necessary and its waste must be disposed somewhere. So, it would be rather selfish of us to reject the repository in Toyo-cho. . . . But if the repository is 100% safe, it should be built under the Diet Building in Tokyo. Rural areas are considered as potential sites of repository because the damage could be held down to the minimum if "something" happens, aren't they?

The residents felt it inequitable that only urban cities enjoyed the economic development that resulted from the power infrastructure, whereas rural towns were always forced to accept risky and unwanted facilities. This perception made the residents think that nuclear waste management was an issue to be considered by the whole nation based on the principle of the user's responsibility, which gave some justification for their NIMBYism and strengthened their opposition.

In addition to the preceding four factors, the grant formulated in the law adversely affected residents' attitudes because of the criticism that the town applied for the literature survey in order to obtain the grant and the subsequent guilty feeling of having received the money at the cost of the town. As the metaphor "slapping cheeks with a wad of bills" by Governor Hashimoto demonstrates, Japanese, and perhaps people in other nations, cannot avoid feeling that they have accepted a bribe when they think of compensation, and they have difficulty justifying receiving money at the cost of accepting hazardous waste. This adverse effect of the grant would be inevitable under the "voluntary-based" siting policy, under which the applicant always voluntarily expresses their willingness to accept a waste repository and it can be considered by the public that they actively apply for money. In order to solve this problem, the Ministry of Economy, Trade and Industry in fact added an "offer-based" siting procedure in 2007 that relieved pressure from applying mayors and enabled stakeholders to negotiate and build consensus in advance. The "offer-based" procedure additionally provides the powerful advantage of giving residents the chance to alleviate their feeling of guilt about accepting the money by giving them the excuse that "[t]he government recommends our town as the HLW repository site, and we obey it against our will. The grant is the only thing we can do to ease our own feeling of being exploited".

Some residents in Toyo-cho, however, recall that they rushed into emotional opposition without calm deliberation; as one resident said, "At the time of the conflict, I thought 'we must reject now'. But now, I also understand what the promoting people said. No financial problems of the town have been solved, and our lives have not been improved at all". It may be true that residents successfully avoided applying for the literature survey. But it could also be said that their emotional judgement strengthened public attention to certain aspects of the issue, such as risk, and drew attention away from other aspects. Many unsolved problems remain in the town that could and should have been discussed calmly during the dispute.

*The case in South Korea (Gyeongju-si, Gyeongsangbuk-do)*

Gyeongju-si finally accepted the siting of underground LILW repository after the simultaneous referenda in four South Korean cities, but the interviews suggest that many residents, especially those with little knowledge of the issue, determined their attitudes at the Emotional Judgement step (Figure 16.3). Indeed, some residents who led the supporting groups formed their attitudes at the Reasoned Negotiation step, after accepting the importance of and need for the repository at the Emotional Judgement step. For example, one of the leading residents in Gyeongju, who was a spokesperson for a supporting group and is now a secretary to a member of the National Assembly, said,

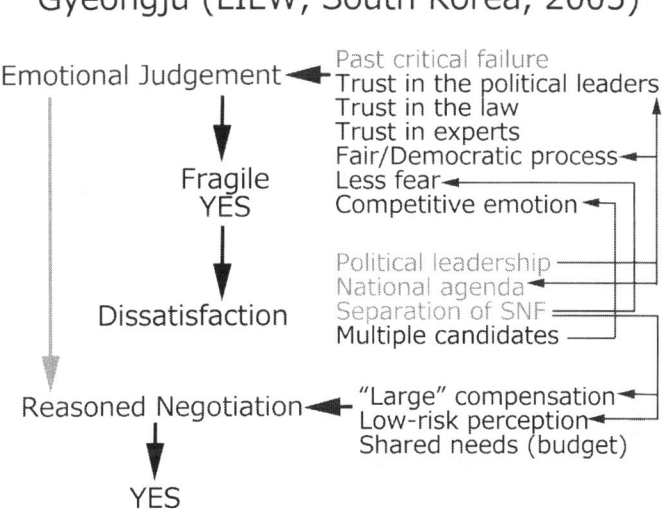

Figure 16.3 The residents' attitude formation throughout the siting process in Gyeongju

The citizens' group[20] I belonged to was established for the purpose of communication with residents about the risks of nuclear power plants. But the legislation of the Special Law for LILW disposal facilities hosting region made me trust the process. I wouldn't have trusted it even if any minister had made promises about it; I trusted it because of the legislation. . . . And the law includes the removal of SNF from the equation, which significantly decreases our perception of risk. Gyeongju keeps a lot of SNF at the Wolseong nuclear power plants [in the city]. It is desirable for us that the SNF stored there will not be a factor, in addition to receiving the economic benefit.

The attitudes of many others were, however, formed at the Emotional Judgement stage, and thus, they regret rushing into the referenda and accepting the repository. One of the residents I interviewed said that he had trusted the legislation of the Special Law and strongly wanted the compensation because the city had failed to invite facilities for local development, but he expressed his current fear and distrust by noting the construction delay due to groundwater leakage, which experts said did not cause any fatal problem. Although 300 billion won (KRW) compensation was given to the city as promised, many Gyeongju residents complained about the safety of the construction and expressed their growing distrust of the government.

Analysis of the interview texts reveals three decisive factors that Gyeongju residents admitted in discussion about their acceptance of the repository, and one factor that drove many residents into an "emotional yes" rather than calm deliberation about the project. The first three factors were (1) the fair and democratic process realized by the past critical failure in Buan and the leadership of certain politicians and administrators, (2) the residents' trust in the newly legislated law and the political leaders and (3) the decrease of fear resulting from the decision not to store SNF at the site. The final "emotional yes" factor was (4) the competitive emotion evoked by the simultaneous referenda.

The first decisive factor was that politicians, administrators and experts thoroughly reviewed the critical failure in Buan in 2003 and 2004 and realized the importance of fairness, democracy and trust. Characterizing the radioactive waste repository siting as a "national problem", they determined the important policy changes that were indispensable to the LILW repository siting in Gyeongju: the decision not to store SNF at the site, legislating the referendum requirement and the establishment of the Site Selection Committee and the Nuclear Plant Project Support Group. Most importantly, then prime minister Hae-Chan Lee and his office exercised strong leadership in implementing those fundamental policy changes. Hae-Chan Lee, as both prime minister and head of the Atomic Energy Commission, not only proposed that SNF be dealt with separately but also formed the two special task forces named earlier. He even selected some of those members himself. His active involvement was so widely known among people concerned with the LILW repository siting issue that many interviewees in Seoul and Gyeongju mentioned it. Moreover, the Site Selection Committee and the Nuclear Plant Project Support Group consisted of "the best members"; for instance, (1) some public officials in those teams were even called back from overseas, (2) not only experts in nuclear science and engineering but also social scientists were represented, (3) the media and non-governmental organizations (NGOs) were represented and (4) the head of the Site Selection Committee was Kap-Soo Han, who had been the minister of agriculture and forestry and took strong leadership. In particular, the Site Selection Committee held intensive discussions, and its attitude and efforts in social communication positively influenced public opinion. In addition, then president Moo-Hyun Roh strongly moved ahead on the Popular Sovereignty Act, the transfer of administrative capital function and the nuclear policy. Although the Popular Sovereignty Act had been an urgent issue since 1994, and it was almost nationally accepted at the 2002 presidential campaign, his leadership, especially after the impeachment issue, might have made policy decisions much easier. All these leading efforts caused a fundamental policy change, which had not been set as a political agenda, and made the nation recognize LILW repository siting as an item on the national agenda.

All the changes were realized because of the critical failure in Buan to identify a radioactive waste repository siting. After each of the nine siting attempts failed, the government made incremental changes in the siting policy, for example, the increase and/or change of compensation and the applications of an "offer-based" selection process and an "application-based" one. Only after the failure in Buan, which ultimately resulted in a 91.83 per cent opposition to the then mayor who supported the repository siting, the Nuclear Plant Project Support Group was established and thoroughly reviewed the causes of the past failures. One of the members of Nuclear Plant Project Support Group maintained in my interview with him that he learned from the failure of Buan the importance of residents' calm understanding about the project and of a democratic decision-making process. He also mentioned that the lack of residents' trust in the government and in KHNP (Korea Hydro and Nuclear Power)[20] caused the strong emotional opposition in Buan. Those recognitions finally led to the policy changes.

The second factor that influenced acceptance was the residents' trust in the newly legislated law and the political leaders who effectively made the residents understand the need and importance of the repository, and some even blindly assumed the repository to be perfectly safe. Then prime minister Hae-Chan Lee received popular support, and the then president Moo-Hyun Roh also recovered his influence through his impeachment dispute as the result of the 2004 national election, in which his administration garnered a more than 50 per cent approval rating. Although most residents still distrusted politicians and administrators, some of the rather "neutral" interviewees (e.g., the president of a local newspaper and a professor of Gyeongju University) said that the residents generally trusted experts and technical information given by the government and the supporting groups. The difference of risk between HLW and LILW was widely and repeatedly explained to the residents, and most residents believed that LILW was much safer than HLW, although very few fully understood the risk of LILW, especially intermediate level 1, and the technical aspects of the project. Above all, however, almost all interviewees mentioned that the Special Law strengthened residents' trust in the project. Regarding the residents' lack of trust in politicians, one of the interviewees said that a change of government could overturn past promises and agendas of politicians. For example, one interviewee said that people in Buan had doubted that SNF, which had been the subject of interim storage, would be permanently disposed of since the government did not clearly state this in a law. The implementation of the Special Law dispelled such doubts by residents, and the contents of the law that were strongly supported also strengthened the residents' trust in it.

The third factor that influenced acceptance was the uncoupling of SNF from the radioactive waste disposal project, which was clearly stipulated in the Special Law and almost dispelled the residents' fears about safety. As most of the interviewees mentioned, Gyeongju has stored SNF in Wolseong nuclear power plants for cooling, and the residents felt much less fear because the Special Law provides that SNF would be moved out of the city. In addition, as noted earlier, the residents generally trusted experts and their explanations about the technical safety of the LILW repository. Dr. Seong-Chun Hwang, professor of geotechnical engineering at Gyeongju University, for instance, assured the safety of LILW management from a technical viewpoint in a public lecture, and the residents believed the relative safety of LILW, compared to SNF, through explanations by such experts, professionals and activists. The reduction of fear and the belief in the safety of LILW made residents calmly evaluate the need of the project and the value of the compensation. The amount of the monetary compensation had already been increased to 300 billion won (KRW) in 2001, but the drastic reduction of the risk perception in the Gyeongju case made the residents evaluate it much higher. Some interviewees in Gyeongju also mentioned other reasons influencing the residents' decision: the Gyeongju residents had a sense of inferiority that Gyeongju had been less developed than surrounding cities[22] due to the strict development restrictions resulting from it having several World Heritage Sites. Another reason put forward was that the city government urgently needed economic development but had failed to invite two national-level projects[23] in the past. Gyeongju residents, especially leading ones, thus decided to accept the LILW repository project at the Reasoned Negotiation step, after calmly evaluating the value of the compensation, the need for economic development and the perceived risk.

Finally, the competitive emotion evoked by the simultaneous referenda, however, drove many residents into an emotional yes, whereas some leading residents calmly deliberated at the Reasoned Negotiation step. The simultaneous referenda not only produced a competitive environment among the candidate cities but also excited the existing rivalry[24] between Gyeongsang-do (Gyeongju) and Jeolla-do (Gunsan). Although many interviewees fully endorsed the referendum as being a direct and democratic decision-making method, it could be said based on the interviews that the referenda process in this case was problematic and deprived many residents of the ability to deliberate composedly; for example, the president of a local newspaper in Gyeongju criticized the referenda for causing hostility among the residents; a leader of the supporting group said, "We should not have made the final decision until we fully understood the risk/safety of the project, the technical knowledge regarding radioactive waste management and underground construction and the value of the compensation. We actually rushed to the referendum and it now causes problems, such as the increasing anxiety and dissatisfaction about the project and the compensation"; another leader of the supporting group and an opposing activist maintained that the simultaneous referenda evoked competition among the candidates and eclipsed the residents' concern about risk. Some interviewees mentioned that the national government should first have investigated safety and made a proposal for the repository siting to the best place from the technical viewpoint and that a referendum should then have been held in a final decision-making step. It might be said that the 2005 referenda obscured the responsibility of the national government, while the residents themselves made the decision of acceptance, which later caused the festering dissatisfaction of the residents. Moreover, according to a few interviewees in Seoul, it might be true that the national government, or the Nuclear Plant Project Support Group, deliberately conducted the referenda process simultaneously, with the intention of driving people into an emotional yes. Although the LILW repository has "successfully" been located in Gyeongju, the remaining antagonism among the residents and the evolving dissatisfaction and anxiety of the residents may have unfavourable influences on the future policy of the SNF interim storage siting and the final disposal siting.

## *The case in France (Bure and surrounding communes in Meuse and Haute-Marne Department)*

The underground research laboratory for HLW management was built according to the agreement of Bure and surrounding municipalities in Meuse and Haute-Marne Department. The residents agreed on the need for and importance of the underground laboratory at the Emotional Judgement step and accepted it based on the deliberation and consideration at the Reasoned Negotiation step (Figure 16.4). In the late 1980s, all attempts at HLW repository siting in France failed due to strong public opposition. One of the interviewees in ANDRA said, "People who were engaged in the site selection at that time could not believe that the ordinary citizen was so strongly opposed". Technocrats determined the candidate sites solely from a technical viewpoint and lacked concerns about transparency and democracy, and a hard-core no was the final result. But after the Bataille Law was enacted in 1991, the residents in Bure and the surrounding municipalities trusted the law, which provided for a fair and democratic process, and the underground laboratory was accepted in 1998 after an eight-year consultation/communication without "emotional" approval or opposition. A mayor of one of

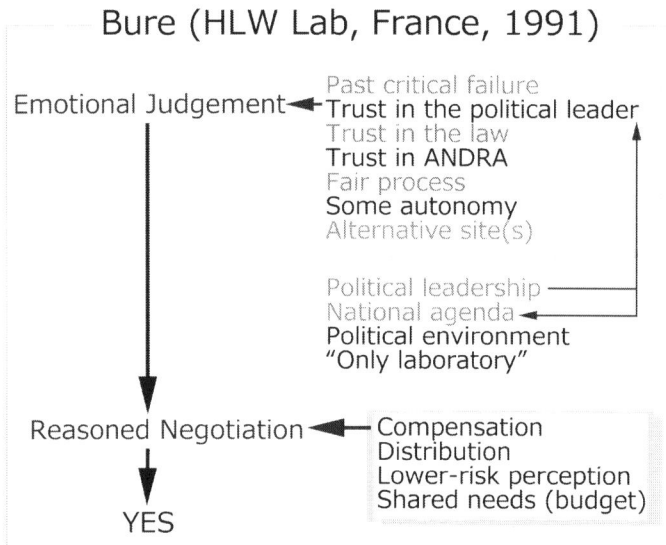

Figure 16.4 The residents' attitude formation throughout the siting process in Bure

the surrounding municipalities, for example, made it clear in the interview that the decision had been made based on consultation and communication in the local area. He, as well as the mayor of Bure, maintained that they would not have agreed on the project if it had included construction of a final disposal site. They concluded after careful deliberation that an underground laboratory was acceptable in exchange for the economic benefit (compensation) but that the benefit was not enough to outweigh accepting a final disposal facility of HLW, and they believed that it would not be automatically located near the laboratory site, as the law provided.

Analysis of the interview texts shows two main decisive factors that enabled the residents to calmly deliberate the underground laboratory siting project: (1) the Bataille Law, which provided for a fair and democratic process based on Bataille's consideration of the critical failure in 1980s, and his leadership, and (2) the residents' trust in the Bataille Law, Bataille himself, ANDRA and local leaders. The interview survey also makes clear that the residents finally accepted the laboratory at the Reasoned Negotiation step, having decided that the value of the compensation was enough for the underground laboratory, which was thought less risky than the final disposal facility, and fairly distributed among the area. The area, especially Bure, had been economically disadvantaged, and people had a shared understanding of the need for economic development. The compensation and the economic benefits associated with the project, such as employment, were thus decisive factors in the residents' decision at the Reasoned Negotiation step.

Without the Bataille Law and Bataille's leadership to create it, no underground laboratory would have been built, and the radioactive waste management in France would still be an unresolved issue. The unexpected critical failure, involving violence, in the late 1980s propelled the then prime minister Michel Rocard to call for a one-year moratorium on site selection in order to conduct a nationwide inquiry and to find a comprehensive policy solution. Rocard displayed leadership, as did Hae-Chan Lee in South Korea in 2004, and it could be said that Rocard's moratorium decision pushed the radioactive waste issue onto the national agenda and triggered the subsequent policy process. Asking OPECST to nominate a proper person to deal with the issue, Rocard and the National Assembly then appointed MP Cristian Bataille to conduct the nationwide inquiry. Some interviewees named one or more of the following reasons for his appointment: major members of Socialist Party, then the governing party, did not want to draw such a "bad lot", and Bataille was the only person who accepted the position; he was a member of OPECST, the parliamentary office which deals specifically with science and technology issues; he did not know anything about the nuclear issue nor had any connection with the nuclear industry; the government also thought it was necessary to involve an MP so that the issue could be controlled by national-level political power. Bataille and his inquiry committee visited all four candidate sites where the past site selection had failed, and they held wide-ranging interviews with local administrators, NGOs, national-level administrators and experts and overseas professionals. The final report of the inquiry (Rapport sur la gestion des déchets nucleaires à haute activité) was submitted to the government in December 1990, only 10 months after the Rocard moratorium was enacted. The report identified the following reasons for the failure: (1) lack of communication to provide information, (2) negative impression by the public of radioactive waste and public fear of a "nuclear garbage dump", (3) economic factors, (4) opposition aroused by ecologists and (5) NIMBYism. Based on the committee's thorough review, the report suggested implementing the following conditions when the project resumed: (1) carrying out research about separation and conversion as well as underground disposal; (2) improving the site selection process by increasing transparency, selecting multiple sites, investing a representative of negotiation with national-level authority and guaranteeing economic benefit; (3) prohibiting the importation of radioactive waste from other nations; and (4) reforming the management organization. Those suggestions were included in the Bataille Law enacted in December 1991. The Bataille Law represented a fundamental change in the philosophy of radioactive waste management policy. The primary criterion of site selection changed from a technical to a democratic one, and an open and fair process replaced the past closed and top-down decision-making. Bataille, who had remained as the negotiation representative with local municipalities even after his Socialist Party had been driven into opposition in the 1993 French legislative election, conducted a nationwide drive to communicate with various local people from the municipalities that had been interested in the project before 1998. Bataille's leadership in creating the thorough review and the Bataille Law and in conducting open communication, such as public hearings, would be the most influential factor in the siting process.

The second factor enabling residents to calmly deliberate the underground laboratory siting project was that residents in Bure and the surrounding municipalities trusted the Bataille Law, ANDRA and local leaders. Despite general distrust in politicians and technocrats, some interviewees in Paris said the Bataille Law and local leaders had the residents' trust. For instance, the interviewees in Bure stressed their trust in the law, and an interviewee in Paris said, "People thought the law would not be changed once it was enacted and would be followed, even though politicians change". Some citizens in Bure expressed their trust in ANDRA, which they thought had become a local economic partner because the staff lived and worked locally since 1991. The ANDRA specialists interviewed in Bure also put great emphasis on their efforts to blend into the local community by living there for more than 10 years, which cannot be seen in the other two cases in Japan and South Korea. The presence of the Bataille Law was the primary source of trust for people concerned with the project and for the local residents, although the residents' trust in Bataille himself, ANDRA and local leaders also played an important role in their attitude formation at the Emotional Judgement step. As the Special Law for LILW disposal facilities hosting region created by the leadership of politicians and administrators in South Korea, the legislation overcame the residents' distrust of politicians and technocrats.

In addition to these major factors, the residents' understanding of representative democracy and the presence of multiple sites might also influence their attitude formation. Indeed, a step-by-step decision-making process and transparent communication would restrain an emotional response by the residents, and the relatively small size of the municipality, compared to those in Japan and South Korea, might affect the relationship among residents. Some interviewees in Paris and Bure, however, mentioned that people had recognized the decision-making process (vote by local assembly members after public deliberation and communication) to be autonomous enough, and there had been no major opposition of residents to the decision made by their representatives. One even said that people followed a representative in the area "like sheep". The social scientist interviewed in Paris mentioned that political representatives had taken the initiative even during the strong opposition in the late 1980s, and it might also demonstrate the strong representative democracy of France. Many interviewees, especially the mayor of Bure, also touched on the influence of the presence of multiple sites, which had been provided under the Bataille Law, on the residents' attitude formation. The presence of multiple sites might influence the residents' perception of fairness at the Emotional Judgement step and had certainly increased the perceived value of the economic benefit at the Reasoned Negotiation step.

Although France has succeeded in selecting the underground laboratory site and deciding the candidate area for HLW final disposal site, potential problems remain that may influence the future site selection process. The attempt to select multiple sites for underground laboratory eventually failed, and some residents in Bure and the surrounding area now criticize the government for breaking its "promise". The concept of "reversibility" has been keenly discussed and studied in France, but those residents express their growing interest in a direct veto right, which may be involved with reversibility because of their discontent regarding the "promise" about the underground laboratory site selection. It could be said that trust is easily eroded and that such erosion may result in wasting any efforts for a long time.

## Synthesis and conclusion

The analysis of the cases in the three nations using the two-step framework of attitude formation has implications for future policy of undesirable facility siting and perhaps deliberative democracy, although the sociopolitical contexts and the objects of siting in each nation are unique. First, political leadership to set a national agenda and initiate a fundamental review of the problem would play an important role in creating a fair and democratic process of site selection, authorizing process and increasing trust in policy. Politicians in any nation would not like to take the responsibility for sensitive political matters at the risk of being ousted at the next election, but in the two "successful" nations, national-level politicians (Christian Bataille in France and Hae-Chan Lee in South Korea) displayed leadership and dared to assume responsibility, whereas leadership and accountability are still lacking in Japan despite the issue's critical failure in Toyo-cho. Second, trust can be said to be the most important factor in people's attitude formation, and a "hard-core no" is likely to be evoked where there is a lack of trust. The three cases demonstrate that the presence of a legal framework produces strong trust even under the condition where people may distrust a politician or administrator. In addition, the cases confirmed that trust is difficult to achieve but easy to be eroded. As the case in France shows, ordinary people hold a deep-rooted fear of radioactive waste and distrust in technocrats. ANDRA has taken more than 10 years to be recognized as a local partner in Bure through long-time deliberation with local people. But even people's strong trust in law can be decayed by careless management. Both in Gyeongju and in Bure, residents started having distrust in the laws and the managing organizations when they felt any promise was broken. Site selection of an undesirable facility is often conducted hurriedly, as in Toyo-cho, but patient and careful management of trust among the persons and organizations concerned should always be secured. Third, a fair, transparent and democratic process of site selection is important, but direct democracy, such as a referendum, may not always be necessary to overcome the Emotional Judgement step. As the case in France demonstrates, the residents can avoid serious antagonism caused by "emotional" attitude formation and experience calm deliberation at the Reasoned Negotiation step without referendum, if a fair, open and democratic process is legislated and if trust in political leaders, managing organizations and experts is carefully secured through thorough communication. The cases in Japan and South Korea suggest that direct democracy, such as referendum and recall, could instead keep the residents' attitude formation at the Emotional Judgement step by limiting the time for communication and cultivating trust, focusing the residents' minds to attend to certain issues, making other concerns fade away and driving residents to a simple yes-or-no decision. Direct democracy may well be legitimate and may cover the potential problems presented by representative democracy; for instance, when an elected mayor, who is generally trusted by residents, arbitrarily makes a decision that residents find unacceptable, direct democracy would effectively work to undo that decision. In order to avoid long-lasting hostility among residents or to resolve potential future anxiety, however, the process before any final decision-making by direct democracy should be carefully designed so that there is enough time for concerned people to be convinced of calm deliberation and to discuss thoroughly the issue.

Although deliberation and decision-making at the Reasoned Negotiation step are important from the democratic and ethical viewpoint, no matter what decision is made, it would also be true from the practical and political perspective that each nation must make every effort to locate radioactive waste repository within the nation that produced the waste, as international convention and/or national law request. Considering the deep-rooted negative attitude toward radioactive waste as seen in all three cases, it might be difficult solely by direct democracy to make a decision to lay such a big burden on a given locale in a nation. The 2011 Tohoku earthquake and tsunami, followed by the Fukushima Daiichi nuclear power plant disaster, keenly evoked people's fear of nuclear power and clearly made it much more difficult for the Japanese to consider the problem of radioactive waste, even though the disaster produced a huge amount of additional radioactive waste to be managed. In addition, as media have reported since May 2011 (for example, "Radioactive Waste Disposal Site Planned in Mongolia" which appeared in the morning edition of *Mainichi Shimbun* on 9 May 2011), the Japanese and the US governments and their respective nuclear industries may have attempted to manage the waste in other nations before the disaster. It is likely that the Japanese would deny site selection of HLW final repository if a national referendum is held, and no municipality would agree to accept even the literature survey if a local referendum is held. The analyses of these three cases in Japan, South Korea and France imply that the leadership qualities of a democratically elected representatives might play a crucial role for breakthrough and political innovation, as the leadership of MP Bataille and PM Rocard created an "innovative" law, which changed the philosophy of policy and had a significant influence on later policies.[25] Leadership and trust, which are also evoked by leader's democratic policies and fair agendas, finally draw residents toward their ultimate decision of acceptance at the Reasoned Negotiation step.

# Notes

1. This chapter relies on my research team's past research about the disputes regarding the siting of facilities related to radioactive waste management in Japan, Korea and France (Komatsuzaki et al., 2010; Saigo et al., 2010; Onga et al., 2011; Yamaguchi et al., 2011).
2. The 2008 administrative reform restructured MoCIE as MKE (the Ministry of Knowledge and Economy).
3. GIP is an administrative body that manages local/regional development and the local/regional budget. Members include local/regional public and business bodies that represent public interests.
4. CLIS is a committee that promotes communication and deliberation. The CLIS for Bure consists of politicians, public officials, non-profit organizations, ANDRA and local residents.
5. CNDP is an independent administrative agency responsible for holding public meetings when asked by the government or a project operator.
6. Different definitions are sometimes given to *affect, emotion, mood* and *feeling* (e.g., Brader, 2006: 51), but following Panksepp (2005: 32), in this chapter, I use *emotion* as a general term that includes affective, cognitive, behavioural, expressive and physiological changes.
7. Ferreria and Gallagher (2010) use the term *hardcore protestor* for a person who categorically rejects the principle of compensation.
8. In the literature survey, geotechnical analysis is done based on aerial photography, literature and past records on earthquakes, tsunamis and other natural disasters without an on-site investigation, such as boring.
9. In Japan, the law allows mayors of municipalities to apply for the literature survey without agreement of their prefectural governor.
10. In Japan, radioactive waste is classified as either HLW or LILW. HLW is a type of waste created through reprocessing SNF.
11. See Chung et al. (2008).
12. A majority of people voted for the disposal siting in every candidate location (Gyeongju: 89.5 per cent, Gunsan: 84.4 per cent, Yeongdeok: 79.3 per cent and Pohang: 67.5 per cent). Based on the policy, Gyeongju, with the highest acceptance rate, "won" the siting of the disposal facility.
13. Japan has sent its SNF to France and the United Kingdom for reprocessing based on the 1977–1978 contracts because the Rokkasho Reprocessing Plant has not been completed, which is expected to be in operation in 2014.
14. The concept of reversibility refers to the retrievability of waste within a certain period before finally sealing a repository and to the possibility of changing any decision and returning to previous decision-making steps.
15. Here, I refer to interviews with then president of the Chamber of Commerce and Industry of Toyo-cho (4 August 2008) in the Hall of the Chamber of Commerce and Industry of Toyo-cho, and then town council member (5 August 2008) in the Town Hall of Toyo-cho.
16. For instance, a supporting resident I interviewed said, "Because the NUMO personnel come from the power companies, they do not make a series effort to solve the problem and neither do the power companies. And NUMO does not cooperate well with the national government. NUMO is ultimately controlled by the national government and has no power and ability".
17. For instance, see the Namitsu blog entry for 20 December 2006 available at http://w1.i92surf.com/blog.pho?e=698#more.
18. Benford and Snow (2000: 627) define two social movement diffusion processes: "Strategic selection encompasses situation in which there is intentional cross-cultural borrowing, with the adopter or importer assuming the role of an active agent in the process, strategically selecting and adapting the borrowed item to the new host context or culture. Strategic fitting encompasses situation in which there is intentional cross-cultural promotion, with transmitter actively engaged in tailoring and fitting the objects or practices of diffusion to the house culture".

19. Then mayor Yasuoki Tashima finally resigned before he could be recalled, and a new election was held. Interviewees' remarks, including Tashima's, suggest that the recall campaign by opposing groups pressed him into resignation and realized the election focused solely on the decision-making regarding the application to the literature survey.
20. The citizens' group is one of the originators of the supporting group.
21. Before the KRMC, the KHNP was responsible for radioactive waste management in South Korea.
22. In particular, Pohang, to the north of Gyeongju (where POSCO, the world's third-largest steel-maker, is based), and Ulsan, in the south (where the Hyundai group is based), have developed rapidly as a result of the enormous income from those giant companies.
23. Those projects are a horse racecourse and a national Tae Kwon Do arena.
24. Gyeongsang-do and Jeolla-do have historically been rivals. For example, Dae-Jung Kim has been the only president ever from Jeolla-do, while Gyeongsang-do produced many presidents, in particular very influential ones, such as Chung-Hee Park, Moo-Hyun Roh and Myung-Bak Lee. People in Jeolla-do believe that one of the reasons that Jeolla-do has been less developed than Gyeongsang-do is because of this political disadvantage.
25. Dr. Yannick Barthe (23 September 2009), in the Centre de Sociologie de l'Innovation, École des Mines de Paris.

## REFERENCES

Barthe, Yannick (2009) "Framing Nuclear Waste as a Political Issue in France", *Journal of Risk Research*, 12(7–8), pp. 941–954.

Barthe, Yannick and Claire Mays (2001) "Communication and Information in France's Underground Laboratory Siting Process: Clarity of Procedure, Ambivalence of Effects", *Journal of Risk Research*, 4(4), pp. 411–430.

Benford, Robert D. and David A. Snow (2000) "Framing Processes and Social Movements: An Overview and Assessment", *Annual Review of Sociology*, 26, pp. 611–639.

Brader, Ted (2006) *Campaigning for Hearts and Minds: How Emotional Appeals in Political Ads Work*, Chicago, IL: University of Chicago Press.

Cacioppo, John T. and Wendi L. Gardner (1999) "Emotion", *Annual Review of Psychology*, 50, pp. 191–214.

Chaiken, Shelly (1980) "Heuristic versus Systematic Information Processing and the Use of Source versus Message Cues in Persuasion", *Journal of Personality and Social Psychology*, 39(5), pp. 752–756.

Chaiken, Shelly and Yaacov Trope (1999) *Dual-Process Theories in Social Psychology*, New York: Guilford Press.

Chung, Ji-Bum and Hong-Kyu Kim (2009) "Competition, Economic Benefits, Trust, and Risk Perception in Siting a Potentially Hazardous Facility", *Landscape and Urban Planning*, 91(1), pp. 8–16.

Chung, Ji-Bum, Hong-Kyu Kim and Sam-Key Rho (2008) "Analysis of Local Acceptance of a Radioactive Waste Disposal Facility", *Risk Analysis*, 28(4), pp. 1021–1032.

Damasio, Antonio (1994) *Descartes' Error: Emotion, Reason, and the Human Brain*, New York: Putnam Publishing.

Dawson, Jane I. and Robert G. Darst (2006) "Meeting the Challenge of Permanent Nuclear Waste Disposal in an Expanding Europe: Transparency, Trust and Democracy", *Environmental Politics*, 15(4), pp. 610–627.

Geki (2006) Available at http://geki1015cocolog-nifty.com/blog/ (in Japanese).
Ferreira, Susana and Louise Gallagher (2010) "Protest Responses and Community Attitudes toward Accepting Compensation to Host Waste Disposal Infrastructure", *Land Use Policy*, 27(2), pp. 638–652.
Fischer, Frank (2003) *Reframing Public Policy: Discursive Politics and Deliberative Practices*, New York: Oxford University Press.
—— (2009) *Democracy and Expertise: Reorienting Policy Inquiry*, New York: Oxford University Press.
Gerrard, Michael B. (1994) *Whose Backyard, Whose Risk: Fear and Fairness in Toxic and Nuclear Waste Siting*, Cambridge, MA: MIT Press.
Harada, Eisuke (2007) *Chronology of Toyo-cho*, rev. ed., Self-published (in Japanese), Aki City, Japan: Aki Type.
Hashimoto, Daijiro (2006) "Don't Slap Cheeks with a Wad of Bills" available at http://daichanzeyo.cocolog-nifty.com/0403/2006/09/post_ce44.html (in Japanese).
Hirota, Noe (2007) Available at http://noe.mo-blog.jp/weblog/ (in Japanese).
IAEA (International Atomic Energy Agency) (1997) "Joint Convention on the Safety of Spent Fuel Management and on the Safety of Radioactive Waste Management", available at http://www.iaea.org/Publications/Documents/Infcircs/1997/infcirc546.pdf.
Johnson, Genevieve Fuji (2008) *Deliberative Democracy for the Future: The Case of Nuclear Waste Management in Canada*, Toronto: University of Toronto Press.
Komatsuzaki, Shunsaku, Akio Yamaguchi and Hideyuki Horii (2010) "NIMBY, Deliberation, and Democratic Decision Making: A Comparative Analysis of Radioactive Waste Repository Siting Cases in Korea and Japan", *International Journal of Policy Studies*, 1(1), pp. 47–70.
Kunreuther, Howard, Douglas Easterling, William Desvousges and Paul Slovic (1990) "Public Attitudes toward Siting a High-Level Nuclear Waste Repository in Nevada", *Risk Analysis*, 10(4), pp. 469–484.
Lau, Richard R. and Mark Schlesinger (2005) "Policy Frames, Metaphorical Reasoning, and Support for Public Policies", *Political Psychology*, 26(1), pp. 77–114.
Marcus, George E (2002) *The Sentimental Citizen: Emotion in Democratic Politics*, University Park: Pennsylvania State University Press.
Masano, Atsuko (2007) "It Was Brought from "Dark World": Report of the Strife in Toyo-cho, Kochi regarding Radioactive Waste Repository Siting", *Ronza* (August), pp. 164–169, Tokyo: Asahi Shimbun Publications Inc. (in Japanese)
Onga, Marie, Shunsaku Komatsuzaki and Hideyuki Horii (2011) "Working Paper: Attitude Formation Towards the Dispute over High-Level Radioactive Waste Repository in France", available at http://intl.civil.t.u-tokyo.ac.jp/res_wp_e.html.
Panksepp, Jaak (2005) "Affective Consciousness: Core Emotional Feelings in Animals and Humans", *Consciousness and Cognition*, 14(1), pp. 30–80.
Pescatore, Claudio and Anna Vári (2006) "Stepwise Approach to the Long-Term Management of Radioactive Waste", *Journal of Risk Research*, 9(1), pp. 13–40.
Petty, Richard E. and John T. Cacioppo (1986) "The Elaboration Likelihood Model of Persuasion", in Leonard Berkowitz (eds.) *Advances in Experimental Social Psychology*, 19, New York: Academic Press, pp. 123–205.
Petty, Richard E., John T. Cacioppo and David Schumann (1983) "Central and Peripheral Routes to Advertising Effectiveness: The Moderating Role of Involvement", *Journal of Consumer Research*, 10(2), pp. 135–146.

Petty, Richard E., David DeSteno and Derek D. Rucker (2001) "The Role of Affect in Attitude Change", in Joseph P. Forgas (ed.) *Handbook of Affect and Social Cognition*, Mahwah, NJ: Lawrence Erlbaum Associates, pp. 212–233.

Saigo, Takahiro, Shunsaku Komatsuzaki and Hideyuki Horii (2010) "Decisive Factors of the Dispute Regarding High-Level Radioactive Waste Repository Siting at Toyo-cho, Kochi, Japan: An Analysis of Political Process and Possible Solutions", *Sociotechnica*, 7(1), pp. 87–98 (in Japanese).

Sherman, Daniel J. (2008) "Disruption or Convention? A Process-Based Explanation of Divergent Repertoires of Contention among Opponents to Low-Level Radioactive Waste Disposal Sites", *Social Movement Studies*, 7(3), pp. 265–280.

Sjöberg, Lennart (2004) "Local Acceptance of a High-Level Nuclear Waste Repository", *Risk Analysis*, 24(3), pp. 737–749.

Tashima, Yasuoki (2008) *"Nuclear War" in a Small Town that No One Knows*, Tokyo: WAC (in Japanese).

Vandenbosch, Robert and Susanne E. Vandenbosch (2007) *Nuclear Waste Stalemate: Political and Scientific Controversies*, Salt Lake City: University of Utah Press.

Yamaguchi, Akio, Shunsaku Komatsuzaki and Hideyuki Horii (2011) "Political Process Analysis of Radioactive Waste Disposal Site Selection in South Korea", *Sociotechnica*, 8, pp. 60–73 (in Japanese).

# 17
# The reintegration of welfare, the economy and the environment: Governance of post-productivist welfare

Taro Miyamoto

In the early twenty-first century, the connections among welfare policies, economic policies and environmental policies have become an issue. Welfare policies are directed toward achieving a sustainable society; economic policies are seeking sustainable economic and financial systems; and environmental policies are dedicated to achieving a sustainable natural environment. These three domains are intertwined, and all of them have fallen into difficulty.

This chapter attempts to survey the relationships among welfare, the economy and the environment, focusing on policies and systems within the larger context of twentieth-century welfare states and their transformation. Particular attention is paid to post-productivist approaches to welfare, which are aimed at forging new relationships between welfare policy and environmental policy. By combining these approaches with economic sustainability, I hope to uncover new possibilities for the integration of welfare, the economy and the environment within a new context.

In the first section, I review the relationships among welfare, the economy and the environment within the context of twentieth-century welfare states. In the second section, I discuss the emergence of new strategies intended to establish mutually supportive, paired relationships among these three domains. In the third and fourth sections, I explore the emergence and development of post-productivist approaches to welfare. Finally, in the last section, I consider what kind of governance is required to realize these approaches.

## Twentieth-century welfare states and productivism

### Twentieth-century welfare states

It has often been observed that the simultaneous realization of welfare, economic growth and environmental conservation is problematic. This difficulty has been defined against the background of the form of the welfare state that supported the lives of people living in advanced industrialized societies in the twentieth century. Twentieth-century welfare states were mechanisms through which excess wealth produced by continuous economic growth was redistributed via social security based on progressive tax systems and cash benefits.

These welfare states were first and foremost dependent on the growth of heavy and chemical industries, which consumed large amounts of natural resources. These industries were in turn supported by the procurement (through an asymmetrical relationship between developed and developing countries) of inexpensive primary resources from developing countries, as well as cheap crude oil under the control of the Seven Sisters (the seven major international oil companies). In the name of free trade, these relationships were codified under the General Agreement on Tariffs and Trade (GATT). In the negotiating process that led to the GATT, Keynes and others in the British Foreign Office put forth a proposal that contained the concept of a system for guaranteeing the prices of primary resources taken from developing countries, but it was never accepted (Oku, 2001). As a result, the heavy and chemical industries of the developed countries realized a "Fordist" economic system based on mass production and consumption, which placed a heavy burden on the natural environment in both developed and resource-rich developing countries.

The social security systems of twentieth-century welfare states were based on this economic system of mass production and consumption. Social security posited the stable employment of a male worker within growing industries, based on the assumption that he would support a family. Therefore, its main function was to ensure that a worker had social insurance to compensate him if his source of income was interrupted because of injury, illness, layoff or retirement. Specifically, it took such forms as workman's compensation insurance, medical insurance, unemployment insurance and annuities. Furthermore, public assistance programs were established to help people who found it impossible to acquire social insurance coverage on their own.

To ensure that this system functioned smoothly, governments applied Keynesian economic policies in an effort to avert the boom-and-bust cycles that accompany mass production/consumption economic systems, thereby securing the conditions needed to sustain the employment of male workers. For example, they engaged in large-scale public works projects in times of economic downturn to stimulate business activity and stabilize employment. This was an important function of twentieth-century welfare states. The welfare systems themselves also functioned to adjust economic cycles by absorbing excess wealth through progressive taxes when the economy was booming, and paying out benefits to supplement people's income when the economy flagged. The stability of workers' incomes was a necessary condition for the maintenance of the mass production/consumption economic system. But strictly speaking, welfare was financed by surplus wealth generated by economic growth and did not in itself function to support economic growth.

*Types of twentieth-century welfare states*

We must remember, however, that twentieth-century welfare states came in many forms. Many different entities (including labour movements and social democratic and Christian democratic political parties) strove to introduce social security systems for many different reasons (including the achievement of social equality and stability). Thus, the way that twentieth-century welfare states were constituted varied.

If we apply the well-known typologies developed by Esping-Andersen (1990), we can discern three regime types: the social democratic regime, characterized by an influential labour movement and an advanced state of social equality (the Scandinavian model); the conservative regime, characterized by strong Christian socialist influence (the Continental European model); and the liberal regime, characterized by a weak labour movement, or one with gradually declining influence, and free-market principles brought to the fore (the Anglo-Saxon model). Whatever the type, however, twentieth-century welfare states all had a productivist aspect that depended on economic growth, as described earlier. That is, they led to a deepening dilemma in which the continued reproduction of the social economy made it difficult to reproduce natural conditions.

This productivist character is even more pronounced in East Asian countries, which emerged as welfare states later than the countries of Europe and North America. In Asia, modernization and economic growth had to be given priority, with no choice but to relegate welfare policy and social policy to a role as supplements of development (Deyo, 1992: 304). Therefore, Holliday (2000) attempted to educe a distinctively East Asian welfare regime in contrast to those found in the West, characterized by social policy that is subservient to an economic policy oriented toward growth. According to this formulation, the East Asian welfare regime is a fourth type that takes its place beside the three regimes identified by Esping-Andersen, and can be called "productivist welfare".

Setting aside for the moment the question of whether or not Holliday's formulation is valid, it certainly does appear that, in Japan's case, public works and other economic policies have functioned as a means of guaranteeing people's incomes (Miyamoto, 2008b). There is no doubt that Japanese-style business management policies have given priority to stabilizing primary incomes within a market context more than social security or social policy, including guaranteeing the livelihood of the male breadwinner and thereby supporting his family. To put it another way, Japan's welfare state has a strong tinge of productivist welfare.

To the extent that all of the twentieth-century welfare state regimes have continued to rely on the expansion of production to support social security, however, none of them is without a productivist character. The Scandinavian countries, to be sure, have lower dependence on primary income than Japan does, and the time people spend outside the labour market is greater. This means that they have made greater progress in post-commercializing labour. However, the various welfare stipends and services provided by the state were developed for the purpose of supporting people's employment, which is assumed. In this sense, the Scandinavian countries were called "productivist" by Esping-Andersen (1999: 80). It turned out that post-commercialization and productivism were not contradictory.

*The crisis in productivist welfare*

The productivist welfare states of the twentieth century face great difficulty, against a backdrop that can be characterized by three points.

First, the necessary condition of continuous growth that provides the basis for the heavy and chemical industries has dissolved. In 1973, the price of crude oil quadrupled with the outbreak of the Yom Kippur War, igniting resource nationalism and initiating a change in the power relationship between developed countries and resource-rich countries. Many of the latter were emerging as new markets themselves, effectively putting an end to the era in which developed countries could expect to grow on the basis of cheap resources. The process that began at this time continues to restrict the manufacturing industries of developed countries today.

Parallel to this, the international mobility of capital intensified, thereby breaking down the Bretton Woods system that made it possible to apply Keynesian economic policies that sought to control capital flows. The United States and other developed countries strategically used this to their advantage by shifting their focus to the financial sector and boosting profits through deregulation. This strategy of financial capitalism, the so-called Washington Consensus, became the foundation for the neo-liberalism that emerged in political and economic trends.

Second, the stable employment of the male worker and the cohesiveness of the family he supported, which was a necessary condition for sustained growth, began to break down. As discussed earlier, twentieth-century welfare states all depended to some degree on the units of employment and family. The fruits of economic growth founded on heavy and chemical industries were passed on to society through the circuits of the stable employment of male workers and the families they supported. But as the economies of the developed countries shifted to the financial and service sectors, male employment became destabilized and the labour market became more fluid. Also, in response to the emerging service economy, more women began to enter the workforce to supplement the incomes of male workers, catalysing change in the family unit. Social security systems could no longer take stable employment and cohesive families for granted.

Third, as a consequence of the preceding, the labour market became increasingly characterized by a repulsive force. As labour productivity increased, less labour time was needed to support the current standard of living. This means that the overall employment rate in developed countries is declining, despite the fact that people are having fewer children and the average age of the population is increasing (Rifkin, 1995). It also means that the tax base for welfare states is shrinking. At the same time, unemployment benefits and public support for people outside the labour market are increasing, putting a strain on welfare state finances. These conditions, coupled with a slackening in economic growth, have exacerbated the financial crisis and threatened the very foundation of productivist welfare.

## Paired relationships of welfare, the economy and the environment

### Triad of welfare, the economy and the environment

Twentieth-century welfare states maintained a precarious balance while creating relationships of tension among the three domains of economy, welfare and environment, as discussed earlier. These states achieved economic growth through heavy and chemical industries that placed a heavy burden on the natural environment, and used the excess "waste" wealth as a financial resource for social security. However, changes in the global market economy pushed developed countries to evolve service economies, thereby removing the conditions that made such a balance possible.

As a result, many symptoms have emerged that indicate the dysfunction of the economy and of social security in developed countries, including rising unemployment rates, a broadening gap between rich and poor, lower birth rates and social isolation. At the same time, the outlook for sustaining the earth's environment has grown increasingly bleak. Far from achieving a successful balance among the economy, welfare and environment, all three of these domains are now faced with crisis.

In the midst of this emergency, is it possible to create a system in which all three domains support each other? How can we change the relationships that such factors as the economy and employment have with social security, and how can we redesign their relationship to the natural environment? At first glance, it seems to be an extremely difficult problem, but there have been several proposed strategies that seek to strengthen the connections between different pairs of these three domains in such a way that they revive each other's functions. The configuration of this discussion is shown in Figure 17.1.

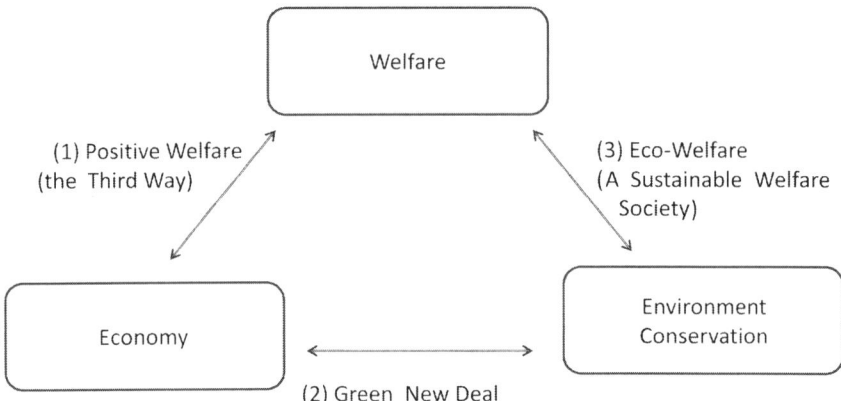

Figure 17.1 Paired relationships of welfare, the economy and the environment
*Source:* Taro Miyamoto

In the following sections, I continue the argument by re-summarizing the various systems involved and making the following distinctions: the domain concerned with the reproduction of the next generation (social security, education), the domain concerned with the reproduction of the social economy (employment, economy) and the domain concerned with the reproduction of the natural environment (natural environment).

*Social security and the economy*

With the twentieth-century welfare states facing crisis, attention has once again focused on how to revise the relationship between social security and the economy on one hand, with employment on the other (see the relationship marked by (1) in Figure 17.1). For many twentieth-century welfare states that have focused their social security efforts on providing public assistance to the poor and pensions to the elderly, social security and the economy have been in a contradictory relationship. However, as mentioned previously, the Scandinavian countries have succeeded in achieving both substantial social security and economic growth.

The Scandinavians have been successful because they supported economic growth through supportive social security systems that were designed to increase people's capabilities and widen their participation in society through such means as public job-training programs, lifelong learning, and child-care and nursing-care services. At this time, the solidity of conventional employment and family has been shaken, intensifying the need for support in the form of employment assistance, child care and nursing care. The supply of such services, however, provides new employment opportunities.

Based on experiences such as these, Anglo-Saxon countries are also pursuing the strategy of trying to improve economic efficiency by supporting employment on the basis of social security. The "Third Way" touted by the Blair administration defined social security as "positive welfare" and attempted to heighten its economic impact. As such, it symbolized an approach based on a new concept.

In Japan, the Kan administration similarly proposed a Japanese-style Third Way, defined as a "strong social security" system that was linked to a strong economy and strong financial system. The Japanese political/economic system, which was rapidly heading toward dissolution, was constituted in such a way as to expand the economy while stabilizing male employment and to nurture families through earned income. These attributes were supposed to serve as a substitute for social security functions as well. However, when the system stopped functioning, the government began to search for a way to strengthen new social security functions while promoting the synergistic development of social security, employment and the economy.

There are three ways to realize a virtuous cycle between social security and the economy. The first is to use social security to enhance people's capabilities in order to heighten the competitiveness of the post-industrial economy. If childcare services provide young people with a high-quality preschool education, it will heighten future abilities and nurture basic cognitive skills that can help people adapt to changing needs for human capital regardless of the economic status of their families. In this context, public vocational education programs and lifelong education outside of schools that are based on positive labour market policies become more significant.

Second, public assistance costs can be reduced if household incomes can be increased through participation and employment in social security. And third, the peace of mind that comes as a result of social security helps to increase spending among seniors and other consumers. With the dissolution of the "trickle down" approach, in which the fruits of economic growth are automatically distributed fairly throughout society, it becomes crucially important to create the previously mentioned conditions in order to stimulate economic growth.

*The economy and the environment*

There has been a contradictory relationship between the expansion/growth of the economy and employment on one hand, and environmental issues such as global warming on the other. Efforts are being made to transform this contradictory relationship into a multiple one. Twentieth-century economies were driven by the growth of heavy and chemical industries that depended on cheap primary resources and oil. However, rises in the price of natural resources, which occurred due to changes in the power relationship between developed countries and resource-rich countries, has pushed up the cost of intermediate input and, particularly in competitive sectors, reduced marginal profits. It has also forced declines in labour costs.

According to Mizuno (2011), Japanese manufacturing industries posted an increase of 48.8 trillion yen in sales between 1998 and 2007. However, a

52.4-trillion-yen increase in intermediate input (higher resource costs) meant a decline of 3.6 trillion yen in profits during that same period. This resulted in a decline in Japan's growth rate, but if renewable energy can be substituted for 10 per cent of the mineral fuel now used, it is predicted that Japan will achieve a 1.2 per cent increase in the growth rate of its gross domestic income (GDI). Reducing dependence on fossil fuels and increasing energy efficiency will help companies achieve profits and increase employment, both directly and indirectly.

The Green New Deal proposed by President Obama of the United States indicated a new connection between economic growth and environmental issues. Progress is being made on doubling the production of renewable energy and building a new smart grid to distribute electrical power. The idea is to create 5 million jobs dedicated to installing solar panels and wind turbines, manufacturing fuel-efficient cars and constructing energy-efficient buildings, thereby linking work undertaken to control greenhouse gas emissions with an expansion in employment and the economy. Government plays an important role in providing incentives for this kind of investment through such means as feed-in law, renewable energy programmes and environmental taxes.

Green jobs created in this way can be acquired through short- and mid-term vocational training and are resistant to overseas outsourcing because they are linked with facilities connected to localized life. To first strengthen the connection between social security and economic growth (see the pair marked (1) in Figure 17.1) Obama insisted that he was enhancing the role of support-type public services, such as government-funded job-training programs in his economic policies outlined on www.change.gov and numerous speeches during the 2008 election campaign. If these efforts lead to the expansion and permanent establishment of green jobs, it will be possible to discern a link between the pair marked (1) with the pair marked (2) in Figure 17.1.

*Social security and the environment*

A new search has also begun for connections between social security/education and the environment. New visions are being espoused that aim for a social security that can coexist with a sustainable natural environment, including the "post-productivist welfare" of Richard Goodin (2001), the "eco-welfare" of Tony Fitzpatrick (2003) and the "sustainable welfare society" of Yoshinori Hiroi (2006b).

Twentieth-century welfare states depended on the growth of heavy and chemical industries, connected mass production with mass consumption through such means as income policy, and redistributed the fruits of growth. It seems acceptable to say that some kind of productivism supported the continuation of the welfare state. However, the market for durable goods, which has until now served as a symbol of people's prosperity, has shown signs of gradual saturation, and with the permeation of information terminals in the wake of the information technology (IT) revolution, people have felt a greater need for consuming "meaningful time" and forming societal relationships. The focus has shifted from income flow to income stock, with greater importance attached to providing people with the basis for living. Concerning the financial sources for social security, as well, there's been a shift from surtaxes on employment to a surtax on the emission of greenhouse gases and other similar changes. That is, the relationship between social security and the economy is undergoing major changes.

In the background of this transformation can be found the advent of "recursive modernization", which is a major change in society. That is, people's lives, which are the foundation of twentieth-century welfare states, have been supported by the existence of a variety of communities, including familial ties and communal connections. In fact, it was precisely because social relationships were supported in this way that attention could be concentrated on income and the consumption of goods.

However, those communal bonds have been loosening, first in the family and then in the community at large, while the labour market has grown more fluid. Under these conditions, people no longer possess a stable place within the social relationships of local communities and workplaces. They become exposed individuals with extremely unstable ties to society. Within this context, the issue of social security changes. As Goodin (2001) emphasizes, certain conditions have arisen in connection with "post-productivist welfare", including people's desire to participate in a variety of communities and spend meaningful time, not only by receiving support for work but also by reducing their work hours and seeking a balance between work and other aspects of their lives.

In recent years, analyses of social consciousness have been conducted from the perspective of happiness research, and the potential for post-productivist welfare has increased. As Frey's (2010) research has recently indicated, once people's income passes a certain point, the importance of human bonds developed in the workplace, the family and the local community increases as a factor in determining happiness. Unemployment is a huge factor in the loss of human happiness, and the existence and the amount of unemployment benefits received are not important variables. The fact that unemployment disrupts the relationship of mutual recognition between people and their society is precisely the source of the damage that unemployment causes (Frey, 2010).

## A vision for post-productivist welfare

### Post-productivist welfare

We have examined three strategies for relating different pairs of the three domains of welfare, the economy and the environment. If, for example, the strategy of post-productivist welfare that connects welfare with the environment as discussed above can be linked to a stable economy, there is a stronger prospect for achieving a complete triad of welfare, economy and environment.

To explore this vision more deeply, let's begin by reviewing the discussions that have been carried out to date concerning post-productivist welfare. Recently in the field of comparative research on welfare states, several researchers have distinguished post-productivist welfare from conventional productivist welfare itself and examined the former's potential. These include Goodin, mentioned earlier, and Van der Veen and Groot (Goodin, 2001; Van der Veen and Groot, 2005). Goodin asserts that all types of twentieth-century welfare states were deeply tinged with productivist welfare. Their respective emphases may have varied (the Anglo-Saxon type could be characterized as "work, not welfare", the Continental European type as "work through welfare" and the Scandinavian type as "welfare and work"), but all of them strongly demanded that people who received state welfare benefits must work. In examples from Japan and other East Asian countries, in which employment serves as a substitute for social security, the productivist tendency is even more pronounced.

In contrast to this, Goodin focuses on trends in the welfare state of the Netherlands, where part-time employment and its attendant rights to social security benefits are treated as equal to that of full-time work, thus achieving a work-sharing system. Although the employment rate is low and total hours worked are comparatively few, the poverty rate is kept under control. There is no unnecessary mobilization in the labour market, and a certain level of welfare is realized. This type of welfare state might be characterized as "welfare without work". It is here that Goodin discerned the potential of post-productivist welfare.

However, Goodin's discussion does not reveal how post-productivist welfare can be linked to a new economic strategy. Even if post-productivist welfare does break free of the work methods generally employed in twentieth-century welfare states, post-productivist welfare itself requires new a economic system which is compatible with natural environment.

*"Ecological modernization" and a "fully active society"*

If it is true that post-productivist welfare can be linked with sustainability in both the natural environment and in the market economy system, how exactly does it work? This issue can be addressed by a variety of standards.

If people can extend the time they spend outside the labour market, it represents an increase in the consumption of time, as opposed to the consumption of goods. This gives birth to conditions that foster the growth of personal service industries, which place less of a burden on the environment. Further, if this extended time is linked to growth in people's knowledge or abilities, it will accelerate a shift toward knowledge industries. The introduction of environmental taxes levied on the consumption of fossil fuels and other resources will promote technical investment in a preference for energy efficiency, which would further accelerate a conversion to a new industrial structure.

In other words, this is a strategy that tries to heighten sustainability by increasing the sophistication of industrial society. One example is found in the discussion of "ecological modernization" that has taken place primarily in Germany (Jänicke, 2008; Nagaoka, 1996). In contrast to this, there is another approach that attempts to achieve the basic reform of industrial society itself.

In their Club of Rome report published in 1996 titled *The Employment Dilemma and the Future of Work*, Giarini and Liedtke assert that a layered structure of new social activity makes it possible to reduce labour hours. Compared with remunerated work, the relative importance of unremunerated work is increasing. Unremunerated work can be further divided into non-monetized work, which is aimed at solving the problems of other people, and non-monetarized work, which is aimed at solving one's own problems or acquiring such things as knowledge, training or healing for oneself.

Non-monetized unremunerated work includes volunteer activities and efforts directed toward solving the problems of others through associations, not-for-profit organizations and the like. Although little of it is mediated through money, such work shares with remunerated work the premise of mutuality among people. In contrast, non-monetarized work corresponds with the self-sufficient activities that people engage in for their own sakes and that of their families in agricultural societies. With the transformation from agricultural through industrial society to today's service society, service consumers have increased their involvement in learning, healing, sports and other activities that relate to partial self-service production. Today, people are expanding the personal activities they engage in for their own sakes.

The Club of Rome report proposes a redesign of our workweek so that 20 hours of work a week provides a guaranteed minimum livelihood. Local governments supply the working conditions for what might be called basic work. People who do not wish to work more than that can expand the time they spend on unremunerated work, including both non-monetized (work for others) and non-monetarized (work for self) work. Through various combinations of these three types of work, it will become possible to solve the day-to-day problems that confront us.

The research of Williams and Windebank (2003) clearly shows that this potential is already becoming a reality. To correctly gauge the relationship between work and poverty, they extracted 44 items that are necessary for maintaining a household, including such tasks as cleaning, house maintenance, cooking and childrearing. Then they conducted surveys in 11 localities in Great Britain, including Southampton and Sheffield, and looked at how many of the items considered necessary were realized in the surveyed households under various employment conditions. Among unemployed households, 43.4 per cent of the items were not realized, whereas in low-income households with dual incomes, 48.9 per cent were unrealized (Williams and Windebank, 2003: 90). The pressure to work breaks down community ties and living capabilities, thus obstructing the fulfilment of various household functions. If this is true, then a shift from a "fully employed" society to a "fully active society" that supports multiple layers of social activity is the key to improving people's welfare.

There is no inherent conflict between the "ecological modernization" concept and the "fully active society" concept, but they do not overlap completely. There is a tension between the two with regard to where the main emphasis lies. The former seeks to generate synergy between economic growth and environmental conservation; the latter seeks to expand the connections among people outside the arena of the market economy. Much debate must still be undertaken to determine what kind of systemic basis is best for post-productivist welfare.

## Post-productivist welfare and social inclusion

### What is social inclusion?

Two visions have been described earlier regarding coping with the crisis faced by twentieth-century welfare states. The first is the reconstruction of productivist welfare; the second is post-productivist welfare. In the following section, I look at how these two approaches are manifested on a more concrete policy level.

The functional failure of the productivism of twentieth-century welfare states began when the labour market became increasingly repulsive, meaning that it became harder for people to find work. In response, particularly in Europe, observers began to debate the concept of social inclusion. This term refers to socially reintegrating people who have been rejected by the labour market and have become socially isolated, instead of just letting them stay in their isolated state. The term *social inclusion*, however, means different things in terms of specific policy options depending on the position of the persons advocating it. To clarify this, I have created the following framework.

The first issue that comes to mind when people talk of social inclusion is the question of where the inclusion occurs. In Europe, it is generally thought that inclusion occurs in the labour market—that is, that people reintegrate by finding jobs. But if the labour market is the only place where people can be subsumed, it seems likely to limit how the problems confronted today by productivist welfare can be addressed. In addition, unless there is some kind of assurance that people can receive education outside the labour market, involve themselves in childrearing and nursing care, or participate in various localized activities, it will be difficult for them to independently participate in the labour market itself. Therefore, many observers today are refuting the idea of social inclusion as a mobilization strategy aimed at the labour market and are asserting that inclusion should mean activity pursued by people outside the labour market (Jordan, 1998).

Another issue is what means should be adopted to achieve inclusion. The first approach is to require people to participate in society in some way, whether inside or outside the labour market. For example, if a person is given a job offer and declines it, he or she might be subject to various penalties. This approach might be called "compulsory participation".

The second approach is to remove difficulties or impediments that prevent participation. An example is vocational training for those who lack the skills to participate in the labour market. We can call this approach "obstacle removal". The third approach is to increase the rewards for participating in society in whatever form. Examples include higher compensation for both labour and for civic activity. Let's call this "rewarded participation". If we combine the two domains and three methods of inclusion, we get the matrix shown in Table 17.1.

Compulsory participation in the labour market (Column I [1] in Table 17.1) is generally called "workfare". A typical example is Temporary Assistance for Needy Families (TANF) in the United States. This system, which was initiated in 1996, requires single heads of households to work in order to qualify for public assistance. They lose their eligibility for public funds if they work fewer 30 hours a week. In Japan, a "new safety net" was proposed at the national governors and mayors conference held in October 2006, which limits the amount of time that livelihood protection is provided.

Policies and programs that fall under the rubric of removing obstacles from the labour market (Column I [2] in Table 17.1) include vocational training and, with a view to promoting female employment, support services for nursing care and childcare. Liberals affiliated with the Democratic Party in the United States fought against I (1)-style workfare, but they were unable to leave unattended the swelling ranks of public assistance recipients outside the labour market. They therefore began proposing I (2) policies that shifted focus away from compulsory labour and toward the removal of obstacles that prevented people from working.

Table 17. 1 Diversity of social inclusion strategies

|  | I Labor market | II Local communities and families |
|---|---|---|
| (1) Compulsory participation | Obligation to work in return for public assistance (Workfare) | Learnfare |
| (2) Assisted participation | Vocational training Child-care services | Shorter working hours |
| (3) Rewarded participation | Negative income tax | Participation income |

Neo-liberalism: Focuses on I (1)
Third Way: Focuses on I (1) and I (2), and partially on I (3)
Post-productivism: Emphasizes II (2) and II (3)
*Source:* Taro Miyamoto

Liberal researchers such as Ellwood, as well as "New Democrats" such as Bill Clinton, who were influenced by them, partially accepted the logic of workfare while asserting the need for vocational training programs and child-care services (Ellwood, 1988).

Policies that fall under the category of creating labour market incentives (Column I [3] in Table 17.1) include economic incentives such as a minimum wage system, and a tax rebate system implemented as a condition of employment, such as the Earned Income Tax Credit (EITC) in the United States. Unlike a conventional income tax, the EITC is a mechanism whereby households (particularly those with children) receive cash from the government if they are employed but have an earned income that fails to reach a prescribed level. When the workfare-style TANF was introduced by the Clinton administration, Clinton himself tried to substantially expand I (2)–type work support policies, but failed to do so because of resistance from Republicans in the House of Representatives. Instead, he significantly improved the standards for EITC benefits. The influence of the New Democrats was felt in Great Britain as well, with the Labour Party instituting welfare reforms under the slogan "From Welfare to Work" and introducing a new minimum wage.

Regarding environmental incentives more broadly, there are systems that offer labour-management incentives such as job diversification and expansion, as well as policies such as codetermination laws that expand economic democracy. When work absenteeism became a problem in Europe, adherents of social democracy focused their efforts on this kind of expansion of economic democracy as a means of creating work incentives.

Let us turn now to the second domain of inclusion, namely a wider participation in various local community activities. It might seem difficult to apply compulsory participation (Column II [1] in Table 17.1) to this category, but in fact, there are examples of it in such places as the state of Wisconsin in the United States. If students attend class fewer than a prescribed number of days, the public assistance received by their parents can be re-evaluated in a system called "learnfare". Even without such tricky examples, we can find similar arrangements in traditional Japanese communities and marriage practices (families), where various social penalties that functioned implicitly were imposed on non-participants. With the hollowing out of these traditional norms, discussions are arising that call for the systematization of mandatory participation in volunteer work, admittedly a somewhat oxymoronic concept.

Let us turn now to column II (2) in Table 17.1, which deals with removing obstacles to participation in local communities. In cases where it is difficult to spend meaningful time in communities and families, obstacles to participation can be broadly divided into the following two types. The first type is characterized by individuals who, because of physical or psychological weakness, do not enjoy the conditions necessary for a vibrant life. In such cases, support services are needed to encourage autonomy in their lives. The second type is characterized by individuals who may have the ability and desire to participate in local communities and families but who find themselves restricted by long working hours or excessive externally-imposed physical or psychological burdens. In such cases, policies and systems are needed that shorten work time and help people achieve a better work–life balance.

Finally, let us consider policies and systems intended to encourage participation in local society (Column II [3] in Table 17.1). Looking first at economic incentives, various mechanisms have been designed to provide an economic evaluation of unremunerated work in the community and family. Beck, for example, proposes a "citizen wage" that is given to people on the condition that they engage in voluntary community activities or participate in politics (Beck, 2000: 143). It is probably possible to also apply, to communities or families, concepts aimed at creating environmental incentives through such means as improving employment conditions in the workplace or expanding economic democracy. If families can shed their erstwhile nature as cramped spaces restricted by the authority of prestigious members and division of labour according to gender roles, they can become venues of rich personal interaction and serve in and of themselves as incentive for participation.

*Three strategies for social inclusion*

The various approaches outlined earlier that aimed at achieving social inclusion in the broad sense have been prescribed as a means of addressing the problems confronting twentieth-century welfare states. Each of the three trends of neo-liberalism, the Third Way and post-productivism discussed in the previous section chooses different approaches or combinations of approaches to social inclusion.

Neo-liberalism centres on inclusion in the labour market and attempts to achieve not through high support costs but rather through mandated labour. In other words, it is a workfare approach centred on I (1), through which people are semi-coerced into staying in the labour market. In contrast, the Third Way not only accepts part of the workfare mentality espoused by neo-liberalism but also advocates various services designed to support labour (I [2]), while boosting the rewards received for work (I [3]). For example, Great Britain's Labour Party advocated, through its "Welfare New Deal" policies, counselling and a number of work experience programs while introducing a minimum wage and providing improved tax exemptions for working households.

Although the emphasis of the Third Way approach is clearly different from that of neo-liberalism, both continue the productivism of twentieth-century welfare states. In contrast, the example found by Goodin (2001) in the Netherlands focused on removing obstacles to participation in society outside the labour market through systemic reforms that induce the possibility of shorter work hours through such means as awarding equal rights to part-time workers. It was hoped that such measures would expand a participatory kind of welfare in which citizens themselves adapt to diverse welfare needs. This kind of systemic reform can be seen as falling under category II (2). The goals set forth in the 1996 Club of Rome report also focus on a shift in the use of human time from remunerated labour to volunteer activities in the local community (including unremunerated work and self-improvement activities; Giarini and Liedtke, 1996).

Basic income is a policy often thought to belong to the lineage of post-productivist welfare. As a variation on that theme, Atkinson and others espouse participatory income, which provides compensation for various kinds of unremunerated work done outside the labour market, such as education and housework (Atkinson, 1996). As discussed previously, Williams and others identify activities such as childrearing and volunteering as appropriate objects for tax exemption benefits; these too, are policies aimed at achieving the same effect. Such efforts can be thought of as belonging in category II (3), which focuses on providing incentives for people to be active in spheres other than the labour market.

## Pluralistic, multilayered governance of post-productivist welfare

### *The normative structure of post-productivist welfare*

The schema of conflict associated with the concept of social inclusion is also associated with the governance of post-twentieth-century welfare states and the normative structures that support it (Miyamoto, 2006).

As the number of people outside the labour market grows, conflict associated with the normative principles that support welfare states expands. The neo-liberal scenario focuses on reiterating mandated labour, with an emphasis on the relationship of correspondence between performance in the labour market and income, including social benefits. Viewed from the perspective of reciprocity, the normative principle supporting welfare states under the neo-liberal scenario is one that demands strong reciprocity between performance in the labour market and benefits received. In terms of governance, this scenario seeks to control disturbances in the financial foundation while cutting back regulations and reducing the size of government.

The Third Way, on the other hand, seeks normative reorganization while taking into account the growing negative reaction against freeloaders who take advantage of the welfare state. As already discussed in relation to social inclusion, the basic orientation of the Third Way places greater emphasis than neo-liberalism does on providing support for labour and enhancing the compensation received in return for work. Therefore, such measures as counselling for the long-term unemployed, vocational training and other support services are considered only natural. At the same time, however, those who receive such services are strongly expected to fulfil their responsibilities by working. In this case, then, the relationship between performance in the labour market and social benefits is not as direct as it is in neo-liberalism, but strong reciprocity still exists.

As described earlier, government functions under the Third Way focus on injecting people into the labour market and improving their quality as human resources. In order to enhance the competitive position of the nation, the size of the government is not in itself a decisive issue. To borrow from Giddens (1998), the goal is to transform the welfare state into a "social investment state".

Then what kind of governance will advance the cause of post-productivist welfare? As noted earlier, many aspects of the systemic vision of post-productivist welfare are yet to be determined. That being said, it seems likely that the post-productivist scenario will bring with it the boldest transformation of governance and normative structure.

The issues related to post-productivist welfare are not the same as those found in neo-liberalism, with its emphasis on forcing people to stay in the labour market, or in the Third Way, with its goals of increasing the rewards received from the labour market and supporting people in their quest for employment. Rather, the role of post-productivist welfare, at least as it stands now, is to expand the conditions under which people who occasionally leave or stay out of the labour market can work to solve a variety of problems in their local communities. Or, its role is to make it possible for people to frequently enter and leave the labour market, and to help them realize their potential abilities and work sharing.

Compared with arguments concerning the norms of neo-liberalism and Third Way, the concept of post-productivist welfare seeks more "diverse reciprocity" (Fitzpatrick, 2003: 46–51). According to Fitzpatrick, reciprocity cannot be thought of as limited to a short-term time frame or to just the labour market. The mere fact of being outside the labour market does not instantly release people from their civic duties. It is also a mistake to inappropriately disparage unremunerated care activities in comparison with wage-earning labour. Restricting reciprocity to a short-term time frame and to relationships between individuals, he argues, makes it impossible to elicit responsible behaviour between generations with regard to the natural environment.

However, not even Fitzpatrick has yet come up with a clear framework for a more broadly defined reciprocity. Not only that, but no agreement has been reached concerning the importance of making reciprocity an issue as well (Jordan, 1998: 61; Fitzpatrick, 2005). This problem, which impinges on the political feasibility of post-productivist welfare, must be discussed more deeply.

*Decentralized, pluralistic governance*

In post-productivist welfare, local governments will play a larger role than before. It will become increasingly necessary for people who leave the labour market to learn new skills, or to receive care or counselling to heal weakened bodies and hearts, or to become involved with nursing care or child care, or to participate in vocational training programs so that they can re-enter the labour market. Public services that meet these diverse needs must be available near the people who need them and be responsive to people's various individualized conditions.

To achieve this, the role of non-profit organizations (NPOs) and cooperatives as the organizations in charge of public services is likely to increase. Neo-liberalism and the Third Way take the same approach toward strengthening the role of private-sector, non-profit organizations. For neo-liberalism, this course is seen as a means of shrinking government; for the Third Way (as seen in the welfare New Deal of the Blair Administration), non-profits are the venue through which people can be reattached to the labor market (Miyamoto, 2005). In contrast, post-productivist welfare, which is concerned with expanding the time that people spend outside the labour market, views NPOs as the venue where people engage in activities that do not fall within the narrow definition of the market.

Post-productivism adopts the strategy of diminishing the relative weight of employment and labour. This strategy broadens the conditions for activity by NPOs and cooperatives. From the very start, emphasis is placed on expanding the domain of volunteer activity within people's portfolio of social activity. In addition (and this overlaps with the reason why the Third Way places emphasis on private-sector non-profits), the role played by private-sector NPOs is particularly large for anyone who wishes to be active, regardless of whether they are inside or outside the labour market.

For local communities, the problem is how to provide support to people with psychological or emotional problems that the people themselves have a hard time defining, or to young people who have shut themselves up at home and are unused to social interaction or to the elderly so that they can maintain autonomous lives. Government administrations don't possess the expertise required to provide this kind of support. This is precisely why private-sector organizations centring on NPOs and cooperatives are needed to take responsibility for providing services that deepen dialogue with the people and families concerned and that respect people's lifestyles.

Fitzpatrick (2003) contends that post-productivist welfare (eco-social welfare) must have an interactive system, and that democracy must be introduced into the welfare system. This is relevant to the point made earlier. Neo-liberalism was critical of the highly centralized twentieth-century welfare states because they transformed recipients of welfare services into passive clients. That criticism was not without merit, but the privatization sought by the neo-liberalists has transformed the recipients of welfare services into consumers. What is needed, however, is the injection of democracy into the domain of welfare services (Fitzpatrick, 2003: 178–179).

According to Fitzpatrick (2005), "welfare democracy" does not stop with the introduction of the logic of existing parliamentary democracy into the domains of social security or welfare. The democracy introduced must itself be a "deliberative democracy" that gives priority to discussion and dialogue or an "associative democracy" that emphasizes participation through groups, or some other new type of democracy. By broadening the scope of activity of diverse associations such as NPOs and cooperatives, it becomes possible to introduce these new democratic elements into the welfare domain.

*The role of the national government*

As we have seen, the role of local government would expand in post-productivist welfare, but the national government's role would also be large because it would continue to provide people with income security. However, that role would be very different from the one that national governments have played in social security and welfare systems in the past. Post-productivist welfare entails the frequent entrance and exit of people from the labour market. It is therefore difficult to support using an income security system that provides social security benefits keyed to job categories and that is closely tied to career earnings. What is needed is a more universal and integrated system.

At the same time, income security will no longer be able to replace the income received from regular employment solely with social security benefits when, for a variety of reasons, regular employment is interrupted. Irregular employment, which until now has been treated as an exceptional form of work, will in fact become the main form of employment. Therefore, it will become necessary to shift the system's emphasis from income replacement to income supplementation.

Adherents of post-productivism often advocate the abolition of income-tested social security and champion the introduction of a single, basic income. This is exemplified by the advocacy of basic income on the part of environmental political parties in Europe. The Green Party of Sweden, for example, calls for the introduction of "a form of citizen income or basic income" that will guarantee a basic income to all citizens regardless of previous income, and regardless of the reasons why income was lost. Then, with the basic security and free time thus achieved, a social economy can be created that is supported by wide-ranging citizen participation and the activities of social corporations and cooperatives that partially replace public-sector agencies that the fourth party program of the Green Party of Sweden adopted at the congress in May 2005.

Pure basic income raises questions concerning the possibility of reaching agreement and the sustainability of basic income as a system. Nevertheless, it will probably prove effective to incorporate the basic income concept to some degree as a means of integrating and universalizing current income security arrangements such as negative income taxes and benefits paid out through tax deduction systems. Furthermore, if social security can be integrated, and the risk that social security is intended to cover can be broadened in scope, a more flexible income security system can be established within the insurance system framework.

## Conclusion

In twentieth-century welfare states, there was a confrontational relationship among the domains of welfare, economy and environment that made it difficult to achieve beneficial results in all three domains simultaneously. This chapter has discussed the concepts and possibilities of a post-productionist welfare that transcends this trilemma. In doing so, it has explored the special characteristics of post-productivist welfare by comparing it with two other scenarios associated with the reform of twentieth-century welfare states, namely, neo-liberalism and the Third Way.

In the wake of the financial crisis that has greatly shaken the prestige of US-style capitalism, neo-liberalism no longer has the legitimacy it once had as dogma. On the other hand, because of ever-deepening financial limitations that have been felt as a result of the financial crisis, many countries are adopting neo-liberalism as the touchstone for welfare reform, just as they did before. Similarly, although champions of the Third Way such as Blair and Schröder have now left the scene, leaving the impression that the Third Way is a thing of the past, it continues to be influential as a liberal political force in many countries, and among policy advisors to the Organisation for Economic Co-operation and Development and other organizations.

In contrast, the post-productivist welfare scenario has not necessarily matured to the point that it should be implemented as a programme. This author does not agree with all of the arguments against productivist welfare either. Nevertheless, the neo-liberalist scenario offers no way to address the growing repulsiveness of the labour market, and the Third Way, which attempts to shift people into more competitive industrial sectors as a way of dealing with that repulsiveness, does not deal with the fact that such sectors are actually reducing the size of their work forces in the context of global market competition (Miyamoto, 2008a). The concept of post-productivist welfare, therefore, is one choice that should certainly be considered in future discussions concerning how to reform welfare.

## REFERENCES

Atkinson, Anthony B. (1996) "The Case for Participation Income", *The Political Quarterly*, 67(i), pp. 67–70.

Beck, Ulrich (2000) *The Brave New World of Work*, Cambridge: Polity Press.

Deyo, Frederic C. (1992) "The Political Economy of Social Policy Formation: East Asia's Newly Industrialized Countries", in R. P. Applebaum (ed.) *States and Development in the Asian Pacific Rim*, CA: Sage, pp. 267–306.

Ellwood, David. T. (1988) *Poor Support: Poverty in the American Family*, New York: Basic Books.

Esping-Andersen, Gøsta (1990) *The Three Worlds of Welfare Capitalism*, Cambridge: Polity Press.

—— (1999) *Social Foundations of Postindustrial Economies*, Oxford: Oxford University Press.

Fitzpatrick, Tony (2003) *After the New Social Democracy: Social Welfare for the Twenty-First Century*, Manchester: Manchester University Press.
—— (2005) "The Fourth Attempt to Construct a Politics of Welfare Obligations", *Policy & Politics*, 33(1), pp. 15–32.
Frey, Bruno S. (2010) *Happiness: A Revolution in Economics*, Cambridge, MA: MIT Press.
Giarini, Orio and Patrick M. Liedtke (1996) *Employment Dilemma and Future of Work: Report to the Club of Rome*, the Club of Rome.
Giddens, Anthony (1998) *The Third Way: The Renewal of Social Democracy*, Polity Press.
Goodin, Robert (2001) "Work and Welfare: Towards a Post-Productivist Welfare Regime", *British Journal of Political Science*, 31(1), pp. 13–39.
Hiroi, Yoshinori (2006a) *The Concept of "Another Japan" as a Sustainable Welfare Society*, Tokyo: Chikuma Shinsho.
—— (2006b) "The Concept of a 'Sustainable Welfare Society': Capitalism, Socialism and Ecology in a Steady-State Society", *Shiso Journal*, 983, pp. 8–26.
Holliday, Ian (2000) "Productivist Welfare Capitalism: Social Policy in East Asia", *Political Studies*, 48(4), pp. 706–723.
Jänicke, Martin (2008) "Ecological modernisation: new perspectives", *Journal of Cleaner Production*, 16(5), pp. 557–565.
Jordan, Bill (1998) *The New Politics of Welfare: Social Justice in a Global Context*, CA: Sage.
Miyamoto, Taro (2005) "Welfare Policy after the Third Way: Three Axes of Confrontation Associated with Social Inclusion", in Jiro Yamaguchi, Taro Miyamoto and Ariyoshi Ogawa (eds.) *The Challenge of Civic Social Democracy: Post-Third Way European Politics*, Tokyo: Nihon Keizai Hyouronsha Ltd, pp. 81–107.
—— (2006) "The Governance of Post-Productivist Welfare States: New Political Opposition", *Shiso Journal*, 983, pp. 27–47.
—— (2008a) "Globalization and Welfare Governance", *Gendai no Riron Journal*, 15, pp. 62–73.
—— (2008b) *Welfare Politics: Japan's Livelihood Security and Democracy,* Tokyo: Yuhikaku Publishing Co., Ltd.
Mizuno, Kazuo (2011) "New World Order and International Coordination System: 21st Century as Struggle between Land and Sea", in Naohiko Jino and Taro Miyamoto (eds.) *Overcoming Self-destructive Society: Visions for New Japan*, Tokyo: Iwanami Shoten Publishers, pp. 1–29.
Nagaoka, Nobutaka (1996) "The Challenge of 'Ecological Modernization' and Social Democracy: Sustainable Development, Social Justice, and New Individualism", University of Economics Thesis Collection, vol. 46, no. 5, pp. 41–70.
Oku, Kazuyoshi (2001) "Functions of International Trade System", in Takekazu Iwamoto, Kazuyoshi Oku, Akihiro Ogura, Jo-Seol Kim and Kaoru Hoshino, *Global Economy,* Tokyo: Yuhikaku Publishing Co, Ltd., pp. 38–74.
Rifkin, Jeremy (1995) *The End of Work: The Decline of the Global Labor Force and the Dawn of the Post-Market Era*, California: J. P. Tarcher,
Van der Veen, Robert and Loek Groot (2005) *Post-Productivist Welfare States: A Comparative Analysis*, ASSR Working Paper, 05/06, Amsterdam School for Social Science Research.
Williams, Colin, C. and Jan Windebank (2003) *Poverty and the Third Way*, London: Routledge.

# Index

Note: Page numbers with $b$, $f$, or $t$ indicate boxes, figures, or tables respectively.

Aalborg Charter, 234, 235, 240
Ackerman, B., 194–95
Adachi, Y., 137–52
adjusted net savings (ADJS), 23
aggregation, policy integration and, 32
Agyeman, J., 112–13, 115
Akizuki, K., 111
Alkire, S., 16, 17, 19–20, 22
Alliance '90/The Greens, 87
All Japan Anti-Nuclear Liaison Association, 258
Amari, A., 298
Amull, A., 68
anti-plutonium movements, 1992-2011, 261–63
antipollution movement, Nishiyodogawa Ward, 124–31
  Aozora Foundation and, 128–29
  compensation/pollution control, political actions for, 126–27
  lawsuit and public empathy, 127–28
  network building and, 130–31
  urban environments improvement and, 129–30
  victims' movements, 124–26
Aozora Foundation, 128–29
  local collectivity, reconstruction of, 133–34
  network building and, 130–31
  urban environment improvement and, 129–30
Argyris, C., 277, 278$f$
Asahi Shimbun, 269
Atkinson, A. B., 332
Atkinson, G., 273
Atkinson, R., 73, 74
Atomic Energy Commission (AEC), 149
Australia
  environmental governance in, 53
  environmental policy integration and, 34–35$t$
Austria, environmental policy integration and, 34–35$t$, 36

Bache, I., 62
Bakir, C., 242
Barbier, E. B., 108

bargaining democracy, 143
Barrett, B., 106, 113
Barry, B., 198
Barthe, Y., 295
Basic Environmental Ordinance (BEO), 111
Basic Environmental Plan (BEP).
    *See also* Environmental governance; Environmental metagovernance
    alternative approach to, 116
    elements of, 111–12
    environmental governance failure in, 112–15
    LA21 as, 111–12
Bataille, C., 309
Bataille Law, 309–10
Bawden, R., 290
Beck, U., 256, 331
Becker, T., 95
Belgium
    environmental governance in, 53
    environmental policy integration and, 34–35t, 36
Bell, S., 57, 243
Benford, R. D., 301
Benhabib, S., 194
Bentham, J., 140
Benz, A., 83
BEP. *See* Basic Environmental Plan (BEP)
Bevir, M., 122
biochemical oxygen demand (BOD), Yahagi River, 286f
Birraux, C., 295, 298
Blair, T., 238
Blaug, R., 190
Block, F., 223
Bohman, J., 194
Bovaired, T., 74
Bovens, M., 74
"Box 2.3 More democracy, better environment?," 155–56
Boyer, R., 66, 239
Bressers, H., 107–8
Brinkerhoff, D. W., 107
Brinkerhoff, J. M., 107
Broadbent, J., 106
Brown, J. W., 231

Browner, C., 37
Brundtland Commission, 30, 61
Buchanan, J. M., 146
Bull, B., 74
BUND, 91, 94, 95
Bundestag, 85, 87
Burke, E., 202
Bush, G. W., 252

Cacioppo, J. T., 295, 296
Cafruny, A., 68
Canada
    environmental governance in, 53
    environmental policy integration and, 34–35t
capability. *See also* human development
    Alkire framework proposal of, 19–21
    equality/expansion of, 16–17
    human development and, 12–13
    Malthusian theory and, 13
    sustainable development and, 11–13
*Capacity to Govern, The: A Report to the Club of Rome* (Dror), 147
Cardiff Process, 30
Chaiken, S., 295–96
Charter of European Cities and Towns towards Sustainability, 234
Chen Shui-bian, 254
Chhotray, V., 66, 106, 109
Chung, Ji-Bum, 294, 295
citizen deliberation, experts in, 197–99
Citizens Jury, 190, 191–92
Citizens' Nuclear Information Center, 258
civil society, global, 229–30
Climate Alliance, 71
climate change policies, in Japan, 97
Clinton, B., 238, 330
Club of Rome, 2
Cohen, J., 194
Collier, U., 32
Comim, F., 15, 21
Commission of the European Communities, 30
Competence Network for Distributed Energy Technologies (deENet), 93

comprehensiveness, policy integration and, 32
Comprehensive Plan (CP), 116–17
compulsory participation approach, 329, 329*t*
Comte, A., 140
Consensus Conference, 190, 192–93
consistency, policy integration and, 32
contemporary capitalism, 222–32
    constraints of, 222
    economic growth and, 225–29
    global governance and, 229–32
    self-regulating market and, 223–25
control of corruption (CC), 160, 161
cooperative governance by various actors strategy, 85
Council of European Union, 68, 73
Covenant of Mayors, 71
CP. *See* Comprehensive Plan (CP)
Crosby, N., 191
Czech Republic
    environmental governance in, 53
    environmental policy integration and, 34–35*t*, 36


*Daigo Fukuryu Maru* (tuna trawler), 257
Daly, H. E., 225–27
Damasio, A., 296
Danish Board of Technology, 192
Darst, R. G., 294
Dasgupta, P., 4, 5
*datsu genpatsu nau* (denuclearization now), 268
Dawson, J. I., 294
decentralization, 234–47
    commodifying and, 240–41
    definition of, 234
    deliberative democracy and, 237–38
    genealogies of, 238–43
    governance theories and, 242–43
    Habermas's steering media and, 241–42
    social system/ecosystem relationship and, 235–37, 236*f*
    sustainable development and, 243–46
Delia, R., 53
deliberate, word origin of, 201–2

deliberation, expert-assisted citizen, 191–94
deliberative democracy, 237–38
deliberative democratic theory, 189–202
    categories of, 194
    experimental, promise and peril of, 194–97
    expert-assisted citizen, 191–94
    experts in citizen deliberation and, 197–99
    objections and responses to, 199–201
    overview of, 189–91
Deliberative Polling, 190, 193–94
*Democracy and Development: Political Institutions and Well-Being in the World, 1950–1990* (Przeworski), 155, 156, 156*f*
democracy and sustainable development, 137–52
    critique of, 139–41
    future generations and, responsibility to, 142–43
    Japanese regulatory reform and, 148–51
    overview of, 137–38
    principle of, 138–39
    reforms for correcting, 143–46
    self-restraint mechanisms for, 146–48
Democratic Party of Japan (DPJ), 82
Denmark
    environmental governance in, 53
    environmental policy integration and, 34–35*t*
Designated Radioactive Waste Final Disposal Act, 296
De Tocqueville, Alexis, 105
"Development by Displacement," 17
development initiatives, 17
Dewey, J., 189
Deyo, F. C., 319
Diedrichs, U., 69, 73
Dienel, P., 192
Dingeldey, I., 66
Directorate-General Environment, 73
Dobson, A., 198
Drèze, J., 24–25
Dror, Y., 147–48
Dryzek, J., 123, 133, 190

Earned Income Tax Credit (EITC), 330
Earth Summit, 30, 31
Easterlin, R. A., 2–3
Easterlin Paradox, 2–3
Eckerberg, K., 106
Eckersley, R., 237, 243
ecological modernization, 326–28
ecological modernization theory, 39
*Ecological Tax-Impasse or a Fine Approach?* (Deutsches institute), 90
Economic and Legal Context Index (ELCI), 157
economic growth and development
 contemporary capitalism and, 225–29
 Daly and, 225–27
 education for (*See* Education for economic development (EED))
 environment and, 180–82, 225–29, 323–24
 global theory and, 227–29
 happiness and, 2–3
 Hypothesis 2 and, 180–82
 system performance, measures of, 13
ecosystem
 defined, 235
 social system and, relationship between, 235–37, 236f
 vitality, 170
Edelenbos, J., 109
education for economic development (EED), 207–11
 burgeoning to fundamental, 209–11
 rapid model of, 207–9
education for sustainable development (ESD), 205, 210, 211–18
 as citizen education, 218–19
 conditions for, 211–13
 critics of, and solutions for, 216–18
 sustainable society and, establishment of, 213–16
EED. *See* Education for economic development (EED)
Elaboration Likelihood Model, 295
Ellwood, D. T., 330
Elster, J., 194
Emotional Judgement, 294, 296f
 France example of, 308f

South Korean example, 303f
Toyo-cho example, 299f
*Employment Dilemma and the Future of Work, The* (Club of Rome), 327
empowerment zones, 238
endogenous development, 275, 276b
*Energy Goal for 2050: 100% Renewable Electricity Supply* (UBA report), 91–92
Environmental Action Plan (EAP), 30
environmental education, 205–19
 as citizen education, 218–19
 for economic development, 207–11
 overview of, 205–7
 for sustainable development, 211–18
environmental/energy policies, 81–101
 in Germany, 86–95
 governance strategies for, 82–86
 in Japan, 95–101
 overview of, 81–82
environmental governance, 154–86
 analytical framework of, 48, 158–59, 158f
 characteristics of, 48–50
 citizen participation and, 112–14
 civil organizations and, 114–15
 criticisms of, responses to, 184–85
 defining, 107–8
 dimensions of, 108
 environmental regulations and, 49–50
 EPI and, 162, 170, 171–75t, 176
 failures of, 108–9
 future research for, 185
 hypotheses of, 176–82, 177f, 178f, 179t, 181f, 183t
 multi-level regulatory governance and, 52–53
 overview of, 47, 154–55
 policy mix and, 52
 Porter hypothesis and, 51–52
 research previously done on, 155–58
 state transformation in, 47–54
 strategies (*See* Environmental governance strategies)
 sustainable development themes and, 114
 typologies of, 52
 WGI and, 159–62

environmental governance strategies, 82–86
  cooperative governance by various actors as, 85
  integrated environmental policy as, 84
  multi-level governance as, 85–86
  overview of, 82–83
  target-and results-oriented governance as, 83–84
environmental health, 162, 170
environmental justice, EPA definition of, 196
Environmental Kuznets curve (EKC), 158, 159
environmental metagovernance, 109–10
  citizen participation and, 115–16
  LA21 and, 115–17
  sustainable development and, local, 116
Environmental Performance Index (EPI), 162, 170, 176
  categories of, 162, 170
  construction of, 171–75$t$
  described, 162
  development of, 162
  GDP and, 181$f$
  vs. other environmental indices, 177$f$
  WGI and, 178$f$
environmental policy, in EU, 68–73
  characteristics of, 70–72
  ICLEI and, 69–70
  monitoring and, 69
  multi-level governance in, 68–73
  regulation methods used, 68–69
  tools and measures of, 72–73
environmental policy integration (EPI), 28–45
  approaches to, 28–29
  definitions and concepts of, 31–33
  described, 29–30
  Fukushima nuclear accident and, 42–43
  Germany and, 39–41
  implementation of, in various countries, 33, 34–35$t$, 36–39
  Japan and, 41–42
  organizational reform and, 37
  origins of, 30–31
  overview of, 28

21st-century power supply system and, 43–45, 44$t$
  vertical and horizontal, integration, 33
environmental quality (Hypothesis 2), 180–82
environmental regulations, 49–50
Environmental Regulatory Regime Index (ERRI), 157
Environmental Sustainability Index (ESI), 157, 162. *See also* Environmental Performance Index (EPI)
Environment Ministers' Conference (UMK), 87
EPI. *See* Environmental Performance Index (EPI); Environmental policy integration (EPI)
ESD. *See* Education for sustainable development (ESD)
Esping-Andersen, G., 240, 319, 320
Esty, D., 154, 155, 157, 185
  EPI and, 162, 170, 171–75$t$, 176
Ethics Commission for a Safe Energy Supply, 90–94
EU. *See* European Union (EU)
European Community (EC), 64, 84
European Court of Justice, 68–69
European Environment Agency (EEA), 30, 69, 73
European Environmental Information and Observation Network (EIONET), 69
European Parliament, 68, 73
European Union (EU). *See also* Environmental policy, in EU
  Europe 2020 Targets of, 92–93
  Sustainable Development Strategy, 30
Evans, B., 70, 112–13, 115

Federal Environmental Agency, 87
Federal Ministry for the Environment, Germany
  national $CO_2$ reduction target and, 89
  Nature Conservation and Nuclear Safety (BMU), 87–88
Finland
  environmental governance in, 53

environmental policy integration and, 34–35*t*, 36
Fischer, F., 189, 190, 294, 296
Fishkin, J., 193–94, 194–95, 198
Fitzpatrick, T., 324, 333, 334
Flasbarth, J., 91
Flinders, M., 62
Fordist Development Pattern, 239
Foreman, C. H., Jr., 201
France
  environmental policy integration and, 34–35*t*
  radioactive waste repository siting and, 298
free riders, 227–28
Frey, B. S., 3, 325
Fukushima Nuclear Power Plant accident
  anti-nuclear movements after, 267–69
  anti-nuclear movements before, 252–55
  Germany and, 81–82, 90–92
  policy integration and, 42–43
fully active society concept, 328
Funabashi, H., 262
functional fragmentation, 114, 116

Gaebler, T., 107
Gardner, W. L., 296
Geki, 294
General Agreement on Tariffs and Trade (GATT), 318
German Council for Sustainable Development, 87
German Council of Environmental Advisors (SRU), 88
Germany. *See also* Germany, environmental governance strategies in
  environmental policy integration and, 34–35*t*, 36
  green cabinets and, 37
  National Sustainable Development Strategy of, 37, 39–41
  red-green coalition, 37
Germany, environmental governance strategies in, 86–95
  Council of Environmental Advisors (SRU) and, 88
  Environment Ministers' Conference (UMK) and, 88–89
  establishment of systems for, 86–87
  Green Party and, 90
  integrating, 89–90
  of Merkel government, 93–95
  nuclear energy and, withdrawal from, 90–92
  renewable electricity supply and, 92–93
  West Germany systems for, 87–88
*Germany's Energy Transition-A Collective Project for the Future* (Ethik-Kommission report), 94
Gerrard, M. B., 294
Ghering, T., 62, 68, 69
Giarini, O., 327, 332
Giddens, A., 333
Gilpin, R., 225, 227
Glasser, H., 274, 288
global civil society, 229–30
global governance models, 229–32
  civil society, 229–30
  post-war, 230*f*
  public policy, new, 230–32
global theory, economic growth and, 227–29
gold standard, 223–24
Goodin, R., 190, 324, 325, 326, 331
Gosseries, A., 198
governance
  concept of, 106–7
  economic prosperity and (Hypothesis 3), 182, 183*t*
  environmental quality and, relation between (Hypothesis 1), 176, 178–80, 178*f*, 179*t*
  WGI definition of, 160
governance for sustainable development, 5–6, 114. *See also* Governance theory
  dimensions of, 108
  local government impact on, 245–46
  metagovernance and, 116
  transformations of, 138
governance theory, 57–75
  described, 57
  European Union environmental policy of, 68–73

governance theory (cont.)
    multi-level governance and, 65–68
    overview of, 57–58
    policy values for, opposition between, 60–62
    reconstruction of, 73–75
    structure of governance and, 62–65
    transition management for, 57–60
governing actors
    diversification of, 107
    relationships among, 107
government effectiveness (GE), 155, 160
government role, in sustainable human development, 24–25
Grabowski, R., 17
grass-roots protests, anti-nuclear, 1986-1992, 259–61, 260*f*
*Great Transformation, The* (Polanyi), 223
Greece
    environmental governance in, 53
    environmental policy integration and, 34–35*t*, 36
green budgeting, 37–38
Green Cabinet, 87
green economic growth. *See* green growth
green growth
    described, 1
    economic growth links to, 1–2
    limits to, 2
    social limit to, 2–3
Green Party, Germany, 90
Grin, J., 273, 277, 288, 290
Groot, L., 326
gross domestic product (GDP), 13, 181*f*
Grubb, M., 30
Gutmann, A., 190, 199
Gyeongju-si dispute, South Korea, 303–7, 303*f*

Haas, E. B., 66
Haas, P. M., 61
Habermas, J., 194, 239, 241–42
Hae-Chan Lee, 304, 309
Hajer, M. A., 190
happiness
    determinants of, 3
    politico-economic system and, 3
    research, 2–3
    social capital and, 3
    social limit to growth and, 2–3
    society conditions and, 3
    sustainable development and, 4–5
    United States level of, 3
happiness paradox. *See* Easterlin Paradox
Haq, M., 13–14
Harada, E., 294
Harris, J. M., 108
Hart, J., 67
Hart, P., 214
Harvey, D., 229
Hasegawa, K., 251–70, 255, 265, 267
Hashimoto, D., 298
Hashimoto, M., 121
Hatoyama, Y., 82
Hayek, F. A., 141, 143
hegemonic stability theory, 227–28
Held, D., 224, 225, 230
Hendriks, C. M., 192
Heuristic-Systematic Model, 295
Hey, C., 88
high-level radioactive waste (HLW), 293
    Designated Radioactive Waste Final Disposal Act and, 296–97
Hindmoor, A., 57, 243
Hirabayashi, Y., 269
Hiroi, Y., 324
Hirose, T., 259
Hirota, N., 294
Hjnal, P. I., 61, 63, 70, 74
Hoffmann, S., 66
Holliday, I., 319
horizontal environmental policy integration, 33
horizontal relations, environmental governance and, 50
Hosoda, E., 41
Hosokawa, M., 95
Hovden, E., environmental policy integration and, 32–33
human development. *See also* capability; sustainable human development
    concept overview of, 9
    definition of, 9
    features of, 11–13

indicators of, 18–19t
in Japan, sustainability of, 17–19
opportunity aspect of, 11, 12–13
sustainable development and, 13–14
well-being and resources of, 11–12
Human Development Index (HDI), 4, 17–19, 18–19t
Human Development Report, 4
*Human Development Report 2010* (UNDP), 25
Humphrey, M., 196
Hungary
environmental governance in, 53
environmental policy integration and, 34–35t, 36
green cabinets and, 37
Huxham, C., 107
Hwang, S -C., 306

Iceland, environmental policy integration and, 34–35t
ICLEI (International Council for Local Environmental Initiatives), 69–70
Imamura, I., 214
Imamura, T., 39
IMPEL (Implementation and Enforcement of Environmental Law), 69
Imura, H., 106, 113
Institute for decentralised Energy-Technology (IdE), 93
Institute for Sustainable Energy Policies, 98
Institute for Wind Energy and Energy System Technology (IWES), 91–92
integrated environmental policy strategy, 84
interest group liberalism, 143
intermestic (international and domestic) theory, 66
International Council for Local Environmental Initiatives (ICLEI), 69–70, 105, 246
International Nuclear Event Scale (INES), 267
Ireland
environmental governance in, 53
environmental policy integration and, 34–35t
Italy, environmental policy integration and, 34–35t

Jacobs, K., 84
Jänicke, M., 83, 84, 87, 89, 327
Japan
Basic Environment Plan of, 36–37
environmental governance strategies in (*See* Japan, environmental governance strategies in)
environmental policy integration and, 34–35t, 41–42
Fukushima nuclear accident and policy integration in, 42–43
LA21, 110–17
Nishiyodogawa Ward, Osaka City case study, 121–34
political and administrative system in, 110–11
radioactive waste repository siting and, 296–97
regulatory system reforms needed in, 148–51
sustainable human development in, 17–19
WGI ratings of, 160, 161–62, 161f
Japan, anti-nuclear movements in, 251–70. *See also* Social movement theory, Japan anti-nuclear
after Fukushima accident, 267–69
characteristics of, 260–61
before Fukushima accident, 252–55
network structure for, 259, 260f
nuclear power generation, stopping, 263–67
overview of, 251
social movement theory analysis of, 255–63
strategies of, 269–70
Japan, environmental governance strategies in, 95–101
Basic Act on Energy Policy and, 96
challenges with, 99–101
climate change policies and, 97

Japan (cont.)
  energy transition challenges in, 99–101
  environmental organizations roles in, 98
  Hosokawa government enacted laws, 95–96
  post Fukushima accident, 96–97
  renewable energies at municipal levels and, 99
  social movements and, 98–99
Japanese Basic Environment Law, 95–96
Jeffery, C., 71
Jere, W. A., 58
Jessop, B., 106, 110, 116, 242
Jickling, B., 214
Jisshi Keikaku (Implementation Plan), 111
Johnson, G. F., 294
Jonas, H., 143
Jordan, A., 29, 30, 33, 34–35t, 38, 41, 52, 84, 106
Jordan, B., 328, 333
Jörgens, H., 83, 84


Kaido, Y., 258, 264
Kaldor, M., 229
Kamanaka, M., 263
Kan, N., 82
Kankyou Kihon Jourei (Basic Environmental Ordinance BEO), 111
Kap-Soo Han, 305
Kaufmann, D., 159, 160–61
Kaul, I., 229
Keen, M., 277–78, 278f
Kemp, R., 59, 64, 65
Kennan, G. F., 148
Kennett, P., 63
Keohane, R. O., 225
Keynesian welfare state, reform of, 238–43
  neo-liberalism theory and, 238
  regulation theory and, 238
Kihon Keikaku (Basic Plan), 111
Kihon Koso (Basic Vision), 111
*Kiken na hanashi: cherunobuiri to nihon no unmei* (Hirose), 259
Kiko Network, 98
Kim, Hong-Kyu, 294
Kim, K., 37, 40–41

Kim Dae-jun, 254
Kirton, J. J., 61, 63, 70, 74
Kjær, A. M., 122
"KKZ" team, 159. *See also* Worldwide Governance Indicators (WGI), World Bank
Kleiner, M., 91
Klijin, E.-H., 109
Kobayashi, T., 193
*Kogai* problems, 275
Kohler-Koch, B., 71
Koizumi, J., 96
Komatsuzaki, Shunsaku, 293–312
Kooiman, J., 83
Korea, environmental policy integration and, 34–35t, 36
Kraay, A., 159
Krongkaew, M, 22–23
Kuks, S. M., 107–8
Kunreuther, H., 294
Kutting, G., 61
Kyokan Hiroba (Sympathy Park), 127
Kyoto Protocol, 245


LA21. *See* Local Agenda 21 (LA21)
Lafferty, W., 32–33, 70, 106
Larat, F., 71
Laslett, P., 198
Lau, R. R., 300–301
lawsuits, nuclear power generation, 263–65
Lee Myung-bak, 254
Lenschow, A., 29, 30, 33, 34–35t, 38, 41, 84
Le Prestre, P., 63
Liedtke, P. M., 327, 332
*Limits to Growth, The* (Club of Rome), 2
lincage politics, 66
Lindblom, C. E., 142
Lipietz, A., 239
Lipschutz, R., 61
Local Agenda 21 (LA21), 110–17
  alternative approach to, 116
  as BEP, 111–12
  as CP, 116–17
  definition of, 105

environmental governance failure and, 112–15
environmental metagovernance and, 115–17
institutional and practical context of, 110–11
overview of, 110
local government. *See also* decentralization
  decentralization role of, 235
  governance for sustainable development and, 245–46
  sustainable development goals of, 235–37, 236*f*
Local Strategic Partnership (LSP), 238
Loeber, A., 290
Loffler, E., 74
Loorbach, D., 57, 59, 60, 64, 65, 73, 123
Loorbach, L., 273
low- and intermediate-level radioactive waste (LILW), 297, 298
low-carbon society, building, 1, 28
Lowi, T., 143
Luxembourg, environmental policy integration and, 34–35*t*

Majone, G., 66
"Make the Rule: Climate Protection Act Campaign Committee," 98
Malthusian theory, 13
Manin, B., 194
Marcus, G. E., 296
Marks, G., 72
Marten, G. G., 235
Masano, A., 294
Mastruzzi, M., 159
Matsumoto, H., 269
Matsushita, K., 28–45, 111, 229
Mays, C., 295
McAdam, D., 255
McGrew, A., 224, 225, 230
McNeill, D., 74
McNicoll, G., 20
McQuaid, R. M., 107
Meadowcroft, J., 106
Merkel, A., 82

energy policy goals defined by, 94
Ethics Commission for a Safe Energy Supply and, 90–94
metagovernance. *See* environmental metagovernance
METI (Ministry of Economie, Trade and Industrie), 96
Meuse and Haute-Marne Department dispute, France, 307–11, 308*f*
Mexico
  environmental governance in, 53
  environmental policy integration and, 34–35*t*
Meyer, L. H., 198
Midwestern Greenhouse Gas Reduction Accord (MGGA), 246
Mill, J. S., 226
Ministry of International Trade and Industry (MITI), 149, 150
Ministry of the Environment
  Global Environment Bureau, 39
  Government of Japan, 36
Miyamoto, K., 275, 276*b*
Miyamoto, T., 317–36, 319, 332, 334, 336
Miyanaga, K., 105–17
Mizuno, K., 323
Moo-Hyun Roh, 305
Morotomi, T., 108
multilayered governance
  behaviour patterns in, 66
  challenge of, 132–33
  characteristics of, 62–63
  concept and theory of, 62
  environmental sustainability policies and, 65–68
  in EU environmental policy, 68–73
  regulatory environmental, 52–53
  strategy, 85–86
  sustainable development and, 63–64
  of transition management for sustainability, 65–68
multilayered governance, of post-productivist welfare, 332–35
  decentralized, pluralistic, 333–35
  national government role in, 335
  normative structures of, 332–33

multiple-loop learning model, 276–78, 278f
Mumford, L., 274, 288
Muneta, Y., 129

Nagaoka, N., 327
Naito, R., 281
Nakasone, Y., 257
"National Environmental Performance Measurement and Determinants" (Esty and Porter), 155, 157
National Liaison Council of Pollution Victims Association (NLCPVA), 126–27
National Sustainable Development Strategy of Germany, 37, 39–41
natural constraint, capitalism and, 222
natural resource depletion, 23
neo-liberalism, self-regulating market and, 224–25
neo-liberalism theory, 238
Netherlands
  environmental governance in, 53
  environmental policy integration and, 34–35t, 36
network structure for anti-nuclear movements, 259, 260f
new functionalism, theory of, 66
Newig, J., 61
New Zealand, environmental policy integration and, 34–35t
Niigata Minamata disease, 126
Niikawa, T., 57–75, 109, 111, 114
Niioka, Satoshi, 222–32
NIMBY (not in my backyard), 266–67, 293
Nishio, B., 300
Nishiyodogawa ESD Commission, 131
Nishiyodogawa Pollution Victims and Families Association, 125, 126–28
  Aozora Foundation and, 128–29
Nishiyodogawa Ward, Osaka City case study, 121–34
  antipollution movement in, 124–31
  Aozora Foundation and, 128–29
  challenge of multilayered governance, 132–33
  compensation/pollution control, political actions for, 126–27
  focus shifts from local to national, 131–32
  governance concept and, 122–24
  lawsuit and public empathy, 127–28
  local collectivity, reconstruction of, 133–34
  network building and, 130–31
  overview of, 121–22
  urban environments improvement and, 129–30
  victims' movements, 124–26
Nogami, H., 9–26
non-governmental organizations (NGOs), 66, 85, 142
non-profit organizations (NPOs), 66, 81, 85, 142
Norway
  environmental policy integration and, 34–35t, 36
  green cabinets and, 37
Nuclear and Industrial Safety Agency (NISA), 151
nuclear energy, withdrawal from in Germany, 90–92
nuclear power generation, methods of stopping, 263–67
  lawsuits as, 263–65
  referendum as, 265–67
nuclear power industry, 254–55
nuclear power plants, construction of, 1973-1986, 257–59
nuclear reactors, in 1995 and 2010, 252–53t
nuclear renaissance promotion, 252
Nuclear Safety Commission (NSC), 149–50
nuclear weapons, abolition of, 1954-1973, 256–57
Nussbaum, M., 16, 22, 25–26, 214

Oakeshott, M., 141
Obara, R., 260

Oberthur, S., 62, 68, 69
obstacle removal approach, 329
Oe, K., 268, 269
Ogata, S., 229
Okereke, C., 63
Oku, K., 318
Onga, M., 295
*On the Risk of Nuclear Power Stations: Chernobyl and Japan's Fate* (Hirose), 260
opportunity aspect
 of human development, 11, 12–13
 of sustainable development, 10
 of sustainable human development, 14–16, 14*f*
Organisation for Economic Co-operation and Development (OECD), 84, 122–23, 246
 EPI and, 33, 34–35*t*, 36–37
organizational reform, environmental policy integration and, 37
Osborne, D., 107
Oshima, K., 43
Ota, Takayuki, 273–90
Otsuka, T., 37
Oulton, S., 214
Oyama, K., 154–86

paired relationships
 of economy and environment, 323–24
 of social security and economy, 322–23
 of social security and environment, 324–25
 of welfare, economy and environment, 321–22, 322*f*
Papadopoulos, Y., 83
Paraskevopoulos, C. J., 68, 74
Parliamentary Advisory Council on Sustainable Development, 87
partisan mutual adjustment, 142
Partridge, E., 198
*Pathways Towards a 100% Renewable Electricity System* (SRU report), 92
Pekkanen, R., 115
"Perspectives for Germany" strategy, 87
Pescatore, C., 294

Peters, B. G., 57, 66, 107
Petty, R. E., 295, 296
Pierre, J., 57, 66, 107, 242
Planning Cell mechanism, 190, 192
planning inflation, 114
Planungszelle. *See* Planning Cell mechanism
Poland, environmental policy integration and, 34–35*t*, 36
Polanyi, K., 223–24, 240
policy integration
 described, 29
 indicators used in, 36
 requirements for, 32
policy mix, environmental governance and, 52
policy-oriented lawsuits, 265
political stability (PS), 160
politico-economic system, happiness and, 3
Pollution-Related Health Damage Compensation Law, 126
Popper, K., 141
Porter, G., 231
Porter, M., 51–52, 155, 157
Porter hypothesis, environmental governance and, 51–52
Portugal, environmental policy integration and, 34–35*t*, 36
post-productivist welfare, 325–26
post-war public policy, 230*f*
poverty band, 22–23
poverty line, 22
poverty reduction, savings and, 21–24
Prakash, A., 67
precommitment-focused theory of deliberation, 194–95
*Primus inter pares* (first among equals), 107
problems, ESD definition of, 215
problem solving, environmental governance and, 50
procedure-focused theory of deliberation, 194
productivist welfare, crisis in, 320–21
Program for International Student Assessment (PISA), 216

Przeworski, A., 155, 156
*Public and Its Problems, The* (Dewey), 189
public governance, characteristics of, 48
public policy, new global governance, 230–32
　freedom and, 231, 232
　justice and, 231, 232
　post-war, 230*f*
　wealth and, 231
Public-Private-Partnership (PPP) policy, 74
Putnam, R., 3, 230

Radioactive Waste Management Funding and Research Center (RWMC), 297
radioactive waste repository siting, 293–312
　analytical framework of, 294–96, 296*f*
　case study findings of, 311–12
　Emotional Judgement step, 294
　France and, 298
　Gyeongju-si dispute, South Korea, 303–7, 303*f*
　Japan and, 296–97
　Meuse and Haute-Marne Department dispute, France, 307–11, 308*f*
　overview of, 293–94
　Reasoned Negotiation step, 294
　South Korea and, 297
　Toyo-cho dispute, Japan, 298–303, 299*f*
rapid economic development model, 207–9
Rawls, J., 194
Reasoned Negotiation step for radioactive waste repository siting, 294, 296*f*, 306–7, 308*f*
Reed, S., 114
referendum, as nuclear power generation, 265–67
regime theory, 228
Regional Greenhouse Gas Initiative (RGI), 245–46
regional survey concept, 274
regulation theory, 239
regulatory quality (RQ), 155, 160

Renn, O., 192
reproduction aspect of sustainable development, 10
resilience, as umbrella term, 246
rewarded participation approach, 329, 329*t*
Rhodes, R. A. W., 57, 107
Rifkin, J., 321
Rio Declaration on Environment and Development, 31
risk society theory, 256
Rittel, H., 139
Robottom, I., 214
Rocard, M., 298, 309
Roh Moo-hyun, 254
*Rokkasho Rhapsody* (movie), 263
Rosenau, J. N., 66
Rosenthal, G., 68
Rossen, J. v., 214
Rothgang, H., 66
Rotmans, J., 58
rule of law (RL), 160, 161
Rydine, Y., 123–24

Saint-Simon, Henri de, 140
Sakamoto, R., 262–63
Samuels, R., 114
Sanders, L., 196
Sanera, M., 214
Sanford, M., 67
Sano, W., 205–19
Satō, J., 17
savings, poverty reduction and, 21–24
Sawayama, Y., 299, 300
*Sayonara genpatsu goman nin shukai* (50,000-person protest for denuclearization), 268
*Sayonara genpatsu issenman nin shomei* (10 million signatures for denuclearization), 269
Sbragia, A., 72
Scharpf, F. W., 85
Schlesinger, M., 300–301
Schön, D. A., 277, 278*f*
Schreurs, M. A., 106, 121, 122
Schröder, G., 82
Schulze, C. L., 145

Schuppert, G. F., 67, 71
Schwartz, F., 112, 113
Science and Technology Agency (STA), 149–51
Scope problem, 195
Scott, W., 214
self-regulating market
　contemporary capitalism and, 223–25
　neo-liberalism and, 224–25
　Polanyi and, 223–24
Sen, A., 4, 12, 15, 16, 24–25
Serageldin, I., 108
Seven Sisters, 318
Shaw, S. S., 214
Sherman, D. J., 294
Shields, M. P., 17
Shimizu, M., 121–34
*Shingikai* (advisory council), 112, 113
Shiokawa, T., 214
Shiraishi, K., 234–47
Shout, A., 52
Shove, E., 59
Sikora, R. I., 198
Single European Act of 1987, 29, 30
Sjöberg, L., 294
Skelcher, C., 60
Slovakia, environmental policy integration and, 34–35*t*, 36
small government, 224
smart grids, 44
Smith, A., 60
Smith, G., 190
Snow, D. A., 301
social capital
　happiness and, 3
　Putnam definition of, 3
social constraint, 222
Social Democratic Party (SPD), 87
social inclusion, 328–32
　described, 328–31
　diversity of, strategies, 329*t*
　strategies for, 331–32
social learning
　Glasser definition of, 274
　types of active, 274
social learning for sustainable development, 273–90

　case study types of, 287–89
　in Japan, 274–76
　multiple-loop learning model of, 276–78, 278*f*
　overview of, 273–74
　regional/local, in Japan, 275–76
　water quality preservation of YWPA and, 280–87
social movements, in Japan, 98–99
social movement theory, Japan anti-nuclear, 255–63
　abolition of nuclear weapons, 1954-1973, 256–57
　anti-plutonium movements, 1992-2011, 261–63
　construction of nuclear power plants, 1973-1986, 257–59
　grass-roots protests, 1986-1992, 259–61, 260*f*
　overview of, 255–56, 255*f*
social planning philosophy, 139–41
social security
　aspects of, 24–25
　economy and, 322–23
　enhancing, 24
　environment and, 324–25
social system, defined, 235
social system and ecosystem, relationship between, 235–37
　co-adaptation type, 236*f*, 237
　co-evolution type, 236*f*, 237
　separate type, 235, 236*f*, 237
society conditions, happiness and, 3
Sørensen, E., 75, 106, 107
Sougou Keikaku, 111. *See also* Comprehensive Plan (CP)
soundness problem, 196
South Korea
　categories of radioactive waste in, 297
　nuclear equipment exports and, 254
　radioactive waste repository siting and, 297
Spain, environmental policy integration and, 34–35*t*, 36
"Speech to the Electors of Bristol" (Burke), 202
spent nuclear fuel (SNF), 297

Speth, J. G., 61
Spork, H., 214
steady state, 226
Steer, A., 108
Stirling, A., 60
Stoett, P., 63
Stoker, G., 64, 66, 67, 106, 242
Strange, S., 230
strategic environmental assessment (SEA), 37, 38
stress test, 96
*Study on the Potential for the Introduction of Renewable Energy in Fiscal 2010* (Japan Ministry of the Environment), 97
Stutzer, A., 3
suspended solid (SS) levels, Yahagi River, 287*f*
sustainability
  described, 63
  environmental governance and, 50
  governance structure and, 62–65
  governance theory and (*See* Governance theory)
  indicators of, 18–19*t*
  multi-level governance and, 63–64
  policy values for, opposition between, 60–62
  problems of governing, 65
  sustainable development and, 10
  transition management for, multi-level governance of, 65–68
sustainability, globalization and, 105–10
  environmental governance and, 107–8
  failures of environmental governance and, 108–9
  governance concept and, 106–7
  metagovernance and, 109–10
  overview of, 105–6
sustainable development. *See also* sustainable human development
  capability and, 11–13
  concepts of, 9–26, 124
  Dasgupta definition of, 4
  decentralization and, 243–46
  definitions of, 122–23
  democracy and (*See* Democracy and sustainable development)
  education for (*See* Education for sustainable development (ESD))
  embedment of, into society, 243–45
  environmental policy integration and, 28–45
  governance for (*See* Governance for sustainable development)
  happiness and, 4–5
  human development and, 13–14
  in Japan, 17–19
  non-representative measures for, 146–48
  opportunity aspect of, 10
  overview of, 9
  principle of, 138–39
  reproduction aspect of, 10
  Sen concept of, 4
  social learning for (*See* Social learning for sustainable development)
  sustainability and, 10
  transition management for, 5–6
  understanding of, as dynamic process, 123–24
Sustainable Development Council, 87
sustainable human development
  concept of, 14–17
  equality/expansion of capabilities and, 16–17
  government role in, 24–25
  in Japan, 17–19
  operational, making, 17–25
  opportunities in, 14–16, 14*f*
  policy framework for, 19–21
  poverty reduction and savings of, 21–24
Sweden, environmental policy integration and, 34–35*t*, 36
Switzerland
  environmental governance in, 53
  environmental policy integration and, 34–35*t*, 36

Takagi, J., 263
Takahashi, H., 114
Takayama, N., 22
Tamas, P., 75

Tanaka, K., 259
target- and results-oriented governance strategy, 83–84
Tashima, Y., 294, 299–300
Taylor, L., 20
Temporary Assistance for Needy Families (TANF), 329
Ten Heuvelhof, E., 124
Teranishi, S., 41
Third Environmental Basic Plan, 176, 177f
Third Way, social security, 323, 332–33, 334
Thompson, D., 190
Thompson, T., 199
Töpfer, K., 90–91
Torfing, J., 60, 75, 106, 107
Toyo-cho dispute, 298–303, 299f
transformation-focused theory of deliberation, 194
transition management theory
  criticisms of, 59–60
  elements of, 59
  environmental governance and, 60
  governing sustainability and, problems of, 65
  multi-level governance of, for sustainability, 65–68
  Netherlands government and, 58
  sustainability policies and, 58–60
Treaty of Amsterdam, EPI and, 29–30
triangular model of social movement (TRIM), 255, 255f
triple bottom line, 63
Trittin, J., 37
Trope, Y., 295
Tsubogo, Minoru, 81–101
Tsuru, S., 106
Turkey, environmental policy integration and, 34–35t, 36
20th-century welfare states, 318–21
  described, 318–19
  productivist, crisis in, 320–21
  types of, 319–20
21st-century power supply system
  conventional vs., 44t
  environmental policy integration and, 43–45

Ueta, K., 1–6, 9–26
Underdal, A., 32
United Kingdom
  environmental governance in, 53
  environmental policy integration and, 34–35t
  green cabinets and, 37
United Nations Decade of Education for Sustainable Development, 216
United Nations Development Programme (UNDP), 4, 9, 12, 225
United Nations Educational, Scientific and Cultural Organization (UNESCO), 193
United Nations Framework Convention on Climate Change, 229
United Nations Millennium Development Goals (UNMDG), 162
United States
  environmental governance in, 53
  environmental policy integration and, 34–35t
  as free rider, 228
  green cabinets and, 37
  Kyoto Protocol and, 228
upstream organizations, YWPA and, 285–86
Usami, Makoto, 189–202
Usui, M., 106
Uzzell, D. L., 214

Van Bueren, E., 124
Vandenbosch, R., 294
Vandenbosch, S. E., 294
Van der Linde, C., 51
Van der Veen, R., 326
Vári, A., 75, 294
vertical administration, 114, 116
vertical environmental policy integration, 33, 43
vertical relations, 50, 53
voice and accountability (VA), 160

Wagenaar, W., 190
Wagner, R. E., 146
Wakamatsu, Y., 193

Walker, G., 59
Wals, A. E. J., 273
Webber, M., 139
Weidner, H., 106
Weiger, H., 94–95
welfare, governance of, 317–36
  ecological modernization and, 326–28
  overview of, 317
  paired relationships and, 321–25, 322$f$
  pluralistic, multilayered, 332–35
  post-productivist welfare and, 325–26
  social inclusion and, 328–32
  twentieth-century welfare states, productivism and, 318–21
welfare democracy, 334–35
well-being
  constituents of, 4
  Dasgupta and, 4
  determinants of, 4
  resources and, distinction of, 11–12
Wenger, E., 277, 289
Western Climate Initiative (WCI), 246
WGI. *See* Worldwide Governance Indicators (WGI), World Bank
Williams, C. C., 327
Windebank, J., 327
Winter, G., 62, 74
World Commission on Environment and Development (WCED), 30–31
World Economic Forum (WEF), 162
World Values Survey, 2
World Watch Institute, 42
Worldwide Governance Indicators (WGI), World Bank, 159–62
  data points distribution, by type, 169–70$t$
  developers of, 159
  dimensions of governance indicators, 160
  EPI and, 178$f$
  governance definition for, 160
  Japan ratings, 160, 161–62, 161$f$
  sources used in obtaining data for, 163–68$t$
Wurzel, R. K., 87
WWF Japan, 98

Yahagi River Basin Water Quality Preservation Association (YWPA)
  activities, 280–87
  area-wide monitoring by, 281–82
  biochemical oxygen demand shift and, 286$f$
  budget of, 280$f$
  case study, 278–87
  effects of, for water quality, 285–87
  features of, 279, 280$f$
  formation of, 279
  organizations involved in, 280$f$
  suspended solid shift and, 287$f$
  upstream organizations and, 285–86
  water pollution causes, 278–79
  Yahagi River Method and, 282–85
Yahagi River Method, 282–84
  described, 282, 284
  for large-scale developments, 283, 282$f$
  number of consultations by, 284, 284$f$
  for small-scale developments, 283–84
Yamaji, T., 298
Yatsuki, Shin-ichi, 41, 47–54
YODOKYO Medical & Welfare Foundation, 125
Yoshizumi, M., 41
Young, I. M., 196
Young, O. R., 228
YWPA. *See* Yahagi River Basin Water Quality Preservation Association (YWPA)